AAL-9327
VC-2057

P9-DMX-791

Please remember that this is a library book,
and that it belongs only temporarily to each
person who uses it. Be considerate. Do
not write in this, or any, library book.

WITHDRAWN

Group Counseling
Strategies and Skills

SECOND EDITION

Ed E. Jacobs
WEST VIRGINIA UNIVERSITY

Riley L. Harvill
NORTH TEXAS STATE UNIVERSITY

Robert L. Masson
WEST VIRGINIA UNIVERSITY

BROOKS/COLE PUBLISHING COMPANY
PACIFIC GROVE, CALIFORNIA

ITP™
The trademark ITP is used under license.

A CLAIREMONT BOOK

Brooks/Cole Publishing Company
A Division of Wadsworth, Inc.

© 1994, 1988 by Wadsworth, Inc., Belmont, California 94002.
All rights reserved. No part of this book may be reproduced,
stored in a retrieval system, or transcribed, in any form or
by any means—electronic, mechanical, photocopying, recording,
or otherwise—without the prior written permission of the
publisher, Brooks/Cole Publishing Company, Pacific Grove,
California 93950, a division of Wadsworth, Inc.

Printed in the United States of America
10   9   8   7   6   5   4   3

Library of Congress Cataloging-in-Publication Data

Jacobs, Edward E., [date]
 Group counseling : strategies and skills / Edward E. Jacobs, Riley
L. Harvill, Robert L. Masson. — 2nd ed.
  p.   cm.
 Includes bibliographical references and index.
 ISBN 0-534-21324-3
 1. Group counseling. 2. Leadership.   I. Harvill, Riley L., [date]
. II. Masson, Robert L., [date]   III. Title.
BF637.C6J34   1993
158′.35—dc20   93-2438
                                                                 CIP

Sponsoring Editor: CLAIRE VERDUIN
Editorial Associate: GAY C. BOND
Production Editor: LAUREL JACKSON
Manuscript Editor: DEBORAH MEYERS
Permissions Editor: MARIE DuBOIS
Interior Design: VERNON T. BOES
Cover Design and Illustration: LISA THOMPSON
Art Coordinator: LISA TORRI
Indexer: CHRIS JAMISON
Typesetting: BOOKENDS TYPESETTING
Cover Printing: SOUTHEASTERN COLOR GRAPHICS
Printing and Binding: THE MAPLE-VAIL BOOK MFG. GROUP

CONTENTS . . . .

CHAPTER TWELVE
Therapy in Groups 291

CHAPTER THIRTEEN
Closing a Session or Group 328

CHAPTER FOURTEEN
Dealing with Problem Situations 361

Group Counseling: Strategies and Skills, Second Edition, provides an in-depth look at group counseling with an emphasis on practical knowledge and techniques for effective group leadership. This book is for counselors, social workers, psychologists and all others who lead groups of one kind or another. Our active approach to group leadership reflects a belief that the leader is largely responsible for the planning and implementing of the group and for its outcome. We have found that in most settings—schools, hospitals, rehabilitation facilities, mental health centers, and so on—the leader must take an active part in facilitating the group. Throughout the book, we discuss many different kinds of groups and describe both basic and advanced skills for leading them. The examples, which include actual dialogue from groups, help the reader understand how an effective leader applies these skills.

The purpose of this text is to integrate traditional theories and concepts of group process with thoughtful strategies and specific exercises that can make groups come alive and can have a dramatic impact on the members. We recognize that group leadership is one of the most difficult types of professional work undertaken by therapists, drug and alcohol counselors, correctional counselors, nurses, and others in the helping professions. We have attempted to address many complex operational issues typically overlooked by texts that emphasize group theory or group process. Our goal is to bridge the gap between theory and practice with a sophisticated how-to approach for both beginning students and experienced practitioners.

ORGANIZATION

The two opening chapters provide an overview of group leadership. In these chapters, we examine various kinds of groups, leadership styles, uses of current theories, group dynamics, therapeutic forces in groups, and group process. In this second edition, we have expanded the section on leadership style to offer the reader a clearer picture of different approaches to leading groups. We also discuss in detail the differences between the interpersonal and intrapersonal approaches to leading. Much of Chapter Two has been rewritten, and a section entitled "Understanding Your Session" has been added. This section contains a discussion of four "maps" used for following interactions within the group.

Chapters Three, Four, and Five cover a range of both basic and advanced leadership skills for planning and implementing a group, as well as specific strategies and skills for initiating the first and second sessions of a group. Among the skills discussed are summarizing, clarifying, using one's voice to set the tone of a group, generating energy in a group, and using one's eyes in effective ways. For the second edition, we have changed the sample plans to make them more specific, and we have expanded the discussion of each plan. The concepts in Chapter Four, which focuses on the first and second sessions of a group, have been clarified further with the use of more examples. We have also presented some additional techniques that are helpful during the opening sessions.

Chapter Six affirms the importance of maintaining a clear purpose for the group and suggests techniques for establishing, holding, and deepening the focus on a topic. In this edition, we have rewritten much of the section on focus and have added discussion about using a depth chart and a "funnel" to monitor the group's focus. We also present additional creative ways to "get the focus." Chapter Seven offers techniques for skillfully drawing out quiet members and cutting off members who ramble or otherwise diffuse the focus of the group. In this edition, we have greatly expanded the discussion of techniques for cutting off group members.

The essential uses of rounds and dyads are outlined and illustrated by numerous examples in Chapter Eight. Other exercises are discussed extensively in Chapters Nine and Ten. Written, movement, fantasy, and creative exercises are among those reviewed in these chapters, and many new and unique exercises involving movement and the use of creative props have been added for this edition. Techniques are presented for introducing and processing the exercises, along with ethical considerations and specific cautions for using them. In addition, our discussion of processing exercises has been revised and expanded considerably.

Chapter Eleven is devoted to the strategies and skills important to the critical middle sessions of a group. We discuss possible ways of dealing in the middle sessions with such topics as sex, need for approval, religion, and self-esteem. We also address issues of trust and commitment as the group experience intensifies, common mistakes some leaders might make during this period, and various strategies for increasing the group's effectiveness. Chapter Twelve focuses specifically on skills and techniques essential for leading therapy groups. This chapter has been completely revised to clarify our model for doing therapy in groups. We discuss the role of the leader, five aspects of therapy groups, the focus of therapy, and the therapeutic paths of therapy groups. We also outline ways of conducting therapy with individual members while involving and enhancing the therapeutic experience for all the members.

Chapter Thirteen contains techniques for closing sessions and groups. Chapter Fourteen offers strategies for handling problem members (the chronic talker, for example) and situations (such as resistance, sexual feelings, and conflicts between members). Chapter Fifteen deals with issues specific to certain populations, such as children, adolescents, couples, older people, and those who are chemically dependent. In this edition, we have added three more specific populations—those who are divorced, survivors of sexual abuse, and adult children of alcoholics. Finally, we have rewritten most of Chapter Sixteen, which offers thoughts on co-leading, legal and ethical issues, research, and evaluation techniques. We have expanded our discussion of ethical issues and added sections on training group counselors and the future of group work.

ACKNOWLEDGMENTS

We wish to express our appreciation to our many friends and students who contributed ideas and insights to the second edition of this book. Very special appreciation goes to Chris Jamison, who spent many hours reading and rereading the drafts of the second edition. Her positive input and attitude were greatly appreciated. We also want to express our appreciation to the many workshop participants who showed us the immediacy and reality of the difficulties inherent in leading groups in the field.

The reviewers who encouraged us to assess various sections of the book also deserve recognition. As a result of their efforts, we consider the second edition significantly more contemporary and relevant to the needs of practitioners today. Our sincere thanks to Richard Blackwell, University of North Carolina; C. Timothy Dickel, Creighton University; Lewis Donovan, West Georgia College; Elise Freed-Fagan, Community College of Philadelphia; and Paul Schmolling, Kingsbough Community College.

We also want to thank Laurel Jackson, our production editor, for her very positive, helpful attitude when discussing editorial changes, design, and so on. Finally, we want to thank Claire Verduin and Gay Bond of Brooks/Cole for their support and help with this project. It is a pleasure to work with them.

Ed E. Jacobs
Riley L. Harvill
Robert L. Masson

CHAPTER ONE.

Introduction

You are probably reading this book because you are interested in leading groups or are taking a course in group counseling or group leadership. If leading a group is a new experience for you, you may be asking yourself several questions: Why should I lead groups? What kinds of groups are there? What happens in groups? You may also be imagining yourself as the leader of a group and wondering, How am I going to prepare for my group? What do I do if nobody talks? What should I do if someone talks too much? What leadership style should I use? You will find in this book many practical examples, hints, and techniques that should increase your understanding and effectiveness as a group leader. Our emphasis is on the art of leading. We hope that reading this book will improve your ability to lead groups and meetings of all kinds.

In this chapter we discuss a number of basic considerations: who should learn to lead groups, why groups are effective, kinds of groups, the place of theory in groups, leadership styles, what makes an effective leader, and possible disruptive things that can happen in a group.

WHO SHOULD LEARN TO LEAD GROUPS?

Anyone in a helping, teaching, or supervisory role may want—or be required—to lead groups. Professionals such as psychiatrists, psychologists, social workers, counselors, ministers, managers, and teachers can all use groups in their work. Because groups are efficient and beneficial, knowing how to lead them can be valuable. If you are interested in an excellent history of group work, starting from before 1900, see Gladding (1991).

WHY ARE GROUPS EFFECTIVE?

There are many sound reasons for using a group approach to problem solving or counseling. Some are common to all groups; others pertain only to specific kinds of groups.

Reasons Common to All Groups

Two reasons for using the group approach apply to almost any kind of group. The first is their efficiency. The second is that there are more resources or viewpoints available in a group setting.

Efficiency

Dyer and Vriend (1980) discuss the concept of efficiency under the heading of "Group Counseling and Counselor Accountability." In their opinion, "counselors are not delivering" (p. 36). They mean that not enough clients are being reached by counselors via traditional one-to-one contact. Bringing together a group of people for a common purpose can save time and effort. Efficiency, therefore, is a sound rationale for group work. For instance, a school counselor who is responsible for 300 students will barely be able to see each student once during a school year in a one-to-one format. However, by developing a well-designed group program, the counselor would be able to offer advising, values clarification, or problem-solving groups in addition to meeting with those students who require individual attention. If a professional has a large population to reach (such as in prisons, industry, hospitals, or rehabilitation centers), setting up groups can be of great benefit. In situations in which there is a need to orient residents, students, or prisoners to a new living arrangement, groups can certainly save time. If a supervisor finds that his or her staff has five different opinions about an issue, bringing those people together for one meeting is more efficient than having individual meetings. In other words, a leader can work more effectively through a well-organized group program than by working solely on an individual basis—there simply is not enough time for the latter in our fast-paced world.

Greater Variety of Resources and Viewpoints

Whether they are sharing information, solving a problem, or exploring personal values, a group of people can offer more viewpoints, and hence more resources. Shulman (1984) uses the phrase *sharing data* to describe the interaction of the multiple resources present in groups. Group members often relate that one of the most helpful aspects of their group is the variety of viewpoints expressed and discussed. When only two people get together, it is possible they will possess similar information, values, or ways of seeing the world. Because of this, it may be difficult to generate new ideas or methods of solving problems. Usually this is not the case in a group setting, especially if the group is not homogeneous. Members usually will have a variety of opinions and ideas, thus making the experience interesting and closer to real life.

Reasons Common to Therapy, Growth, and Support Groups

A leader who decides to conduct a therapy, growth, or support group does so for many different reasons. We discuss seven advantages: (1) the feeling of sharing common ground; (2) the experience of "belonging"; (3) the chance to practice on one another; (4) the opportunities for varied feedback; (5) the vicarious learning from others' concerns; (6) the approximation to real-life encounters; and (7) the peer pressure to maintain commitment.

Experience of Commonality

One of the major reasons for having people get together in a group is that they will frequently discover that they are not alone—that other people have thoughts and feelings similar to theirs. Yalom (1985) uses the term *universality* instead of *commonality* when he discusses the value of people getting together. But whatever the terminology, there is almost total agreement among writers in the field about the benefit of sharing common experiences. Some examples of groups in which shared common experiences can be helpful are the following:

- Parents whose children have died
- Pregnant teenagers
- Recently divorced women
- Vietnam veterans

The feeling of commonality is helpful and therapeutic for most individuals and cannot develop in individual counseling. Many people carry around fears they believe to be unique to them. As group members grow comfortable with one another and begin to take risks in sharing personal concerns, thoughts, and feelings, they are often amazed that others in the group have similar concerns. This provides a sense of "we-ness" that is greatly reassuring.

Sense of Belonging

Many writers in the fields of counseling and psychology have commented on the powerful human need to belong (Adler, 1927; Berne, 1964; Maslow, 1962; Rogers, 1961). This need can be satisfied in part by being in a group (Kottler, 1983; Trotzer, 1989; Yalom, 1985). Members will often identify with each other and thus feel part of a whole. Some examples of groups in which this sense of belonging has been reported to be beneficial are those for Vietnam veterans, women, ex-convicts, troubled adolescents, people with disabilities, and the elderly. Members of those groups have said that the experience of being accepted was one of the most important features of the group. This certainly would be congruent with the findings of the personality theorists cited earlier in this paragraph, who believe that a sense of belonging and, in Rogers's (1958) words, "unconditional positive regard" facilitates the development of a healthy personality.

Skills Practice

Groups provide an arena for safe practice, as many writers point out (Corey, 1990; Dyer & Vriend, 1980; Kottler, 1983; Trotzer, 1989). Members practice the new skills and behaviors they have learned in a supportive environment before trying them in real-world contexts. The range of new behaviors to explore is nearly infinite; leaders can set up role-play situations in which members can practice being assertive; interviewing for jobs; developing social skills; asking for a raise; or talking to teachers, parents, or spouses. Practicing these interactions and skills will greatly enhance members' chances for better communication in their individual environments. Assertiveness groups, communication groups, and parenting groups are all examples of groups in which members might experiment with new behaviors.

Aside from role playing, another form of practicing in the group is experimentation with new behaviors while relating to one another during the session. Members may share personal facts about themselves, confront others, talk about sex, look at others when they talk, cry in front of others, laugh with others, sing with others, or disagree with others. Teachers' groups, employer-employee relations groups, and police riot-training groups exemplify arenas in which members can authentically practice behaviors they have never attempted before.

Feedback

Groups provide an opportunity for members to receive feedback. In groups in which behavior rehearsal is a major component, the suggestions, reactions, and perceptions of others can be valuable. Only in groups do members have so many chances to hear how others experience them. Frequently members will have the opportunity to hear both first impressions and updated impressions. Group feedback partly differs from feedback during an individual counseling session by generally being more powerful. When only one person is giving feedback, the receiver can dismiss that person's viewpoint. When six or seven people are saying the same thing, it is hard to deny what's being said. Often clients have an unrealistic perception of themselves, and feedback from the group can cause them to expand and alter their self-perceptions.

There are many kinds of feedback and ways of giving feedback in a group. Leaders need to be aware of how and when to conduct feedback activities. Because these activities are very complex and valuable, we have devoted an entire section to feedback exercises (see Chapter Nine).

Vicarious Learning

In many kinds of groups, clients frequently discuss issues that are very meaningful to other members. That is, they have the opportunity to hear another present concerns similar to their own. The positive value of vicarious learning has been discussed by a number of authors (Bandura, 1977; Corey, 1990; Kottler, 1983; Yalom, 1985). Often a member will sit in silence and yet learn a great deal by watching how fellow members resolve their personal concerns. On countless occasions members say such things as, "That's exactly the same problem I have. It was helpful to watch how you learned to be stronger." Other members have said, "Hearing you has really made me aware of the fears and hangups I have."

Leaders should always be aware of the vicarious learning aspects of groups. Members who are quiet can still be learning about themselves. For example, in a group consisting of five women living in the same college residence hall, one member said very little throughout the eight sessions. The leader felt he had not reached her at all. About six months later, he got a short note from her saying she had changed a number of things in her life because of the group. She thanked the leader for allowing her to be in the group even though she did not contribute much. You can see from this example that it is not always necessary to push for active participation.

Real-Life Approximation

Groups come closer to replicating real life than does one-to-one therapy. This is so because people are not islands, but rather they live in an environment composed of others. Different writers have discussed groups as a microcosm or reflection of society (Dinkmeyer & Muro, 1979; Gazda, 1981; Yalom, 1985). Trotzer (1989) calls groups "minisocieties." While interacting with others, people experience fear, anger, doubt, worry, and jealousy. In the comparatively safe atmosphere of the group, those same emotions can surface and be identified and, it is hoped, resolved. The group setting becomes a temporary substitute for the community, family, work site, or organization in which those feelings repeat themselves fruitlessly.

The social context of the group experience is valuable in many other ways. Not only are maladaptive emotions and behaviors scrutinized and corrected, but members also are given the opportunity to discover how people honestly react to them over a period of weeks or months. In addition, they are exposed to a variety of human behaviors and attitudes: encouragement, support, anger, confrontation, genuineness, rigidity, and so on. Being exposed to these in a group environment enables individuals to learn methods of relating and coping that may in turn carry over into their everyday living.

Contracts and Commitments

The group can be a place to make important and helpful commitments or contracts to work on specific, individual concerns. A contract is essentially an oral or written statement indicating what a member is willing to do either in or outside of the group session. Although such commitments are often made in one-to-one situations (counselor-client, nurse-patient, supervisor-supervisee), the motivation to honor them seems to be stronger when they are made with a number of people. This is obviously one of the most helpful aspects of such groups as Alcoholics Anonymous, Weight Watchers, Gamblers Anonymous, and groups that help people become more assertive, stop smoking, or find a job. In these groups, members make at least an implied commitment to stop drinking, smoking, or overeating; to make a certain number of job contacts; or to practice assertiveness.

The combination of support, subtle expectations, and fear of letting down the group if the commitment is broken is a powerful motivator for behavioral change. Trotzer (1989) discusses the value of contracts under the heading of "The Group As Power" (p. 32). He points to the many ways the group can become a powerful force in a member's life, pressing for fidelity to commitments undertaken.

Summary of Advantages of Using a Group Approach

   A. For all groups:
      1. Efficiency
      2. Variety of viewpoints and resources
   B. For growth, support, and therapy groups:
      1. Experience of commonality
      2. Sense of belonging
      3. Skills practice

4. Feedback
5. Vicarious learning
6. Real-life approximation
7. Contracts and commitments

After considering the various reasons for forming a group, the leader must then decide which kinds of group would best serve the potential members.

KINDS OF GROUPS

Some people think the term *group* refers only to one kind of group: a counseling or therapy group for troubled individuals who have many self-defeating problems. In fact, groups have many different purposes. A group is two or more people who have come together for the purpose of some designated interaction. A person may form a group for educational purposes, to discuss or decide something, to complete a specific task or achieve a specific goal, or—yes—to explore personal problems. During your professional career you may have the opportunity to lead many different kinds of groups and to assume many different leadership roles. These roles will vary from one kind of group to the next. Many leaders make the mistake of having only one style or role; this can impede the optimal functioning of some groups. Although the techniques discussed here apply to all kinds of groups, they are ideally suited to groups of 5 to 15 people.

Educators have classified groups differently. Trotzer (1989) divides groups into six major categories: guidance and life skills groups, counseling groups, psychotherapy groups, support and self-help groups, consultation groups, and growth groups. Gladding (1991) lists groups as group guidance, group counseling, and group psychotherapy, along with some additional categories. Other kinds of groups were popular during the 1960s and 1970s. Gladding (1991) and Trotzer (1989) discuss these groups and the many ways that groups have been categorized.

Recently, groups have been formed that focus on multicultural issues. Group leaders need to be aware of such dynamics as they determine the kind of group they are leading (Corey, 1990; Newlon & Arciniega, 1992). It is very important for the group leader to be clear as to the purpose of the group. Very often groups are unsuccessful because the leader, the members, or both are confused about the purpose of the group.

We have created seven categories of groups, based on the different goals of each. Some goals reflect what we hope the members gain from the group and others what we hope the members will do in the group. The seven categories are as follows:

1. Support
2. Education

3. Discussion
4. Task
5. Growth and experiential
6. Therapy
7. Self-help

Support Groups

A support group is usually composed of 4 to 12 members and meets monthly, weekly, or even twice weekly. In this type of group, members share thoughts and feelings about themselves. Sharing with and listening to others furnishes a variety of viewpoints from which to examine issues and develop a feeling of commonality among members. Thus, support groups enable members to learn that other people struggle with the same issues, feel similar emotions, and think similar thoughts. Recently, men's support groups have developed throughout the country as a result of the work of Robert Bly and others (Capuzzi & Gross, 1992). Other examples of support groups include the following:

- Prisoners brought together to share their concerns about their loss of freedom, upcoming release, or loneliness.
- Children of divorced parents who wish to talk about their experiences and adjustment.
- Victims of a natural disaster, such as a flood or tornado, who may share feelings about the loss of loved ones, loss of property, or their sense of helplessness.
- Elderly people confined to convalescent centers. Growth or support groups allow them to support each other in their efforts to cope with loneliness and alienation.
- Homemakers seeking comfort and friendship from others who have chosen not to work outside the home.
- Those whose loved ones are dying of cancer. These individuals may find comfort in hearing that others are also experiencing grief and hopelessness and are struggling to carry on with their lives.
- Individuals with a disability coming together to share their feelings and fears about their disability.
- War veterans who share their feelings of alienation and horror and mourn the loss of their buddies.
- People with AIDS.
- A group of stepparents who find it helpful to share the specific difficulties experienced in a stepfamily.
- Recently divorced individuals who wish to discover how others are coping.
- Burnout and stress-management groups.

The role of the leader in a support group is to encourage sharing interactions among participants. Ideally, these interactions are personal, and members speak directly to one another. This is not to suggest that leaders should not speak up. They may be quite active and wish to share personal experiences of their own. However, it is important that leaders of these groups keep in mind that mutual sharing is the group's purpose and goal. It cannot be achieved if the leader or any one member dominates discussion.

EXAMPLES . . . .

This group is taking place in a community that has recently experienced a disaster. A fire in a local movie theater killed 50 people. Of the ten members present in the group, some were in the theater and managed to escape, and some lost loved ones in the fire. It is 45 minutes into the third session.

Leader: How are you sleeping?

Joe: I'm still not sleeping through the night. I have this anger at God, and I don't know what to do with it.

Carol: I have the same feeling. I haven't been to church since the fire, and I don't know if I'll ever go back.

Leader: (*Seeing that Bill is shaking his head "no"*) Bill, you seem troubled by what Carol and Joe said.

Bill: (*In a tentative, gentle manner*) Well, I am troubled. I guess my faith in God has been the thing that has pulled me through this. I don't know why He did what He did, but I guess He had a reason. I wish Carol and Joe could see their way clear to going back to church.

Leader: Does anyone else want to comment on that?

Jack: The priest gave me a book to read that helped me cope. The main point in the book was that you just have to go on and not ask "why." I guess that book really has helped and I did sleep last week for the first time.

At this point the leader's purpose is not to work therapeutically with the members' anger toward God, but rather to facilitate interaction and let people hear how others are coping. Now the leader invites another member into the discussion.

Leader: Ralph, what has helped you the most?

Ralph: I'm staying busy. I'm back at work, and at night I've made it a point not to be alone, at least in the early evening. I've arranged to eat meals with friends and family. I've also planned weekends well, and I'm making myself do things even though they don't seem to have much meaning. A friend of mine said, "Ralph, you've just gotta start living again." He was right!

Joe: You know, hearing you say that is helpful. I think that's what I need to start doing. I guess I haven't really thought about it, but I'm not trying to live in the present; I'm just staying in the past.

Betty: Joe, I hope you'll start living now because it's true for me, too. Just a week or so ago, I started living again, and it really made all the difference. I really do believe that as long as we're here on earth we've got to focus on our life and not on why it was *our* husband or son or loved one who died. (*Pauses and says with pain*) But believe me, it's not easy.

Leader: You know, I do have to agree with Betty and Ralph that focusing on the present and future is really the way to go. Does anyone else want to comment?

The leader is doing an excellent job of facilitating the group and seems to be providing a valuable experience for the members by allowing them to share and learn from each other. Notice that the leader is not overly involved in the discussion. Many leaders make the mistake of overleading, which sometimes prevents members from sharing.

. . . .

This group is composed of eight elderly people living in a convalescent center. It is the third meeting.

Carl: Nobody came to visit me this weekend.

Three members simultaneously: They didn't?

Carl: (*Dejectedly*) They called at the last minute and said something else came up and that they weren't going to be able to come.

Claude: That's too bad. I didn't check on you this weekend because I thought you were gone.

Wayne: I wish you had come down to my room. I certainly would have spent time with you.

Bob: We oughta get up a system to check on each other during the weekends. You know, they're the hardest.

Bertha: Boy, that's for sure.

Jim: I guess I'm beginning to count on this group more than on my family.

Claude: You know, I enjoy this group because you all care. It's not that my family doesn't care; it's just that it's a burden for them to come here. Yeah, I *do* like this group.

Leader: (*Realizing that Sam hasn't talked*) How about you, Sam? Are you feeling better about the group? I know the first couple of times you weren't sure if you were going to like it.

Sam: Oh, I think I like it. We just talk. I guess I was afraid people were going to tell me what to do. It feels good here.

The leader realizes that the purpose of this group is to generate member-to-member interaction in the hope that the day will be a little brighter for these people. Because this appears to be happening, she is staying out of the discussion except to draw out comments from quiet individuals or generate discussion if the interaction starts to decline. Eventually the leader may initiate discussion of Bob's suggestion that they develop a system to check on each other during weekends.

. . . .

This group is composed of eight teenage girls who are all at least six months pregnant. The leader is a high school counselor who decided to form the group to help the girls cope with their situation. It's the second meeting.

Leader: Let's talk about two things tonight. First, the reaction you're getting from peers and family; second, let's follow up on last week and any decisions you have made regarding keeping the baby or giving it up for adoption.

Julie: Can we start with last week first?

Leader: Sure.

Julie: Well, the decision is so hard. I thought I knew for sure that I was going to keep the baby, and then I saw a show on TV about a teenager giving up her baby. Did anyone see that movie?

Connie, Linda, and Carol: I did.

Julie: Did it affect you at all?

Linda: Yes, it did. I've wanted to give up the baby, but my mom doesn't want me to. She thinks giving up the baby would be a horrible thing to do. (*Turns to leader*) What do you think?

Leader: No doubt the decision is a tough one, especially when your family is putting pressure on you one way or another. I hope that what we can do is take a look at all the forces that come into play in this decision and then try to help each one of you. I hope you realize that although each of you is in the same situation in that you are pregnant, each of you must make your own decision. I hope that what we do in the group will be helpful and support you in making that decision.

Cindy: But what do you do when you have pressure from your mom or dad? They want me to keep the baby, but I really don't want to be reminded of this. There are a lot of people wanting to adopt babies, and I don't want a baby.

Leader: (*Knowing that Cindy is a fairly strong person, she decides to spend a little time with her, believing the others will benefit*) Cindy, why don't you list for the group the pros and cons of giving up the baby?

Cindy: The real con, as I see it, is that my parents will be mad. Other than that, I see it as a good idea for me. I'm not saying you all should do this.

Leader: Okay, can you deal with your parents being mad at you—and how mad would they be?

Cindy: Well, they would be mad, but I think they could get over it. I guess I do wonder, too, if in ten years I will regret my decision.

Leader: Cindy, let's talk about how bad feelings can creep up on you without you realizing it. (*Leader teaches Cindy and the rest of the group that thoughts can cause feelings*)

Even though this seems a little like therapy, it is mainly a support group in which some education and some therapy are also taking place. This vignette is an example of how one kind of group will sometimes overlap with others.

.   .   .   .

These three examples should give you a good idea of the type of dialogue heard in support groups.

Education Groups

Often, helping professionals are asked to provide clients with information on various topics. That is, the leader has information to share and facilitates group interaction among members to enhance their learning. Examples of educational groups include the following:

- Rehabilitation clients learning how to use a wheelchair
- Students learning study skills
- Diabetics acquiring information on a special diet and nutrition
- Women learning about rape and how to protect themselves
- Managers learning how to supervise employees better
- Sixth-graders learning about the harmful effects of drug use

In each of these groups, the leader provides information and then elicits reactions and comments from the members, thereby serving sometimes as an educator and other times as a facilitator. It is very important that the leader conceptualize this dual role. There is no set formula for how much to play each role—it will depend on the amount of information to be covered, the amount of knowledge the members already have, and the amount of time available. Likewise, there is no set format for the number of sessions or length of meetings. Often, educational groups are held just once for two to eight hours. Others meet for a number of weeks, two hours per week.

EXAMPLES. . . . .

The setting is a college counseling center. The group is composed of eight first-year students who want hints on how to study more efficiently. It is 20 minutes into the first session.

Leader: OK, let's talk about the different ways of going about studying a chapter in a text. What are the ways that you do it?

Jerry: Well, I just read the chapter and underline.

Bill: I do the same thing.

Kevin: I try to outline 'em, but it takes me too long.

Bobbi: I just read it twice and hope for the best.

Leader: Let me give you some ideas. One of the best things you can do is sit down and skim the chapter for the main idea of what you are going to be reading. Often, there is a summary at the end of each chapter. Then decide the kinds of questions that the professor might ask. If you can, look over your other tests and try to get a sense of the kind of questions you have been asked before. How does that sound?

Becky: Well, I never thought of skimming the chapter.

Jim: I like that idea.

Chu: Me, too. Would you suggest underlining or taking notes or what?

Leader: It's quicker to either underline or mark in the margin. Many people, however, don't learn from underlining.

Kevin: That's true for me. It's not helpful for me to underline. But when I take notes as I read, I remember.

Jim: Yeah, I like that idea. I've been underlining too, but it hasn't helped. I think I'd better take notes or try something else.

The leader's role in this group is to offer helpful suggestions and ideas concerning ways of studying. A second rule is to get members to share those methods of studying that do and do not work for them.

. . . .

This group is composed of five women who weigh over 200 pounds. The purpose of the group is to educate the women about behavior-modification methods of losing weight. It is the second meeting, and it's ten minutes into the session.

Leader: Get out your list of things other than food that are reinforcing for you—let's talk about them.

Rhonda: I realize that I do like to read, although I don't do it, and there are three or four TV shows that I like. I also put on my list that I have two friends who live back in Missouri that I would like to call but don't.

Phyllis: Gosh, that's strange. I also put down that I have some friends who live in California that I would like to call. The other thing that I like to do that would be good for weight control is walking early in the morning. Gee, I'll bet I haven't gone for a good walk in the morning for over a year.

Sally: Oh, I'd go with you! I get up early, but I just sit around and watch the news.

Leader: How about others? Margie, what about you?

Margie: My list doesn't make sense.

Leader: Do you mean that the activities you listed are strange or that you did not do it exactly right? I'm not sure what you mean.

Margie: Well, I've got things like sleeping, exercising, washing my car, cleaning my house—you know, dumb things like that.

Leader: I don't really see those as dumb. In fact, let's talk more about how you can use your "reinforcer list" to help you. Let me go into a little more theory. . . .

In this example, the leader is both educating by providing information and facilitating interaction by bringing up topics, clarifying comments, and getting members to share.

. . . .

Discussion Groups

In a discussion group, the focus is usually on topics or issues rather than on the members' personal concerns. Its purpose is to give participants the opportunity to share ideas and exchange information. The leader serves mainly as a facilitator because he or she does not necessarily have more knowledge about the subject than the members do. The goal of the discussion group is to get members involved. Its value is that usually a greater number of viewpoints are expressed. Here are some possible examples of discussion-group topics:

- Whether or not to have children
- The prevalence of drug abuse in the local schools
- The benefits of religious thought
- The possibility of nuclear war
- The pros and cons of marriage

The following examples should help you conceptualize the leader's role in discussion groups.

EXAMPLES . . . .

This group is composed of nine high school students taking a class in marriage and the family. The topic of discussion is "How the Family Is Changing."

Leader: Let's list all the different forms in which families exist in our town. Each of you make a list. (*After a couple of minutes*) In looking at your list, what stands out to you?

Eddie: To me, the effects of people getting divorced stand out because we have single mothers with kids, single fathers with kids, and stepfamilies. A lot of these exist because of divorce.

Lynn: I never realized how many families aren't just the regular kind; that is, a mom, a dad, and some kids.

Don: You know, I think we need to be more accepting of all these kinds of families.

Charles: I agree, because I'm currently living with just my mom, and I remember that last year I was kidded about it.

Lewis: Yeah, well, what can we do in the school to make everyone more accepting?

Leader: (*Intervening*) Wait, let's just discuss the different kinds of families today. I don't think we should try to take on changing attitudes here in the school just yet.

Billy: The thing I wonder about is all those single fathers. What do they know about babies?

Sarah: I saw a thing on TV just the other day. . . .

The leader's role in this group was to generate discussion on the topic of the changing family. The leader was acting appropriately by not dominating the discussion and not letting Lewis shift the focus of the group to ways of making other people more accepting.

.   .   .   .

It is the monthly meeting of the Personal Growth Book Club. The book being discussed is titled *Love and Addiction*.

Leader: Let's do a quick round of 1 to 10. If you liked the book a whole lot, give it a 10; a 1 means you did not like it at all.

Leslie: I'd give it a 7.

Ralph: 9.

Steve: 10.

Tuyen: 7.

Cindy: 8.

Lendon: 9.

Fred: 6.

Leader: Let's talk about what stood out for you, since most people did like it. What were the main two or three points that really hit you?

Steve: There was just so much in there that helped me to understand the crazy relationship I'm currently in. I felt that the authors were talking directly to me. I thought it was really interesting the way they described how people get into bad relationships.

Ralph: Yeah, me too. I thought the description was excellent. It really helped me to think through an old relationship that I'd had. On page 27—everyone look at that for a minute—. . . .

In this group, the leader uses the 1-to-10 ratings to generate discussion. Once the discussion gets going, he simply tries to keep members involved by seeing to it that the discussion is relevant and meaningful. The leader may or may not choose to enter into the discussion.

. . . .

Task Groups

The task group is one in which a specific task is to be accomplished, such as discussing a patient in a psychiatric ward, resolving conflicts among house residents, or deciding policies for a new hospital wing. It is called a *task group* because its purpose is very specific and clear. This kind of group usually meets once or just a few times and is terminated when the task is completed. Staff meetings, faculty meetings, organizational meetings, planning sessions, or decision-making meetings about rules or nominations are examples of task groups.

The leader's role in a "pure" task group is to keep the focus on the task at hand. In some task groups, the members stay focused on their own; then the leader's role is more facilitative. In other task groups, discussion becomes unfocused, or conflict breaks out among members. In such instances, the leader intervenes and deals with the disruptive members to bring the group back to the task. Sometimes the leader even lets the focus blur in order to resolve other issues. Although some task groups take place without a leader, often one is needed to monitor the focus. The following list should give you a better idea of what task groups are:

- Members of an organization who are choosing a slate of officers
- Houseparents who are deciding rules and policies
- Professionals who are all involved in the treatment of one student (for example, a counselor, two teachers, a social worker, and a special-education coordinator)
- Professionals who are collaborating on a year-end report
- Concerned citizens who want to do something about drunk drivers
- People who are planning their ten-year high school reunion
- Students who are trying to change some policies at their school

E X A M P L E S . . . .

The purpose of the group is to discuss Johnny, who has been labeled a juvenile delinquent. To determine a future placement solution (the child is currently residing in an emergency crisis shelter), a houseparent, Johnny, Johnny's mother, a social worker, and a counselor have been brought together. The leader of the group is the social worker.

Mother: I want Johnny at home, but I don't know if I can get my husband to agree. I know that if Johnny continues to do what he was doing, I just can't have him there.

Houseparent: Johnny was not cooperative here, and I don't think he's ready to go home.

Johnny: But wait a minute! I'm more cooperative than Carol Ann.

Houseparent: (*In a condescending voice*) Now, Johnny, how can you say that? Carol Ann has done a lot around here lately that shows me she is more cooperative than you. She's swept the hall. She cooked and she—

Leader: (*Seeing that they're off the task*) Wait a minute. Let's get back to our task, which is deciding where Johnny should go come Monday morning. (*To the counselor*) What is your evaluation of Johnny?

Counselor: I have seen Johnny for five sessions now, and he's still a very angry kid. My own opinion is that he will not do well at home.

Johnny: What do *you* know!

Counselor: (*Starts to answer, but the leader jumps in*)

Leader: (*To the group*) Is there anyone here who feels that Johnny could make it at home?

Johnny: I do.

Leader: OK. Is there anyone else? (*Silence*) Then it looks like we need to figure out a temporary place for Johnny to go.

. . . .

The purpose of this group is to select one of three applicants to fill a vacant position in a small community agency. To make the decision, the director has brought together her staff of six to discuss the interviews.

Dave: I feel that we need a female, so I think we should hire Sarah.

Sheri: I agree that we need another female.

Tom: (*Angrily*) Hold on just one minute. That's a bunch of crap. Why did we interview two guys if we were going to hire a woman? We never said anything about hiring a woman.

Director: (*Recognizing a potentially volatile situation*) Let's talk about what we *do* need. I think both points are well taken. We never decided that we needed a woman. However, all things being equal, I think hiring a woman would be in our best interest. Let's go over each candidate's strengths and weaknesses.

Filip: I didn't like the fact that Sarah smoked. None of us smoke. In fact, I think we should get the secretary to stop smoking.

Tom: Oh, I agree. Let's do that. Let's make a policy about smoking. (*Turns to the director*) How do we pass such a policy? I make a motion—

Director: (*Realizing that the group is off the intended task*) Wait! We're here to decide on the three candidates. We need to choose one of them. At the next meeting, we can set policies on smoking or whatever. Let's go over each candidate, listing strengths and weaknesses.

. . . .

In each of these groups, the leader made clear what the task was and tried to keep the group working on the task. Even though the members got sidetracked, they too were aware that the purpose of the group was to work on a given task.

Growth Groups and Experiential Groups

Growth groups consist of members who want to experience being in a group and who have the motivation to learn more about themselves. T-groups, or *training* groups, were the first popular kind of growth group; the first one was held in Bethel, Maine, in 1947. Sensitivity groups, awareness groups, and encounter groups would all be considered growth groups. These names were given to certain kinds of groups popular in the 1960s and early 1970s. In these and other growth groups, members are given the opportunity to explore and develop personal goals. Often those goals include changes in lifestyle, a greater awareness of feelings about oneself and others, improved interpersonal communications, and an assessment of values—all accomplished in an atmosphere of honest sharing and listening.

Depending on the specific goal of the group, the leader may need knowledge of a broad range of issues, including divorce, sex, parents, the grieving process, stepfamilies, religion, and the intrapersonal dynamics of anger, guilt, worry, anxiety, and the need for approval. These are some of the issues that are often discussed. Corey (1990) discusses in some detail structured growth groups. He describes social competence groups for youngsters, self-esteem groups, anger-control groups for Vietnam veterans, groups that engage in adventurous activities, and many other structured growth groups. Growth groups are conducted in settings such as schools, colleges, community centers, and retreat centers.

One form of growth group is the experiential group, in which the leader designs several experiential activities for the members. Often these are conducted outdoors and involve physical challenges, risk taking, and cooperation among members. Perhaps the best known is the "ropes course," in which members are challenged on a number of activities that involve ropes.

EXAMPLES. . . . .

This group is composed of ten teenagers who are out on the ropes course.

Leader: What have you learned so far?

Buz: That fear is more in the mind!

Eden: I agree. I never thought I could do the cross walk, but when I saw Amiel do it, I thought, "I can do it."

Steve: The group support has been what stood out for me. I was really scared, but everyone kept telling me I could do it. That really helped.

Leader: Let me pick up on what Steve is saying about group support and the value of it.

. . . .

The purpose of this group is to examine values. This kind of group could meet in a school, a church, or a community center.

Leader: Today we are going to take a look at some of the things you value. First, let me have everyone stand up and get in a line behind Serj. (*Everyone is now standing in the center of the room in a straight line, with the leader standing in front where everyone can see him*)
  On the count of three, I am going to ask you to move to the position that is most like the way you are. Toward the wall to your left is "spender," and toward the wall to your right is "saver." That is, if any time you have money you spend it, you would move all the way to the wall to your left. If you spend some and save some, you may want to position yourself in the middle, and so on. Everyone understand? (*Everyone nods*) Okay, on three. One, two, three. (*Everyone moves*)

Leader: Any comments?

Doug: I am glad to see I am not the only spender because my mom says I spend, spend, spend.

Toni: I wish I could spend. I always feel like I must save my money. That's why I'm up against this wall. Have you spenders always been able to spend?

Leader: (*After letting several members comment*) The main point of doing this is to see that people are different and to help each of you get a better understanding of why you are the way you are. Let's now talk about why you are the way you are and whether you want to change.

Later, the leader might use other examples, such as "big city versus small town" or "high risk taker versus low risk taker."

.   .   .   .

In each of these examples, the leader is attempting to help the members explore aspects of their personality. The group is structured in that the leader has initiated activities that will involve the members in relevant self-exploration and self-growth.

Therapy Groups

The purposes of therapy groups are similar to those of growth and support groups. Each tries to promote growth through sharing personal concerns and listening to the concerns of others. There are differences, however, in the role of the leader as well as in the needs of the members. In the kinds of groups we have discussed thus far, the leader functions mainly as an educator or facilitator, attempting to generate verbal interaction among participants. The rationale for limiting the leader to a facilitative role is the assumption that, with guidance, group members possess the ability and resources to help themselves and one another. In contrast, in many therapy groups, members are unable to solve their own problems and are often unable to objectively help others. Examples of therapy groups include inpatients diagnosed as having emotional disorders, juvenile delinquents in an institutional setting, a group of clients with eating disorders such as bulimia and anorexia, and alcohol and drug abusers.

It is important to realize that group therapists do not all agree on how therapy groups should be conducted. Opinions vary widely on the role of the members, the role of the leader, the appropriate tone, and the use of theory in the group. Some believe that members should conduct the majority of the therapy, with supportive probing and encouragement from the leader (Rogers, 1970; Yalom, 1985). Others feel that a confrontive, aggressive approach works best, such as in positive peer culture groups (Vorrath, 1974) or Synanon groups (Casriel, 1963). Some believe that individual therapy by the leader while the majority of the group observes is very beneficial (Dyer & Vriend, 1980; Perls, 1969). Some leaders strictly follow one of the theoretical models, such as rational emotive therapy, transactional analysis, or psychoanalytic theory. Others use none of the individual counseling theories as their theoretical base, but rather believe it is the power of the group interaction—sharing, involvement, and belonging—that serves as the main agent for change (Yalom, 1985).

In Chapter Twelve, we discuss in greater detail some of the ways of leading therapy groups and give the pros and cons of each approach. We also outline our own model, which places primary responsibility in the leader's hands.

E X A M P L E S . . . .

This group consists of five women whose husbands routinely beat them. It is 20 minutes into the third session.

Leader: A number of you have talked about your poor self-concept. Rather than us just talking about self-concept, I'd like for someone to volunteer to work on her self-concept so that we can help her and at the same time get others in the group to go deeper.

Katelyn: I will, but I'm sort of scared.

Leader: I think all of us understand your fear. Why don't you start by telling us more about how you felt growing up?

Katelyn: I always felt like a nothing. My parents definitely favored my brother and sister. They even told me that if they'd known I was going to be so much trouble, they would have never had me. (*Starts to cry*)

. . . .

This group consists of five teenagers who all recently attempted suicide. It is 15 minutes into the third session, and the members have been discussing their relationship with their parents.

Carl: At least your parents care! Hell, my old man hasn't been here since he brought me here. When he left, he said to me, "I'm done with you!"

Dione: At least you have a dad. My mom has all these men over all the time. I can't stand it.

Leader: (*In a caring tone*) Look, we could sit here and talk about how bad things are, but I am not sure that is the most helpful thing. What do the rest of you think?

Trudy: I think we have to learn to feel good about ourselves no matter what our parents say and do. Like you said last time, we all need to learn how to cope with our feelings.

Leader: Let's focus on the feelings you have about yourself and talk about how you can change your feelings by changing some of the negative "self-talk" that is in your head. I want each of you to think of the negative things you tell yourself throughout the week.

. . . .

In the first example, no specific theory was demonstrated, although the leader was most likely thinking in terms of Adlerian, rational emotive therapy, transactional analysis, reality therapy, or some other theory. In the second example, the leader obviously was using rational emotive therapy to help these teenagers examine their poor self-concept.

Self-Help Groups

The last kind of group we want to discuss is the self-help group, which is now very popular (Corey, 1990; Gladding, 1991; Trotzer, 1989). These groups often follow the model of Alcoholics Anonymous groups and the Twelve Steps. We feel that all counselors should be aware of these groups because they have proven to have tremendous value for thousands of people. It is unfortunate that some professionals have negative feelings about these groups. Although we realize that they are not for everyone, many people take advantage of these helpful, no-fee groups. If you are not familiar with these groups, please be sure to seek further information. Because the purpose of this text is to discuss group leadership and these groups have no permanent leader, we will not focus on self-help groups here.

GROUP VERSUS INDIVIDUAL COUNSELING

It is important to realize that group counseling is not for everyone (Corey, 1990; Yalom, 1985). Not only can participating in a group be harmful for some people, but an individual who does not want or is not ready to be in a group can disrupt it. When leaders recognize that a member needs more than the group can provide or that the member is going to be disruptive, they should discuss with the member options for individual counseling instead of group counseling or for both individual and group counseling. In a later chapter, we discuss the problems of dealing with nonvoluntary members, which is a slightly different issue.

USE OF THEORIES

Many of our students have asked us if there are any specific group counseling theories. The answer is "no" except for psychodrama, which we will discuss in Chapter Twelve. Although labels have been given to many groups—encounter, T, sensory awareness, here-and-now—these names simply describe what takes place in those groups; they are in no way to be construed as specific group counseling theories. However, this does not mean that a leader does not use theory in working with growth, support, or therapy groups. Theories originally developed for one-to-one settings, such as rational emotive, behavioral, or reality therapy, have been successfully adapted for groups.

Throughout this text, and especially in our discussion of therapy groups in Chapter Twelve, we mention various counseling theories. To cover them in detail is beyond the purpose of this book. If you desire further information about specific theories as they apply to group work, see Corey (1990) or Gladding (1991).

We cannot stress enough the importance of being able to use at least one counseling theory when leading therapy or growth groups. Those who do not have a good working knowledge of at least one theoretical perspective often lead a very shallow group; that is, the group never goes beyond surface interaction and sharing. If the members do become more involved, the leader who does not have a theoretical base is usually overwhelmed.

On the other hand, certain kinds of groups do not require that leadership be based on a counseling theory. Discussion, education, and task groups require instead that the leader possess a variety of basic leadership skills in monitoring and directing the flow of conversation and interaction.

For human relationships training groups, there are some organization and development theories that may apply. Kormanski (1991) discusses these and presents a strong argument for the use of theory with these kinds of groups.

GROUP LEADERSHIP STYLES

Much has been written regarding leadership style (Capuzzi & Gross, 1992; Corey, 1990; Gladding, 1991; Trotzer, 1989). We believe that the style or role of the leader will always depend on the purpose of the group. As Gladding (1991) states: "Most effective group leaders show versatility" (p. 154). However, some people are taught only one style of leadership, regardless of the kind of group they are leading. Many model their group leadership style after the style of a group leader they had in graduate school. This is not a good idea because the groups they are leading in their work are often very different from groups in an academic program.

The major leadership debate seems to center on how active, directive, and structured the leader should be. Until recently, many group-leadership educators were hesitant about telling students to be active and directive in group leadership. A similar situation existed in the 1960s regarding individual counseling, when educators debated the relative merits of directive and nondirective counseling. Now most educators encourage their students to be active and reasonably directive in their individual counseling.

For group counseling, our position is that an active style of leadership works best for most groups. The reason is that most members of most groups need some structure, organization, and direction. In fact, most members expect the leader to lead. This is especially true of groups in schools, mental health settings, hospitals, prisons, and rehabilitation centers, and of issue-focused groups such as those concerning divorce, abuse, incest, or addiction. We strongly believe that *people don't mind being led when they are led well.*

Leader Direction versus Group Direction

A related question is "Should the group be leader-directed or group-directed?" Many writers express concern regarding the leader-directed approach (Capuzzi & Gross, 1992; Gladding, 1991; Posthuma, 1989; Starak, 1988). They fear that the members will have to cater to the leader. However, good leaders who follow the leader-directed model never demand that the members follow them as if they were gurus; rather, they lead in a manner that is valuable for the members. The concept of *leader-directed groups* does not mean that the leader is on an ego trip or that the group has to serve the personality of the leader. It simply means that the leader has an understanding of the members' needs and structures the group to meet those needs.

Leaders using the group-directed approach often will turn the group over to the members and have the members determine the direction and content. This can waste much time, especially for a group that is meeting only once or for only a few sessions. Often the members don't know what they need. For example, parents of teens in a drug treatment center or victims of some kind of disaster often attend a group to find help, but they are not at all clear as to how the group can be helpful. A leader-directed style can be of great benefit by providing thought-provoking questions, group exercises, and structure.

The question is not really whether the approach is group-directed or leader-directed, but rather who is primarily responsible for the group—the leader or the members? We believe the leader is responsible for the group. As Trotzer (1989) states:

> Leaders, because of their training and professional commitment, are remiss if they do not exercise their responsibility to prevent negative consequences in the group. Leaders can share responsibility to a very large degree, but they can never abdicate their responsibility. Doing so completely undermines the nature of the helping profession and is detrimental to positive therapeutic intervention. Leaders must be willing to divert topic and conversational trends that seem to be shaping into negative and damaging content (Blaker & Samo, 1973). They must be willing to intervene to protect members and to serve as a reality check if the group does not do so. As Lakin (1969) noted, responsibility must be consciously exercised and modeled by the leader if the group is to qualify as a professional therapeutic venture. [p. 218]

Even though the leader is responsible, the level of involvement will depend on the kind of group and the composition of its members. For certain groups, the leader may primarily want the members to direct the group; for other groups, the leader will want to assume much of the direction. It is important for the leader to remember that the amount of active leading necessary can vary according to the stage the group is in. In the middle stage of a group, often the members are fully aware of how the group should be run and therefore are actively involved in choosing the topics and direction.

Interpersonal versus Intrapersonal Leadership Styles

Another way to view leadership style is as a continuum from focusing on the group as a whole to focusing on the individuals in the group (Shapiro, 1978). Corey (1990) states that the *interpersonally oriented* leader "emphasizes the here and now, the interactions among the members, the group as a whole, the ongoing group dynamics, and the obstacles to the development of effective interpersonal relationships within the group" (p. 79). The *intrapersonally oriented* leader focuses primarily on the needs and concerns of the individual members.

Understanding both styles of leadership is very important. Leaders must be able to adopt a style along this continuum, depending on the kind of group, the needs of the members, and the dynamics occurring within the group. You might want to think of the continuum as a 1-to-10 scale:

Interpersonal   Intrapersonal

| 1 | 2 | 3 | 4 | 5 | 6 | 7 | 8 | 9 | 10 |

When the purpose of the group is to improve relationships among members or to accomplish a task, the leader will probably use an interpersonal leadership style within the 2-to-5 range. Some experts (Carroll, 1986; Rogers, 1970; Yalom, 1985) have strongly advocated the interpersonal model (1 to 3 on the continuum) for therapy groups. Group leaders who follow this model place strong emphasis on the stages of the group and on the members' being the primary agents of change.

We believe the intrapersonal model (6 to 8 on the continuum) is better for therapy, growth, and support groups because members in most of these groups have intrapersonal conflicts they want to or need to deal with. In most therapy groups, the members need to address issues such as unfinished business from the past, problems with parents or a lover, sexual abuse, abandonment, low self-esteem, fear of failure, guilt, shame, or need for approval. Many therapy groups deal with clients who have deep-seated emotional problems. The intrapersonal perspective seems better suited to helping clients obtain a better understanding of the issues they are struggling with. The intrapersonally oriented leader will address these issues directly, whereas the interpersonally oriented leader will wait until the issues emerge and then may only focus on them as they apply to the here-and-now experience within the group. For these reasons, we find the interpersonal leadership style somewhat limited. On the continuum, we feel that the style of most therapy group leaders should fall between a 6 and an 8.

In using a style ranging from 6 to 8 on the continuum, the leader primarily would encourage members to examine their issues, concerns, and feelings and share them with the group. Once a member discloses a concern, the leader would use several techniques and theories to help the disclosing member. Those leaders operating at a 9 or 10 on the continuum might only do one-on-one counseling while other members watch (Perls, 1969). Those operating at a 6 to 8 would involve members in many different ways when focusing on a member or an issue. More emphasis would be placed on individual needs and less on group interaction and group development. Leaders using a style in the 2-to-4 range focus more on what is happening in the group in the present moment and less on pressing personal issues or on the past.

Even though we feel that for most therapy groups a style of 6 to 8 on the continuum is best, we want to qualify this by saying that at all times the leader must pay attention to the group dynamics. There will be times when the leader will need or want to focus on the dynamics and interaction.

We also want to point out that for some groups this continuum will be of little importance. For instance, leaders of education and discussion groups will usually not need to pay too much attention to the stage of the group, the group dynamics, or the intrapersonal dynamics of the members, but rather will need to use various leadership skills and techniques to impart knowledge or generate discussion.

LEADERSHIP FUNCTIONS

Another way to view leadership style is to consider leadership functions. Yalom (1985) points out that the leader may provide emotional stimulation, caring, praise, protection, acceptance, interpretations, and explanations. The leader also may serve as a model through self-disclosure and as a person who sets limits, enforces rules, and manages the time. In other words, depending on the kind of group, the leader may perform many different roles and functions. The following list of different groups and possible leadership behaviors may clarify this point further:

- In a group of elementary school children who recently have had someone close to them die, the leader would want to provide support, explanations, and acceptance. He or she might want to use structured exercises to help the children talk about different issues pertaining to their loss.
- For a group of unemployed people trying to improve their job-finding skills, the leader would want to provide helpful information and activities. The leader might also provide structured exercises and practice sessions with feedback.
- In a support group of adults with a parent suffering from Alzheimer's disease, the leader would want to facilitate member sharing and caring. The leader might also provide some information and would probably not need to use many structured activities.
- For a group of adult children of alcoholics who feel they are still affected by growing up in an alcoholic family, the leader would want to provide information, caring, and protection. In addition, the leader might serve as a model if he or she were also the child of an alcoholic. Through his or her own self-disclosure, the leader could also use group exercises to help members recognize and experience some well-hidden but intense feelings.

These are just four examples. We could list many more, but these demonstrate that different kinds of groups require different styles and functions. Education, discussion, and task groups often dictate a facilitative or educational role, or both on the part of the leader. In these kinds of groups, there are times when the leader needs to be directive to keep the group focused on the task or topic. Therapy, growth, and support groups often require that the leader provide support and caring, and sometimes confrontation and structure.

WHAT MAKES AN EFFECTIVE LEADER?

A number of writers have described what makes an effective counselor and group leader (Cavanaugh, 1990; Corey, 1990; Egan, 1990; George & Dustin, 1988; Trotzer, 1989). Among the characteristics discussed are caring, openness, flexibility, warmth, objectivity, trustworthiness, honesty, strength, patience, sensitivity, and self-awareness. Each of these characteristics is important, and we urge you to refer to the works cited in this paragraph or to any other beginning counseling text if you desire further clarification of ideal helper characteristics.

Additional leadership characteristics include comfort with oneself and others; a liking for people; comfort in a position of authority; confidence in one's ability to lead; and the ability to read others well—that is, to be tuned in to others' feelings, reactions, moods, and words. Finally, the effective leader is psychologically healthy.

Leading groups successfully requires a great deal from the leader, and often people lead groups when they simply do not possess the necessary leadership characteristics. Besides those already mentioned, six other traits warrant further discussion.

Experience with individuals.   Effective leaders have spent much time talking with people at work and at social, sports, cultural, or religious events and functions—and with all kinds of people, not just those like themselves. The broader the leader's range of life experiences, the greater the chances for understanding the diverse members of a group.

The effective therapy group leader has not only general experience with people but also considerable experience in one-to-one counseling. This is necessary because all kinds of situations arise with specific individuals while leading therapy groups, and the more experience the leader has working with individuals, the easier it will be to work with an individual and the group simultaneously. Without a foundation of individual counseling experience, one would very likely find leading therapy groups very difficult.

Experience with groups.   In the development of any skill, practice and experience increase one's effectiveness. Effective leaders have led many groups; there is no point, therefore, in novice leaders' being overly self-critical. Due to lack of experience, they probably will not be highly skilled, but they can try to learn from their mistakes and from each leadership experience. Novices who do this will most likely improve their skills. It is advisable to begin, if possible, by leading groups other than growth or therapy groups and to restrict the number of members to four or five. Once beginning leaders are comfortable, they should increase the number of members or try a growth group centered either on a topic such as stress or assertiveness or on another with which they are comfortable and familiar. When novice leaders feel they can comfortably facilitate growth groups, they might try co-leading several therapy groups before leading one on their own.

Planning and organizational skills.   A major reason groups go well is that their leaders have thought through the plan for each session based on how long the group has been meeting, the purpose of the group, the various members' needs, what has been discussed, and what is going to be discussed. Effective leaders can plan a session and a series of sessions in such a way that the group is interesting, beneficial, and personally valuable. When leading discussion, education, task, or growth groups, effective leaders give considerable thought to relevant topics and to activities and exercises that pertain to those topics. Effective leaders organize sessions in such a way that all topics are covered and there is a flow from topic to topic.

Planning is different for support or therapy groups because the members contribute most of the content, but leaders still need to plan for these groups. For instance, during each session, a leader usually will allow time for warming up, progress reports from various members, sharing among members, and summarizing at the end of the session or following the discussion of an important issue. Because planning is essential to effective leading, we devote an entire chapter to it (see Chapter Three).

Knowledge of the topic.   In almost any kind of group, the leader who is well informed will naturally do a better job of leading than the one who lacks information. The leader can use information to stimulate discussion, clarify issues, and share new ideas. For example, in a group centered on the topic of divorce, the leader ideally would know about the pertinent legal issues as well as the practicalities of dealing with children in that situation.

A good understanding of basic human conflicts and dilemmas. The leader of almost any kind of group must be prepared to deal with a number of human problems and multicultural issues (Corey, 1990; Newlon & Arciniega, 1992); this is especially true in growth and therapy groups. Issues such as guilt, fear of failure, self-worth, parents, anger, love relationships, and death often emerge in such groups. Effective leaders will have an understanding of those issues and know several ways to help others who are struggling with them. Again, novice leaders may not yet have gained a thorough understanding of some, or perhaps most, of the issues mentioned. They should not criticize themselves for this, but rather should read material that will offer new insights and perhaps seek out counseling in an effort to better understand those issues as they pertain to them personally. Also, paying attention to the lives of other people and to the issues presented in the news, movies, and on television is equally important.

A good understanding of counseling theory. A knowledge of counseling theory is not merely background but a pragmatic key to understanding people and the world in which we live. Theories of therapy, such as person-centered, rational emotive, transactional analysis, Adlerian, and behavioral, help us understand why people do what they do in their lives and in groups. Theories offer group leaders a variety of ways to grasp what people are saying and doing. Corey and Corey (1992) state: "Group leaders without any theory behind their interventions will probably find that their groups never reach a productive stage" (p. 7). During group interaction, many things surface for each member and between members; the effective leader must be able to recognize these dynamics quickly. Knowledge of theories will help the leader to do so (Gladding, 1991). If you do not feel you have a good working knowledge of the various counseling theories, seek out workshops and books that relate to the theories. Study one or two of the theories until you master them and feel confident in their application.

POTENTIAL GROUP PROBLEMS

So far, we have discussed basic issues that pertain to the general field of group work. We hope that exposure to the rationale for using a group approach and to the various kinds of groups has cleared up some of their mystique and has better prepared you to lead them. To give you an idea of some of the challenges that arise in leading groups, we have compiled a partial list. Some of these occur in certain kinds of groups; others, in all kinds of groups. This list of problematic member behaviors and situations further illustrates the need for learning effective leadership skills. Group members might do any of the following:

- Skip from topic to topic
- Try to dominate the discussion
- Be "chit-chatty" rather than personal and focused
- Attend sporadically
- Be shy and withdrawn
- Get angry at the leader
- Get angry at each other
- Try to force others to speak
- Try to preach morals and religion to the group
- Be resistant because forced to attend by a court, principal, warden, and so on
- Dislike other members
- Stop attending the group

As you can see, leaders must be able to deal with all kinds of members and situations. In the rest of this book, we teach ways of approaching not only these situations, but many more.

CONCLUDING COMMENTS

In this chapter, we discussed who should learn to lead groups and the reasons for using groups. The advantages of group work include efficiency, belonging, feedback, vicarious learning, and a setting that is close to real life. In addition, we categorized and discussed seven kinds of groups: support, educational, discussion, task, growth, therapy, and self-help. It is important for leaders to identify what kind of group they are leading so that its purpose is clear. We also discussed the use of theories as they apply to groups. In our discussion of group leadership styles, we stressed the importance of not being limited to one style because different kinds of groups have different purposes and require that leaders adjust their style accordingly. We concluded with a portrait of the effective leader and a list of difficult situations that typically arise in groups.

CHAPTER TWO

Group Dynamics, Therapeutic Forces, and Group Process

In the literature on group counseling, three aspects are almost always addressed: group dynamics, group process, and therapeutic forces. *Group dynamics* usually refers to the attitudes and interaction of group members and leaders; *group process* refers to the stages of a group. *Therapeutic forces* are the factors that influence the group dynamics and group process. In this chapter we discuss the importance of understanding each of these aspects of group counseling and how they are interrelated. We close the chapter with a description of three important ways to view a group session.

GROUP DYNAMICS

Group dynamics have been studied by sociologists, social psychologists, and group therapists and researchers. Because this book is about group counseling, our discussion here will primarily focus on group dynamics as they relate to groups we outlined in Chapter One. If you are interested in a discussion of the sociological view of group dynamics and a brief history of the study of group dynamics, see Johnson and Johnson (1991); they discuss the contributions that Kurt Lewin made in this area.

Group dynamics refers to the interaction and energy exchange between members and leaders. We use the term to describe the forces operating in a group. Gladding (1991) describes group dynamics as "the forces in a group that either benefit or harm it. . . . It is by understanding these forces that group specialists come to discern more about the nature of groups and how interactions between members and leaders affect group development" (p. 129–130). These forces can be obvious or hidden and include how members feel about themselves; how they talk to each other, feel about each other and about the leader; and how the leader reacts to the members.

It is important for leaders to realize that when they lead a group, they must attend to much more than just the verbal exchange among members. Hansen, Warner, and Smith (1980) describe the "group dynamicist" as a person who closely observes the "potent group currents" that influence the members. Some of these currents are lack of trust, lack of commitment, power plays, conflicts between members, strong alliances between members, and attention-seeking behaviors. Group dynamics may be affected by members' expectations if some members have been in a group before. The degree to which members understand how to behave in a group is also a factor in developing group dynamics.

Dynamics of Interaction Patterns

One of the most important group dynamics to observe is who talks to whom and how often each member speaks. It is not unusual in the beginning stages of a group for a couple of members to try to dominate. If this occurs, the leader should alter the pattern by using the cutting-off and drawing-out skills discussed in Chapter Seven. Sometimes members will fall into the habit of talking only to the leader or selected members instead of to the entire group. The leader will usually want to change this dynamic and get members to address the entire group because members' talking only to the leader or a few other members will not lead to group cohesion.

Silent members may or may not create negative group dynamics. In most groups, participation of all members is desirable. When a member is almost totally silent, some of the others may become uncomfortable, especially if this pattern continues for several weeks and the group is a therapy or support group. In certain education, discussion, and task groups, the silent member may not produce a negative dynamic, because in these groups the members are not usually as sensitive to the silence. We discuss dealing with silence and silent members in Chapters Seven and Fourteen.

Another pattern the leader should watch out for is that of one member speaking, followed by the leader, then a second member, then the leader, then a third member, then the leader—rather than member-to-member interaction. The leader should avoid establishing a pattern of responding after each member's comment.

EXAMPLE . . . .

Sam: I like my mother, but I don't feel close to her.
Leader: I hope that gets better for you.
Bill: My mom and I fight all the time. I can't talk to her about anything.

Leader: So it is hard for you to talk to her.
Nan: I feel that my mom favors my brother but she won't admit it. We have a terrible relationship.
Leader: So you feel hurt by your mom's favoritism.

This leader has made the mistake of responding to each member's comment. A more skilled leader would have let more members comment before commenting herself.

. . . .

Other patterns that the leader wants to look for include the following:

• Members "ganging up" on other members.
• Members arguing with each other.
• Members always discounting one another's suggestions.
• Members presenting problems and others trying to rescue.
• Members presenting a problem and the rest of the group giving advice. (It is important for the leader to realize that groups are *not* advice-giving sessions.)

E X A M P L E . . . .

Larry: . . . so I don't know whether to call her or not.
Steve: I don't think you should call her for at least a week.
Nancy: I don't know. I think you could wait a week and then send her a nice card.
Sandy: Why not a funny card?
Craig: I personally think you should let her make the next move.

. . . .

Sometimes advice and suggestions are beneficial, but often leaders mistakenly let groups turn into advice-giving sessions. In this example, the members are giving advice from their own frame of reference, which is probably not helpful.

THERAPEUTIC FORCES
AND GROUP DYNAMICS

Ohlsen, Horne, and Lawe (1988) describe a number of the forces present in almost any group situation. Members want (1) to feel accepted by the group, (2) to know what is expected, (3) to feel they belong, and (4) to feel safe. When these forces are absent, members tend to be negative hostile, withdrawn, or apathetic. A leader will often find that these forces operate in a positive way for most but not all the members. Negative leaders create dynamics that require the leader's attention.

The leader can tune in to some of the group dynamics by considering the following questions:

- How does each member feel about being in the group?
- Do the members seem to know what is expected in the group?
- Is each member clear about why he or she is in the group?
- How does each member deal with being in the group?
- Do the members seem to like one another?
- Do the members seem comfortable with one another?
- Do the members have a sense of belonging to the group?
- Do the members seem comfortable with the leader?
- Are there any power plays for the leadership role?

The answers to these questions can be very helpful to the group leader in understanding how members are feeling about the group and the leader.

Yalom (1985) discusses group dynamics in terms of *curative factors* operating in groups. He cites 11 different factors:

1. Altruism (giving to other members)
2. Group cohesiveness (feeling connected to each other)
3. Interpersonal learning (learning from other members)
4. Guidance (receiving help and advice)
5. Catharsis (releasing feelings and emotions)
6. Identification (modeling after members or leader)
7. Family reenactment (feeling as if one is in a family and learning from the experience)
8. Self-understanding (gaining personal insights)
9. Instillation of hope (feeling hopeful about one's life)
10. Universality (feeling that one is not alone)
11. Existential factors (coming to understand what life is about— the ebb and flow of living)

Yalom's factors are especially helpful when looking at group dynamics in support and therapy groups. If all these curative factors are operating in a group, the group more than likely is helpful to the members. On the other hand, if many of these are not operating, the group probably is only minimally successful or possibly not successful at all.

Therapeutic Forces

When leading any group, it is helpful to think in terms of what forces are working for you and what forces are working against you. Awareness of the therapeutic forces is essential to good leading. Described in this section are 16 forces that we feel the leader should attend to. These forces can be either positive (therapeutic), neutral, or negative (antitherapeutic). Groups that are not successful will have one or more antitherapeutic forces operating. As a way to understand this, think of any group you have ever led or been a member of; then go through the 16 therapeutic forces, considering if the force was positive, neutral, or negative for the group. Most likely you will find that if the group was successful, most of the forces were positive or neutral. If the group was not successful, one or more of the forces were negative. We say "one" because some-times a single antitherapeutic force can destroy a group. The 16 forces include the following:

1. Clarity of purpose for both the leader and the members
2. Relevance of purpose for the members
3. Size of the group
4. Length of each session
5. Frequency of meetings
6. Adequacy of the setting
7. Time of day for both the leader and the members
8. The leader's attitude
9. Closed or open group
10. Voluntary or nonvoluntary membership
11. Members' level of goodwill
12. Members' level of commitment
13. Level of trust among members
14. Members' attitudes toward the leader
15. The leader's attitude toward the members
16. The leader's experience and readiness to deal with groups

Clarity of Purpose

Probably the single most important therapeutic force is clarity of pur-pose; that is, the leader and the members clearly understand the pur-pose of the group. In unsuccessful groups, the leader often is unclear as to the purpose and thus confuses the members. For instance, a leader might say the group is educational but spend most of the time doing therapy, or the leader might say the group is for support but spend the majority of the time focusing on one person or on one topic that is not relevant to most of the members. Unfortunately, groups often are led in which the members are not sure what the purpose is. It is important that the leader always makes sure that both leader and members clearly understand the purpose of the group. Much of Chapter Six deals with clarity of purpose.

Relevance of Purpose

Not only should the members and leaders be clear regarding the purpose, but the purpose must be relevant for the members. An antitherapeutic force is created when the leader allows the group to focus on irrelevant material. Leaders of mandatory groups such as DUI (driving under the influence), prison, or dropout prevention groups often have to work hard and be creative to make the group relevant for the members because the members do not come to the group believing it will have any relevance to their lives. It is the leader's responsibility to show the members that the group is in fact relevant for them. This is no easy task!

Group Size

The size of the group will depend in part on its purpose, the length of time of each session, the setting available, and the experience of the leader. Education groups usually have from 4 to 15 members; discussion groups usually have from 5 to 8. Ideally, personal growth groups, support groups, and therapy groups have from 5 to 8 members, although there can be as few as 3 and as many as 12.

The size of the group can be antitherapeutic. If the group is too large, members very often will hesitate to share or will not have time to share. Too often, leaders form large groups out of necessity without realizing that an antitherapeutic force is being created. Groups that are too small, on the other hand, can cause members to feel too much pressure to participate, creating an equally negative force.

Group size can definitely affect group dynamics, so the leader should take care with this decision. We suggest five to eight as the ideal number of members for most groups. If the group is going to be one hour or less, the leader will want to keep the group relatively small (no more than six), unless it is an educational group.

Length of Each Session

If a group session is not long enough, members may feel they did not get their chance to share; this becomes an antitherapeutic force. Another problem that arises when insufficient time is allowed is that the group never really accomplishes much and the sharing never gets very personal. For members to feel invested in the group and in one another, enough time must be allotted for each session.

For education, discussion, and task groups, the usual session lasts from one to two hours; it can be longer in certain instances. For therapy, support, and growth groups, at least one and one-half hours—and usually not longer than three hours—is advisable. However, there may be times when the leader and members decide to meet for a more extended period—five or six hours, or for as long as an entire weekend. For groups composed of children, the length of time may be much shorter; 30 to 45 minutes is usually a good length for younger children.

Frequency of Meetings

The number of meetings per month will depend on many different factors, the most important ones being the purpose of the group and the composition of the members. Groups in residential settings often meet daily or two to three times a week. Most outpatient groups meet once a week or once every two weeks. Support groups usually meet twice a month. The key to the frequency of meetings is that they not be so frequent that they become boring and not so infrequent that each meeting is like a beginning first session. A leader should pay attention to the effect of the interval between sessions and, if at all possible, adjust the frequency so that it is a positive rather than negative force.

Adequacy of the Setting

There are a number of things to consider regarding where the group meets. One is convenience. Is it suitably located? Members will tend to come regularly if the location is easily accessible. Of course, the choice of location is not always within the leader's control, but when it is, the convenience factor should be weighed.

Another consideration is the privacy of the meeting room. Ideally, the leader will have a room that is closed to any other traffic during the meeting time. Sometimes, especially in schools and some institutions, this is not possible. When faced with an inadequate setting, the leader must do as much as possible to ensure privacy, recognizing that an antitherapeutic force is operating. The leader should also continue impressing upon the administration the importance of having a private room for group work.

Other things the leader needs to consider about the setting are whether the room is comfortable, what the wall decorations are like, what the lighting is like, and whether the seating arrangements and chairs are comfortable.

The relative size of the chairs also must be considered. They should all be approximately the same size. If not, the leader will want to remedy this if at all possible, especially in a therapy group, in which members sitting at various heights may create a negative group dynamic. An option in such a case is to have everyone sit on the floor. The leader would only want to do this if there were a comfortable carpet to sit on and if the members agreed. More than likely, a leader would not use the floor for education, discussion, or task groups. In most group situations, it is best that the chairs not be lounge chairs because members might simply relax and not get involved in the process.

Another consideration is whether or not to use tables. In most cases, it is better not to because they tend to serve as barriers between members. But there will be times when the leader may want to have tables, particularly in certain educational and task groups.

Once these details are taken care of, the leader still has some other factors to consider. Usually the best seating arrangement is a circle, in which all members can see each other. The leader will want to be careful that some people are not blocked by others who are sitting up slightly. If this occurs, the leader can simply ask them to move back so that no one feels excluded. If the group is widely spread out, it usually doesn't matter for discussion, educational, or task groups, but it could for support and therapy groups. A tighter circle often creates a more intimate feeling, and members may tend to share more.

Time of Day

The time that the group meets can be a negative force; if the group meets right after lunch or late in the day, the leader and the members may be tired. When setting up a group, the leader should choose a time that seems best for the majority of those involved. This may seem like a simple matter, but often leaders find themselves leading a group in which the members have little energy because of the meeting time.

The Leader's Attitude

The leader's feelings about leading a group definitely affect how the group will go. If the leader has a positive attitude, a positive force is created. On the other hand, an antitherapeutic force is created by the leader who dreads going to group or is tired on the day the group meets. Too often this is the case with leaders who have a hectic schedule or are required to lead many groups in a given week.

Closed or Open Groups

An important group-composition decision for the leader is whether the membership will be *open* or *closed*. Many groups are conducted as closed groups—that is, no new members are admitted once the group is established. Closed groups can be time limited and goal oriented. Groups are also conducted on an open basis, in which members join and leave periodically. The purpose of the group and the population being served usually dictate the leader's choice. In most cases, especially for support and therapy groups, the closed group is better because the members develop trust and caring as the group evolves. The only time a closed group becomes a detriment is when the group is getting stale and new members would add new life.

In some settings, such as hospitals or residential treatment centers where there are usually new arrivals weekly, groups with an open membership are mandated. This does not have to constitute a negative force if the leader's style is adjusted for this dynamic. That is, the leader must keep in mind that the group will not evolve through various stages because members will always be at different places in their feelings about the group. The leader will want to develop ways of introducing new members that do not detract from the flow of the last session. Often leaders will spend too much time on introducing and orienting new members, thus creating a negative force. We discuss ways of bringing in new members in Chapter Four.

Voluntary or Nonvoluntary Membership

Perhaps the most basic force to consider is whether the members are voluntary or nonvoluntary. Naturally, it would be nice if all groups could be held on a voluntary basis. However, settings such as correctional institutions, residential treatment settings, and schools often mandate group participation. When a leader must organize a group in which there are nonvolunteers, it is important to accommodate this dynamic.

A leader who ignores the fact that some members do not want to be there is not addressing one of the most critical factors: the attitudes of the members. Both Yalom (1985) and Corey (1990) state that often negative attitudes about being in a group can be transformed by the leader's ability to prepare members for the group. Corey further states that the leader also has to *believe* in the group process. Often some nonvoluntary members will change their negative attitude if the first couple of sessions go well. To make those first sessions successful, the leader must plan the group on the assumption that there will be negative attitudes. The following are three examples of what a leader might say to nonvoluntary members during the first session:

I realize many of you do not want to be here and probably are thinking this is going to be a big waste of time. All I can say is that I hope you will at least give it a chance. I think I have some things planned that should be of interest to all of you.

or

Since you did not volunteer for this group, I imagine you may have some strong negative feelings about being here. You will have a chance to air those feelings in a few minutes, but first I want to tell you a little about what we will be doing in the hope that you will see that the group can be interesting and may be helpful to you.

or

Every time I lead one of these groups, there are members who fight being here at the beginning, but by the end they thank me for providing a place for them to share their thoughts and feelings. I know that some of you right now are angry about being forced to be in this group. All I can say is that these groups have helped some people, and they can help you if you let them. If you will give the group a chance for a couple of weeks, I will do all I can to make it a good experience.

There will be times when no matter what the leader does, some members will remain negative and antitherapeutic. When faced with this situation, the leader should accept that the group will not go as well as desired. It is sometimes a good idea, when possible, to divide the group and let those who are totally negative sit in a corner and do something else, such as read, rest, or play some quiet game. Another strategy is to meet with the entire group for less time, then excuse the negative members and have those who are really interested remain. The point to remember and plan for is that there will definitely be some negative group dynamics at the beginning of the group and perhaps throughout the sessions if you have nonvoluntary members.

Members' Level of Goodwill

One of the forces to consider when thinking about the members is the group's level of goodwill. By goodwill, we simply mean the members' attempts to be helpful rather than resistant, disruptive, or hostile. It stands to reason that a group made up of members with goodwill will be much easier to lead than one with members of little goodwill. Goodwill usually produces a high level of commitment. Members lacking goodwill are usually those who are forced to be in the group or those who want to direct the group or be the center of attention. Such members have little or no commitment to the group.

How do you know if there is goodwill? The best way to assess this is simply to observe your members. You can nearly always tell how they feel about being in the group. If you are not sure, bring the topic up for discussion. Simply ask, "What is your feeling about being in the group?"

Members' Level of Commitment

As we have just suggested, the group's level of commitment is closely tied to its level of goodwill. When commitment is low, members will tend to get off the track, show little interest, contribute very little, do disruptive things, argue with the leader, or attack each other. In other words, all kinds of negative group dynamics will occur when there is little commitment. As a leader you must expect to have difficulty if you are leading a group of members who are not committed. In later chapters we suggest some ways to deal with low commitment.

Level of Trust

Many groups will start out with the therapeutic forces of goodwill and commitment, but that does not automatically mean that there is a high level of trust. For a group to start with a high level of trust, the members must already know and trust each other. In groups whose members have goodwill and commitment, trust will usually develop over time if the group is moving in a positive direction. Problems of trust often occur when members have relationships with each other outside of the group, such as living together, being in the same classes, working together, and so forth. If the group contains members who do not like each other, the leader will want to try to change this by meeting with them to see if their differences can be resolved or by asking one or more members to drop out of the group. If the lack of trust does not change and, due to administrative policy, the members cannot be asked to leave the group, the leader will have to accept the fact that a difficult task lies ahead.

In almost any group, the trust level increases or decreases as the group progresses, and it is important for the leader to pay attention to the evolving trust level. This increase or decrease is usually dependent on the ways in which members are reacting to one another. Obviously, if members are being hostile or are saying things that put other members off, the trust level will be low. Some members may not like each other, or cliques may have existed before the group started. Sometimes the trust level is low due to members' not trusting one or more members to keep disclosures confidential.

In therapy and support groups, the leader must focus on very judgmental statements about subjects such as affairs, abortion, or homosexuality. The leader needs to discuss these statements in such a way that other members can recognize when they represent the opinion of only one or two members. Ideally, the leader would help the judging member or members be more open. If the leader allows very negative statements to go by without clarification, the members will probably tend not to disclose much personal information for fear of being criticized.

Members' Attitudes toward the Leader

The attitudes of the members toward the leader have to be considered when leading any group. What do the members think of the leader? Do they like him? Do they respect him? Do they trust him? Do they respect his group leadership skills? In most groups, members will have a variety of feelings toward the leader. Sometimes all the members may have negative feelings about the leader. In such a case, the leader needs to examine this dynamic, since it may have something to do with style or experience as a leader. Often negative feelings are harbored by only one or two members, but one person who is out to "get the leader" can really interfere with positive group dynamics.

EXAMPLE. . . . .

> **Leader:** I would like to take a few minutes to discuss how you are feeling about the group.
>
> **Melvin:** (Angrily) Why do you always ask us that? It's your job to know how we feel! Let's do something fun. All the things you have us do are boring!

In this situation, the leader would not want to focus on the negative member, especially if she knows that the member is mainly out to "get" her. The leader can deflect the negative dynamic by saying in a soft, firm voice something like this:

> **Leader:** Melvin, I think most of the others feel differently. (*Turning to the rest of the group*) How are you feeling?

. . . .

The most important thing for leaders to realize is that negative attitudes about them as leaders definitely affect the interaction and disclosures in the group.

The Leader's Attitude toward the Members

A force that is often overlooked but is of great importance is the leader's attitude toward the group members. During workshops on group leadership, it is common to hear group leaders express their dislike for some of their members. There are a number of reasons why this dynamic occurs. One is that members who are forced to be in the group devote their entire time to disrupting it. It is no wonder that leaders would not like this kind of member. If the group contains hostile, involuntary members, the leader should try to figure out a way not to have them present.

Otherwise, the leader will end up resenting and possibly fighting with them, which rarely is good for the group.

Another possible reason is that the leader is being required to lead a group for people he simply does not like. If the leader cannot avoid leading the group and cannot change his feelings about the members, he may try adding a co-leader. If that is not possible, the leader should spend extra time planning the sessions in the hope that the exercises and activities will help make the group more interesting for both members and leader. If the leader does not do this, the group surely will go poorly.

The Leader's Experience in Leading Groups

For those who are just starting out, the therapeutic force of experience needs to be mentioned here. If the leader is new to leading groups, this may be an antitherapeutic force because the leader will be learning from the experience and may be nervous. It is important for the novice leader to recognize this and, if need be, to mention it to the group.

Along these same lines, in a therapy group, an antitherapeutic force will be present if the leader is inexperienced in therapy. For a good therapy group to occur, the leader must be experienced in individual counseling and knowledgeable about counseling theories.

Ideally, beginning leaders should work with a more experienced co-leader, but this usually is not the case. If you find yourself leading without the benefit of prior experience, do the best you can and learn from the experience by discussing your group with your supervisor or a colleague.

GROUP PROCESS

The study of group process is the study of stages in a group (Corey, 1990; Gladding, 1991). The literature contains much about the number of stages, the characteristics of each stage, and how much time each stage takes (Corey, 1990; Gladding 1991; Maples, 1988). If you are observing group interactions and want to study the development of the group, reading the literature on group process will be quite valuable. However, some of the literature can become confusing if the more detailed description of stages is applied to certain groups, such as discussion, education, or task groups; our description of group process applies to any kind of group.

Three Stages of Group Process

All groups go through three stages, regardless of the type of group or style of leadership. The three stages are the beginning stage, the middle or working stage, and the ending or closing stage. Whether a group meets for 1 session or 15 sessions, it will go through these stages, and it is important that the leader attend to each. Many of the dynamics described earlier in this chapter can occur during any of the stages.

Most of the literature describing numerous stages of group process has been written about groups whose leader is mainly using the interpersonal, facilitator model (Yalom 1985). Groups in which the leader does not actively lead or does a poor job of leading will go through many of the additional stages described in the literature. We believe that certain leadership models tend to create some of the additional stages, such as storming. (*Storming* usually refers to the members being upset with the leader, other members, or both.)

Leaders who use an active, intrapersonal approach to groups usually do not create these stages or dynamics. Skilled leaders will curtail many of these occurrences because they will be trying to ensure that the members clearly understand the purpose of the group, the ground rules, and the leader's approach. Also, the intrapersonal approach does not promote as much transference and projection as the interpersonal approach. If the leader does not have the characteristics of a good leader outlined in Chapter One, then most certainly all kinds of dynamics will occur during any of the stages.

The Beginning Stage

All groups go through a beginning stage. (Chapter Four is devoted to beginning groups.) By *beginning stage,* we mean the time period used for introductions and for discussing such topics as the purpose of the group, what may happen, fears, ground rules, comfort levels, and perhaps the content of the group. In this stage, members are checking out other members and their own level of comfort with sharing in the group. For some groups, such as certain task, education, and discussion groups whose topics or agendas have not been predetermined, this is the period in which the members determine the focus of the group.

The beginning stage often lasts the entire first session and part of the second session. It is not uncommon for the members of certain groups to take more than two sessions to feel enough trust and comfort to share beyond the surface level. For instance, in groups in a prison, in a work setting, or with teenagers, it may take as many as three sessions to develop an atmosphere that lends itself to productive group work. For groups in a residential setting, "agendas" between members must sometimes be confronted.

The leader knows the beginning stage is over when the members seem willing to focus on the purpose of the group. For some groups the beginning stage lasts only a few minutes, because the purpose is clear and the trust and comfort levels are high to begin with. For example, members who meet to share feelings about a recent suicide, death, or disaster can move through the beginning stage in just a few minutes if the leader structures the group so they can share their feelings. We have seen leaders spend far too long on this stage, conducting ice-breakers and talking about ground rules and the purpose of the group. On the other hand, we have seen leaders move too quickly into the working stage, causing members to feel uncomfortable and even angry.

A leader who provides very little structure tends to create a group that stays in the beginning stage for several sessions and that has dynamics that could be avoided. As stated in Chapter One, we question the value of this approach for most groups.

The Working Stage

The middle, or working stage, is the stage of the group in which the members focus on the purpose. In this stage, the members learn new material, thoroughly discuss various topics, complete tasks, or engage in personal sharing and therapeutic work. This stage is the core of the group process; it is the period when members benefit from being in a group.

During this stage, many different dynamics can occur, because the members are interacting in many different ways. The leader will want to pay particular attention to the interaction patterns and attitudes of the members toward each other and the leader. This is the time when members decide how much they want to get involved or share. (This stage is discussed in greater detail in Chapter Eleven.)

Corey (1990) discusses the transition stage as separate from the working stage. According to Corey, this is the period when the beginning stage is over, but members are not yet ready to share on a highly personal level. Members contribute and interact, but they are still checking things out. Many, but not all, groups go through a transition stage; that is why we did not include it as a separate stage. When it does occur, it is good for a leader to recognize it and refrain from pushing the group ahead too quickly and thus causing discomfort.

The Closing Stage

The closing, or ending stage is devoted to ending the group (see Chapter Thirteen). During this period, members share what they have learned, how they have changed, and how they plan to use what they have learned. Members also say goodbye and deal with the ending of the group. For some groups, the ending will be an emotional experience, while for others the closing will simply mean that the group has done what it was supposed to. The length of the closing stage will depend on the kind of group, the length of time it has been meeting, and its development. Most groups will need only one session for this stage.

GROUP DYNAMICS OF DIFFERENT KINDS OF GROUPS

Any discussion of group dynamics has to take into consideration the kind of group and the style of leadership. If the leader does not play an active role, usually someone in the group will try to take the leadership role. Even with an active leader there can be a bid for power by one or more members. Members may challenge the active leader's authority or competency. Throughout the book, we discuss skills for handling these dynamics if they arise. In this section, we discuss dynamics unique to the seven kinds of groups described in Chapter One.

Education Groups

In an education group, the leader usually is presenting some information. Although the members will probably interact with each other, this is not the most important dynamic. Often, those attending education groups are eager to learn the material being presented. In some education groups, however, the members are not interested in the topic because they have been forced to attend, such as those attending a DUI (driving under the influence) group. In these groups, if the leader does not plan well or is not dynamic, the group may be "dead."

The dynamics become difficult when members are at different levels of understanding regarding the subject matter or when some are much more comfortable with the topic than others. A good example would be in dealing with the topic of sex. The leader of a sex-education group must be aware that some members will be more open and comfortable than others. It is important for the leader to observe how the members are relating to the material.

Education groups usually will not go through long beginning or closing stages. The leader does, however, have to plan for these stages. Although this may seem obvious, we have observed beginning leaders who pay no attention to group process in their planning.

The middle stage of an education group will usually include delivery of the content and discussion of the material. As members get to know each other, they will usually become more comfortable and willing to share their reactions, questions, and feelings.

Discussion Groups

Discussion group leaders will mainly want to be aware of any member who tries to dominate or distract the group. They will also want to pay attention to how comfortable members are in sharing, because if many are not comfortable, only a few members will be contributing, and a good discussion will not occur. Another dynamic related to the members' hesitancy is the leader's becoming uncomfortable. A leader might deal with discomfort by talking more than is appropriate for a discussion group. Also, because the leader should be using a facilitator style of leadership in discussion groups, she needs to watch for possible power plays for leadership.

Discussion groups are often led in conjunction with a workshop or class and are therefore one-time experiences that last anywhere from 15 minutes to an hour. The tone set at the beginning of a discussion group is usually crucial, so the leader should try to get everyone to share something in the first few minutes if at all possible. This gets members involved and gives the leader an idea of each member's thoughts on the topic.

Task Groups

In a task group, the ways in which members interact may be the most important dynamic to monitor. This is especially true if the leader's task is one of team building. The leader will want to be aware of how members feel about the other members. Often, task groups accomplish nothing because the members cannot get along well enough to work together. If this is the case, the leader must do some conflict resolution work or team building before getting to the task of the group. The leader will also want to be aware of the formation of cliques and plays for power and control.

Johnson and Johnson (1991) discuss three core activities that leaders can use to assess effectiveness of the task group: (1) accomplishing its goals, (2) maintaining itself internally, and (3) developing and changing in ways that improve its effectiveness. Observing these dynamics is excellent for the leader of task groups. As Johnson and Johnson state, "A successful group has the quality and kind of interaction among members that integrate these three core activities" (p. 8).

The beginning stage of task groups is often brief. Usually, the task is clarified during this stage. Most of the group's time is spent in the middle stage—working on the task. The closing stage of a task group can be very brief, sometimes coinciding with accomplishment of the task. However, some kinds of task groups will require a longer closing stage.

Growth and Experiential Groups

This kind of group varies greatly. In groups whose purpose is values clarification or personal self-exploration, the most important dynamic would be how the members feel about one another, since they will be sharing either in small groups or with the entire group. Also, members might become jealous of other members or become angry with the leader because they don't like what they are learning about themselves.

In some growth and experiential groups, individual members' needs and expectations can vary so widely that negative forces are created. If this occurs, the leader will want to focus on issues and concerns that are relevant to the majority of the members. The leader will also want to look for any members who are not appropriate for the group— members who would be better served in a therapy group, individual counseling, or some other group experience.

In experiential groups in which members are engaging in some activity and the purposes are teambuilding and cooperative interaction, struggles for leadership can occur. Also, members may form factions or cliques that create antitherapeutic forces. Competition among members may arise, which can also be a detrimental dynamic. Depending on the actual experience, sometimes members will angrily turn on other members or the leader as a result of frustration with the activity.

The beginning stage of a growth or experiential group will usually last only one or two sessions because the leader will probably engage the members in some activities during one or both of those sessions. Most members will get more comfortable as the group progresses, and the working stage will be reached fairly quickly. The closing stage will last no more than one session and will usually consist of people sharing what they have learned about themselves and how they have grown.

Support Groups

In this kind of group, the leader wants to create a safe environment in which members can share. The leader will also want to make sure that members feel they have opportunities to share their ideas and concerns with the group. Therefore, the leader will not want to let any member dominate. Trust, commitment, and true caring of members for one another are important dynamics for this kind of group. When members do not trust one another or there are members who are at odds with each other, the support group will not be effective. If these dynamics occur, they must be worked through for the group to succeed.

Other dynamics that are important to watch for include members being nonsupportive, members rescuing other members (that is, trying to solve members' problems for them—there is a difference between caring for members and "rescuing" them), and lack of commonality. For instance, a leader might form a divorce support group believing that the only relevant criterion for membership is having been divorced. The group could consist of recently divorced members who are in a great deal of emotional pain as well as others who have been divorced for two years and want to share stories about being single. Sometimes this works, but other times leading such a group would be quite difficult because members' needs are so different. For a support group to work, members must feel a common bond. For example, Alcoholics Anonymous is perhaps the best-known support group; it is effective for a large number of people.

The beginning stage of a support group usually will last one to three sessions. During this stage, the sharing is usually not as personal as in the middle stage, when sharing is more intimate and caring is greater because the members now know each other. The closing of a support group can be an emotional experience for its members. Some may even feel frightened of losing the group as a support system. Because of this, the leader will want to allow plenty of time for terminating the group— maybe as much as two entire sessions.

Therapy Groups

In a therapy group, the leader must be keenly aware of how members feel about each other and about the leader. Members may resent others for being too quiet, too open, or too "together." Because members of therapy groups vary in their degree of mental health, the chances for complex dynamics are far greater than in any other group discussed. To prevent the occurrence of some of the complex dynamics, we advocate screening through individual interviews of potential members whenever possible.

Some leaders mistakenly ignore the dynamics and lead the group as if everyone were comfortable with everyone else. This often results in a boring, superficial group whose members are not willing to share personally due to their lack of trust in other members, the leader, or both. Also, one negative or hostile member can create impossible dynamics unless the leader does something to neutralize the effect of the acting-out member. This can be done privately, which is usually best, or in the group if the leader sees value in this kind of intervention.

Much skill, knowledge, and courage are needed to lead an effective therapy group. Because members are being pushed to deal with personal issues, attacks on the leader are not uncommon. Unfortunately, sometimes the attacks are warranted because the leader does not have the knowledge or skills necessary to lead a therapy group but is doing so because it is part of the job. As we say throughout the book, leaders should not lead groups they are not trained to lead.

The beginning stage of a therapy group can last two or three sessions. Although some therapeutic discussion or work will probably be done during these sessions, the members usually will still be warming up to the idea of sharing their problems with others. The working stage starts when members begin to share and work on their issues. The leader can ease the transition to the working stage by selecting relevant, important themes to discuss or conducting exercises that help members recognize their pressing concerns. This can become very intense. If the group develops properly during the working stage, new members joining the group (in open groups) will usually not be too much of a hindrance because they will see the productive work going on. However, any member who is not willing or able to be in a therapy group can create tremendous problems.

The closing stage will usually last one session, although there may be occasions when the leader sees a need to allow more time. The leader should pay careful attention to members' feelings about ending the group, especially if being in the group has been a very emotional, supportive experience for them.

Self-Help Groups

Many different dynamics can occur in self-help groups, and without a leader to resolve these dynamics, some groups will not be productive and can even be harmful. We strongly believe in the self-help group and feel that generally these groups are very helpful and supportive. However, we recognize that usually few restrictions exist in these groups and that all kinds of dynamics can arise among the members as a result. If you are involved in setting up self-help groups, you should be aware of several dynamics. Members may attack each other or may take over the group. Cliques may form, causing other members to feel excluded. Members may need individual therapy in addition to or instead of a self-help group.

Once self-help groups have formed, they usually are ongoing, with new members coming and others leaving constantly. There is no trained leader in self-help groups. If you are in charge of establishing a self-help group, you might want to attend the first couple of meetings to ensure that they get off to a good start. We suggest that you then drop in periodically to see if the group is being productive. Sometimes the groups have strayed far from their intended purpose and need to be redirected.

UNDERSTANDING YOUR SESSION

Because groups are complex, it is helpful for the leader to have several ways of understanding what happens in them. We offer three ways to view any given session. One view, or *map*, consists of dividing the session into phases. Another way is to use what we call a *10–1 depth chart*, with 10 being surface level and 1 being the deepest level of interaction. A third way to view your group is to think of it as funneling down as the group goes to a deeper level of interaction. These maps, which aid in understanding the development of a session, are discussed in this section.

Phases of a Session

Each session has three phases: the beginning or warm-up phase, the middle or working phase, and the closing phase. During the beginning phase, the leader gets a sense of the members' energy and interest for the session and any topics or issues they may want to talk about. In some groups, members give progress reports or report on some follow-up work done in the previous session. A leader should always consider how she is going to begin a session and how long the warm-up phase should be. Too often, leaders let the beginning phase last too long or become boring, thus setting a negative tone for the rest of the session. We discuss this phase in detail in Chapter Four.

In the middle or working phase of the session, members focus on the group's purpose. We call it the *middle phase* when referring to an education or discussion group and the *working phase* if the group is a support, task, growth, or therapy group. It is important for leaders to be aware of this phase, in which something productive takes place. Otherwise the group might wander aimlessly, never getting to its purpose. Chapter Eleven is devoted to this phase.

The closing phase is devoted to summarizing and ending the session. During this phase, the leader tries to help members integrate what they have learned during the middle or working phase of the group. It is very important that the leader allow enough time for this phase. Some leaders do not watch their time well and end up having to stop the group without a closing phase; this is not good leadership. Chapter Thirteen deals with closing a session.

The Depth Chart

The depth chart is a gauge for measuring how "deep" the group is. By *deep*, we mean how helpful or productive the group is; that is, the amount of impact the experience has on the members. Depth is measured differently for various groups—for education and discussion groups, depth is measured by assessing learning and exchange of ideas. Task group depth is measured with regard to productivity and how well members are working together. Therapy, growth, and support groups are measured by the level of personal exploration and insight. When using the depth chart the lower the number, the greater the depth—a 10 is surface-level talking, discussing, or sharing; a 1 is deep, intense, personal sharing.

During the life of a group, the depth of discussion will vary. In the beginning phase, the depth is usually a 9 or 10 because members are telling stories or talking superficially about some topic or issue. As a group moves to the middle phase, the depth should reach below 9 to at least an 8, and for most groups, the leader will want the group to reach

Depth*	Leader's Behavior	Comments

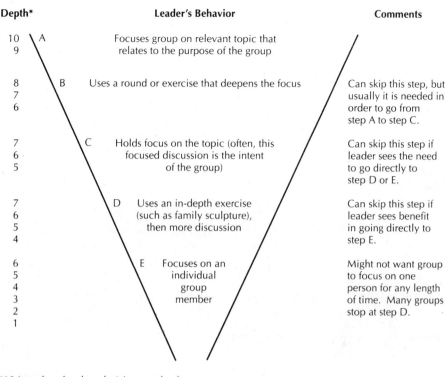

10 9	A	Focuses group on relevant topic that relates to the purpose of the group	
8 7 6	B	Uses a round or exercise that deepens the focus	Can skip this step, but usually it is needed in order to go from step A to step C.
7 6 5	C	Holds focus on the topic (often, this focused discussion is the intent of the group)	Can skip this step if leader sees the need to go directly to step D or E.
7 6 5 4	D	Uses an in-depth exercise (such as family sculpture), then more discussion	Can skip this step if leader sees benefit in going directly to step E.
6 5 4 3 2 1	E	Focuses on an individual group member	Might not want group to focus on one person for any length of time. Many groups stop at step D.

*10 is surface-level work; 1 is great depth

The funnel effect for growth, support, and therapy groups.

a depth of 7 or below. By using the depth chart as a guide, the leader can gain a sense of how meaningful the group is for members. That is, if the group is staying at the 8–10 level, the leader may want to try something different to move the group to a deeper level. Often a group exercise is helpful. In therapy groups, the desired depth during the working phase is 7 or deeper, with some groups going to an intense level of 3, 2, or even 1. Throughout this book, we refer to the depth chart and the funnel, which is discussed next.

The Funnel Effect

Another way to think about the development or progression of the group session is to envision a funnel based on the premise that as a session evolves, it has the potential to "funnel down" to greater depth. The funnel in the illustration shows the development of a group and its depth (using the depth-chart concept). You will notice that on the left, the depth levels overlap somewhat, depending on the level of discussion, sharing, or personal work. The benefit of thinking about the group as "funnel-ing down" is that the leader can gain a sense of what he is trying to en-courage in his group. In most groups, the leader's goal is to funnel the group to at least a level of 7. At the beginning of the group or of discus-sion on a new topic, members may have diverse agendas, or even lack of awareness of an issue. Funneling helps establish an agenda to which most members can relate. That is, the focus is narrowed and deepened. To bring this about, the leader may use an exercise or introduce some topics for discussion. The leader of a therapy group may want to funnel it to a deeper level by using an exercise that encourages members to explore an issue in greater depth. Processing the exercise can lead to individual work at a very deep level.

By using the depth chart and the funnel, a leader will be able to gauge her group's progress. Too often, groups follow a pattern of 10, 9, 8—10, 9, 8—10, 9, 8, bouncing from topic to topic and never going deep enough to derive any benefit. With the chart and the funnel, the leader may be able to identify and correct the problem. In some groups, the leader may even explain these two "maps" to members and periodically ask them about their perceptions of and responses to the group's depth.

CONCLUDING COMMENTS

In this chapter, we discussed the group dynamics, therapeutic forces, and group process that leaders must be aware of to be effective. *Group dynamics* refers to the attitudes and interaction of members and leaders. *Therapeutic forces* refers to the many different elements operating in a group, such as its size, its setting, the time of day it meets, its member composition, the trust and commitment levels of its members, and its leader's experience.

Group process refers to the stages a group goes through. We dis-cussed the three stages: beginning, working, and closing. It is impor-tant that leaders be aware that groups go through these stages, even though the amount of time for each stage will depend on the kind of group and its purpose.

We also discussed three maps for viewing a session: the three phases of a session, the 10–1 depth chart, and the funnel. Each of these can help leaders understand their groups and better plan each session.

CHAPTER THREE.

Planning

The importance of carefully planning a group cannot be overemphasized. Corey (1990) states: "If you want a group to be successful, you need to devote considerable time to planning. In my view planning should begin with the drafting of a written proposal" (p. 86). We agree that there are two stages of planning: the planning that goes on when forming a group and the planning of each group session.

PREGROUP PLANNING

In Chapters One and Two, we discussed several considerations for the formation of a group: who should lead it, how large it should be, whether it should have open or closed membership, how long sessions should last, and where it should meet. The following list enumerates four additional decisions to be made when establishing a group.

1. Who should the members be?
2. How will the members be screened?
3. For how many sessions will the group meet?
4. When will the group meet?

Who Should the Members Be?

Any time a group is being formed, a number of considerations arise regarding its membership (Corey, 1990). Probably the first one is whom the group will serve; that is, from where its members will come. Will they be hospital patients, prisoners, clients of a mental health center, interested persons in a community, or schoolchildren? Once the population to be served is determined, another decision to be made is whether the entire population will automatically constitute the membership or whether the members will volunteer or be selected. For example, in an orientation group at a university residence hall, will the group consist of all 15 new students in a wing, or will it include only those who want to be in a group? In a unit in a hospital for mental patients, will the group be for everyone, or will only selected patients be allowed? There are no absolute guidelines for deciding whom to include; usually the purpose of the group, kind of group, time constraints, and setting will help the leader decide whether and how to limit membership.

Another consideration is whether to place members who are very different in age or background in the same group. For instance, in various hospital situations, patients in the same unit often include young and old people or people with varying educational or socioeconomic backgrounds. Sometimes mixing the ages or backgrounds is beneficial; at other times it can be detrimental. If the leader were planning a group for the unemployed, it would not be beneficial to place college-educated individuals and high school dropouts in the same group because their needs would differ. In a marital-problems group, mixing ages and backgrounds would probably prove beneficial because members might benefit from hearing different views and ideas. As Corey (1990) says: "The key point is that screening needs to be done within the context of the type of group that a practitioner is offering. Whether a client is to be included or excluded has much to do with purposes of the group" (p. 90). Unfortunately, one of the biggest problems faced by counselors in agencies and institutions is that administrators do not let them select the members, and therefore, groups are often conducted with members who should not be in the group. We encourage you to lobby hard for the right to screen your members if the goal for the group is to benefit the participants.

How Will the Members Be Screened?

Closely related to questions about composition of membership are decisions about screening members. The obvious first question is whether to screen or not. The reason for screening is that not everyone is appropriate for every group. Also, often the leader will be seeking certain kinds of members; screening allows selection of appropriate members. But with certain kinds of groups, screening is either unnecessary or only slightly beneficial. For education, discussion, and task groups, screening may not be necessary—it depends on the specific situation. In addition, in certain situations screening is not possible. When it is both possible and desirable, however, the leader has several procedural options.

The Personal Interview

The best, though most time-consuming, screening method is the personal interview. It is valuable for three reasons. Certainly the main reason is that it allows the leader to assess most easily the appropriateness of the member for the group. A second reason is that it gives the leader a chance to make individual contact with potential members. Third, the leader has an opportunity to inform the prospective member about the group: the rules, content, membership, and so forth.

Assessment of appropriateness. By asking questions relevant to the type of group being formed, the leader can determine whether the potential member is appropriate for the group. In the personal interview, the leader can often spot those people whose needs and goals differ from those of the group. For educational groups, the leader tries to determine if the individual knows either too much or too little about the subject matter. For support groups, the leader may find that a potential member needs individual or group therapy rather than a support group, which is not designed for in-depth therapy. Screening for therapy groups allows the leader to determine if the person's needs can best be met by group or individual therapy. If a potential member is seriously disturbed, the leader may want to exclude that person from the group.

Individual contact with the potential member. Personal interviews permit the leader and member to meet each other before the group actually begins. (Sometimes the leader will conduct "screening" interviews after the first or second meeting if it was not possible before the group began.) It is important for the leader to make this experience more than just a question-and-answer session. The leader should realize that the interview is the beginning of his relationship with the member. He will want to use many of the same skills used in an individual counseling session: positive attending, listening, and reflecting. The leader will not want to let the interview become a counseling session, however, because that is not the stated purpose of the meeting; the potential member is coming to interview for a group. Too often leaders alienate candidates by making the interview too formal or by turning it into a therapy session. The interview should be as comfortable as possible while the leader assesses the potential member's needs and goals.

Informing the member about the group. During the screening interview, the leader can explain the purpose of the group, how it will be conducted, some of its rules, and any other relevant information. If the group is a therapy group, the leader can tell the member about the theories that may be used and offer some idea of the roles of the members and the leader. If it is to be a support group, the leader can give the member examples of what might be shared. Some leaders have gone as far as showing a videotape of a group so the prospective member can see what the group will be like.

Other Forms of Screening

Another method of screening is by using a written form, completed by the prospective member, that gives the leader the information necessary to decide if the person is appropriate for the group. Sometimes the only information the leader needs is biographical: age, grade level completed, sex, marital status, diagnosis, length of illness, kind of illness, living situation, and age of children. When basing choices on biographical data only, the leader must remember to ask all the pertinent questions. Questions that are sometimes overlooked include the candidate's availability for meetings and whether the candidate needs child care and transportation.

Another form of screening calls for potential members to respond in writing to certain questions. Some examples are as follows:

- Why do you want to be in this group?
- What are your expectations of the group?
- What concerns do you want the group to help you with?
- How do you think you can contribute to the group?
- Write a short autobiography that describes the important events and people in your life.

Naturally, the questions asked will depend on the purpose of the group. If the topics to be covered are sensitive ones, such as sex, death, divorce, or religion, you may want to list them and ask prospective members to comment on how they feel about talking about those subjects. You may also want prospective members to comment briefly on those topics so you can get an idea of how they view various issues. The key to effective screening is to remember that you are attempting to find out certain information in order to form a group of members who can work together, share, and learn from each other.

Another form of screening occurs when the leader informs possible referral sources, such as other therapists, teachers, or hospital staff, about the group, its purpose, and the kind of member sought. These people, in a sense, do the screening by telling appropriate potential members of the availability of the group. The leader who uses this method of screening will want to make sure that those making referrals fully understand the purpose of the group and the kind of members sought.

A leader conducting several groups in the same setting—such as in a prison, hospital, company, or school—can "screen" by assigning members to any one of the groups. Assigning members according to their knowledge, age, experience, or some personality characteristic often increases the likelihood of the group being valuable to the members. The leader can also sort members according to their interaction style or level of mental health; the leader might even place some highly verbal members in a group with some nontalkers. At times, it is useful to mix certain characteristics in that way. In other words, there really are no absolute guidelines for making these decisions because each situation and purpose is so different. The main thing to realize is that these kinds of screening decisions can be instrumental in enhancing positive therapeutic forces.

For How Many Sessions Will the Group Meet?

Many groups will be established for a certain length of time. For instance, parenting groups, childbirth groups, assertiveness-training groups, certain growth and therapy groups, and many educational groups are set up to meet for a specified number of sessions. Therapy groups, growth groups, task groups, and support groups sometimes begin with no set number of sessions planned, although we recommend that a limit be set because it gives members an idea of how long they have to complete any personal work. Another option is to leave the decision about the number of sessions up to the members once the group has been meeting for a while. Often the number of sessions is dictated by other considerations, such as the length of a school term, the leader's availability, the needs of the population being served, or the amount of educational information to be covered.

When Will the Group Meet?

Two factors must be considered: time of day and frequency of meetings. Ideally, the meeting time will not conflict with members' other activities. If the setting for the group is an agency, school, or hospital, the choice of meeting time should cause as little disruption as possible in the institution's daily routine. Choice of meeting time is especially important in a school, where the students would be coming from different classes. The leader would want to make sure the same class is not missed on a regular basis. This can be accomplished by having the group meet during different periods each week.

The members' schedules also need to be considered when setting the time. If the members work, perhaps the evening is best, or maybe even early morning or noon. If they are in a residential center, such as a prison, hospital, or detention center, a careful examination of the daily routine is helpful. Beginning leaders often make the mistake of planning a group without fully considering the many factors that might make the meeting time of the group inconvenient.

The leader's schedule, naturally, is also important; she must always be available to lead the group, and in most work situations some days are better than others. Days when the leader tends to be very busy with such things as staff meetings, paperwork, or intakes should be avoided because she may have to either miss the group or be late. In the case of therapy groups, it is inadvisable to lead one group right after another— it is too taxing on the leader. Ideally, any therapy group leader would lead no more than one group a day; the maximum should be three.

Besides deciding on the best time to meet, the leader will usually be the one to decide how often the group will meet. Some groups meet daily; others meet twice a week, once a week, or once every two weeks; still others meet once a month. The number of meetings per week or month depends on the kind of group, its purpose, and the availability of members and leader. There is no set formula for how often a group should meet, but the leader must ensure that the meetings are properly spaced. It is important that the group meet neither so often nor so infrequently as to defeat the overall purpose.

Additional Considerations for Pregroup Planning

The leader will want to ascertain whether any additional materials are needed for the group, whether any resource people must be contacted, whether any permission forms must be signed, and whether an evaluation procedure should be designed for the conclusion of the group. It may also be useful to consider whether any kind of oral or written contract for members is needed or desired.

PLANNING THE INDIVIDUAL SESSION

Planning a specific session involves deciding on its topics and group activities as well as delegating an approximate amount of time needed for each. Most groups require a good deal of planning, although only a minimum of planning is necessary for certain kinds of therapy, growth, and support groups after their initial sessions. Minimal planning is necessary when the members come to understand the purpose of their group and arrive at the sessions eager and ready to share and discuss concerns important to them and relevant to others. But even in groups in which the planning of exercises and topics is minimal, the leader will want to give considerable thought to what kinds of exercises and what topics would be helpful. Many beginning leaders make the mistake of coming to the group without thinking about what may be valuable for the members, and when the members have little energy the group falls flat. Other kinds of therapy, support, and growth groups will require more planning: members benefit from the leader's introduction of various topics when they do not bring issues to the group to discuss.

Discussion groups, educational groups, and task groups are often more effective when thoroughly planned by the leader. The thoughtful leader can organize the session in a way that makes the group both interesting and productive. In the rest of this chapter, we discuss the considerations that go into planning an effective group session.

Certainly one of the first things to consider is whether the session is the first, the second, a middle, or a closing session. Planning a first session is very different from planning a middle or closing session. During the first session, there are a number of things that the leader will need to do, such as having members introduce themselves, clarifying the purpose of the group, setting a positive tone for the group, helping members get over any uneasiness, and going over any guidelines or ground rules for the group. (Chapter Four discusses the first and second sessions of a group.) During the closing sessions, the leader will want to make sure the members are saying and doing the things necessary for ending the group (see Chapter Thirteen).

Another consideration is for how many more sessions the group will meet. Some groups only meet for one session; the planning for that kind of session is obviously different from that for a group that will meet for ten weeks. Planning the fifth session when only two sessions are left will be different from planning a fifth session when six more sessions remain.

When planning a session, the leader will want to consider its format. Some groups work well with the same format each week: for instance, the entire time is spent on a member telling his or her "story," or discussing the reading assignment, or on hearing a report from one of the subgroups. In other groups, the session has some variety, but the format for each session is the same: the group starts with progress reports, moves to an activity, then to a discussion, and concludes with members summarizing what they learned. For still other groups, a varied format seems advantageous because it keeps the interest level high. By a varied format, we mean that, for example, one session might consist of two different exercises, a short film, and a discussion; the next session might include three exercises, and then some role-playing practice. Doing different things in each session keeps members interested and curious. The leader should always consider whether the format is getting stale.

A common way to vary format is by using exercises, but the leader will want to be sure that he does not plan too many and that enough time is allotted for processing them; that is, for discussing the members' thoughts, feelings, and reactions. The leader should also make sure the exercises within a given session are compatible. As a rule, leaders should try to vary the type of exercise used in a session; for example, exercises should not all be rounds or sentence-completion exercises.

The leader also needs to anticipate potential problems when planning. For example, if she has asked members to read something for the session, she can anticipate that some members will not have done the reading and can plan ways of processing the material that will not alienate those members. Additionally, it is a good idea to have a backup plan in case an exercise does not go well or a vital member does not come.

Leaders should keep specific planning guidelines in mind for each phase (beginning, middle, and ending) of any given session. The process of leading members through each of the phases is covered in great detail in later chapters, but we want to give a brief overview here.

The Beginning Phase

When planning the opening moments of a session of an open-membership group, the leader will need to allot time and choose a method for introducing new members. The leader may either introduce them or have them introduce themselves. Another method is to have the established members introduce themselves. Chapter Four contains several examples of how to introduce members to the group. These first minutes are also used to update anyone who has missed the previous session. The leader will need to decide how much time to devote to this to avoid spending too much of one session rehashing the previous one.

No matter what is planned for the session, the leader must evaluate the members' interest, comfort level, and commitment level in the first minutes. If interest or trust levels appear low, the leader can avoid mistakes such as starting with personal sharing and can spend more time trying to "warm up" the group. The leader can even suggest the issues of trust or interest for discussion, perhaps incorporating an exercise that helps to build comfort and trust.

When planning the session's beginning, the leader should always consider whether time is needed to warm up the members. Some groups require almost no time: the members come ready to talk, share, discuss, or listen. In other groups, the leader must plan to spend time at the beginning to let the members get focused on being in the group. There are a number of ways for a leader to do this:

- Talk about the last session, mentioning the key issues that were discussed, and then talk about the plan for the current session.
- Ask the members to comment on their past week—any thoughts, feelings, reactions, or observations.
- Get members to talk about current events, the weather, movies, television shows, and so on for about five minutes.
- Ask certain members (ones who seem ready to respond) to give progress reports on what they have been working on.
- Ask members if there are any questions they would like answered and then spend the first five minutes answering them. This is common in education and discussion groups.

If the group needs little warm-up, the leader has a number of options for beginning a session. Any of these options may be used, depending on the group's purpose and composition.

EDUCATION OR DISCUSSION GROUPS
- Today we are going to talk about _____ . To get you thinking about the subject, I'd like you to do the following. . . .
- I'd like to talk for a few minutes about _____ , and then we'll discuss your reactions, feelings, and thoughts.
- We're going to start with a 15-minute film. Afterwards, we'll discuss any questions or reactions.
- Before we get started on today's subject, does anyone have any questions or comments about last week or about that handout I gave you?

TASK GROUPS
- Let's start with progress reports from each of you. Who wants to go first?
- Let me review briefly where we are and what seems to be the next thing we need to decide. . . .
- Before we start, do any of you have something pertinent you want to share?

GROWTH OR SUPPORT GROUPS
- How has the week been?
- Any reactions to the last session, progress reports, or updates?
- What would you like to talk about tonight—any particular topic or issue you would like to discuss?
- Let's start by thinking about the most significant thing that has happened to you since our last meeting. In a minute, we'll go around and let each of you share this. Who wants to go first?— we'll hear from everyone.

THERAPY GROUPS
- Why don't we start? First, does anyone have something they'd like to bring up?
- Let's begin. Last session, a number of you talked about some very important personal issues. I think it would be good if you shared any reactions or thoughts you've had since then. We might do that for a few minutes, then move on to other people and topics.
- I want to start the group a little differently. I want each of you to think about whether you have something you would like to talk about. In a second, we'll go around the room. I'm going to have you simply say "yes" or "no" if there is something you would like to bring up. This is just a quick way to find out how many of you have something on your mind. I hope many of you will have something you want to discuss, but it is perfectly OK to say "no."
- Let's start. I was talking with Sammy out in the hall just now, and he said he had something that was really bothering him. I hope we can help. Sammy, you said you wanted to tell the group what happened when you saw your son.

In the last example, the leader decided not to stay with his planned opening, because he realized that focusing on Sammy would be a good way to begin the group. Some leaders make the mistake of being unable to adjust their plans when something arises spontaneously that is as good as or better than what was planned. On the other hand, some leaders are overly spontaneous and allow members to go on tangents at the very start of the group, which makes refocusing on the planned activities more difficult. In the two examples that follow, the leader made the mistake of "going with the flow" instead of with the planned beginning; consequently much of the session was spent in an unproductive way.

E X A M P L E S . . . .

The group is for recently divorced women. Its purpose is to help the women begin living a single lifestyle. It is the beginning of the third session, and after making brief comments about how the previous week was, the leader has planned to discuss starting to date again. A couple of members have already commented.

Leader: Any other comments?

Myra: I had a real crazy week. My daughter said she wanted to go live with her dad. I didn't know what to say. She was mad because I wouldn't let her have a dog—I just don't need that now!

Jan: I've heard that pets are good for children, especially after a loss. Is that true?

Pat: My daughter spends more time with our cat than she ever did. It is interesting how pets may be able to help during this time.

Vicky: I would think that there are many reasons for that. I can think of at least three. First, . . .

If Vicky is allowed to discuss the reasons for children's positive reactions to pets, the leader may have a difficult time shifting the focus of the group from pets to dating.

. . . .

It is the second of four sessions in a group for men who are not satisfied with their current occupation and who want a change. The leader plans to focus on ways to assess skills and to research occupations that use those skills.

Leader: Today I thought we would focus on what skills you have and what occupations would fit those skills.

Omar: Can I say something? I have never believed I was good at anything because my father always cut me down. I really think that had an effect on me.

Bill: My problem is my oldest brother. He could always do things better than me.

Ted: I think I put myself down because my wife has always wanted me to be more than I am. She really has been on my case.

Sam: Mine, too. My wife nags me constantly. The other day she was on my case about my salary, my car, and the mess in the garage. Let me tell you what happened the other day when I got home from work. . . .

At this point, the leader should use a cut-off skill (see Chapter Seven). Because the leader did not interrupt, the members are now focused on their wives. Because the group is only meeting four times, the leader needs to stick to the planned topic rather than to allow the members to discuss their past or their wives.

. . . .

The Middle or Working Phase

Planning for the active middle phase will vary somewhat, depending on the type of group you're working with, so we will discuss each in turn. The sample session plans that appear later in this chapter should also give you a good idea of how to plan for the bulk of the session.

Discussion and Education Groups

Planning a discussion or an educational group session requires that the leader decide, first, what topics or information to cover, then the order to which the topics should be presented or discussed and how they are to be covered. The leader also has to estimate the amount of time needed for each.

A leader has many options for covering a topic. She can give a mini-lecture on the subject to educate or stimulate discussion. She can invite a guest speaker or show a videotape. She can simply introduce the topic for discussion, and have the members discuss it in pairs before discussing it in the entire group. She can use one or more exercises (see Chapters Nine and Ten); sentence-completion exercises are often very useful in discussion groups.

Task Groups

The planning of a task group depends mostly on its purpose, but it is always the leader's responsibility to plan each session so that it is relevant and productive. Topics and exercises may be useful for some task groups; for example, in a group meeting to improve communications between management and workers, the leader can plan various exercises that help members understand their own communication patterns and style. In a group deciding policies for a new treatment unit, certain exercises might be useful if the group has trouble focusing on the task; the leader can conduct a brainstorming activity or a round, or can have the group break into two or three smaller discussion groups. Planning ahead of time often ensures that the time will be well spent. It is important to decide how much planning is needed for a task group session because without the proper amount, the session may be nonproductive.

Support Groups

In some support groups, members come eager to share their common concern, whether it be drugs, divorce, weight problems, or their disability; therefore, little planning is needed. In others, the leader may have to provide topics or exercises that encourage members to share. For instance, in a group for disabled veterans, the leader might introduce topics such as how members' disabilities affect family relationships, what the hardest times are for the disabled, or how to handle stress. In a group for spouses of people with Alzheimer's disease, the leader may introduce topics such as accepting the illness, getting some relief time, or dealing with the loss of the partner as a companion. The important thing to remember in planning a support group is to make sure a variety of topics are covered and not introduce the same one week after week. If the members are constantly bringing up new and relevant topics, very little planning will be necessary.

Growth Groups

Although the leader will usually be the one to plan each growth group session, the topics may be decided either by the group the week before or by the leader. In either case, the leader should come to the group with a plan for the beginning, middle, and ending phases of the session. The leader should plan for the group to focus on either a number of topics or a specific topic and decide whether the group should focus on one or two individuals or on the whole membership.

Therapy Groups

The planning of therapy groups varies greatly. Some require almost no planning because the members are ready, willing, and eager to share their concerns. In other groups, members are in pain and in need of therapy, but they need exercises and other activities to encourage them to share. In therapy groups that require planning, the leader will want to consider what topics have yet to be covered. The leader may even cover certain topics hoping to help one or two specific members. For instance, a leader who knows that a few group members are having trouble dealing with anger might plan an exercise to work on anger. Leaders will also want to make sure the topics vary; if the members keep talking about the same thing over and over, the leader probably will want to plan an exercise that focuses the members on some other issue.

Ending Phase

For certain kinds of groups and for certain group sessions, planning the ending phase is very important. Certainly, leaders should give extra thought to planning the ending of the first and last sessions of any group. Because this stage is so critical, we have devoted Chapter Thirteen to ending a session as well as to ending a group. If you are currently leading a group, we urge you to turn to that chapter for ideas on how to end your sessions. At this point, however, we want to stress that planning the ending is crucial; a common mistake is to fail to plan adequately for this phase. Some leaders even simply let the clock announce the ending: when the designated time to stop comes around, the group ends. The leader should always allow five to ten minutes for summarizing and "processing" the session—that is, for discussing it in a focused, conscious manner. He might want to use one of the ending exercises or activities discussed in Chapter Thirteen to do this.

Sample Session Plans

This section contains sample plans for sessions in different kinds of groups. Note that an estimated time is given for each activity to help the leader gauge how the flow of the group might go. This guideline helps greatly during the session, because otherwise the leader has little idea whether too much time is being spent on a topic. It is important to allot specific amounts of time for exercises and activities, but we also want to caution you against becoming a slave to your plan. Realize that the plan can be and often will need to be changed as the session progresses. The plan's purpose is merely to help you organize a session in a logical sequence.

As you read through the sample plans, you may see terms with which you are unfamiliar. However, because our purpose here is simply to give you an idea of how to plan a session, it is not necessary that you completely understand each activity; these activities are explained in later chapters. We tried to include a variety of techniques and activities to show the many different ways to plan a session. After each plan is a discussion of its features.

PLAN 1
The first session of a parenting group consisting of ten members: two couples, three mothers alone, two single mothers, and one single father.

5 min.	Introductions—round (name, age of children, why they came to the group).
7 min.	Discuss the group—format, purpose (stress that it is mainly an educational and support group and not a therapy group). Have members share their needs and any fears or questions about the group. (Sandwich in the ground rules of confidentiality, attendance, no attacking of others.)
3 min.	Dyads—share problems and feelings as a parent.
5 min.	Have members share these in large group (use their examples in discussion below).
5 min.	Discuss Adlerian principles of child behavior (use charts and handouts):
	All behavior is purposeful.
	Children are not bad—they are discouraged.
	Four goals of misbehavior.
5 min.	Have members share in triads their thoughts about the Adlerian principles.
10 min.	Discuss in large group, then continue overview of principles:
	Parent's reaction to each of the goals.
	Natural and logical consequences.
5 min.	Triads (make sure members are getting with different people)—discuss their parenting in reference to the comments regarding the Adlerian approach.
5 min.	Discuss comments from the triads.
10 min.	Focus on the first goal of misbehavior—attention getting:
	Use short role-plays to demonstrate.
	Discuss ways to deal with situations.
5 min.	Dyads—discuss this goal in relation to their children and how parents may handle situations differently.
15 min.	Process dyads. (If not much time is needed, discuss the second goal of misbehavior.)
10 min.	Summarize—what stood out, feelings about the group, one thing they plan to do differently:
	Hand out reading material.
	Remind them of next meeting time.

In this plan, the introductory exercise is brief because it is for an educational group and the group is only meeting for an hour and a half. Also, the leader knows that the members will be interacting in dyads and triads during the sessions, so they will have several opportunities to get to know each other better. The introductions and discussion about the group are useful because they allow members to share some important information and to mention their fears and expectations regarding the group. The purpose of the group and the format are clarified during the first 15 minutes. Ground rules are minimal so no specific time is established to review them; they will probably be mentioned during the first few segments. The dyad gives members a chance to share their individual problems with one other person (this helps some members get more comfortable and "warms them up"); the large-group processing allows the leader and other members to hear each member's concerns. In discussing the Adlerian principles, the leader can use examples from the processing of the dyads. Because it is the first session, the leader chooses to use many dyads and triads so that members have opportunities to interact with many different members. Also, using triads instead of the entire group to discuss some topics enables more members to talk. (Usually, some members are more comfortable sharing in triads than in the large group.) The leader varies the format to keep members interested. Also, the leader's plan includes some interesting and immediately useful content that is relevant to the group's purpose. (Too often, leaders mistakenly plan first sessions that have very little content; thus some members do not return.) It is the first session, so more time than usual is allowed for the summary. Ordinarily, the summary would take five to eight minutes. Remember, time periods are approximate but are necessary to give the leader some idea of how long to stay on any activity.

PLAN 2

The second session of a growth and support group for fifth- and sixth-graders who don't seem to make friends easily. There is one new member this week.

5 min.	Introduce new member to the group—have members tell their names and what they remember about last week. Leader comments about the group and its purpose. Also, remind members to look at others besides the leader when they talk.
2 min.	Have members list things they can do to make friends.
3 min.	Discuss lists in dyads.
15 min.	Process ideas in large group: List ideas on chalkboard. Discuss the ideas. Role-play some of the ideas. Get each member to practice.
3 min.	Have each member tell one thing he or she will try this week.
2 min.	Summarize—each member completes "One thing I learned. . . .

In this plan, the leader uses welcoming a new member as a way to review last week's session. The opening segment is short because the session only lasts 30 minutes. Next, the leader uses a written exercise because this is a good way to get the children focused and involved. For the middle phase of the session, the leader has thought of several interesting ways to focus on making friends. The use of dyads is a good idea because it gets each member talking to another member, which is part of the purpose of the group—that is, to learn how to talk with other children. To close the session the leader plans a simple but focused ending—having members commit to trying something new and asking them to comment on what they learned in the session.

PLAN 3
The third session of a six-week assertiveness-training group with eight members.

10 min.	Progress reports, observations from the week, questions.
15 min.	Reenact some "assertiveness" situations from the week (this could last longer if there are a number of situations).
5 min.	Dyads—process thoughts from the reenactments.
15 min.	Present the "broken record" technique: Demonstrate. Practice.
10 min.	Reactions, comments, and questions.
1 min.	Round—(1–10; 10 = very much): how guilty do you feel when you are being assertive?
15 min.	Discuss their numbers and how not to feel guilty—teach RET: Show ABC model. Write on board their irrational self-talk and then rational self-talk.
5 min.	Dyads: discuss the use of RET when being assertive.
10 min.	Discussion: things I plan to try this week regarding being assertive.
5 min.	Summary: what stood out for you today? Any wishes for anyone in the group.

Progress reports are helpful both for the member who shares and for the rest of the members, who hear how others are using what they learn in the group. Also, progress reports help members see the continuity and flow of the group experience. Plan 3 includes a review, the introduction of much new material, and periods of focus on the past, present, and future. The plan uses a varied format that includes a round, dyads, teaching, demonstrating, practicing, interacting, and committing to trying new behavior during the coming week. The leader also introduces a theory and model that members can use during the rest of the sessions. In closing, the leader asks the "wishes for anyone" question so that members can say encouraging things to each other and feel the support of other members; this helps build cohesion in the group.

PLAN 4

The third session of a weekly therapy group for outpatients of a mental health center; the group has six members.

5 min.   Progress reports—ask about Bob's mother's visit, Ruth's exercise program, Tandy's contract to talk with two people each day.

5 min.   Thoughts, comments, reactions to the week.

10 min.   Review Ellis's ABC model—use examples from their week.

60 min.   Personal work—do yes/no round of who wants to bring up something; if all no's, use backup plan—focus on love relationships:

Rate love relationship on a scale of 1 to 10 (10 = great).

Ask what keeps it from being a 10 (discussion and personal work should come out of this).

20 min.   Introduce TA model if it did not come up during the personal work or continue the personal work if others want to work.

10 min.   Share (in triads) reactions to TA model.

5 min.   Summarize.

5 min.   Write in journals.

In this plan, the leader starts by having specific members report on some of the work they have done in group. This fosters continuity; also, when members know they are going to report to the group or be asked if they did something, they tend to think more about it. The leader asks about the week to see whether anyone has something to share. This allows members to share positive or negative things that happened. Personal work could be started here, but the leader wants to spend a few minutes reviewing the RET model and uses the members' comments about the week to show how RET could be helpful. Note that the review is brief because the leader wants to allow enough time for individual work. In therapy groups, members often come wanting to talk about some concern. The round helps the leader to learn quickly how many members have something to discuss. Two things to note in this segment are that the leader has a backup plan and that an hour, plus more time if necessary, has been allowed for personal work. The leader introduces transactional analysis (TA) to the group because it is a theory that most patients find interesting and helpful. This leader also has members write in a journal that they leave with her; this gives them a chance to express what they may have wanted to say in the group but for some reason did not.

FREQUENT MISTAKES IN PLANNING

Before closing this chapter, we want to comment on some typical mistakes leaders make in planning. Some of them have been alluded to in the commentary on the sample plans; others are new.

Not Planning

The biggest mistake made in planning is not doing it. Very often, at the end of workshops that we give, counselors comment that they now realize their problems with their groups stem mostly from not planning. Unfortunately, some professionals still subscribe to the notion that planning will detract from the group. It is very important to understand this simply is not true. *Plan your groups.* Good planning is the best way to ensure that the session will be valuable to the group members.

Irrelevant or Meaningless Content

Too often, leaders choose activities, exercises, or topics that do not interest the members of a specific group. Leaders sometimes use introductory exercises that are irrelevant and thus fail to set the appropriate tone, or they conduct activities that are not related to the members' concerns. Leaders might also introduce topics to which only one or two members can relate; this causes the others to lose interest or become resentful. It is absolutely essential that the leader do everything possible to ensure that the session will be relevant and valuable to most or all of the members. The following are examples of *poor* planning.

- For the first session of a weight-loss group, the leader plans 45 minutes on the topic of the biochemical makeup of foods.
- In a group for teenagers, the leader plans to focus on how to select the right college to attend, even though only two members are planning to go to college.
- For a 1½-hour session for stepparents, the leader plans a 15-minute minilecture on society and the family.
- In a group for couples with marital problems, the leader plans 30 minutes on dealing with children. Only two of the five couples have children.

Inappropriate Exercises

Leaders will sometimes plan an exercise for which members are not ready. For example, during a first or second session, often members are not ready for an exercise that involves sharing about sexual concerns, nor are they ready for certain kinds of feedback exercises.

Too Many Exercises

Another mistake leaders make is to plan too many exercises for a given session. This prevents members from having enough time to process and learn from the exercises, thereby robbing them of much of the value of the exercises. Too, the session will seem like a series of exercises rather than a group in which members can share and exchange reactions, feelings, and thoughts. Inexperienced leaders are especially prone to this error, perhaps due to their fear of leading less structured discussions.

Poor Planning of Time and Order

Many beginning leaders make the mistake of planning their available time poorly. A common example is planning warm-up or introductory activities that last too long. This means that not enough time is allowed to do more meaningful, productive work in the middle part of the session. It is *imperative* that the leader plan the group so that the most time is spent on the most important issues.

A good plan has a reasonable order to it. Some leaders forget this and plan topics or exercises that are not related to each other. For example, a leader would not want to conduct an exercise that focuses on fun followed by one that focuses on death. Also, leaders sometimes arrange the topics or exercises in a sequence that makes them less beneficial than they could be. For instance, it would be a mistake for the leader to plan a long feedback exercise followed by a discussion of how members see themselves. Rather, the order should be reversed, because it would benefit members more to consider how they see themselves before hearing feedback from others.

Planning Negative Activities at the Beginning

Some leaders allow the start of the group to be negative. This is especially true for groups run in institutions, such as prisons or mental hospitals. The leader will ask for opening comments, and often members will offer some complaint about the institution or the program. Leaders of groups in which the members tend to be negative will want to plan interesting openings that do not allow negative comments to surface at the beginning. The leader might even establish that the last few minutes of each session will be available for members to air their complaints.

Allowing Too Much Time for Warm-Up

Some leaders mistakenly plan long openings to sessions as a way to review the previous session. The idea is good, but allowing as much as fifteen to twenty minutes is usually a mistake because most people want to move on to new material. It is very important to make sure that the opening is productive and not so long as to bore the members.

Not Allowing Enough Time for Warm-Up

When leaders have much to cover in a session, they sometimes forget to plan for the warm-up phase. Members need time to get focused, which is the purpose of the first few minutes of any group. Groups will vary as to how much time is needed for the beginning phase of the session, but it is important that the leader allot whatever time is needed.

Not Allowing Enough Time for Closing

Many leaders fail to plan for the closing and either let the group end when the time has run out or conduct a hurried closing. For some groups, this may be acceptable, but for most groups, we strongly suggest that the leader plan for the closing. The closing can be a productive time in which members share what they learned and make commitments to the group about actions they are going to take before the next session.

Vague Plans

Many beginning leaders plan their groups too vaguely to be of much help. For instance, the leader will plan to deal with the subject of anger and will allow 45 minutes for the topic but will neglect to plan in detail how to introduce the topic and what exercises and activities will be used. The leader will also want to list possible spin-off subjects, such as anger at parents, self-talk and anger, and ways to deal with anger.

Lack of Flexibility

Some leaders rigidly follow their plan even when members have raised issues that are more meaningful and appropriate than those planned. Others fail to recognize when their plan is not working. It is challenging yet necessary to be flexible enough to deviate from a plan whenever it becomes clear that members are not benefiting from it. For example, imagine the toll in group commitment and interest in the following scenario.

E X A M P L E . . . .

The leader has planned two activities to improve family communication for a group of teenagers who live together in a detention center. The members tell the leader how angry they are at two of the residents who are not in the group. Their anger is due to a stealing and lying incident. Rather than changing the plan and focusing on their immediate needs, the leader forces the members to try the communication-skills activities. They listlessly role-play their mother or father.

. . . .

CONCLUDING COMMENTS

In this chapter, we discussed how to plan for a session and for a series of sessions. We discussed who group members should be, how they are screened, and when and for how long the group should meet. We stressed that a leader must plan the beginning, middle, and ending phases of any particular session: not only the activities and topics, but the time to be devoted to each. The leader should also consider whether particular members could benefit from certain topics or from having the group focus on them. Members do not mind a group that is planned if it is planned well. Remember that although we emphasize the importance of having a plan, the effective leader is never a slave to that plan. If members become very involved in a topic or exercise, the leader should probably adjust the plan. If a valuable new topic emerges during a session, the leader might want to alter the plan; conversely, if the plan is not working, the leader should abandon it and use a backup plan.

CHAPTER FOUR.

Getting Started:
The First and Second Sessions

The first and second sessions of any group are probably the most important and usually are the most difficult to lead. For those reasons, we will discuss them separately and in detail.

THE FIRST SESSION

The first session is difficult because the leader has many different dynamics and logistics to manage: starting the group, introducing the content to the members, and monitoring the members' reactions both to being in the group and to the content. Some of the dynamics and logistics the leader must contend with include the following:

1. Beginning the group
2. Helping members get acquainted
3. Setting a positive tone
4. Drawing out members
5. Clarifying the purpose of the group
6. Explaining the leader's role
7. Explaining how the group will be conducted
8. Helping members verbalize expectations
9. Addressing questions
10. Explaining the ground rules
11. Explaining any special terms that will be used
12. Checking out the comfort levels of the members
13. Assessing members' interaction style
14. Introducing and focusing on the content

After discussing each of these in turn, we'll present exercises useful during the first session, some focusing issues, and hints for closing the session.

Beginning the Group

One of the most important considerations for the first session is how to begin the group. The manner in which the leader opens the session will have an important bearing on the tone of the group and the comfort level of the members. The leader should convey warmth, trust, helpfulness, understanding, and positive regard. This is the stage at which members form their impressions of the group and the leader and assess whether or not they think the group is going to be helpful to them. Unfortunately, members sometimes leave groups that could be helpful simply because the opening few minutes were boring or intimidating. Others may be put off if the leader inappropriately uses a formal, businesslike manner in the opening moments. For some groups, a formal opening is appropriate, but for many others, it is less effective. Remember, the opening two or three sentences and the way they are presented do matter!

Some leaders make the mistake of opening with a minilecture on issues such as the ground rules for the group, the meeting time for each session, and the frequency of meetings. Such minilectures usually get the first session off to a poor start because they set a "leader-dominant" tone and simply bore the members.

Another common error is to ask for members' expectations when they are uneasy about being in the group and have not yet met one another. A leader who starts by saying, "To begin the group, I would like each of you to comment on why you came," may get no response because the members are not yet comfortable. At the beginning of most groups, a brief opening statement about the group, followed by member introductions, is usually helpful.

The following are seven possible openings; some of them include the use of an introduction exercise.

Options for Opening the First Session

Start with an opening statement about the group and its purpose; then conduct an introduction exercise.   This type of opening is often used for education or task groups, although some leaders use a long opening statement for therapy and growth groups as well. By an opening statement, we mean that the leader will spend the first two to three minutes describing the purpose and format of the group and then will present an overview of the planned content. During this opening, the leader will usually give some background information about himself and his experience in leading groups similar to the present one. Leaders should be cautious about boring members with too lengthy an opening. On the other hand, a practical reason for using a long opening might be to capture the interest of the members who are present when other members have not yet arrived.

EXAMPLE. . . . .

The group consists of teachers in a large school district. It is the first session in a series of four on teacher burnout.

Leader: I'd like us to begin. I am Sarah Daniels. I am a counselor at North High School. Over the last several years, I have been studying teacher burnout. As a result of my studies, I have developed what I think is a helpful way of understanding burnout. Over the next four weeks, I will be going over the material. Briefly, I'd like to share what each session will be about. Today we will start by. . . .

After going over the material for two or three minutes, the leader concludes the opening statement.

Leader: I hope you now have an idea of what will take place here and how this group can help. Now, before getting started with definitions of burnout, I'd like to take a couple of minutes and let you introduce yourselves. I'd like each of you to tell us your name, how long you have been teaching, what you teach, and a sentence or two about why you came.

. . . .

Start with a brief statement about the group; then conduct an introduction exercise. This type of opening is perhaps the one most frequently used. The leader gives a brief (one- to two-minute), well-thought-out opening statement and then has the members participate in an introduction exercise. This prevents members from settling into a "listening" frame of mind; they become active almost immediately and quickly feel that they are participants in a group rather than listeners in a class. This opening is especially useful for groups in which the members do not know each other.

EXAMPLE. . . . .

The group is for teenagers whose parents have divorced or separated in the last four months.

Leader: I'm really glad you are here. As you know, this group is for sharing thoughts, feelings, and reactions to your parents' divorce or separation. It is my understanding that each of you has experienced your parents either divorcing or separating within the last four months. Through this group, I hope you will realize that you're not the only one feeling the way you do. Having your parents split up causes all kinds of feelings—chances are many of you are having a variety of those feelings.

We 'll explore them in this group. To get started, I thought we'd do an introductory exercise to learn people's names, since most of you do not know each other. I am going to say my name; then, Ted, you say my name, then your name. Then, Yolanda, you say my name, then Ted's, then yours. We'll go around the group like this.

Leader: OK, I'm Mike.

Ted: This is Mike, and I am Ted.

Yolanda: That is Mike. This is Ted, and I am Yolanda.

. . . .

Start with a long opening statement; then get right into the content of the group.   This opening can be used in discussion, education, and task groups in which the members already know each other or in groups in which personal sharing will be minimal. A long opening statement is used when the leader feels the members need an explanation or clarification of the group's content or purpose. The long opening statement would be similar to that in our first option, in which the leader outlines the content and shares some information about himself. It differs from the first option in that the leader does not plan an introduction of the members but rather starts right in with the content.

E X A M P L E . . . .

The group is for helping unemployed people find a job. The leader opens the session.

Leader: I am glad you decided to attend the group. I think you will find the information helpful in getting you back into the work force. The goal of these group sessions will be to give you information about how to find potential jobs, how to interview for jobs, how to fill out applications, and how to keep a positive attitude while looking. Before we get started, I want to tell you a little about myself and about each of the five sessions. . . . (*After going over the proposed content of the five sessions, the leader continues*)

Leader: Now let's get started on today's material. We're going to discuss how to find potential jobs. I want each of you to think of three ways that you go about looking for work. . . .

. . . .

Start with a brief statement about the group; then get into the content.   This opening would be used when no introductions are needed (members already know each other) and the purpose of the group is already clear to the members. This is a good opening for many discussion, education, and task groups, especially if they are meeting for a short period, such as an hour.

EXAMPLE . . . .

The group's purpose is to decide on policies for a new treatment unit for adolescents. The leader begins.

Leader: Let's get started. We have a number of policies to decide on regarding the new unit. The current plan is to meet each Tuesday for an hour and a half at this time for the next four weeks or until we feel we are finished. Why don't we begin by listing the kinds of policies we think need to be written? I'll write them as you call them out.

. . . .

Start with a brief statement about the group; then have the members form dyads.   This opening can be used when no introduction exercise is necessary. The leader describes the group briefly and then has members form dyads to discuss either the content of the group or why they have come to the group. This kind of opening is useful when the purpose is already clear to everyone and the members are comfortable being in the group. It is also useful in certain kinds of task, education, discussion, and support groups.

EXAMPLE . . . .

The group is for parents who have learned that their children have been sexually abused at a day care center.

Leader: I am glad you came tonight. I think that all of you will benefit from sharing your feelings with each other. When something like this occurs, a group can be helpful in getting support and exchanging ideas for helping your child. Since you all know each other, I want us to start by pairing up. Do not pair up with your spouse, if he or she is with you, or with someone you know very well.

Now that you have a partner, I want you to share the feelings that you have experienced since this incident and why you chose to come to the group—that is, what you hope to gain from being here.

. . . .

Start with a brief statement about the group; then have members fill out a short sentence-completion form.   When no introductions are needed, using a sentence-completion form is an excellent way to open certain kinds of groups because it tends to help members focus. This kind of opening is helpful in leading task groups, discussion groups, and some education groups. It can also be used in growth and therapy groups in which the members already know one another.

EXAMPLE . . . .

The group's purpose is to improve staff relations in a hospital unit.

Leader: As you know, the purpose of this meeting is to improve working relations within the unit. I'd like to start by having you fill out, as honestly as you can, this form, which consists of five incomplete sentences. The sentences have to do with the unit: your feelings, your perception of the problems, and so on. I'll give you a couple of minutes to complete it.

. . . .

Start with an introduction exercise.   Starting with an introduction exercise instead of a statement about the group should only be done when the members have a clear idea of the group's purpose. If an appropriate introduction exercise is used, this type of opening can serve a dual purpose: members can introduce themselves and begin immediately to focus on the content of the group.

EXAMPLE . . . .

The group is for single fathers.

Leader: Why don't we begin? As a way of starting, I'd like each of you to introduce yourself and tell us in two or three sentences how you came to be a single father. Who wants to go first?

. . . .

We hope the examples and discussion have helped you see that there are a variety of appropriate ways to open a beginning session. The right kind of opening, combined with enthusiasm on the part of the leader, can have a strong positive effect on how a group starts.

Helping Members Get Acquainted

If members do not know each other, it is usually beneficial to have members get acquainted soon after the session begins. Members tend to feel more at ease after learning one another's names (name tags can help) and spending some time getting to know one another. In groups in which personal sharing will take place, more time should be spent helping members get to know one another. This is important for two reasons. First, in growth, therapy, or support groups, members are much more curious about those with whom they will be discussing personal issues. Second, a thorough introduction helps the group develop cohesion and trust. In most education and discussion groups and in many task groups, only a minimal amount of time needs to be spent on introductions because members either know one another or will not be discussing personal issues.

The type of introduction exercise the leader uses will depend on several factors, including the size of the group, the amount of time the session is to last, the purpose of the group, and whether or not the members are already acquainted.

The size of the group can limit the options for the kind of introduction exercise chosen. If the group has more than ten members, the leader will probably not want to use an introduction exercise involving each member sharing about himself or herself for two to three minutes because it would take too long. When groups are meeting for a rather short period (an hour or less), the leader will not want to use any introduction exercise that lasts more than five minutes. This applies especially to education, discussion, and task groups and to groups meeting for only one session.

The purpose of the group is probably the most important factor in determining what kind of introduction exercise to use. With groups meeting for educational or discussion purposes, the leader might want to use an exercise that helps people remember names. In growth, task, support, and therapy groups, the leader might choose an exercise that gets members to share relevant information about themselves. The leader might also have members share their reasons for attending the group or their expectations of the session.

It is the leader who determines whether the introduction exercise is to be light or serious. A "fun" activity is perfectly appropriate for certain kinds of groups, but it could be a mistake in others—for example, in therapy groups or those dealing with such issues as abuse or addiction. The leader must be sure, too, that the opening used is relevant to the purpose of the group. For instance, in a group for patients with cancer, an introductory activity in which the members share their names, the names of their family members, where they work, and their favorite hobby would not be relevant. Instead, the leader could have the members state their names, how long they have been receiving treatment, and one fear or feeling about having the disease.

The following are descriptions of several introduction activities.

The Name Round

This is probably the most frequently used exercise for learning people's names. In the name round, members simply introduce themselves, sometimes giving names only and other times sharing additional information, such as place of origin, occupation, reason for joining the group, or things they like to do. Naturally, what is shared will depend partly on the purpose of the group. For instance, in a parenting group, the leader would have members state the number of children they have and their ages, but the leader would not have them state where they work because it would not be relevant to the purpose of the group.

The Repeat Round

The repeat round is a name exercise in which the first member says his or her name, the next member says the first member's name and then his or her own, and so on. This exercise is good for helping members remember everyone's name. The leader should also use members' names frequently during the first session.

The Introduction Dyad

This exercise consists of two members pairing up and telling each other certain things about themselves, usually based on suggestions from the leader. Then all the members come back together in a group, and each one introduces his or her partner to the group. For example, in a group for children who have trouble making friends, a member might say, "This is Carlos. He likes football and fishing. He has two younger stepbrothers. His favorite subject in school is math."

Repeated Dyad

This exercise consists of having members pair up with every other member and spend two to five minutes sharing such things as why they are in the group and what they hope to get from it (this is good for certain kinds of support, growth, and therapy groups). This exercise should only be used when there are fewer than seven members; otherwise, it would take too much time to allow each member to form a dyad with every other member.

Milling

For large groups (12 or more members), we sometimes have members mill around and meet each other during the first four to five minutes of the first group session. The instructions are usually quite simple, such as, "To help you get acquainted, I'd like you to stand up and mill about the room meeting the other group members. Try to learn everyone's name and why he or she is here." A simple activity like this provides an opportunity for members to have contact with one another and speeds up the process of getting acquainted.

These are just some of the ways a leader can help members get acquainted. Large name tags are also helpful for remembering names. A good introduction exercise shows that the leader thought about how members will get to know one another. Also, a good introduction exercise is one that is appropriate for the members, the kind of group, and the amount of time the group is meeting.

Setting a Positive Tone

Another important task for the leader during the first and second sessions is to establish a positive tone for the group. The tone is the prevailing atmosphere; it stems from several sources, including the leader's and members' energy and enthusiasm and the comfort and trust experienced among the members. The leader can establish a positive tone by drawing out members, by holding the focus on interesting topics, by shifting the focus when the topics are irrelevant or only interesting to a couple of members, by cutting off any interactions that are hostile or negative, and by being enthusiastic.

It is very important that the leader not let the group focus on negative members or negative issues for a major portion of the first session. A member who is complaining about being in the group or questioning its value can establish a negative tone that may be difficult to alter. Allowing extended hostile or heated interaction between members also contributes to a negative tone. Certainly some time might have to be devoted to those kinds of dynamics, but the leader will want to make sure that most of the time is spent in building rapport, sharing, and discussing in a positive way.

If a negative tone is set during the first two group sessions, members will usually never come to trust one another enough to share personal data about themselves. Also, they may feel that the group is a place to "nail" other members and therefore will either focus on others or fear being attacked by the group.

Drawing Out Members

It is advisable that the leader, during the first and second sessions, try to make sure that everyone has a chance to contribute. The leader should not force each member to speak; rather, members should feel that they can participate if they so desire. They may feel left out if they believe they haven't had an opportunity to verbalize their thoughts, feelings, and ideas.

During the first session of a growth, therapy, or support group, the leader should, if at all possible, get each member to share something somewhat personal. This is important because by sharing, members often reduce their anxiety about being in the group. It is also important because members of these groups are usually curious about each other. Disclosures usually help listening members feel more comfortable with the disclosing member. Be aware, however, that some members will be so uncomfortable or fearful that they will not share very much during the first meeting.

A number of leadership skills and activities are helpful in drawing out members. Introduction exercises, rounds, dyads, and some written exercises usually will get each member to comment. These activities, if properly conducted, allow members the opportunity to participate as much as they feel comfortable with. We discuss these skills in detail in Chapter Seven.

Also discussed in Chapter Seven is the skill of cutting off, which is extremely useful for containing members who want to dominate. If the leader does not restrain those members, others will feel that they do not have a chance to contribute.

Clarifying the Purpose

The leader must be sure that the purpose of the group is clarified during the first and second sessions of a new group. Clarification is particularly important if there has been no screening interview before the first group meeting. Even if the leader has screened the members and has already spent time discussing the group's purpose, it is still a good idea to review it as a group. The purpose of some groups may require more clarification than others. In a group that has been advertised as a weight-loss group, the purpose is probably clear to all members; on the other hand, one called a divorce group could be intended for singles to meet others for support or for therapy. Therefore, the specific purpose of that group will have to be clarified during the first session.

It is a good idea to reiterate the purpose throughout the first two sessions. Members often are anxious or preoccupied at first and thus are not always listening. After the second session, it usually is not necessary to review the purpose unless new members are added to the group or the purpose changes during the life of the group.

Explaining the Leader's Role

During the first session, the leader should explain what her role will be throughout the sessions: a teaching role, a facilitative role, an active leadership role, a therapeutic role, or some of each. Offering this explanation helps members form a picture of what to expect from the leader.

E X A M P L E S . . . .

- Let me take just a minute to explain my role to all of you. As you know, during the next six weeks, we will be meeting every Monday evening so that you can share your experience of being a single parent. My role in this group will be to facilitate sharing and provide some information. On some occasions, the situation may call for me to vary somewhat from a facilitative role to a role in which I am actually doing some counseling with one or two members.

- In this group I mainly will be helping you share your experience as a newly divorced woman. Since the purpose is support, I will try to facilitate discussion among you. Sometimes I will attempt to draw some of you into the conversation. Please realize that it is your group and that I am not here as an expert or as the person responsible for making meaningful things happen.

- In this group, I will be introducing you to the dangers of alcohol and drug use. To do this, I will be giving you information, facilitating discussion, and answering questions.

- My role in this group is to see to it that you make the decisions outlined on the handout in front of you. I will push you to be open and honest with each other, and I will try to get you to express how you feel about the issues. Also, I will try to structure the time wisely so we can accomplish something each time we meet. My participation will be minimal; that is, I will not offer my opinions or ideas, since I do not work here and do not know your agency as well as you do.

. . . .

The leader might also want to explain some of his leadership behaviors, such as cutting members off at times and drawing members out:

Leader: Something that I may do from time to time is cut you off if I feel you are off on a tangent. I won't do this often, but one of my tasks is to give everyone a chance to talk. Also, there will be times when I may try to get you to talk. Please realize that you don't have to, but I may try to draw you into the discussion.

If the leader plans to do therapy, he might want to explain the techniques he plans to use with which members may be unfamiliar. Some leaders may use psychodrama techniques that need explaining, "the empty chair," or a therapeutic round (see Chapter Twelve). Explaining these procedures in the first or second session reduces the chances of confusion or misunderstanding when they are used in later sessions.

Explaining How the Group Will Be Conducted

Closely allied to explaining the purpose of the group is explaining what will happen in it. It is important to clarify during the first session how the leader plans to conduct the group. Describing the kinds of discussions and activities that will take place in the group will help ease tension and ensure the smooth functioning of the group. For example, in an education or discussion group, the leader might want to explain that the format for the group will require that the first ten minutes serve as a review time for the previous session's topic. Then a new topic will be presented by a speaker or by the leader, followed by members sharing their opinions and reactions.

In certain kinds of support, growth, and therapy groups, the leader will want to inform members that at times they will be asked to do certain group exercises. If there is going to be discussion and sharing during the first half of each session and exercises and therapy during the last half, the leader would want to explain this. Also, she may want to explain how she intends to do therapy in the group if that is part of her agenda. Hearing this explanation during the first and second sessions will give members a much clearer understanding of what will take place in the group.

Another reason for stating what will happen in the group is that after hearing a description of how the group will be conducted, some members may decide they do not want to be in the group. If a member decides not to join the group, the leader will want to speak privately with that member to determine the reason. Depending on the reason, the leader may or may not encourage the member to stay. That is, the leader would not want to urge a member to stay who definitely wanted a different kind of group, but she might try to encourage a member who feared that something bad might happen to him in the group.

The following are examples of how a leader might explain how she plans to conduct the sessions.

IN AN EDUCATION GROUP

Leader: All of our time will not be spent with me just providing you with facts and information. We will be doing a variety of activities. There will be times when I may ask you to break into pairs to discuss some issue, or I may ask you to write down some of your ideas. Near the end of each session, we'll deal with any questions you might have. At the very end of the session, I'll ask each of you to share what you learned from it.

IN A THERAPY GROUP

Leader: At different times in this group, someone will bring up something very personal. We will focus on that person for several minutes and try to be helpful. At times, I may even do some one-to-one counseling while the group watches, or shares only minimally.

Helping Members Verbalize Expectations

During the first session, it is important to let members share their expectations of the group. In this way, the leader learns what the members want and can further clarify the purpose of the group by commenting on those expectations. At times, the leader will reinforce some of the expectations voiced if they are in line with the purpose. At other times, the leader will need to point out that certain members' expectations will not be met by the current group due to its structure and purpose.

EXAMPLE . . . .

This group is for teenage girls who have had a baby in the last three months. The leader has just finished an introduction exercise and decides to use a round to get members to verbalize their expectations. Note also how the leader comments on some of the expectations as they apply to the group.

Leader: OK, now that we know a little more about each other, I want to talk about your expectations for the group. I want you each to think of what you are hoping to get from the group. We'll go around and hear from each of you.

Angela: I just look forward to talking to kids my own age about having a baby. Talking to grown-ups all the time just isn't fun.

Leader: Certainly one of the main reasons for the group is just that—all of you will get a chance to share with one another, and you do have things in common, that's for sure.

Donna: I am overwhelmed. Trying to handle the baby, school, my boyfriend, friends! I don't know if I can do it, and I hope to get some ideas.

Leader: I think all of you will find that the group can really be of help. I think each one of us has some ideas that can help others, and that's the benefit of the six of us meeting.

Nilda: I came because it sounded like something I could learn from.

Tandy: I need help with childrearing. I am scared that I will screw up my kid and I don't want to do that.

Leader: We will spend some time each week talking about childrearing, since I think each of you probably want to hear about that. We'll also spend time sharing about anything you want to that pertains to being a teenage mother.

. . . .

Along with being able to comment on how this group will be conducted as different expectations are expressed, the leader has the opportunity to clarify what expectations cannot be met. Sometimes members attend a first session having expectations that are not in line with the purpose of the group. If this situation arises, the leader will want to reiterate the purpose. If a member remains insistent that the purpose should be different, the leader may have members get into pairs and discuss why they came or some other relevant question; the leader pairs up with that member, which avoids a long discussion or debate in the group that may create a negative tone.

E X A M P L E S . . . .

In this first example, the member has an expectation that is not in line with the group's purpose, which is to help first-year college students with study skills. The students are expressing their expectations.

Bud: I want to learn how to prepare for essay exams. My high school was such a breeze, and all my tests were fill-in-the-blank or multiple choice.

Akira: I need help with my math problems—I don't understand equations and the instructor said I should get a tutor, so when I saw the announcement about a study skills group, I thought I would give it a try.

Leader: Well, Akira, let me clarify something for you and for others of you. This group is not really for tutoring as much as it is for teaching you how to study. That is, we will not work on any specific course but will talk about how to study for certain courses, including math. I guess what I am saying is that if any of you are looking for specific help in a course, then probably a tutor would be better. We are going to talk about how to take notes, how to prepare for exams, and basically how to study. Akira, now that you are here, you may want to stay or you may really just be looking for math help. If you want a tutor, I'll help you find one.

. . . .

In this example, one member's expectations are different from the others'. The purpose of the group is for parents to discuss what to do about the many pregnancies in the school. Members are discussing their views of the goal of the group.

Carla: I think it's good that we are meeting. I don't want my daughter to become pregnant, but I don't know the best way to prevent it. So I am hoping that as a group we can come up with some good ideas for educating our kids about sex.

Betsy: That's why I came. To try to come up with something that either the school or community can do.

Dot: I can tell you what we have to do, and that's to stop these kids from having abortions! They gave some statistics about teenage abortions on TV that horrified me. I am here to see to it that the school does something about all these abortions!

Leader: I really don't see this group as focusing on abortions. The purpose of this group is to decide how to prevent so many from getting pregnant.

Dot: I can't buy that. It is our moral duty to stop kids from even considering abortion!

Leader: (*In a very calm voice*) Let's do this: I want you to pair up with someone you don't know very well and discuss what you think are the different topics that we need to discuss in this group. Dot, I'll be with you.

. . . .

The leader could tell that Dot was not going to let the issue die, and he did not want the group to focus on a side issue. By using dyads, the leader is able to keep members focused while talking to Dot about the purpose. The leader would want to be careful not to spend the next half-hour trying to convince Dot of the purpose. He probably should not spend more than five minutes, if for no other reason than that the other members will likely run out of things to say. This is a situation in which the leader might ask Dot to leave if she insists on talking about the abortion issue.

A leader can make several mistakes regarding the expectations of the members. Some leaders spend as much as half or three-fourths of a session on the question "What do you hope to get from this group?" This usually happens when expectations are highly varied and the leader feels obligated to discuss each one. Probably no more than 10 to 15 minutes should be spent on expectations, and often they can be covered in 5 minutes or less.

Another mistake leaders make is to ask members for their expectations when they really don't have any. This might be the case in groups led in settings such as prisons or rehabilitation centers, where members are required to attend or are attending in order to avoid some other activity, such as a class. The leader might want to ask about expectations but should be prepared for little or no response—or responses that are not in line with the purpose.

E X A M P L E . . . .

This is a mandatory group at a 30-day juvenile crisis center.

Leader: I'd like to hear from each of you about why you are in the group and what you hope to gain from it.

Don: Hey, man, I don't want anything—they made me come.

Alton: There's nothing the matter with me—I hate this group therapy crap!

Leader: This isn't crap. Hopefully it will be helpful.

Mel: I want to talk about rock music—the houseparent said we can talk about anything we want to.

Leader: Come on, be serious. What can you get from this group?

. . . .

In this group, the leader should not have mentioned expectations or should have expected some negative reactions because the members did not volunteer for the group.

Addressing Questions

In the first session, members will often have a wide variety of questions that should be answered. Some of their questions will pertain to the purpose of the group, others to the meeting time and place, the leader's credentials, and other details. Though this point may seem elementary, there are leaders who do not anticipate these possible questions and fail to allot time for members to ask what they consider to be important questions.

Another mistake is taking a long time to answer a question in which only one member is interested. If the leader feels too much time is being spent on specific questions that are not relevant to all the members, she can offer to stay around to answer additional questions when the session ends. The leader must not allow the first session to become a question-and-answer session rather than move on to the purpose of the group.

Explaining Ground Rules

Certain ground rules need to be discussed during the first and second sessions. Rules about the confidentiality of the information shared among members and about eating, drinking, or smoking during group sessions are usually mentioned in the first session. Many groups set forth rules during the first session prohibiting attacking others and putting others on the spot. However, these rules do not always have to be covered at the very beginning; this is a mistake that many novice leaders make. When all the ground rules are covered in the initial moments of the group, members may become bored or anxious for something to happen. It is usually preferable to cover ground rules as needed rather than opening up with a speech or discussion about them.

EXAMPLES . . . .

It is 30 minutes into the first session of a therapy group.

Jake: I want to hear what David thinks. He hasn't said anything about his problems.

Leader: Let me jump in here. I know that some of you may want to hear from other members, but one ground rule that I have in groups that I lead is that no one will be forced to talk. So, rather than putting David on the spot, you might say that you are curious about what others are thinking. The reason for that rule is that I want people not to have to worry about being attacked or singled out. Any comments on that or on what we have been talking about?

In this example, the leader saw the need to mention a ground rule and stated it in a natural manner. He also spared David by shifting the focus from him to the ground rule and then back to the topic. Introducing ground rules when they are relevant helps members remember them better.

. . . .

This group is in its first half-hour, and the members are discussing fears about being in the group. They are using a sentence-completion form containing a sentence that reads "One thing I am afraid of in groups is _____ ."

Beth: I wrote that I am afraid of looking foolish.

Leader: That is a very common feeling. I would imagine that others feel the same way. (*Several heads nod*)

Fern: I put down that I am afraid of being attacked by other members for something that I say.

Leader: I want to comment on that. I'd like to establish a ground rule that no one is allowed to attack another member. We are here to try to listen to and learn from each other, not to attack those who differ from us. How do all of you feel about having that as a rule?

The leader asks the question to hold the focus on "no member will be allowed to attack another member" because she feels it is a very important issue for the group.

. . . .

It is close to the end of the first session, and a member says he has something he would like to bring up. It is obvious that what he is going to say is very personal, and he is the first member actually to say that he wants to talk about a concern. Up to now, members have shared only "safe" things about themselves.

John: I think I want to share something that happened here at the plant that I have never told anyone.

Leader: John, before you do I want to mention something very important. In the beginning, we discussed briefly that we should keep things confidential. I want to emphasize that rule, since John obviously is about to share something important and personal to him. It is imperative that we keep the content of these group meetings confidential if there is to be a feeling of trust. Is this suitable to everyone? (*Looks around the room*) OK, John, let's get back to you.

. . . .

The point is that the leader should not spend an inordinate amount of time explaining ground rules unless there is some reason to do so. If a member tries to argue about a rule that the leader feels is necessary, the leader should calmly explain why it is important for the smooth running of the group. If he anticipates any disagreement with some of the ground rules, the leader will want to be careful in presenting them.

Sometimes it is best simply to say what the rules are and why they exist rather than opening them up for discussion. For example, if a leader decides that there will be no smoking or eating during the group, she can tell the group the reason.

Leader: Since the room is small and some of us are nonsmokers, there will be no smoking during the session. If you feel you have to smoke, you may excuse yourself for a couple of minutes. Also, I'm going to ask you not to eat or drink during the session, since it can be distracting.

In other words, though some leaders spend a few minutes discussing the ground rules so that the members feel involved in the decisions, it is easy to make the mistake of discussing issues like the preceding ones for 15 to 20 minutes. This is usually not necessary and detracts from the purpose of the group. In many kinds of groups, it is appropriate and helpful for the leader to decide the ground rules alone, based on prior experiences.

Explaining Terms

If the leader plans to use special terms, she should explain them to the members. Some terms that might confuse members are *rounds*, *dyads*, and *exercises*. If the group is a therapy, support, or growth group, the leader will want to explain the terms she might be using, such as *RET*,

TA, or *alter ego.* This ensures that members won't feel they are miss-ing something. The leader could explain the terms when she is explain-ing her role or at any other time that seems appropriate, such as the first time they naturally occur. For example, before the first round, the leader could explain the concept and any other terms she feels necessary.

Checking Out the Comfort Level

Feeling apprehensive or uncomfortable during the first session of a sup-port, growth, or therapy group is quite common. To help reduce this discomfort, the leader might spend a few minutes focused on the topic of comfort level. By inquiring about members' comfort level, the leader lets members know he is aware that there may be some anxiety and that it is to be expected. In addition, hearing that others are anxious often eases members' anxiety by showing them they are not alone. The leader may want to introduce the topic of comfort during the warm-up phase—that is, within the first half-hour—if members seem extremely uncom-fortable. If the leader does not discuss comfort in the beginning, he can in-troduce it almost any time throughout the session. For example, he can raise the topic during a period of silence—especially since silence can re-flect discomfort—or when he wants to shift the focus of discussion. At any point, the leader can say, "Let's focus for a few minutes on the topic of comfort in this group," then continue with any of the following:

- In terms of comfort in the group right now, what is the word or phrase that best describes how you are feeling?
- On a 1-to-10 scale, with 10 being very uncomfortable and 1 be-ing very comfortable, how would you rate how you are feeling in the group right now?
- On a 1-to-10 scale, with 10 being very uncomfortable and 1 be-ing very comfortable, how would you rate how you were feeling in the group when we started and how would you rate your feel-ing now?
- Does anyone want to comment on how he or she is feeling about being in this group?
- I'd like you to pair up with a person whom you would like to get to know better and talk about how you feel about being in the group. Discuss your comfort level and why you feel the way you do. Naturally some of you are more comfortable than others. You'll have about three minutes to do this; then we'll come back to the large group for discussion.

Any of these activities will help members talk about the comfort level in the group. Such discussions often help members feel more com-fortable, both through sharing their feelings and hearing that others feel some discomfort. The leader also gains a better idea of the source of discomfort (for example, members still not knowing each other very well or some members knowing others from outside the group). The leader may choose not to draw out those who rate themselves as very uncomfortable, because focusing on them could make them more so. The leader will want to make sure that he does nothing to increase the group's discomfort level at this point.

It is essential to be aware that the comfort level might be low if members know each other outside the group, such as is common in a school setting. In these groups, some members may feel that the others don't like them, or believe that what they share may negatively influence a relationship outside the group.

Some people are simply not used to speaking up in front of others. For example, a group of unemployed steel workers may feel uncomfortable talking in front of others about the problems they are having finding work, dealing with family stressors, and maintaining their image in the community. If the leader senses that group members are uncomfortable, he will want to spend extra time trying to increase the comfort level by using exercises, rounds, and dyads to get members to share.

Assessing Members' Interaction Styles

During the first session, the leader will want to note the different ways that members interact in the group. This is extremely helpful for leading the session and planning for future sessions. Every member has a certain style or manner. Some members may be very quiet, others may try to dominate, others may be supportive, and still others may be very critical. By observing these styles, the leader will be able to adjust the session plan if some activities would not be appropriate or effective due to the mixture of styles. Any leader who fails to assess the interaction style of members will make the task of leading much more difficult.

Leaders assess interaction styles through paying attention to what members say, how they say it, and how often they say anything. Too often, a beginning leader will get caught up in the content of the group and fail to observe that not all members are participating or that certain members are trying to dominate.

Focusing on the Content

In this context, *content* means the topic being discussed in the group. All groups have a content area; some are very specific, such as assertiveness, coping with divorce, or study skills, while others are less specific, such as personal problems or personal growth. The leader will want to be sure to focus some of the first session on the content or purpose of the group. Devoting too much time in the first two sessions to explaining ground rules, making introductions, getting acquainted, or explaining the leadership role will cause members to become bored and to lose interest, because their need for coming to the group is not being met.

To focus members on the content of the group, the leader can use an introduction exercise that causes them to think about why they came to the group, as in the example below. As the round ends, the leader focuses the group on content by "spinning off" from one member's comment—taking the comment and elaborating on it. The leader then focuses the members on the elaboration.

EXAMPLES . . . .

It is the first session of a group for battered women. The leader has briefly discussed the purpose of the group and has had each of the five women introduce herself and tell a little about her situation. The introduction round is on the next-to-last person.

Jane: I'm Jane. I have been married for four years. I have two children. My husband has beaten me five times and each time has been worse than the others. He says it is my fault—I'm confused.

Diane: I'm Diane. My husband verbally and physically abuses me daily and I can't take it any more.

Leader: Now that we know each other's names, I would like to go back to what Jane said about being confused about whose fault it is. I think that discussing the idea of fault is important, since many women often do think it is their fault that their man gets so out of control. I think it would be helpful if each of you shared your ideas about whether you think it is your fault and why.

In this example, the leader focuses the group on a topic relevant to everyone. The discussion could last for 10 to 20 minutes and probably would be very helpful.

. . . .

The purpose of this group is to provide help for people who have recently been released from the state psychiatric hospital. The members are discussing their expectations of the group.

Barry: I hope that people here can help me stay out of the hospital. I really want to make it.

Leader: I think what Barry is saying applies to all of you—that you want to stay out of the hospital. Is that right? (*Sees all the heads nodding*) Let's talk then about what it is going to take to stay out and what might cause you to go back. What do you need to do to keep yourself out of the hospital? Who wants to comment on that?

Rico: I will. I realize that I have got to. . . . (*A valuable discussion follows for the next ten minutes about all the things that can help them stay out of the hospital: working, friends, and attending the group are all discussed*)

Leader: A while back we were going over expectations, and took off on what Barry said. Does anyone else have an expectation for this group that hasn't been discussed?

Martha: I do. I hope that the group can be a place where I can learn to say "no"! I really need to learn this.

Leader: That's a good thing to learn and I think we can talk about that in here. How many of you also have trouble saying "no"? (*Looks around*) Seems like quite a few. We have about 45 minutes left; let's talk about that for a few minutes. I'd like you to think about who is the hardest person for you to say "no" to. We'll go around the group and get each of you to comment—your spouse? your child? your mother?

. . . .

In each of the preceding examples, the leader has spun off to a relevant topic. There are countless ways for the leader to spin off during introductions, expectations, and questions. It is a very useful as well as complex skill in support, growth, and therapy groups, because the leader must pay attention to the dynamics of the first session while at the same time introducing members to the group's content. Spinning off makes the flow of the group much smoother because there is a natural interplay between the start-up dynamics and the content of the group.

Another way to move from the logistics and dynamics to the content is simply to introduce an issue or present some information. In a task group, the leader might say, "Why don't we start by discussing the different options that are available? Then we'll discuss the pros and cons of each." In an education group, the leader might shift from introductions by saying, "OK, now that you know names and why people are here, I'd like to begin by showing this 12-minute film that I think gives some good information." One other simple way to make the transition from logistics and dynamics to content is to use a group exercise.

Use of Exercises during the First Session

A number of group exercises may be useful during the first session. Three of the more useful ones are dyads, sentence completions, and rounds. (These are discussed in detail in later chapters.)

Dyads are pairs; in this context, members are paired with one another to discuss their reactions, feelings, ideas, answers, or some other relevant point. Dyads are very valuable in the beginning stage of groups because they give members the opportunity to talk with each other, which tends to facilitate comfort. However, make sure dyads do not last too long (no more than five minutes) in the first session. Long dyads do not allow members to have contact with many others; also, the leader cannot be sure how members are going to react to each other initially. If two very diverse members are paired in a dyad for a long time, one may feel annoyed or intimidated and thus conclude that the group is not helpful.

Sentence-completion exercises have also proven very helpful in facilitating interaction during the first session. This kind of written exercise gives members a base from which to comment. Also, as members are usually very interested in hearing how others responded to the same incomplete sentence, sentence completion gets them sharing with one another in a natural manner. The following are examples of sentence stems that could be used. Note that each group of sentence stems needs to be created by the leader and tailored to the group; different kinds of groups require different kinds of sentences.

In a new group, I feel most comfortable when _____ .

In a new group, I am most afraid of _____ .

In a new group, I will usually _____ .

For a group on stress, a set of sentences might be the following:

The biggest stress for me at work is _____ .

The biggest stress for me at home is _____ .

One way I cope with stress is _____ .

For a group of elementary school children whose parents are divorced, these sentence stems might be used:

The hardest thing about my parents' divorce was _____ .

The person I blame the most for the divorce is _____ .

When I think of my parents' divorce, I am most angry about

_____ .

Rounds are probably the most valuable exercise that we use during a first session. A round consists of having each person comment. The value of rounds is that everyone speaks, which is important in the first session. Earlier in this chapter, we discussed the name round and the comfort round. Other rounds can consist of 1-to-10 scales on some issue or feeling, such as guilt or worry. Rounds can be used at the beginning and end of the first session; the possibilities are endless. We discuss the use of rounds in detail in Chapter Eight.

These are just a few examples of exercises that may be helpful at the start of the group. Certainly other exercises—written or verbal—are beneficial. However, some exercises are not appropriate for the first session. Certain fantasy exercises, which help members get in touch with feelings of sorrow, guilt, anxiety, or fears, will not help members become comfortable and, in fact, may cause members not to return to the group. The leader should always keep in mind when selecting exercises for the first session that their purpose is usually to help members get acquainted and feel comfortable, or to focus on the content in a meaningful but not too stressful way.

A good rule to follow for exercises during the first session is not to use too many. Some leaders make the mistake of doing one right after another, which does not leave much time for interaction or for processing the exercises.

Other First-Session Considerations

In many kinds of groups, the opportunity may arise during the first session to focus on one member's ideas, opinions, stories, or concerns. In certain educational, discussion, and task groups it is very appropriate to allow the focus to be held on one issue for an extended period of time. However, in most support, growth, and therapy groups, it is usually not a good idea to spend more than 15 minutes focused on one member or one topic. The purpose of the first session is to get people involved, to give members a chance to share, and to get them warmed up. Focusing on one member may cause others to feel left out.

Another reason to be careful when focusing on a member during the first session is that others may become unsure about being in the group if they see a member really struggling with a concern. When in-depth therapy takes place during the first session, members may simply not be ready for it. Also, the discussion of certain topics may be inappropriate for the first session. Beginning leaders can make the mistake of focusing on any topic that arises or of focusing on issues that require more trust and comfort than is present in a first session. For instance, in a group for helping members find employment, the leader would probably want to focus the group on skills assessment or how to locate places of potential employment rather than on how to present oneself during an interview. The latter topic is a good one but should not be approached until later. Other examples of inappropriate topics for the first session of a growth or therapy group might be sexual issues or death. Usually the leader should wait at least two or three sessions before introducing topics such as these.

Closing the First Session

Closing the first session is similar to closing any other session except that the leader will want to allow more time to hear members' reactions and clear up any questions or other matters that need clarifying. Depending on the kind of group, the leader may want to ask some of the following questions during the closing phase of the first session.

- How was the session for you?
- How was it different from what you thought was going to happen?
- What stood out to you?
- Was there anything that happened that you didn't understand or didn't like?
- Do you have questions about the group, its purpose, or what is going to happen?
- What did you learn from group today?

During the close of the first session, the leader will probably want to summarize the session and comment again on the purpose of the group and what the possibilities are for the future. For a full discussion of how to close sessions and groups, see Chapter Thirteen.

THE SECOND SESSION

Certain dynamics in the second session require the special attention of the leader, though many are similar to those of the first session. The leader continues setting the tone of the group during the second session and must remain aware that some members are still uncomfortable during the second session. In addition to these general considerations, others unique to the second session include the following:

1. Opening the second session
2. Planning for the letdown
3. Ending the second session

Opening the Second Session

Two important considerations for opening the second session are the introduction of new members and the evaluation of the first session's success.

New Members

If new members join the group, it is usually a good idea to begin with introductions. Several methods can be used to introduce new members.

If time is of the essence, introductions can be accomplished in a round in which all members state their names and something about themselves. Or the leader may simply introduce the new members to the group and then ask the returning members to introduce themselves. Certain kinds of groups will require no planning beyond having members give their names; others will call for some kind of introduction activity.

EXAMPLE . . . .

Leader: (*After asking members to get settled for the beginning of the group*) There are two new members joining us tonight. I have asked them to tell us their names and some relevant information about themselves.

Melvin: My name is Melvin Conrad, and I'm glad to be here. I am an accountant here in town. I am recently divorced and am having trouble adjusting.

Leader: OK, Melvin. (*Looks toward Rhonda*)

Rhonda: My name is Rhonda. I am here because I want to get over my fear of people.

. . . .

This is perhaps the simplest and briefest method of introducing members. After the new members give a short description of themselves, a round can be used in which the other group members tell their names.

It is possible for a leader to introduce a new member in a manner that gives that person an opportunity to hear what happened in the previous session as well as to get to know the names of the other members. This type of introduction also serves as a review for the other members. At the beginning of the second session of an education group, for example, the leader could say:

Leader: This is Ralph. He was unable to make our meeting last week. I thought as a way to get Ralph caught up I'd ask each of you to take a minute to think of one or two things that stood out to you about what we discussed last week, and then I'll ask each of you to share that. Be sure to say your name also.

This method can be combined with one that gives the new members a chance to share their own situations. For instance, at the beginning of a support group for battered women, the leader could say:

Leader: Since Carol is new tonight, and as a review, I thought we'd start by having each of you share how your week was and what thoughts you had as a result of what we covered last week. To help Carol, you may want to comment on what was most helpful last week in the group. Also share your name and any information about your situation that you feel comfortable sharing.

At the end of this round, the leader would then say:

Leader: Carol, if you feel comfortable, you may want to share some of your story, or you may want to wait a few minutes. It's up to you.

Another method of introduction is for the leader to tell the group about the new members. This can only be done if the leader has had the opportunity to meet with the new members and gather information before the group has begun. The reasons a leader might choose this approach are (1) to keep the time spent on the introduction to a minimum; (2) to tell the group something specific about the member that the member might not include in the self-introduction, or (3) the member is very anxious about speaking to a group of people and needs time to ease into the group. For example, if a new member were frightened about joining the group, the leader might say the following:

Leader: This is Ted. He's going to be joining the group. Ted told me that he was really apprehensive about coming today so I told him that he would not have to say anything if he didn't want to. Let's start by talking about any thoughts or reactions to last week's session. What thoughts or feelings did you have about coming back the second time? I'd like each of you to share something and also state your name.

The amount of time spent introducing new members will often depend on the kind of group. In most therapy, growth, and support groups, an introduction of five minutes or less is all that is necessary for new members. In this time new members can tell the group their name and a little bit about why they are there, what their interests are, and what they hope to gain from being part of the group. In task, discussion, and educational groups, merely having new members give their names may be sufficient. In a residential drug and alcohol treatment program, in which members are in daily treatment for up to eight weeks, the leader might allot up to half an hour allowing a new member to introduce himself by telling some of his story to the others. An introduction of such length would not be used in most groups, however, because of the time factor.

When new members join at the second session the leader must also decide how much time should be spent informing them of what has happened during the previous session. If there is a lot to explain, the leader should try to do so before the second session rather than during it; returning members could become bored by a lengthy recap of the first session. Informing new members of the events of the first session helps them adjust more quickly to the group and keeps them from feeling in the dark when other members talk about something that happened during the first session.

The Success of the First Session

If the first session was reasonably successful—a positive tone was set and most of the members seemed to like the session—the leader will simply plan to do more of the same in the second session. On the other hand, if it did not go smoothly, the leader will have to plan a second session that takes into account what the members did not value in the first one.

Probably the first step in doing this is to consider why the session went poorly. Some possible reasons follow:

- Members were afraid to talk or share.
- Members were confused about the purpose of the group.
- The group was held at a bad time of day.
- Members came to the group late and disrupted what was going on.
- The leader was unclear about the purpose of the group or the members' needs.
- The room was not conducive to groups.
- Members were forced to attend the group.
- Members reacted negatively to the leader.
- The session was not planned well.
- The focus moved from topic to topic too quickly.
- The focus was held on a person or topic too long.
- Too much or too little time was spent on warming up.

If the first group did not go well, the leader may change the room, the meeting time, or the membership. It may be necessary to ask certain members not to return because they are not appropriate for this kind of group. When planning for the opening of the second session, the leader may choose from three options: (1) to address what went wrong in an effort to explain that future sessions will not be similar to the first one; (2) to restate the purpose of the group and make no attempt to verbalize any of the negative events of the first session; or (3) to elicit from all members their reactions to the first session.

The advantage of the leader's addressing what went wrong during the first session is that she honestly acknowledges that the first session was not a good one and can point out ways that the group can be better.

EXAMPLES. . . . .

Leader: OK, let's get started. I'd like to say something about the first session. When the group ended the other night I was concerned that some of you may have left feeling discouraged. I realize that not enough people got to share, since we focused so much on a couple of you. I sensed that some of you felt a bit frustrated, because as we were wrapping up you asked if every group was going to be like this and whether you would get a chance to talk. Let me assure you that not every group will be like the first one. All of you signed up to be in this group because you felt a need to get support and hear ideas from people who are struggling with the same issues that you are. I know that the group will be most beneficial if you share your thoughts and feelings concerning your common situations. I will make sure that the group does not focus on only one or two members unless a majority of you indicate a desire to do so.

The leader, aware that some members might have left the first session feeling frustrated, is attempting to inform them that the first session was not indicative of the remaining sessions and, at the same time, to set a tone of sharing.

. . . .

The leader can also restate the purpose of the group without delving into the proceedings of the bad first session.

Leader: Let's begin. I want to mention again that the purpose of this group is to discuss problems that you are having with your teenagers. I'm going to ask each of you to share briefly one or two concerns pertaining to your son or daughter; then we will discuss as many of them as we can.

. . . .

The leader might want to elicit comments from the group members about their reactions to the first session.

Leader: I want to begin this session by getting your reaction to the last one. I feel that our first session was OK, but I do believe these next sessions can be better. Please share honestly any reaction or questions that you had about what we did here last time.

In this last example, the leader gives the members a chance to react so that she can comment on their reactions in a positive, clarifying manner.

. . . .

Our point is that the leader needs to consider how the first session went when planning the second session. If the group did not go well, the leader will definitely need to plan to counteract the bad beginning. One leader we know decided to use name tags on the chairs to break up the cliques of eighth-grade girls. She knew she could have a good group with the girls, but the first session did not go well because of where the girls were sitting. She assigned seats for the next few sessions and had a very successful group.

Even if the first session does not go very well, a leader can come back with a good second session by planning one that is relevant and interesting to the majority of the members. The leader will also want to remember that it is usually necessary and helpful to reiterate the purpose of the group during the second session.

It is also helpful for the leader to arrive at the second session early and talk informally to members before the group begins. This provides some idea of how members reacted to the first session. It also gives the leader a chance to answer members' questions about the group and to get to know them.

Planning for the Possible Letdown

A skilled leader will anticipate a letdown during the second session. By letdown, we mean that the excitement exhibited among members during the first session is not always present in the second. This letdown is often disconcerting to a beginning group leader if he has made the mistake of thinking that the energy present in the first session will be present throughout the rest. As a result, he often fails to plan the group adequately or to anticipate the change of atmosphere. One reason for a change in the members' energy is that much of the first session is spent on members getting acquainted with each other, discussing why they are there, what their expectations are, and the format and ground rules for the group. Given these topics, the first session of a group is often filled with a lot of sharing and excitement. In the second session those topics are not the focus of the group. Instead, the focus moves toward personal sharing, and members often experience anxiety about participating. They become hesitant to interact, thus causing a letdown.

To help prevent this, the leader can mention at the end of the first session that there is a strong possibility that members may not feel as enthusiastic the next time. If it is appropriate, the leader could give them some task to accomplish before the next session. This may help to keep the second session interesting and create a higher level of energy among the members.

Another way to prevent the second-session letdown is to set aside additional time for warming up. During this warm-up phase, which is the opening phase of the second session, the leader might mention the potential decrease in enthusiasm from the first session. Several kinds of exercises seem to be particularly well suited for warming up members and getting them to share. Lists and sentence completions are excellent for this purpose in that they facilitate members' talking to each other and sharing information about themselves. Rounds and dyads are also effective in getting members to talk and share with each other.

Ending the Second Session

The leader should plan to spend a considerable amount of time ending the second session, because this is the first opportunity to gather feedback. Often, the first session is not a good indication of how members view the group and what it will be like; the second session is much more reliable. Members' reactions will tell the leader what changes need to be made. Critical information the leader will want to gather during the ending of the second session is what the members perceived as being helpful and unhelpful. A round in which the leader asks the members to describe their reactions to the group is a good closing activity because it involves everyone.

E X A M P L E S .   .   .   .

> **Leader:** Let's take a few minutes to wind up the group. We're going to do a round in just a moment. In this round I would like each of you to talk about what your reactions are to this group or what stands out to you the most. In addition, if there is anything that you would like to see us do differently, please say so.
>
> **Timothy:** The thing that stands out to me the most is that I get to hear other people struggling with the same issue that I am. I would also like to talk more in pairs like we did at the beginning of the session.
>
> **Pauline:** I liked the movement exercise that we did today. It really caused me to stop and think about my situation. I too would like to do more stuff in pairs. I feel as though I get to know that person better when we talk in twos.
>
> **Bert:** I'm still a little bit hesitant about speaking up. I've always had difficulty being in groups. I think the dyads help me feel a little bit more comfortable.

.   .   .   .

The leader could also use a variation of this round by getting members to rate the group on a 1-to-10 scale, 10 meaning that the group meets all expectations and 1 that the group is far from meeting their expectations.

> **Leader:** I want to take a bit more time to end the group today so that I can get some idea of how you are reacting to it thus far.

> Think of how you would rate this group on a 1-to-10 scale. (*Leader explains the meaning of the scale*) If your rating is not a 10, think what it would take to move the group up to a 10.

Kevin: I give the group an 8. I think that to make it a 10 we just need to feel more comfortable with each other.

Becky: I give it a 10. I really like the way we shared with each other today. I feel a lot more comfortable and I feel as though I know these people very well. I also liked the way you started the group with that exercise that got us to list things.

. . . .

In both of these examples, the leader is using a round for two reasons: (1) to obtain information about how members are perceiving the group; and (2) to get members to share their reactions with each other. In the follow-up to these examples, the leader would spend time discussing the various responses, clarifying anything that needed clarification and answering any questions.

CONCLUDING COMMENTS

In this chapter, we pointed out the importance of the first and second sessions. It is very important that the leader plan these sessions well, since they set the tone for the rest. We discussed the various ways for members to introduce themselves and a number of good exercises for the first session. We discussed the need for the leader to pay attention to the content or purpose of the group as well as to the comfort level. It is important that the leader not focus too long on one person or topic during the first sessions, as it is usually better to get more members involved and sharing. In most groups, the leader should let the ground rules emerge and not spend too much time on them. Another first session caution is not to go too deeply into therapy during the first session. Many of the members may not be quite ready for "heavy" work.

In planning for the second session, the leader needs to be prepared for the typical letdown. If the first session did not go well, the leader will want to specifically prepare to counteract that in the next session. Most important is to plan these first two sessions and be prepared to put out a great deal of energy and effort, since they often determine how the remainder of the sessions will go.

Basic Skills for Group Leaders

Throughout the first four chapters, we have referred to various leadership skills but have not discussed them in great detail. In the next few chapters, we describe specific skills that we feel are essential for good leading. Some of these are basic human-relations skills that you may have developed on your own or through specialized training. If you have had some training in interviewing or counseling, you will recognize the names of many of these skills.

1. Active listening
2. Reflection
3. Clarification and questioning
4. Summarizing
5. Minilecturing and information giving
6. Encouraging and supporting
7. Tone setting
8. Modeling and self-disclosure
9. Use of eyes
10. Use of voice
11. Use of the leader's energy
12. Identifying allies

ACTIVE LISTENING

Active listening entails listening to the content, voice, and body language of the person speaking (Corey & Corey, 1992). It also involves communicating to the person(s) speaking that you are really listening. Most of you have probably been trained to listen on a one-to-one basis. For some of you this was fairly easy to master; for others it may have been somewhat difficult. Active listening as a group leader is a much more complex task, since you listen to more people. The skilled leader actually tries to listen to all the group's members at the same time and not just to the one who is talking. To the extent this is possible, the leader wants to be aware of what members are feeling and thinking even when they are not speaking. The main technique the leader uses for this is to scan the room for nonverbal gestures, especially facial expressions and body shifts. We hope you can appreciate the complexity of this skill. It is difficult to convey to the speaker that you are really listening while you are at the same time communicating with other members by picking up on their silent messages. We urge you to practice this skill whenever you are with a group of friends, family, or colleagues. See if you can take in more than just the content of the person who is talking: try to pick up on what the others are thinking and feeling. This skill, perhaps more than any other, is essential for good group leadership, and yet many students try to become skilled leaders without first becoming active listeners.

REFLECTION

In counseling, to reflect a comment is to restate it, conveying that you understand the content, the feeling behind it, or both. As a group leader, you will find it helpful and necessary to use the skill of reflecting both content and feeling. The purpose of reflecting is twofold: (1) to help the group member who is speaking become more aware of what he is saying, and (2) to communicate to him that you are aware of how he is feeling. As a group leader, you will use reflection at times with individual members, at other times to reflect what two or more members may be saying about a topic or issue, and at still other times to reflect what the entire group is experiencing.

EXAMPLES. . . . .

> **Alicia:** I'm not sure how I'll do here. I'm a little uncomfortable with all this, but I sure want to get started to make some changes in my life.
>
> **Leader:** Alicia, you seem to be feeling that the group is both an exciting and a scary experience for you at this point.

. . . .

> **Martin:** Looking for work is tough on me. I hate going into places and feeling like I've got to beg for anything they can give me.
>
> **Randy:** Yeah, that's how I feel about it. Some days I'd rather stay home. I dread the thought of having to face those pompous receptionists.

Leader: You both seem to be saying that one of the hardest things in looking for work is having to deal with the feeling of being one down.

If the leader is on target with her reflection, it is likely that other members can relate to it. The leader may follow up her reflection with something like this: "I wonder if other people here are having similar feelings as they go out job hunting." As she watches for responses, the leader may find that the reflection she has directed to two members has actually encouraged others to become aware of their similar feelings.

. . . .

Anita, a member in a group of abused women, has been talking for five minutes about how she dislikes herself for having remained in an abusive situation. The members have been very attentive, and as Anita finishes, it is apparent that the others are feeling strong emotions. The leader tries to reflect the entire group:

Leader: From your reactions, I'd guess that most of you are in touch with what Anita is experiencing right now.

The leader may add:

Leader: Some of you may be having similar feelings about yourself.

. . . .

This last reflection, while general and tentative, can help members become more aware of their own feelings.

In summary, the use of reflection with a single member, several members, or the entire group clarifies and deepens members' understanding and communicates that the leader is in tune with what is happening. One word of warning comes from Corey and Corey (1992), who state that "many neophyte group leaders find themselves confining most of their interactions to mere reflections" (p. 21). The warning is a good one, because in many instances the use of reflection does not cause members to delve more deeply into the discussion at hand.

CLARIFICATION AND QUESTIONING

Several authors have discussed clarification and questioning as necessary group skills (Corey & Corey, 1992; Dyer & Vriend, 1980; Trotzer, 1989). Often, the leader will find it necessary to help members clarify their statements. Clarification may be done for the benefit of the entire group or for the speaker's benefit—that is, to help the member become more aware of what he or she is trying to say. There are several techniques for clarification that you may find useful: questioning, restating, and using other members to clarify.

E X A M P L E S . . . .

    Stan: I don't think we should accept the proposal. It has too many hidden agendas.

    Leader: Stan, can you tell us a little more about what you mean by that?

Here the leader is attempting to clarify by gathering more information. He is using an open-ended question to encourage the member to clarify his statement.

. . . .

    Ellen: There are times when I think I'm going crazy and yet I know I'm just off balance because of my divorce. My mom says, "What about the kids?" Carla, my 8-year-old, was crying last night. It's my life, though! I have got to get out. I don't know how my husband will make it.

    Leader: Ellen, you've just said a lot. I'd like to try to clarify how you might be feeling at this point—do tell me if I am off base. There is a part of you that says this divorce is right and then there is a part of you that says, "Maybe I'm being selfish."

In this example, rather than questioning further, the leader has taken jumbled information presented by a member and used a statement to reorder it in an attempt to clarify the key issues. This clarification helps Ellen and the others become more aware of what she now needs to work on. We cannot stress enough the importance of clarification. If a member's thoughts are vague, confusing, or incomplete—as they often are in moments of stress—the rest of the members will have difficulty understanding him. As a result, some members will lose interest, and their minds will start to wander. The leader has the responsibility of trying to maintain clear communication in the group; this can be done by using the skill of clarification.

. . . .

    Danny: I want a dog, but my mom says "no." I know it'd be good for me. She says I wouldn't take care of it—like the rabbit. But I was only 8 then, and I'm 11 now. I know I'd do better in school. I wish my mom wasn't so mean to me.

    Leader: Does anyone think they know how Danny is feeling about his mom and about having a pet?

Sally: I think I do. Danny is lonely sometimes and feels like having a pet friend would help him. By having a dog he would have
someone to talk to and play with and that would help him feel
better. Then he would do better in school. He says he thinks
his mom is mean but I think he knows she's not—she just
doesn't want to take care of the dog. She's probably like my
mom and feels that kids are enough to take care of.

Leader: That sounds right, Sally. Danny, how did it sound to you?

The method of using a member serves the dual purpose of
clarifying what the member was saying and also involving other
group members, thus generating interest and energy.

. . . .

In summary, the skill of clarification is important for ensuring clear
communications in the group. Confusing messages create frustration
and drain group energy if they are not adequately clarified.

SUMMARIZING

The skill of summarizing is a must for all group leaders (Corey & Corey,
1992; Dyer & Vriend, 1980; Ohlsen, Horne, & Lawe, 1988; Shulman,
1984). Groups often generate material from a wide range of viewpoints.
Because members are busy listening and sharing during the session,
they often do not pick up on or remember many of the details. Therefore,
thoughtful and concise summaries are very helpful to them.

There are several occasions in a group session when summarizing
can or should be used. A summary may be helpful when you have
allowed a member to speak uninterrupted for several minutes. Without
a summary, members may pick up on small or irrelevant points. The
summary tightens the focus and allows the leader to stay with the issue
or move on, depending on the needs of the particular member.

A concise summary is also useful in making a transition from one
topic to another. The summary can highlight key points in a discussion
or in the work done by a member and can serve as a bridge to the next
activity in the group. A summary is especially important if the discussion has been diffuse or has involved overlapping points or ideas. A good
summary will pull together the major points and can serve to deepen
or sharpen the focus. For example:

Leader: So far, we've been talking in general terms about changes we
would like to make in our lives. Juan and Al both talked about job
changes. Betty, you said you wanted to improve your relationship
with your husband in some major ways. Someone said they wanted
to go back to school. Margaret, I think that was you. A couple of

other people wanted to be happier. Now I would like each of you to take a minute to think about this change you want. . . . What is one thing you will have to give up to get what you want?

In this example, the summary serves to highlight each member's desire for change and sets the stage for the leader to deepen the focus. A summary can also be used at the opening of a session and is especially helpful if there is unfinished work from the last session or a strong interest on the part of the members to continue the topic. However, the summary should serve to get the group focused on the current session rather than to encourage a rehash of the previous session.

Leader: A lot happened last session. We talked mainly about prenatal care. Betsy talked about smoking and Jane talked about drugs, and they both wanted to quit. Others talked about things they were doing that might not be good. We discussed stress, food, and exercise. We finished with a discussion of what to do during the ninth month. Today I want us to continue talking about the ninth month, especially the last couple of weeks and the delivery. First, I want to report that I have been talking with Jane and Betsy, and they are doing great! (*Group cheers*)

Another good time to use summarizing is at the end of a session. Because many ideas will have been discussed during the session, a skillful summary can be helpful. In our discussion of ending a session, in Chapter Thirteen, we address the different ways to summarize and how to use the members to summarize.

MINILECTURING AND INFORMATION GIVING

Sometimes the leader will need or want to provide information to the group. In educational groups, the leader most often is the person who is providing the expertise on subjects such as diet, health, birth control methods, or types of post–high school education. In situations in which you are the "expert," you will want to do several things when giving a minilecture:

- Make it interesting.
- Make it relevant.
- Make it short (usually no more than five to eight minutes).
- Make it energizing.
- Make sure you have current, correct, and objective information.

The purpose of giving information is to enable people to learn from you and from the discussion that follows. By keeping your comments relatively short, you can provide good information without turning your group into a class. Probably the key to successful minilecturing is to briefly provide new and interesting ideas. Very often, beginning leaders will be afraid to give any information or will give boring minilectures. A good leader has to have good things to say. In discussion, educational, and task groups it is important that the leader be well informed about the subject. In growth or counseling groups, the skilled leader needs to have information on all kinds of topics, such as guilt, marital affairs, children, the value of hobbies and pets, and so forth. In almost any group there will be times during a session when a 2- or 3-minute minilecture on some subject will help focus the group, or deepen the focus, or simply help members understand something about which they are confused. Our point is that providing information is helpful in many groups and the skilled leader not only has beneficial things to say but knows when and how to say them.

E X A M P L E . . . .

The focus of this group is marital enrichment for young couples who have been married less than two years. In the second session, a member asks a question.

Member: Can marriages go smoothly without working so hard? When does it get easy?

Leader: Let me comment about that. Most marriages require work, especially during the first couple of years as the partners get to know each other in a different way. Also, differences continue to emerge that have to be discussed. Having to work hard during these first two years does not mean it is not a good marriage. Let me tell you three or four ways that each of you can benefit from working on your marriage now. . . . (*Leader talks for a couple more minutes*)

. . . .

ENCOURAGING AND SUPPORTING

Because you are interested in the helping professions, you have most likely already learned to provide encouragement and support to others. As a leader, this ability will be especially important in helping members deal with the anxiety of being in a new situation and sharing their ideas or personal feelings with others. Members are often concerned with how they will appear to others and sometimes fear they will say something "wrong" or "stupid" in the group. In growth or therapy groups, members sometimes fear they will reveal something about themselves that they will later regret. The skilled leader must take the initiative in providing support and encouragement that will help put members at ease (Dyer & Vriend, 1980). Acknowledging that some discomfort is normal often eases members' anxiety. For example, a leader might make an encouraging statement like, "People in groups may feel a little nervous. That feeling usually goes away as we get to know each other better and learn more of what the group is about."

In addition to the content of what you say, it is important that you communicate your support with warmth in your voice, a pleasant facial expression, and an "open" posture. Your encouragement must be genuine and congruent with your actual feelings.

As the level of personal sharing in a group increases, members may require additional encouragement in their struggle to talk about themselves. Members' primary concern often will be how the other people in the group will react to them if they reveal something very personal. Your encouragement can help members get over their "scared" feelings and can help them take risks that they otherwise might not take. The following is an example of an encouraging and supportive statement:

Leader: John, you've started to tell us about the problems you have regarding sex. You seem troubled and also scared about the prospect of sharing such personal things with us. I think you will find that we'll listen without criticism. We're not here to be critical of you or anybody—we're all trying to be helpful and supportive of each other.

In this example, the leader is supportive and delivers a message to the other members that no criticism or judgment will be allowed. This is an additional form of protection that the leader provides as part of her role.

Keep in mind that giving support and encouragement to members in your group does not mean that you should reinforce inappropriate or self-defeating behaviors. As the leader you would not support or encourage excessive talking, interrupting of others, or members' decisions that you know not to be in their best interests.

TONE SETTING

"Tone setting is subtle but crucial to the atmosphere and attitude of the group" (Trotzer, 1989, p. 207). By tone setting, we mean the leader's establishing a mood for the group. Some beginning leaders are not aware of the tone-setting dimension of group leading; thus, without realizing what they are doing, they set a very "serious" tone. Other beginners, wanting to be liked, set a very "light" tone and end up frustrated because no one seems committed to the group. It is important to realize that the leader sets the tone by his actions, words, and what he allows to happen. If the leader is very aggressive, he will create an atmosphere of resistance and tension. A leader who allows members to attack and criticize others permits a negative tone to emerge. If the leader encourages sharing and caring, a more positive atmosphere is established. The thing to remember is that the leader is responsible for setting the tone and should consider the following:

- Should the group be serious or sociable?
- Should the tone be confrontive or supportive? (Some groups for addicts, juveniles, and certain kinds of criminals are conducted effectively with very confrontive tones.)
- Should the tone be very formal or informal?
- Should the group be task-oriented or more relaxed?

If you ask yourself these questions and then lead according to your answers, you will probably achieve the desired tone for your group. The following examples show how a leader can set different tones for the group.

EXAMPLES . . . .

SERIOUS TONE
Leader: Let's begin. Before we start, I'd like us to pull in so that we are not all spread out. Also, I'd like you to put away any food or drinks for now. (*Members do this*) OK, let's start by having different members introduce themselves and tell why they are here.

. . . .

SOCIAL TONE
Leader: Let's begin. (*Members remain spread out and continue eating*) I'd like to start by having you tell a little bit about who you are. Tell anything that you think is important or anything you'd like.

. . . .

CONFRONTIVE TONE
It is the first session of a group of teenagers who have been caught using drugs. Joe has been talking about how he does not think he has any problem with drugs.

Leader: Joe, I think you have a serious problem! In this group I think we can all help each other by making sure that people are honest with themselves. (*In a rather confrontive voice*) How many of you feel that Joe has a problem?

. . . .

SUPPORTIVE TONE
Leader: Joe, I hope the group can be of value even though you don't feel that you have a problem. Others of you may feel

the same way. Also, I believe some of you do realize that you have a problem. The purpose of the group is to be helpful and I am hoping that you'll help each other by listening, sharing, and hopefully caring for one another. For some of you to say that you have a problem will be tough.

. . . .

FORMAL TONE

Leader: I am Tom Smith. I'm from the mental health center and am here today to serve as the leader of this group. Before we get started I would like to go over some of the ground rules for this group. The first thing that I would like you to do is to introduce yourself. State your name, where you work, and why you decided to attend the group.

. . . .

"ON-TASK" TONE

Leader: I'd like us to get started. We have a lot to cover and only an hour and a half to do it. First, . . .

. . . .

In the preceding examples we outlined a number of possible "tones" for a group. In workshops that we have conducted, we have asked participants to describe the tone of groups they have led or been members of and state whether the group was successful or not successful. Some of the tones reported for the not-successful groups are "hostile," "boring," "frustrating," "combative," "slow-moving," and "confusing." For the successful groups, tones such as "warm," "serious and caring," "interesting," and "energizing" were reported. Remember, the leader sets the tone, and without the proper tone, your group most likely will not be as effective as you would like it to be.

MODELING AND SELF-DISCLOSURE

As a group leader, you will find modeling and self-disclosure to be important skills for setting the tone. These skills are also useful for getting members to do more of what you want them to do in terms of their sharing, responses, and feedback. Corey and Corey (1992) state that "one of the best ways to teach desired behaviors is by modeling those behaviors in the group" (p. 16). Your style of effective communication, your ability to listen, and your encouragement of others will serve as a model for your members to emulate. Your energy and interest in a subject or in the group itself can serve as a model for others. If the purpose of the group involves more personal sharing, then your self-disclosure can be used to demonstrate how to disclose and that you are willing to risk and share yourself. Your self-disclosure can also indicate that you are human and that you have dealt with many of the same issues in your life that they are presently exploring.

Self-disclosure in the group can serve as a model of what you want from the members. Let's look at the following example of self-disclosure.

Leader: Now that you have had a chance to think about the three people who have the most significant impact on your life in terms of who you are now, let's begin sharing. I'll go first to show how this might work. The most significant person in my life was my mother. She was significant because she supported me and sort of protected me from my father, who was an alcoholic. My brother. . . .

Here the leader demonstrates the depth at which sharing can take place and shows the members that she is willing to do herself what she is asking of them. Self-disclosure can be used to reveal past events, present events, and present feelings about the group or about some members. The following examples show two different kinds of self-disclosure.

Leader: In my current relationship, my partner and I have some trouble with how we like to socialize. She likes to spend time with lots of people, whereas I really only enjoy one or two people at a time. I think this is one of many concerns that couples deal with. Does anyone have that concern or have other concerns about a relationship?

or

Leader: I want to share how I am feeling about the group tonight. I feel that people are holding back. I am not sure why. Does anyone else feel that?

It is not necessary for the leader to self-disclose on every issue or topic that is discussed in the group. Frequent self-disclosure may, in fact, be distracting and confusing to the members. In addition, self-disclosure by the leader should not be of such intensity that the leader becomes the focus of the group. The preceding excerpts are good examples of how leaders can self-disclose yet make sure that the group does not focus on them.

USE OF EYES

Knowing how to use your eyes is very important when leading groups. The leader needs to be aware of how her eyes can gather valuable information, encourage members to speak, and possibly deter members from speaking (Harvill, Masson, & Jacobs, 1983). The leader can use her eyes in four ways:

1. Scanning for nonverbal cues
2. Redirecting members' comments to the group
3. Drawing out members
4. Cutting off members

Scanning the Group

Leaders gather valuable information by scanning the group with their eyes. Although scanning seems easy, most group leaders find it difficult because when people are talking to you it is natural for you to look at them. Picture a beginning leader leading a group of ten members. The member closest to the leader's left starts talking, and the leader naturally turns to look at the speaker. Let's say the member talks for two minutes about a personal situation. During those two minutes, our beginning leader will have made contact only with the speaker and perhaps with the next two members to the speaker's left. For the entire two minutes, the leader has made no observation of the remaining seven members. Here are some of the problems and difficulties this leader might have:

- Some of the other members may feel excluded because the leader did not make eye contact with them.
- The leader has no idea how most of the members were reacting to what was being said.
- The leader has no idea who may want to speak next.
- Some of the other members may have lost interest because the member talked only to the leader.

These points suggest that if you do what is natural, which would be to look exclusively at the person speaking, you miss information that is very helpful in facilitating the group. Seeing members' reactions and knowing who wants to add comments or react makes leading a lot easier. Most beginning leaders can learn rather quickly to scan the group while they are talking. However, learning to scan when someone else is talking is a skill that takes practice.

Of course, there are situations in which you would want to attend almost exclusively to the talking member, but those situations should be the exception rather than the rule. The rule is to *keep your eyes moving.* Scanning is the best way to pick up the various immediate reactions of the members. Among the most important nonverbal cues to observe are head nods, facial expressions, body shifts, and tears.

Head Nods

It is very helpful to look for head nods indicating both agreement and disagreement when someone is offering an opinion or describing some concern. The leader can facilitate discussion simply by saying something like, "Biff, you're nodding—what are your thoughts?" or "I notice that some of your heads are nodding in agreement and some in disagreement—let's continue the discussion, realizing that there are differences here." Picking up on head nods can also be useful for drawing out and linking one person with another: "Jodi, you were nodding when Diane was mentioning leaving—are you also having similar thoughts?"

Facial Expressions

While head nodding implies some degree of agreement or disagreement about an issue, facial expressions may mean that the member has had a similar experience or is in some way relating positively or negatively to the issue. Facial expressions can suggest disapproval, confusion, or some other reaction that the leader may want to clarify.

EXAMPLE . . . .

Barbara: He really believes that I should be home from work at 5:00 and his dinner should be on the table by 6:00. I am not obligated to make dinner!!

Sue: I agree with you.

Jane: There are no wife's duties!!!

Leader: (*Picking up on Ann's expression*) Ann, by your expression I'm guessing that you might be having mixed feelings about what Barbara and the others are saying.

Ann: Well, ah, I am. You see, I'm all confused about this. I want to believe what's being said and yet I sure was raised differently. And, too, there are things I like to do as a wife.

Dee: I feel the same way you do, Ann.

Ann: You do? I thought I was the only one here who was somewhat traditional.

. . . .

If the leader had not picked up on Ann's reaction, Ann might not have volunteered her thoughts because she was fearful of being different.

Tears

Tears or "tearing up" on the part of a member is an important clue for the leader. While some members may break into tears and sob audibly, often people merely tear up while they are either talking or listening to another. The leader needs to be aware of members' tears because they are usually indicative of strong feelings. Whether the leader deals with the tears directly by drawing the member out or chooses simply to acknowledge them or ignore them will depend on the purpose of the group and other factors such as the time remaining, who the member is, and the leader's guess about what is causing the tears. The skilled leader who scans the group will, on occasion, observe members who are expressing their pain silently through tears. Not scanning the group causes the leader to miss this valuable information.

Body Shifts

Members often express themselves through the way they sit and move. Body shifts during the group frequently indicate confusion, boredom, or irritation. By observing these reactions the leader can often become aware of what members are feeling and can devise some strategies for dealing with a member or a number of members. For instance, if two or three members are noticeably confused, the leader may want to use the skills of reflection and clarification; give a minilecture that may provide valuable information; initiate a group exercise; or even have the group take a ten-minute break. One body shift that is important to observe is the forward lean, which often indicates "I've got something to say." Beginning leaders frequently miss this and other signals from members. As a result, they may ignore those who are ready to speak and resort to calling on members who may have less to say.

Redirecting Members' Comments to the Group

Very often, members will speak mainly to the leader unless the leader encourages them to talk to the entire group. Getting members to address everyone can be helpful in building interest, getting members involved, building group cohesion, and creating an atmosphere of belonging. To get members to look at the entire group or to get them to avoid looking only at the leader, any or all of the following are appropriate:

• Tell your members you would like them to look at the group rather than exclusively at you when they are talking. You can explain this in the beginning or after someone has spoken directly to you. Ask the speaker and the rest of the members to look at everyone in the group.

• Explain to the members that you are not going to be looking at them all the time when they are speaking because at various times you will be scanning the group. You can also tell them to let your scanning serve as a signal to them to address the entire group.

• Scan the group, because the talking member will tend to seek eye contact with someone; if you are scanning, the speaker will usually look elsewhere.

• Signal the member to talk to everyone by making a sweeping motion with your hand. A sweeping motion consists of bringing your right hand to your left shoulder and then bringing it slowly around until it is more or less pointing to your right.

Sometimes the leader will need to be persistent in redirecting members. If they address only the leader, there is a good chance that a leader-member-leader-member interaction pattern will develop, making leading much more difficult. In most groups, the leader is trying to get members to work together and to feel support and concern for one another. Having members look at other members when talking helps develop cohesion.

Drawing Out Members

Another way a leader might use his eyes is to make eye contact with those whom he is trying to draw out. By scanning the entire group and contacting particular members, the leader's eyes can serve as an invitation to talk. Beginning leaders sometimes make the mistake of maintaining eye contact only with those who are talking and not with those who are silent. The leader's eyes can really encourage members to join in and share. Let's say you have a member who has not spoken much and it is already the third session. Observation has shown you that this member is scared and shy. Your kind and encouraging eye contact may help this person venture into the group. Once drawn out, this type of member may speak only to you. You may want to allow this at first and then, as the member becomes more comfortable, ask him or her to talk to the entire group.

The leader's eyes can also be helpful when a member is revealing something very painful. Encouragement through eye contact and body language may be just what the member needs to fully disclose some previously hidden aspects. This is another example of an appropriate time for the leader to maintain eye contact with only one member for a longer period. Usually this does not result in others feeling ignored, since members are very attentive when someone is doing intense personal work.

Another way for the leader to use his eyes to draw out a member is to make eye contact with that person a number of times while speaking to the group as a whole.

EXAMPLE . . . .

The group has been in progress for 45 minutes, and the leader is aware that Claire has said very little. The discussion has been about people's different values. The leader decides to shift the focus and to try to draw Claire into the group.

Leader: OK, now that we've generated a list of different values, let's talk more about you and where your own values come from. (*While scanning the group, the leader intentionally has been*

holding eye contact with Claire a little longer than previously)
Think about different people or institutions, such as the church
or scouts, that have had an impact on you. (*The leader, noticing that Claire nodded at the word* church, *decides to say
more about religion while looking often at Claire)* For some,
religion may be the major source of your value system. Some
of you may be very religious. (*Claire nods, and the leader nods
back)* Sharing that would be helpful in the group. Who would
like to share about where values come from? Let's take the influence of religion first. (*The leader ends the comments while
looking at Claire)*

Claire: My family was very religious. In fact, . . .

. . . .

In this example, the leader intentionally ended the introduction
looking at Claire, increasing the likelihood that she would speak up. Of
course, sometimes this will not be effective, and you need to be aware
that this technique should be used with care and concern for your
members. Unfortunately, some beginners misunderstand the technique
and end up using eye contact as a "spotlight," thus creating undue
pressure on a member to respond.

Cutting Off Members

Often, there will be one member who tends to speak first on any issue
or question. There may be times when the leader will want someone else
to comment first, perhaps just for a change or because the talkative
member is negative or long-winded. When the leader knows that she
is going to pose a question to the group, she can use her eyes to control
the talkative member. By looking at the member as she starts to ask her
question and then slowly shifting her eyes around to other members,
she finishes her comments totally *out of eye contact* with the talkative
member. This technique subtly invites others to respond and avoids the
talkative member's nonverbal overtures to comment. Certainly this does
not work all the time, but it can be very effective.

E X A M P L E . . . .

The leader, wishing to get members to share their fears about leaving the hospital, starts by looking at Joe, an overzealous member
on the leader's left.

Leader: All of you probably have some fears about leaving this
hospital. I hope that a number of you will share those fears.

(Now scanning the middle of the group) Who would share some of those fears, no matter how big or small? *(The leader's eyes are now fixed on the members on the right)*

In this example, the leader is hoping that members in the middle or on the far right side of the group will comment first. By finishing the question with Joe outside his range of vision, the leader increases the chance of someone other than Joe initiating the discussion.

.   .   .   .

Leaders can also use their eyes to help cut off a member who is speaking. If a member has gone on for a while, a very subtle but often helpful cutting-off technique is for the leader to avoid making eye contact with the speaker. Members frequently will "wind down" sooner when the leader is not attending to their comments.

To summarize, by moving your eyes you will be in contact with your members and more aware of the energy of the group. By scanning the group, you will have a better sense of what to do next. All in all, the leader who scans will have much more data than the leader who doesn't.

When co-leading, the need to scan is reduced, since both leaders will be observing members' reactions. In situations in which one leader is "working" with a member, the other should be scanning the group.

To conclude this section, try practicing the two training exercises provided below. Also see the additional examples following the exercises; they are offered as a way of reviewing how the use of your eyes can be of great value to you as a group leader.

Practice Activities

The following two exercises will help you develop more effective use of your eyes in working with groups. Try each several times. The key to these exercises is to make them fun and interesting. See what you can learn.

1. In a group (one you are actually leading or simply a group of as few as three people standing around talking), move your eyes comfortably from face to face. Study expressions and reactions to the speaker. See if you can guess who will speak next. Also see if you can tell by the data you are gathering from head nods, smiles, and other facial expressions whether the other people are agreeing or disagreeing with the speaker. Try to guess whether the next person will maintain the topic or go off in a new direction.

2. In a group, move your eyes comfortably from face to face. Think about each person's expression. What feeling do you get from it? If you

were to make a statement about each person based on his or her expression, what would it be?

The following examples should help you further understand reasons for scanning the group when you or other members are talking.

EXAMPLES. . . . .

A SUPPORT GROUP FOR CANCER PATIENTS

Carl is talking about his recent diagnosis of cancer and his family's denial of the whole matter. While scanning the group, the leader notices that Sue's head is nodding vigorously. He asks Sue to share, and she comments on her family's denial reactions and how she dealt with them. Carl listens intently.

. . . .

A GROUP FOR ELEMENTARY
SCHOOLCHILDREN WHO LIVE IN STEPFAMILIES

The leader is talking about how the first few months are hard because of the blending of two families. She notices that Mike, Karen, and Bob are nodding and Jane is looking down. (The leader knows from Jane's teachers that Jane is having a hard time in her new stepfamily.) The leader then gets Mike, Karen, and Bob to talk about their hard times while she continues to observe Jane. Toward the end of Bob's comments, the leader notices that Jane seems more relaxed, so she invites Jane to share.

. . . .

A THERAPY GROUP FOR ALCOHOLICS

Gloria is into a long story about her history of drinking that she has told twice before. By scanning, the leader notices that the members are not paying attention and are starting to drift off. He decides to cut Gloria off by saying in a gentle, caring voice, "Gloria, you seem to be losing us. Are you aware that people aren't listening? My guess is that they are not listening because you have told us this twice before. How can we be of help to you?"

. . . .

A DIVORCE ADJUSTMENT GROUP

Mary is talking about how things are better for her now—she and her ex-husband are even talking about possibly dating each other. In scanning, the leader notices some questioning looks and also notices that Betty is starting to tear up. The leader decides to shift to Betty, who reveals that her ex-husband told her yesterday that he was going to get married.

. . . .

A PERSONAL GROWTH
GROUP FOR GRADUATE STUDENTS
The leader has just introduced an exercise on family of origin and, scanning, notices a confused look on one of the members' faces. She asks the member about his confusion, and he tells her he was raised in an orphanage. The leader then says, "Think of those people to whom you were closest. It may have been your houseparents and some of your peers in the orphanage."

. . . .

USE OF VOICE

Use of voice is another skill that many leaders overlook. Our discussion here will cover how the leader's voice can be used to influence the tone and atmosphere of the group as well as its pace and content. In later chapters, the use of the voice to draw out and cut off members is explained.

Setting the Tone

A leader conveys how a group will be led both by the content of his words and the tone of his voice. A very strong, dominating voice usually indicates that the leader is going to run everything, whereas a firm yet caring voice communicates a responsible and facilitative role on the part of the leader. It is not that one voice pattern is better than another or that you should develop only one pattern. Different kinds of groups with different member needs demand different styles of leadership. Some leaders have what could be called a very "warm" voice; others have a somewhat formal voice. Try to listen to your voice pattern, perhaps using a tape recorder. You will want to develop more than one voice pattern, because at times you will need to vary the tone of the group, and your voice can help in that process.

In task, education, and discussion groups your voice can communicate a serious or a light tone; be aware of the message your voice is sending. Sometimes you want the group to be serious, yet your voice indicates something else. In support groups, the leader usually wants to communicate caring and encouragement with her voice. She will also want to express through both words and tone that the members will be playing a major role in what takes place in the group. A very strong, stern voice may be experienced as intimidating by the members, and they may not share as much. A nonassertive voice may cause members not to respect or believe in the leader, which naturally would make leading difficult. A warm, encouraging voice certainly helps the scared, troubled, or withdrawn member.

Energizing the Group

In many kinds of groups, the leader's energy and enthusiasm will help to energize the members. Frequently leaders who complain that their group is "dead" are those who have not learned to use their voice to their advantage. Discussion groups, educational groups, and task groups can be nearly ruined if the leader himself does not demonstrate by his actions and voice that he is interested in the topic and the group. An enthusiastic voice will affect most members in a positive way as long as the leader is sincere. Very often, at the beginning of a new group, and even at the start of a given session, the leader's voice can be a key factor in generating interest and energy. We suggest that you observe various teachers and group leaders and notice how the energy level of the leader usually affects the listeners' or members' energy levels. Also, we recommend that you listen to your own voice when leading and determine whether you are using it to energize the group. If you are not, you can practice using different energy levels in your voice, thus changing your voice patterns and habits. Although this will take some effort, you will find the effort worthwhile.

Pacing the Group

Closely linked to the tone and energy of the group is its pace, which can also be influenced by the leader's voice. Often, a very slow-talking leader will influence members in such a way as to slow the pace down—perhaps to such a degree that the group moves too slowly. Although there are exceptions, it is best to assume that your voice is having some influence. At times, you will want the group to move faster or slower; by learning to manipulate your rate of speech you may be able to regulate the pace of the members. Practice this, and evaluate your effectiveness as you are leading. You will likely be surprised at how much influence your voice can have.

In summary, the leader's voice pattern—which includes tone, pitch, volume, and rate—can be instrumental in leading an effective group.

USE OF THE LEADER'S ENERGY

So far, we have discussed several skills that a leader finds useful. Another skill—perhaps we should call it a characteristic—is the leader's energy. Good leaders have enthusiasm for what they are doing. Unfortunately, leaders often hold group sessions at the end of the day when they are very tired. If at all possible, leaders should take a break of an hour or two before a group session. You need to be excited about leading, because if you are not excited, the group members probably will not be, either. There really is no way to practice increasing your energy level, but it helps to be aware that your energy level affects that of the group.

IDENTIFYING ALLIES

A very useful skill is that of discovering who your allies are in the group; that is, which members you can count on to be cooperative and helpful. It is important to identify them, for there will be times in the group when you will want someone to start a discussion or an exercise or when you will need someone reliable to play a role or take a risk. Also, when leading therapy groups, you may encounter a situation in which one member is working at a very intense level on some issue, and another member becomes very emotional and needs immediate attention. A good therapy group leader has to be prepared for such occurrences. One way to handle this so as not to disrupt the work in progress is to ask your ally to be with the member who is very upset. This allows you to feel confident that the member who has become very emotional is getting some support while you are dealing with the "working" member and the rest of the group.

There are some important things to know about identifying your allies. Some members start out being very cooperative and are seemingly allies, but as the group progresses the desire to take over the group or focus the group on themselves. Sometimes your best allies are members who are quiet at first and don't stand out at the very beginning of the group. It usually takes at least a couple of group meetings to identify the members who will be especially helpful and cooperative in facilitating the group's purpose.

In some groups, there really isn't a need to be concerned about allies, but in others it becomes very important to identify them. You will, however, want to be careful not to play favorites in the group.

CONCLUDING COMMENTS

Our purpose in this chapter has been to describe a number of basic skills for leading groups, such as active listening, reflection, clarification, summarizing, minilecturing, encouraging, and modeling. Beginning leaders often fail to realize that these fundamental counseling skills are also useful in group leadership. We also discussed the importance of using one's eyes to draw members out, cut members off, and notice important nonverbal gestures. We covered the proper use of voice, including ways in which the leader may affect the tone of the group, the energy of the members, and the pace of the session. All of these skills are essential for good leading. If you conscientiously practice them, in time their use will become second nature to you.

Purpose and Focus

PURPOSE

Being clear about the purpose of the group and then sticking to that purpose is perhaps the most important group leadership concept to be learned. All of the other skills and tasks discussed in this book, such as holding and shifting the focus, cutting off and drawing out members, and planning a group, are based on the leader having a clear understanding of the purpose of the group. By clarity of purpose we mean that it is clear to the leader why the group is meeting and what its goals and objectives are. (The terms *goals* and *objectives* will sometimes be used in place of *purpose.*) When the leader fully understands the purpose of the group, it is easier for him to decide such things as its size, membership, session length, and number of sessions. Also, when the purpose is clear to the leader, he will know if the content he has chosen is appropriate.

The purpose of the group serves as a "map" for the leader, with which he guides the members. Members and leader must be clear about both the general purpose of the group and the specific purpose of each session, if any. The leader keeps the members "on course" by suggesting relevant activities, asking relevant questions, and cutting off irrelevant discussions. Groups whose objectives are not well defined—or in which the leader does not follow the stated objectives—often result in sessions that are confusing, boring, or unproductive. The following are examples of groups whose purpose is either unclear or is not followed by the leader.

EXAMPLES . . . .

Kind of group: Support/therapy group
Stated purpose: Learning to survive the pain of divorce

It is the first meeting. Members have been talking about their loneliness, self-doubts, and fears. Alan interrupts abruptly and starts talking about his children and how he plans to care for them when they visit. The leader says to the group, "What are your thoughts on how Alan can handle the upcoming visit?" For the next 30 minutes, the group gives Alan suggestions on how to handle the situation, with much of the talk centering on what to feed the kids.

This leader made a mistake by asking for comments on what Alan was saying. The stated purpose was support and therapy to survive the pain of divorce, so the leader should not have focused the group on one person by asking that particular question. Rather, the leader should have halted the discussion and redirected the group back to a discussion of the members' feelings about their divorce. Allowing the discussion to continue probably resulted in some members becoming bored and frustrated. Members might also have become angry and left the group or cut in on the discussion and attacked Alan or the group for being "shallow and petty." Such responses could have been prevented had the leader been clear about the purpose and then used his skills to redirect the group. For example, the leader could have said something like this: "Alan, that's an important topic; however, it does not fit with the purpose of the group at this time. I would like to talk with you later about your situation."

. . . .

Kind of group: Educational/informational
Stated purpose: Orientation to the rules of the prison

The group starts with the leader going over the procedures for meals, visits, and weekend passes. One man brings up the prison's policy of no passes for the first month. Another inmate chimes in about the lack of places to be alone when he has visitors. Another asks the group what they think of that situation. Different members offer their opinions and ideas about it. Following this, the leader brings the discussion back to the policies and procedures by discussing mealtime procedures. One inmate mentions that he is a vegetarian and two others ask him a number of questions about why he doesn't eat meat. Another inmate says he thinks the meals are terrible. The leader asks what other members think about the meals. Two inmates then start complaining about the food, the heating in the rooms, and the lack of television sets on the units. The group ends with very little having been said about procedures in the prison.

Because this leader did not stick to the educational/informational purpose and was more worried about whether people would talk, he let the group wander. There is a good chance that some members will be resistant at the second meeting because the first was boring and irrelevant. The leader could have stopped the discussion of visits and meals and brought the group back to its intended purpose by saying, kindly but firmly: "The purpose of this group is to discuss the rules and procedures of the prisons. I'd be more than happy to arrange a time to discuss these other matters. However, for now let's get back to our topics—let's talk about the procedures for having a visitor."

. . . .

Kind of group: Discussion
Stated purpose: Adult Sunday school discussion group on church-related issues

It is the fourth session, and the topic scheduled for discussion this week is "ways in which the church can be more responsive to the changing family—the single-parent family and the stepfamily." The discussion has been interesting and relevant. Then a member asks, "Why is the divorce rate so high now?" The leader mistakenly throws the question open to the group and, for the next 25 minutes, four of the nine members argue about the many reasons. When the group returns to the original topic of the church being responsive, there is little energy for it. People seem anxious to get home.

Again, the leader's lack of clarity caused this group to go awry. If the leader had been clear about the purpose of this meeting, she would not have let the members discuss the causes of divorce. Rather, she would have said something like, "That might be something we could discuss at a later meeting. However, let's stay with the topic for this week."

. . . .

Clarifying the Purpose

To ensure that leaders achieve a clear understanding of the group's purpose, they can follow these steps that will help them think it through.

1. Gather information.
2. Determine the kind of group.
3. Think about possible topics, issues, and exercises.
4. Check that the purpose fits the members' needs once the group begins.

Gathering Information

When considering leading a group, a leader should begin by asking, "Why should this group exist?" If the purpose is not yet determined, it is imporant that the leader gather information about members' needs. This can be accomplished in a number of ways, depending on the situation. In situations in which the potential members are readily available, such as in a school, prison, or hospital, obtaining information directly from those persons is usually the best policy. This can be done either by meeting with them individually or by having them complete a short questionnaire about why they might want to be in a group, what they would like to get from a group, and specific things about which they would want to talk. When the leader cannot gather information directly, she can talk with those who are in charge or who know the potential members: counselors, teachers, principals, directors, and so on. The leader would want to ask why the prospective members are interested in being in a group or why they are being put in a group. Such information tells her what their particular needs are, their likely level of sophistication, and their probable level of commitment to the group. Assessing members' needs is the first and most important step in clarifying the purpose of a group, for those needs define both the kind of group that will be led and its specific goals.

Sometimes the purpose is obvious immediately; when potential group members have only one need, such as weight loss, quitting smoking, overcoming a phobia, or learning study skills, the leadership task is simplified. The group's goal is automatically defined, and interviewing members is less important. More often, however, members' needs will not be so specific. Leading groups of people with a variety of needs means that the leader will have to help the group decide which needs are reasonable and possible to address. Focusing the group on specific goals saves time and effort and ensures that the group maintains both order and a forward movement.

Determining the Kind of Group

Once the leader has assessed the members' needs, she must decide which kind of group (see Chapter One) will be most helpful. Identifying the kind of group to be led also helps her to define its overall purpose and the kind of group behavior and dynamics she wants. For example, a leader working with a group of mentally retarded teenagers might decide on an educational group covering such topics as sex, money, and job hunting, or a support group to help them explore their feelings. Gathering information about the members' needs, deciding which needs can be met by the group, and then conceptualizing the kind of group that will ideally meet those needs enables the purpose to become more clearly defined in the leader's mind. The next example illustrates the process of clarifying the purpose of a group by determining what kind it will be.

EXAMPLE . . . .

A leader has been asked to lead a group for pregnant teenage girls. First, she tries to find out if the group's goal, such as providing abortion information or sharing common experiences, has already been determined. The leader finds there is no predetermined purpose. She then gathers information about the members' ages, length of pregnancies, the attitudes of their parents, their marital status, abortion options, and reasons for wanting to be in a group. She finds that the five girls range in age from 14 to 17. They are all at least four months pregnant, and all plan to keep the baby. They've volunteered to be in the group because of conflicts at home and a desire for information. The leader also discovers that their needs are varied: sessions might cover dealing with their peers, handling guilt associated with religious beliefs, nutrition information, parenting skills, coping with pregnancy, planning for the baby, and the effects of drugs, alcohol, and smoking on the fetus.

Given these needs, it appears that an educational/support group is called for. The overall purpose, therefore, will be to educate the girls on various aspects of pregnancy and nutrition, as well as to facilitate personal sharing in an effort to establish support among members.

. . . .

Thinking about Possible Topics, Issues, and Exercises

Once members' needs and the kind of group are determined, the leader must give thought to what topics, issues, and group exercises are appropriate for the group. By doing so, she mentally prepares for leading the group and will be better able to avoid drifting away from the purpose. The leader could begin by writing down all the ideas that might be relevant. For instance, for a study skills group, her list would include such topics as study schedules, different ways to study, and how to prepare for tests. For groups whose purposes are less specific, her list might be longer and contain all the possible areas that could or should be covered in the group. This clarifying exercise helps to focus the leader on the group and the possible directions in which it can go.

Making Sure the Purpose Fits the Members' Needs

Once the group begins, the leader needs to clarify with the members what the purpose is. By doing this, the leader ensures that the purpose in fact coincides with what the members want or expect. If the leader has planned well and has followed the first three steps, the stated goals should meet the needs of the group members. It is important to note that it is not always the leader who determines exactly what is to happen in the group. However, the leader can and often does initially decide on the very broad purpose and kind of group, such as "educational/informational," or "support." Along with checking the group's goals with the members, the leader may also have the members outline the format, choose the topics to be covered during the next few sessions, or both.

Common Questions about Purpose

Certain questions often come up regarding the purpose of groups. Although some of them may seem similar, each one addresses slightly different issues.

Can the Group Have More Than One Purpose?

Yes; many groups may have multiple purposes, such as providing support, information, and therapy. The pairing of values clarification with counseling or drug information is compatible and can set the stage for an effective and interesting group experience. Another example of multiple purposes is a group for people just released from a state hospital, in which the leader has two purposes: to encourage support and to provide information on such subjects as budgeting one's income and how to interview for a job. Another example is a group for pregnant teenagers, with multiple purposes of providing support and information, and helping with the task of deciding what to do about their pregnancies. Eventually the purpose could shift to teaching parenting skills for those who choose to keep their babies. The main thing to consider when developing multiple goals for your group is whether or not they are compatible.

So far our discussion of purpose has mostly centered on the content of the group. There are other ways to conceptualize purpose; it can also be one or more of the following:

- To have fun
- To be informative
- To build trust
- To increase commitment
- To be thought-provoking
- To provide a place for contact with others
- To accomplish a task

Each of these is a valid reason for conducting a group and may be either part of a multiple purpose or the sole purpose for one or more sessions. For instance, a leader who discovers that the group lacks trust or commitment would probably want to focus part of the next meeting on those issues rather than on the overall purpose, such as personal growth, getting out of prison, living with cancer, or learning assertiveness. If members do not trust one another or if their commitment to the group is low, they will usually not get involved in the topic and overall purpose.

Another example of a multiple-purpose group session is the first session, for which the leader always has at least two purposes in mind. One is introducing the general content of the group (study habits, communications skills, weight loss) and the other, managing the dynamics of beginning a group (introductions, assessing comfort level, getting everyone to share). There are also two purposes for the last session: finishing the content and finishing the group.

Two important things to make sure of when a group has multiple purposes are that the members are clear that there *are* several purposes and that those purposes are relevant for most members. Sometimes leaders mix purposes in incompatible ways. For example, a leader might take 30 minutes of the group's time to do one-to-one counseling with a woman complaining about her husband, although the group's purpose is to discuss childrearing. Ideally, the leader would meet with that woman at the end of the session or the next day but not during the group, since the other members have come for a totally different purpose. Another example of mixing incompatible purposes is common in residential settings such as halfway houses, juvenile centers, or prisons. In these settings, leaders sometimes try to deal in a single session with issues such as tensions between residents, house rules, and disciplinary procedures. These leaders should divide those issues into two or three separate meetings, because each has a tone and agenda that does not really mesh with the others.

Can the Purpose Change?

Yes; there are times when changing the purpose of the group can benefit the members. For example, say a group of teenagers has been meeting together for fun and educational purposes. After six weeks, the leader sees the need and benefit of doing more counseling and growth-oriented activities. Probably the best way for him to make the shift would be to express this idea to the group and explain how the group could change direction. If the group decided to switch its emphasis, the leader would need to be aware that it will probably take one or two sessions to completely change the direction.

Another common shift is toward more intensive therapy. Groups often start out as support or growth groups and, as they develop, the members begin to share on a more personal level. If a group has had discussion, education, or support as its purpose and the leader sees a need to shift to therapy, it is best to discuss this in the group. Often leaders make the mistake of shifting the purpose of the group without informing the members. As a result, members feel frustrated, confused, or resentful. As we have said throughout this chapter, it is important that both leader and members remain clear about the group's purpose, and the leader should reiterate the purpose whenever necessary. If the leader decides to shift the purpose, he must be sure that the members are aware of his intent and that they, too, desire the shift.

Can There Be No Purpose?

This is inadvisable. Groups without a purpose usually dissolve due to lack of interest and direction. While you may choose to bring together a group of people having no predetermined goal in mind, the purpose of the first meeting should be to decide in what direction the remainder of the meetings will go. In fact, a group with no purpose cannot really be termed a group. Rather it is a social gathering.

Must Each Session Have a Purpose?

Yes; a good group leader will have in mind the purpose or purposes of each specific session. One purpose might be to clarify what the rest of the sessions will be like—or to address the group's trust or commitment level. Other purposes can be to give feedback to each other; to discuss a specific topic such as religion, sex, or the need for approval; or to get to know each other better. Sometimes the leader, the group, or both will decide beforehand what the purpose of the next session will be.

Here are some examples of the specific purposes of several group sessions.

EXAMPLES . . . .

It is the fourth session of a discussion group composed of high school students exploring different postgraduate options. The predetermined topic of discussion is the military. The students have been asked to gather as much information as they can to share in the group.

. . . .

This is a growth group consisting of three women and five men. The leader starts the session by saying,

Leader: Tonight we are going to spend the entire two hours talking about love relationships. We'll discuss our current love situations, what works for us, and what doesn't work.

. . . .

In the fifth session of a therapy group, Sandy starts rambling again. The leader decides that the group is far enough along to start giving feedback to one another. He says the following to the group and to Sandy:

Leader: I want to pick up on something that I think will help you and the other members of the group. I want to do a feedback exercise in which we tell each other how we experience them in the group. That is, for the next hour and a half, we are going to give each other feedback. Here's what I'd like you to do. I need a volunteer to go first. We will spend three minutes talking about that person, first listing the person's strengths and then the things the person may need to change. Who will go first?

.   .   .   .

It is the third session of a support group composed of juveniles in a detention center. The leader notices that there is no energy, although the group began only ten minutes ago. She decides, therefore, that the best purpose for this session is to work on commitment and trust. She says to the group,

Leader: On a 1-to-10 scale, with 10 being a lot and 1 being none, how much commitment do you have to this group?

After the information is gathered, the leader will focus for the remainder of the session on why members are not committed and what would increase their commitment.

.   .   .   .

It is the third in a series of five sessions of an educational group whose overall purpose is to teach nursing supervisors new ways to deal with their staff. The leader starts by saying,

Leader: Today we are going to focus on nonverbal behavior. I want to go over some of the latest research, which I found to be quite useful; then I'll ask for reactions and comments. Jefferson and Smith studied the nonverbal behavior of 22 nursing supervisors and found. . . .

.   .   .   .

A therapy group in its third session is composed of mental-health patients having outpatient status. The leader opens the group by saying, "Who has something to bring up tonight?" Two of the seven members respond. Joe says he wants to talk about his mom and her desire to control him. Molly mentions her anxiety at work. The leader says to the group,

Leader: Tonight we'll focus on Molly's and Joe's concerns, and then during the last hour we'll spend time talking about learning to control our feelings by paying attention to the things that we tell ourselves.

. . . .

As you can see, a leader can establish the session's purpose by a variety of methods. The simple, direct approach is often a very good way to make the purpose clear.

If the Leader Is Clear, Will the Members Be?

Not always. Often, members have their own ideas of what the group should be about, and they try to steer it in that direction. In addition, some members will come to groups for reasons other than the stated purpose; that is, they come to complain, to preach, or to attack, and will not follow the leader's direction. Another reason members may not be clear about the group's purpose is that some find it hard to understand what is going on. Due to their anxiety, they are not able to listen well. By reiterating, the leader can do much to clarify the intent of the group for the members. If she sees that some of the members are working at cross-purposes, she will probably want to do one of two things; (1) meet with those members who seem confused, or (2) discuss the problem in the group. Often, this clears up the confusion.

Purpose in Single-Session Groups

Most of our comments have implied that groups meet for a number of sessions. Many, but not all, do. Many groups meet only once. When leading a single-session group, clarity of purpose is even more essential. The leader will want to be very clear about why this group is meeting and then plan a group that will accomplish the desired objective in the time allotted. The group's purpose may be to staff a patient (discuss and determine a treatment plan), to resolve a conflict, or to plan an event. Being clear will help the leader use the time effectively and accomplish the desired outcomes. Often at single-session group meetings, little is accomplished because the members skip around and the leader fails to keep the flow of ideas within the boundaries of the purpose. Another problem is that the members may focus for half the meeting on something that is irrelevant, thus necessitating a second meeting. A good leader will have thought out what needs to be done and then decide how much time should be spent on introductions, warm-up, background information, and the various topics.

Clarity of purpose, then, is crucial no matter what type of group is led. Once you have mastered the process of clarifying the purpose, the next important aspect to understand about effective group leadership pertains to getting and holding the focus.

FOCUS

If clarity of purpose is the most important concept to understand about group leading, then focusing is probably the next most important aspect to understand. It can be said that group leading is about focusing—establishing the focus, holding the focus, shifting the focus, and deepening the focus. The focus is on whatever is being discussed. At any given moment in a session, the focus is either on a topic, an activity, or a person. That is, the discussion or interaction will be about either some topic—"love relationships," "ways of dealing with your parents," "trust within the group"—or a group activity, such as a guided fantasy or a written activity, or on a person's ideas, issues, or problems.

In Chapter Two, we introduced you to many different ideas for understanding your group: stages of the group, phases of the session, the depth chart, and the funnel. These "maps," along with clarity of purpose and focusing, give you many helpful ways to view the interactions and development of your group. A summary of these concepts is:

- *Purpose:* Why the group is meeting
- *Stage:* Where the group is in its development
- *Phase:* Where the session is
- *Focus:* The content of the group:
    Getting the focus
    Holding the focus
    Shifting the focus
    Deepening the focus
- *Depth chart:* A way to gauge the depth of the focus
- *Funnel:* A way to view the focusing

A skilled leader will always observe where the focus is and make sure it is in line with the purpose. Usually, the leader will not take the focus too deep during the beginning phase. At times, the leader will focus the group on certain topics or individuals, hold the focus on topics or on members, or shift the focus if the topic or the person talking is not in line with the purpose. (As we have pointed out, members can very easily get off the purpose of the group and end up talking about movies, the weather, other people, or various other unrelated topics.) The leader should always be aware of the depth of any discussion or personal work and should, when appropriate, try to funnel the group to a deeper level. The leader should also be alert to the tendency of groups to skip from topic to topic. In the remainder of this chapter, we discuss establishing the focus, holding and shifting the focus, and deepening the focus.

Establishing the Focus

There are many different ways that the focus is established in a group. The most important thing to remember is that the leader is often the one to do this. Often, the members will be discussing different ideas when the leader sees the value in holding the focus on one topic. There also will be many times when the leader establishes the focus with comments or by introducing a group exercise. Methods of getting the group focused are discussed below.

Comments to Focus the Group

Sometimes establishing the focus is accomplished by simply stating to the group what the topic or activity is going to be for the next few minutes.

- Let's focus on the topic of guilt for the next hour.
- Let's focus on Julio for the next 20 minutes and try to help him with his dilemma.
- I'd like us to summarize what this last 30 minutes has meant.
- Let's really zero in on one of these topics. It doesn't matter which one, but let's pick one rather than trying to talk about all three.
- The topic for tonight is learning how to budget your time. Who wants to share what they learned from doing the homework on time management?

Often comments regarding the focus are coupled with some activity or exercise. Many different ways to focus the members are discussed on the following pages.

Activities and Exercises to Focus the Group

Using visual aids and having members write or draw something are excellent ways to get members focused. The following are just a few examples of the activities you can use.

1. *Use posters, charts, or diagrams relevant to the topic or task of the group.* Having a carefully made drawing or list can be very helpful in focusing members. Visual aids tend to get the members involved both visually and auditorily.

2. *Use a chalkboard or a large pad to list items or characteristics.* For instance, if the group members were talking about drugs you could go to the chalkboard and say, "Let's list the pros and cons of drug use." Or if you were leading a high school group and the topic was friends, you could say, "Let's list the characteristics of a good friend." While looking at the list on the board, members often get more focused by trying to generate new items to add.

3. *Use a chalkboard to draw pictures or visual analogies.* For example, group members could be discussing all the ways in which they

feel they are being held down. You could go to the chalkboard (or a large newsprint pad) and sketch a large hot-air balloon with various lead weights hanging off the sides. Each weight would be labeled in terms of pounds (200, 100, 50, 25, 10), and there would be space under each to fill in what that weight represented. This image might prove helpful to members and allow them to focus on what is holding them down and to what degree. Another drawing for that discussion might be of a road with various roadblocks and choices on it. Having the picture in front of them often helps members focus on the discussion. The visual image also keeps members focused in that they continue to look at the image and think of new things to add or new meanings for the image.

4. *Have members list or write something.* A very helpful focusing technique is to have members write answers on sentence-completion forms. For example, a leader who wants the group to focus on the topic of parents could make up a list of five sentences for members to complete, such as the following:

When I think of my mom, I _____ .

When I think of my dad, I _____ .

I wish my dad _____ .

I wish my mom _____ .

The biggest problem I have with my parents is _____ .

Another focusing technique that involves writing is to have each member make a list of something. For instance, the leader could have a group of first-year college students list their worries or have elementary schoolchildren list their favorite activities.

5. *Have members draw something.* Drawing such things as their favorite scene, the house they grew up in, or their earliest memory helps members focus on topics such as "what I like and value," "what my family was like," and "the impact of childhood on present-day living."

6. *Put a large piece of paper on the floor in the center of the group with a stimulus word or phrase on it.* This is a good way to get the members zeroed in on one concept. With this phrase in the center of the floor to stare at, they will usually stay focused. Some examples of words and phrases that you might put in the middle of the group are "Dad," "Mom," "work," "responsibilities," "fears I have," "changes I can make in my life," and "things that make me happy."

7. *Use handouts that contain information you want to cover.* Handouts give members something to look at and relate to. Also they are useful in that the members take them with them when the session is over.

8. *Place an empty chair in the center of the room.* The empty chair can represent many different people. If you want to focus on

parents, you could have the chair represent one or both parents. If you want to focus on anger, you could have the chair be someone with whom they are angry.

9. *Place a small child's chair in the center of the room.* The small chair can represent the "free child," the "inner child," or the "hurt child." By having the chair present, members tend to focus on that part of themselves much more easily than if simply asked to imagine being the child.

10. *Stand on a chair.* The leader can usually get members focused on such issues as need for approval, whom they see as "above" them, or codependency by standing on an empty chair and asking a few questions about the people they have "above" them.

Other creative techniques include the use of such items as shields, beer bottles, rubber bands, audiotapes, and videotapes. For a complete description of these and other creative techniques, see *Creative Counseling Techniques: An Illustrated Guide* (Jacobs, 1992).

When used properly, all of these techniques can prove very helpful to the leader. The point is that there are many direct and creative ways to get groups focused, and it is important to have a number of techniques from which to choose. Different situations call for different techniques; through trial-and-error experience you will learn which ones work best in particular situations.

Rounds and Dyads to Focus the Group

Rounds and dyads are two additional ways to get members focused. A round is an activity in which the leader asks each member to briefly respond to the same stimulus. A dyad is an activity in which members pair up to discuss some issue or reaction. (See Chapter Eight for a thorough explanation of both.)

Rounds.   The round gets members focused in two specific ways: (1) they have to think of what they are going to say, and (2) they hear others comment on the topic.

Here are just a few examples of how rounds can be used to focus the group. The leader could say any of the following:

- Think of what has been the biggest change since your accident. In a minute I'm going to have each of you comment briefly on this. Take a few seconds to think about the biggest change.
- How much effect do your siblings have on you today—a lot, a little, or none? Think about this, and then we'll do a round.
- In a word or phrase, what stood out to you the most about tonight?

These examples should help you see how rounds can be used for focusing. Rounds are very useful because they involve everybody and get members to think.

Dyads.   The dyad helps focus members on a topic because they are paired with one another and instructed to discuss various ideas. The following examples illustrate how dyads can be used to get members to think about and stay with certain issues.

- Pair up and talk about ways you can benefit from the group.
- Pair up and talk about your reaction to the reading for the week.
- OK, let's break into dyads and talk about your ideas for a solution to the problem.

The intent of this section on establishing the focus has been to give you ideas about how to get your group on course. The techniques mentioned will help in focusing the group, but the focus rarely stays constant or clear for long periods of time without the aid of the leader. Therefore, knowing how to *hold* the focus is essential for good group leadership.

Holding the Focus

Once the leader has the group focused, he can pay attention to the flow of the group. The leader is constantly deciding if the focus is skipping around too much and needs to be brought back and held on the topic or person, or if it needs to be shifted to some other person, topic, or activity. Holding the focus means sticking with the content. For example, if Mac is discussing the pain he's experiencing over his wife's death and Melvin tries to interrupt and discuss his brother's visit, the leader "holds" the focus by directing the group back to Mac. Another example might be a personal growth group for teenagers in which a good discussion of dating is taking place. Someone asks a question about the best five movies to see with a date. The trained leader does not let the topic shift to movies, but rather holds the focus on dating interactions because it is in line with the purpose of the group.

There are three considerations to keep in mind for holding the focus: when to hold it, how long to hold it, and how to hold it.

When to Hold the Focus

Deciding when to hold the focus is not simple because each group has a different purpose and is made up of members whose needs vary greatly. The first thing the leader considers in deciding whether to hold the focus is where the focus is. Is it on a person or on a topic? The leader's approach will be different depending on the answer to that question.

Focus on a topic.   The following five questions are helpful in determining whether to hold the focus on a topic. (By *topic*, we mean such things as parents, vanity, the value of staying in school, how to budget money, or any other subject the group is discussing.)

1. Is the topic relevant to the purpose of the group?
2. Are the members interested in the topic?
3. How many members seem interested? If most members are not interested, you will probably want to shift the focus, although there are times when you may decide to stay with it a little longer.
4. Has the focus been on the topic too long? This will usually depend on how much you planned to cover in the session. If there are five major issues to discuss and the group is still on the first one with only half the session remaining, the focus should probably be shifted.
5. Has the group discussed the topic before? Sometimes a group will go over the same issues week after week.

The answers to these questions will give leaders a sense of whether to hold or shift the focus. When you are unsure about whether to stay with a topic, another way to decide is to do a "quick 1-to-10." Simply say "I want to get a quick reading from you on whether we should continue to discuss the issue of _____ . On a 1-to-10 scale, with 10 being very interested and 1 being very disinterested, what number best describes your attitude?"

Usually the numbers will indicate whether there is enough interest. If all are low numbers or high numbers, the decision is obvious. If there is a range, a number of things can be done. The leader may ask those who indicated high interest what they specifically would like to discuss, then focus the group there with a time limit of 5, 10, or 20 minutes. She could split the group and let those with high interest meet for 20 minutes (depending on the time remaining) while the others discuss another topic. Splitting the group would be appropriate only in educational or discussion groups, where group cohesion is not a major goal. Skilled leaders would rarely do this in a growth or therapy group. Another thing the leader could do would be to give a break to those who rated their interest as low while the high-interest members continued with the topic. As you can see, the quick 1-to-10 round can offer information that generates a number of options for the leader.

Focus on a person.   When the focus is on a person, there are three questions to consider.

1. *Who is talking, and how much "air time" has the speaker had recently?* If the person talking has not spoken in a while, or has spoken very little throughout the group's life, it is usually better to hold the focus

on that individual. If, on the other hand, the person has had the group's attention often in the past, the leader may choose to shift the focus.

2. *Does focusing on one person serve the purpose of the group?* Some groups meet for the purpose of doing therapy or personal growth work; in such groups, focusing on one person is appropriate and definitely in line with the group's purpose. Others meet for discussion, sharing, or accomplishing a task; thus, to focus on one person would not be in line with the established goals.

3. *Is the person benefitting from having the focus?* Certainly one of the major benefits of groups is that members have the opportunity to share with others—hearing feedback and ideas that pertain to them. If a member is the focus of the group and appears to be benefiting, hold the focus unless (1) the group has gone on for a long time and others are restless, or (2) the content is no longer relevant to the group's purpose, such as if a member were talking about whether or not to get braces during a weight-control group.

How Long to Hold the Focus

One question you may be asking is "How long is the focus held on a person or topic?" There is no single answer, because it depends on the purpose of the group, which session it is in, what has happened in previous sessions, and how much time is left in the current session. Also, different factors must be considered depending on whether the focus is on a person or on a topic.

Focus on a person. The amount of time to hold the focus on a person depends partly on the kind of group being led. For therapy, growth, and support groups, where holding the focus on one person is appropriate, the upper limit is probably 20 or 30 minutes. Naturally, there will be exceptions: sometimes the leader may even stay with one person for an hour or more. However, this should be the exception rather than the rule. In other kinds of groups (discussion, education, or task) a good rule of thumb would be not to hold the focus longer than 5 minutes on any one person, since you would probably want an exchange of ideas or information from all the members.

Holding the focus for a long period of time also depends on which session it is. Leaders do not want anyone to dominate the first couple of sessions, because they are trying to get people to feel comfortable being in the group. If one person dominates, other members may tend to sit back and listen rather than think and contribute. If one person is the focus for most of the first or second session, members will probably not experience the desired bonding or feelings of commonality. Beginning leaders often make the mistake of focusing for too long on one member in early sessions, probably due to their own nervousness and/or not knowing how to cut off or draw out other members.

Focus on a topic.   How long to hold the focus on a topic depends on a number of things. If the group is an education, discussion, or task group in which there are a number of things to be covered, the leader will want to budget the time wisely. Many beginning leaders get so caught up in the content or interaction that they forget that other topics need to be covered.

A second factor is what the topic is. Focusing on a "heavy" issue in the early stages of a group is usually not wise. Also, topics such as sex or death should not be focused on unless there is ample time to process them. A discussion of death can stir up a number of feelings, memories, and fears, so it is probably wise not to hold the focus on death if it comes up during the last 30 minutes of the session. The leader would probably want to say something like "Let's hold off discussing the topic of death until next week, since we really don't have enough time to fully discuss it and I wouldn't want us to get started on something that might leave some of you hanging."

How to Hold the Focus

When the group is flowing and the focus starts to shift, the leader has access to several skills and methods for holding the focus. The main skill is cutting members off. (See Chapter Seven for a complete discussion.) Whether you are using that skill or one of the methods described below, remember that the most important thing is to *act quickly*. The more quickly something is said or done when the focus starts to shift, the better. The longer you wait before bringing the group back to the topic or person the harder it will be, since the members' energy and attention will have become invested in the new person or topic. The most common method for holding the focus is simply to address the group directly. The examples below should give you some idea of what to say.

- Let's stay with Sandy.
- I want to go back to what Joe was saying. Joe, when did you start feeling that way?
- Can we put that on hold until Karen finishes with her list?
- I believe we may have left Manuel hanging—Manuel, do you want to say more about that situation?
- Let's finish this topic before we start a new one.
- I think if we're not careful we'll get too many things going at once—let's go back to the topic of _____ .

If you decide that you want the group to stay with a certain topic or person for a while, it is sometimes helpful to verbalize this. If, for example, your group has been discussing religion, you might say, "Let's spend the next 20 minutes talking only about religion and how it affects your life."

Another way to hold the focus is to do a group exercise or use a focusing prop such as the chalkboard or a newsprint pad. For instance, if the members were discussing their fears about cancer and the focus shifted to financial concerns, this statement could bring them back to the topic of fears: "I'd like to list on the chalkboard the different fears that you are experiencing. Financial fears is one; what are some others?" Or imagine a task group in which eight members are trying to resolve their differences on how the probation office and welfare office can work together. The discussion has turned momentarily to the local judge and how her recent rulings have been inconsistent. Seeing the need to hold the focus on the task, the leader could say to the members, "I'd like to do something a little different. I want each of you to pair up with someone from the other office and come up with a list of suggestions for improving the working relationship of your two offices."

As you have probably gathered, the possibilities for holding the focus are actually unlimited. With experience you will develop more techniques. Until then, try to use some of the ideas provided above plus others you will learn later on in this book.

Shifting the Focus

Although holding the focus and shifting the focus are very much tied together, it is important to clearly conceptualize them as separate skills. You consciously shift the focus when you decide that it needs to change. The shift can go in many directions:

- From a topic to a person
- From a topic to another topic
- From a topic to an activity
- From a person to another person
- From a person to a topic
- From a person to an activity
- From an activity to a topic
- From an activity to a person

"From an activity to another activity" is not listed because group exercises need to be processed and not just done one right after the other. The following is a discussion of when and how to shift the focus.

When to Shift the Focus

As you might guess, when to shift the focus depends on the same considerations listed in the section titled "When to Hold the Focus," because the two skills are so interrelated. You may wish to take a moment to refer to that section. There are two main ways to conceptualize shifting the focus: (1) as a shift *away* from some person, topic, or activity or (2) as a shift *toward* some person, topic, or activity. The leader shifts the focus when the following is the case:

- The focus has been on one person for too long.
- The focus has been on one topic for too long.
- The focus does not fit the purpose of the group.
- The time left dictates the need to change.
- The leader feels the members need a change to reenergize the group.
- The leader wants to draw another member into the group.
- The leader wants to introduce a new topic or activity.

How to Shift the Focus

How to shift the focus depends on which of the categories mentioned under "Shifting the Focus" the desired shift belongs to.

From a topic to a person.   Leaders often want to shift the focus from a topic to a person in therapy groups and growth groups but certainly may also do so in all kinds of groups.

EXAMPLE . . . .

The group has been discussing jealousy and a number of members have commented on how they handle it. The discussion has been going on for three or four minutes.

Missy: I just can't help it—I'm a jealous person. If Frank is talking to some woman at a party, I lose it.
Bill: But why? My wife does that to me, too. I don't like it at all.
Ted: I'm a lot more jealous than my wife. In fact, I don't think she gets jealous, and that makes me mad sometimes!

The leader decides to focus on one person for a few minutes rather than continue to let the interaction go from one member to another. Here are two ways the focus can be shifted to a person.

Leader: Missy, I'm wondering if you would want to explore your jealousy further. You seem to be bothered by it and I think I detect a desire on your part to get better control of it.

In this response, the leader shifts directly to a specific person who appears to have some interest in going deeper.

Leader: Would anyone like to spend a few minutes talking specifically about their concerns with jealousy? It is apparent to me that many of you are concerned about it. Ted, you and Missy and John and Bill all have talked about how jealousy is interfering in your relationship.

In this example, the leader merely indicates the desire to shift to a person but does not focus on any one individual.

. . . .

Here are some additional comments that leaders can make to shift to a person.

- I'd like each of you to think about what we have been talking about for the last few minutes. Does anybody want to work on anything regarding this issue?
- Who wants to take this issue deeper? There seem to be several things that you could work on.
- This discussion is good; however, I feel that some of you may have something personal that you want to discuss. Does anyone have something they would like to bring up?

In the last example the shift would not only be to a person but possibly to a new topic. If the leader doesn't want the topic to shift, a comment like the first example, which is more specific, should be used.

From one topic to another.   In discussion, task, and educational groups, the leader will usually need to shift the focus from time to time to cover the necessary material or accomplish the task. To shift the focus the leader might say any of the following:

- Let's take a minute or two to finish this topic, because we need to move on to something else.
- We seem to be about finished with this issue. Who has some other issues or points to bring up?
- We have a lot to cover tonight, so let's go on to something else.
- I would like to change the discussion to focus on what Kay was talking about. She mentioned the effects of the decision. Let's talk about what the rest of you think the effects would be.

In task groups and educational groups there is often certain material to be covered. The leader can help shift the focus by letting the members know the agenda and an estimate of the time needed to cover the topics. For example, the leader could say:

Leader: Today we are going to talk about diet and exercise as they relate to stress. We'll try to spend 45 minutes on each topic.

For a task group, the leader might say:

Leader: First we need to decide which proposal we want to accept. Then we need to decide who will do what, and discuss the necessary schedule changes that will be required. We only have an hour and a half, so we'll need to watch the time.

In each of these examples, telling the members what the agenda is helps the leader. It will still be the leader's responsibility to budget the group's time and to shift the focus when needed, but the clock can be used to do so—that is, by allowing so many minutes for each topic and, when the time has run out, simply saying to the group, "Time is up."

Here are some additional ways that leaders can shift to a new topic.

- We have a lot to cover today, so let's move on to the next chapter.
- Let's turn to another issue that is equally as important as the one we are now discussing.
- There are two more topics that we need to cover today. Let me throw them out to you and then let's decide which one we want to do next.

From a topic to an exercise.   Often when the group is discussing a topic, a group exercise may be useful to further the discussion or to get members more involved. The leader can introduce the exercise by saying something like, "I want us to stay with what we are discussing, but I think an exercise could be helpful now." Or the leader can say, "I want to change the format a little bit. There is a group exercise that fits in with what we are talking about."

Another way to shift from a topic is to use rounds. For instance, if the group has been discussing a topic for some time, you might say, "In a word or phrase, what are you thinking about right now?" Other rounds that you can use after a discussion are "How meaningful was this discussion, and why?" or "What did you learn from this discussion?"

Another easy way to shift from a topic to an activity is to have members form dyads to further discuss the topic that was being explored in the large group.

From one person to another person.   If the leader has determined that the focus needs to shift to another person, there are a number of possible things to say. Below are some examples of different situations and different responses.

- Lori, I think it would be good to let you just think about what you have been saying these last 15 minutes; then maybe we'll come back to you later on. What did this bring up for the rest of you? Who wants to explore their reactions or feelings?
- Joe, I'd like to shift to Cindy. (*The leader turns and addresses Cindy*) You seem to really be relating to this. I noticed a couple of times that you wanted to say something. Do you want to share that now?
- Bill, we'll stay with you for another couple of minutes; then I'm going to give others a chance to share their ideas.

In these examples the leader addresses the person who has the focus and then shifts it. The leader who wants to cut off the member who has the focus will address the group directly. In such situations, the leader might say something like this:

- Does anyone want to comment on what Joe has been saying?
- Let's not focus on Joe, but rather on yourselves.
- Cindy, how about you? You seem deep in thought.
- Can anyone relate to what Lori has been saying? (The leader would look away from Lori and would have some idea of who might want to speak.)

From a person to a topic.   There will be times when the leader will want to focus on the topic that a person is addressing. This may be because the topic is one to which he thinks most of the members can relate or because he wants to subtly shift the focus from the member who currently has it. Here are some examples:

- Dean, I want to pick up on what you've been talking about. I think the issue is a good one and I want to hear how others think and feel about it. What do others of you think about the issue—how do you deal with it and what reactions have you gotten? (Throwing out so many different questions invites discussion, which in this case is the intention.)
- Carol, you have brought up many concerns that certainly relate to others. I'd like to spend the rest of the session discussing some of those issues. Let's take the one you mentioned first. (Mentioning Carol by name and using some of the content she has been discussing increases the likelihood that she will not feel cut off.)
- Ted, your thoughts are interesting. However, I am aware that we are running out of time, and we still have one more major item to discuss. Why don't you summarize your position, and then we will move on.
- I want to shift the discussion to the whole group, since we really want to hear a number of ideas and views. What do the rest of you think?

As you can see in these examples, shifting the focus often involves cutting off. The next chapter covers that skill in detail.

From a person to an exercise.   As mentioned earlier, the use of rounds and dyads is a very good way to shift the focus. The leader can simply ask the members to respond to a member's question, to pair up and discuss what the member has been talking about, or to talk about any thoughts or feelings they had when the member was speaking.

Many other group exercises may come to mind. The following are some ways to introduce such exercises:

- I want to take what you are talking about and get the whole group to think about it. Everyone get out a piece of paper and something to write with. I want you to do the following. . . .

- Ruth, your energy and enthusiasm are appreciated. I want to see if I can get everyone as excited and interested as you are. Everyone stand up—I want you to move to this side of the room. Now, here's what I want you to do.

Deepening the Focus

In the discussion of holding the focus, we referred to deepening the focus. In most groups, the leader will want to take the group to a depth of at least a 7; that is, to a level that is not superficial. For many groups, the leader will want to funnel the group down to depths of 5 or below because the deeper the group, the more impact it has on its members. A leader deepens the focus by using several different techniques:

- Conducting an intense exercise that gets in touch with some deep, personal issues
- Asking very thought-provoking or challenging questions
- Asking members to share at a more personal level
- Facilitating sharing by members in a more personal way
- Working with a member in a more intense manner

In later chapters on middle sessions and therapy, we discuss in detail ways to take the focus to a deeper level.

CONCLUDING COMMENTS

In this chapter, we have discussed the importance of purpose and focus. Being clear about the purpose is perhaps the most important factor affecting the outcome of a group. It also affects the leader's choice of the kind of group, makeup of the membership, topics, dynamics, depth of intensity, and the leader's role. Throughout the first section we discussed the steps for getting a clear picture of the purpose as well as how the purpose varies with each kind of group. Many common questions about purpose were answered, covering such issues as multiple-purpose groups and specific purposes for each session.

In the second half of the chapter, we discussed paying attention to the focus of a group and techniques for getting the focus, holding it, and shifting it. Being aware of where the focus is and whether it needs to be shifted or held enables the leader to maintain control over what is happening in the group. That control in turn allows the leader to maximize the potential of the group so that it is productive and beneficial.

Cutting Off and Drawing Out

CUTTING OFF

An essential skill to know and use when leading groups is cutting off. *Cutting off* is the term we use to describe the leader's stopping a member from talking (Harvill, Masson, & Jacobs, 1983; Masson & Jacobs, 1980). Other terms used to describe this skill are *blocking* (Trotzer, 1989) and *intervening* (Dyer & Vriend, 1980). While the term *cutting off* may seem to have negative connotations, as though we are advocating that the leader be rude or authoritarian in the group, we merely mean that there are instances in which the leader must verbally intercept a member's flow of words in a nonpunitive way in order to move the group in a purposeful direction. Of all the skills we present in this book, cutting off is probably the hardest for leaders to use because they often fear that they will hurt a member's feelings or that members will become angry. In addition, the skill may be difficult because it is far from being a naturally acquired one. We don't learn as we grow up to stop others from talking when their remarks are boring, long-winded, or inappropriate. However, a group leader is responsible for ensuring positive group outcomes, and when group members' behaviors are counterproductive to those goals the leader should intervene.

In this chapter we discuss some of the reasons for cutting off and the many ways in which it can be done.

Situations Calling for Cutting-Off Skills

There are a number of situations in which a leader may want to use the skill of cutting off. We will discuss seven of them:

1. When a member is rambling
2. When a member's comments conflict with the group's purpose

3. When a member is saying something inaccurate
4. When the leader wants to shift the focus
5. When it is near the end of the session
6. When members are arguing
7. When members are rescuing

When a Member Is Rambling

We have all been in group or classroom situations in which a group member or student lost our attention by talking on and on and repeating himself. Leaders will invariably encounter such "talkers" in their groups. Some members drone on and on, totally oblivious to the effect that their rambling is having on others. If left unchecked, these members will effectively kill the energy and enthusiasm present in the others.

One way to conceptualize cutting off the rambler is in terms of three possible decisions that the leader can make. The leader can (1) cut and stay with the person, (2) cut and stay with the topic, or (3) cut and leave the person and topic.

Cutting and staying with the person.   Many times, the leader sees value in continuing to focus on the rambler if the leader can get the member more focused. There are a number of techniques that can help do this.

1. *Ask the person clarifying questions.* The leader may interrupt and either ask or have the members ask some questions to break up the monologue of the rambler. The leader will want to be sure that the questions are not ones that allow the rambler to keep on rambling.

E X A M P L E . . . .

Danie: (*Who has been telling stories for a couple of minutes about her alcoholic father and is not expressing her feelings much*) And another thing he did was. . . .

Leader: Just a second here. Let us ask you some questions about you and your dad. I want each of you to think of something you can ask Danie that will get her to explore more deeply her feelings about her situation. One question I want to ask is, "How much do you blame yourself for his drinking?"

. . . .

2. *Have the person do some focused activity (could use chairs, drama, or some experiential activity).* In the preceding example, the leader could put a chair in front of Danie and ask her to pretend that her father is sitting there and to have a conversation with him. Or the

leader could ask Danie to act out one of the scenes she has been describing, using members of the group to play her father and other family
members. Many other activities could also be tried. The point is that
Danie's storytelling is stopped, but the focus is still on her.

    3. *Have the person complete a round (from her seat or by having
the person sit in front of each of the members in turn).*

EXAMPLE . . . .

> **Leader:** Danie, let me get you to do this. I want you to turn to Lilly
> and complete the following sentence: "When Dad drinks,
> I . . ."
>
> **Danie:** (*Looks at Lilly, who is sitting next to her*) When Dad drinks,
> I feel that it is my fault.
>
> **Leader:** Now look at Amos, and start with the same phrase.
>
> **Danie:** When Dad drinks, I get scared that someone will get hurt.
> (*Begins to cry*)
>
> **Leader:** Stay with these feelings. I believe we can help you.

. . . .

    4. *Have the members give the person feedback.* If the member is
not benefitting from talking, the leader can interrupt by asking the
members to give some feedback:

Leader: Danie, I want to stop you for a second, and I am going to ask
the group for some feedback. What do you think Danie is trying to
say?

or

Leader: What do you think Danie needs to explore but is avoiding?

    5. *Have the members become the person.*

Leader: I want you to become Danie. Try with your voice and body to
be her. Start with, "I'm Danie, and here's what I am trying to say."

    This activity can be valuable in that the focus stays on Danie, but
she is not the one talking. Some members actually can benefit more by
listening to themselves being discussed than by talking. The leader could
even ask a member who is playing Danie a number of deepening questions. If a member can role-play Danie's feelings and behaviors well, this
can prove to be very enlightening to her.

    Cutting and staying with the topic.   There will be times when
the leader will want to shift the focus away from the member who is talking but stay with the topic. When the leader makes the decision to intervene in this manner, the member usually does not feel so cut off. In

the preceding example, the leader might say, "Danie, let me get other members' comments about their relationship with their parents. Can any of you relate to what Danie is saying?"

Cutting and leaving the person and the topic.   Inevitably, there will be times when the leader will need to cut off and redirect the group because it is off on a tangent or it is time to start closing the group. In such instances, the leader might say something like, "I think we need to move on. I want to shift our attention to an exercise that I think you will find interesting."

When a Member's Comments Conflict with the Group's Purpose

One of the main uses of cutting off is to ensure that the group's content fits with its purpose. Whenever a member's comments are not in line with the group's purpose or when the group is discussing a nonproductive or nonrelated topic, the leader should use the cutting-off skill to refocus the group on a more relevant issue. Too often, a member will get going on some irrelevant topic and the leader will let that speaker continue until other members join in. Cutting off is then in order.

When a Member Is Saying Something Inaccurate

In discussion, education, and task groups things can be said that are inaccurate, misleading, or simply inappropriate. For example, in an educational group about birth control, a member might say, "The pill should never be used because it has been proven to cause cancer. I have two friends now who are suffering from its side effects. Let me tell you about them." The leader would want to use cutting-off skills to correct this member's exaggerated statements. Whenever something is being said that is not accurate, do not feel that you have to wait until the person is finished before you can comment. In fact, it is best to cut off "speeches" that are not beneficial to the group as soon as you identify them as such.

Another example of this situation might be a discussion group about Carl Rogers's client-centered therapy. Dave, who is obviously anti-Rogers, comments as follows:

Dave: Rogers's therapy doesn't work. It's not possible to be that genuine in a relationship. Also, who wants to be a parrot? That's all Rogers is—he's just a parrot. I don't see how anyone would benefit from his stuff!

This member does not understand the theory, and to let him go on would be a mistake. It is necessary and appropriate to cut off this member. The leader could say something like "Dave, I think what we are trying to do here is discuss the merits of Rogers's theory. I think when all of you come to understand the theory you will realize that it is a lot more than just parroting."

In therapy and growth groups it is especially important to listen for inappropriate comments or advice, since members can say things harmful to others. For instance, a member might say to another, "I think you should divorce her immediately. Any woman who won't go to church with her husband is not a good woman." In this situation the leader needs to cut off the member for giving inappropriate advice.

A common phenomenon in many groups is the guaranteeing of someone's behavior. That is, a member will say to another, "If you do X, then your wife (son, boss, parent, and so on) will do Y." It is important that the leader not let anyone make promises about how another person will think, feel, or behave. Here are some examples of such promises:

- If you get mad a couple of times, she'll change. You just need to let her know who's boss.
- Go home and tell your mom you're sorry for what you did. She'll understand, and all will be fine.

In these examples, members are promising some behavior over which they have no control. The leader should cut off any comments similar to this. One cardinal rule for leaders to follow and one to teach members to follow is *Do not guarantee anyone's behavior other than your own.* Human behavior is highly unpredictable, and what may seem to be the most likely outcome will not always come to pass.

EXAMPLE . . . .

The group is composed of stepparents who are sharing feelings and experiences about their particular situations in the hope of discovering new ways of coping.

Jim: My stepson Jeff seems to prevent himself from getting emotionally close to me because of his loyalty to his biological father.

Edgar: (*Dogmatically*) You should spend more time with him, Jim. If you'll limit his time with his father and use it for the two of you, he'll grow to love you more. That's what I did with my stepson and it's working out okay. I guarantee you that Jeff will respect you if you take a little control over the situation. Besides, . . .

Leader: Edgar, let me stop you here to say a couple of things. First, I appreciate your attempt to help. I'm glad that it is working out well between you and your stepson. I'm not so sure that your particular method will work for Jim and Jeff. It is actually a very common and normal thing that Jeff is experiencing.

Many stepchildren experience divided loyalty between their absent parent and the new stepparent. Each of you may want to think about this issue as it applies to your children. . . .

In this example, the leader was aware that Edgar was making guarantees to Jim based on his own experience and that his advice was not appropriate.

. . . .

Extreme, value-laden comments about certain issues also need to be cut off. Members may attempt to lecture each other about such things as the evils of having an affair or an abortion. A member may want to comment at length about how everyone should be religious or about how divorce is the ultimate failure and all marriages can be saved. These types of comments usually represent one particular member's point of view; to let that member go on and on would be a mistake on the part of the leader, especially since other group members could be greatly offended.

When the Leader Wants to Shift the Focus

Many times in the group, the leader will decide that the focus needs to shift. Sometimes, a natural break occurs in the interaction, and the shift is easy. At other times, the leader will need to use cutting-off skills to accomplish the shift. When one member is talking and another appears eager to talk, the leader may feel that it would be beneficial to shift to the second member. The leader might have noticed that the member's facial expressions, body posture, and nods indicated a desire to talk but inability to do so because someone else "had the floor." In this case the leader would, at a strategic point, stop the person speaking, explain why, and draw out the person wishing to speak.

E X A M P L E . . . .

This is a growth group for beginning counselors in a master's degree program. The purpose of the group is to heighten self-awareness and discuss personal concerns that might detract from the members' ability to counsel others. The issue being discussed is love relationships. While Amy is telling a story about her sister, the leader notices that Sherry seems to want to speak.

Amy: I just don't understand. Tom and Cindy got along so well in the beginning. They were so happy together. They could talk to each other about anything. I thought it was for keeps, but after a couple of months things were not so rosy. I think they maintained the relationship for several months because they kept hoping they could regain what they once had. Let me give you an example. They were—(*The leader notices that Sherry is listening intently and nodding her head in agreement*)

Leader: Amy, let me stop you before you really get into the story, unless there is a personal note to your comments. It seems that Sherry is reacting to what you are saying and I want to give her a chance to comment. Sherry, would you like to offer some comments?

Sherry: Oh, yes. What Amy was saying about the relationship being so good at first and then changing also happened to me. My boyfriend and I ended our relationship two months ago. It just seemed that we suddenly had nothing in common anymore. I. . . .

In this example, the leader decides to cut Amy off and shift to Sherry for two reasons. First, although Amy was telling an interesting story, she appeared to have no personal investment in the topic. Therefore, it was not something about which she needed to receive help from the group. Second, Sherry appeared interested in the discussion and seemed to relate to it personally. In growth groups it is usually more beneficial to engage members in personally relevant discussions than in stories about others.

. . . .

A leader might also want to cut off a speaker when an exercise would be appropriate at that point. Many times the leader can simply wait until the action has died down, but in other situations timing is essential; that is, it would be detrimental to wait. Some exercises are meaningless if done at the wrong time—they seem out of place. Since leaders want exercises to have maximum effect on the members, they will sometimes need to stop the current action of the group in order to introduce them.

E X A M P L E . . . .

The members have been discussing their families of origin. The discussion has been going on for about ten minutes, and the members still seem to be on the surface. The leader decides that the "Family Sculpture" exercise would be a way to get members to really focus on their home environments. The members are currently discussing vacations they had with their parents when they were young.

Leader: Let me jump in here. I'd like to make this discussion about families more meaningful. An exercise that I have used before and one that is quite helpful in getting you to look at how you were affected by your early family experiences is called "Family Sculpture." This involves having you pick members of the group to represent your family as it was when you were growing up. . . .

· ·

Cutting off in order to move to a structured activity can sometimes help to deepen the focus and funnel the group from merely conversational to more insightful reflections.

Frequently, when a topic has been thoroughly covered or the focus has been held on one member too long, members will not realize that the interaction is no longer productive. The leader's task in these situations is to cut off the prolonged discussion and shift the focus.

EXAMPLE. · · · · · · · · · · · · · · · · · ·

The group has been discussing religion and its influence on their lives. The leader recognizes that the focus on the members' parents and religion has been thoroughly discussed and some members seem to be bored. A member is into a story about how her parents are now more religious than ever. She has paused to give some thought to a question asked of her. The leader takes the opportunity to cut in.

Leader: I wonder if it would be possible for you to conclude in the next moment or two. I sense that we have thoroughly covered this issue and need to move on to a fresh topic.

The leader uses cutting off to change the focus in hope of generating some energy. Group members will often become bored and apathetic if a topic is focused on for too long.

· ·

When It Is Near the End of the Session

There are two situations in which cutting off is necessary near the end of a session. When leading a group with a designated ending time, the leader will sometimes have to cut off members in order to allow time for summarizing and ending the group promptly. It is very important to have enough time to close the group, and it often becomes the leader's responsibility to get the members focused on ending. Sometimes the only way to do this is by cutting off what is going on.

The second situation is when a member brings up an emotional issue with only a short time remaining in the session. Skilled leaders will quickly cut off these members before they get too far into their stories. Obviously, this is a very difficult situation to handle, but there are times when the group simply has to end and there is not enough time for dealing with the concern.

E X A M P L E . . . .

There are approximately five minutes left in the first session of a group made up of adults who were adopted when they were very young and who are now trying to find their biological mothers. Tracy starts to talk about her fears and the problems her search has already caused.

Leader: Tracy, could I ask you to hold that until we meet next week? I don't think we have enough time now to really deal with that issue, and I think it is one that everyone can relate to. Now in the last few minutes left, I'd like us to summarize tonight and get different reactions to this first session. I think we are off to a good start.

In this example, Tracy's concern is obviously a sensitive and personal one, and the leader is wise to hold off on it until the next session. The leader also does the right thing by cutting her off quickly, before the momentum of the group shifts to the topic of fears and problems.

. . . .

When Members Are Arguing

Any time people come together to form a group there is the potential for arguments. This is especially true of groups whose purpose is to resolve conflicts, in which the issues being discussed are volatile ones, or whose members live or work together. Cutting off in such groups entails preventing the argument from continuing and getting the group back on the topic that preceded the argument, if it is appropriate. Members usually leave it to the leader to stop arguments; if left on their own, some members would spend the entire session arguing. Therefore, the leader has to intervene and come up with better ways of discussing or resolving issues. Some of the things that the leader can do are the following:

- Get some of the nonvolatile members to discuss the issue.
- Ask the volatile members to continue the discussion but tone down their remarks.

- Discuss the issue calmly herself.
- Shift the focus to a new issue.

Ordinarily, it is best to cut off arguments quickly because they are usually not productive and are often detrimental to the group; they do nothing to build cohesion and can erode trust. Arguments can also set a negative tone for the group and use up time that can be spent in a much more productive manner.

In a few situations a leader might allow an argument to continue for a short period; for example, the leader might want to observe the argument and then use the skills of immediacy and feedback to help the antagonists and perhaps the others learn about their style of interacting and arguing. The rule, however, is: *Don't let members argue unless it is productive in some way for them or the group.*

E X A M P L E . . . .

The group is composed of clients at a mental-health center. Members are discussing their different living arrangements; it is the third session.

Rita: I live in a communal-type situation with three men and four women.

Sam: (*Sits bolt upright*) I think that's disgusting!

Rita: What do you mean by that?

Sam: I mean I think that's wrong—God didn't put us on this earth to live in sin!

Rita: Who says it's a sin?

Sam: God does! In the Bible—

Leader: (*Calmly*) Hold on. Let me say something to everyone. Maybe I haven't touched enough on the subject of attacking one another. Our purpose here is not to judge whether others are right or wrong in their actions or beliefs but rather to listen to the variety of ideas expressed and learn about differences in the way people live. Human relationships require listening without judging. I hope in this group you will learn to get along with people who are different from you. Rita, you were saying. . . .

In this example, the leader recognizes that the exchange is not productive and that it requires cutting off the argument. The leader then engages in a brief minilecture on the purpose of the group, which serves both to cut off the rapidly escalating argument and to inform the members that making moral judgments about the actions of others is inappropriate. By speaking in a calm way, the leader is able to defuse the hostile tone being created.

. . . .

When Members Are Rescuing Other Members

By *rescuing* we mean that members try to smooth over the negative emotions someone else is experiencing. This usually sounds something like "It'll be okay; everything is going to work out" or "Don't cry; you can do it." Members rescue other members more often in growth/support groups and therapy groups than in other kinds of groups. Some members on occasion present a helpless, "poor me" self-portrait in which they paint themselves as victims of their environment. When this happens, other members will often want to rescue them by saying certain soothing things or by offering all kinds of advice. This kind of member behavior is usually not productive, because it indicates that the "working" member is in fact helpless and in a situation that can only improve through a miracle or the efforts of someone else. Rescuing tends to reinforce these members' belief that they can't do it themselves.

Certainly it is desirable for members to help each other, but there is a difference between helping and rescuing. Leaders often mistakenly let rescuing go on when such behavior should be cut off. A similar mistake is to allow members to hug or touch another who is crying because of a "poor me" attitude. This kind of physical support can serve to reinforce the "I'm weak" position taken by that member.

E X A M P L E . . . .

A group of recent divorcées is meeting for the purpose of support.

Alice: (*Crying*) I'm just no good to anyone. I'm not pretty and obviously not interesting. The divorce was all my fault. I'm sure no one will ever ask me out.

Terri: (*Patronizingly*) There, there, Alice. (*Patting her on the arm*) Everything will be OK. There are lots of men out there who are just waiting for someone like you to come along. There's no need to cry. I'll bet your husband—

Leader: Wait a minute, Terri. I don't think that Alice needs to be cheered up right now. (*To the entire group*) Helping someone doesn't always involve making them feel better immediately. Alice, I'm not sure if you are asking for help or just telling us your current feelings.

The leader quickly steps in to prevent Terri from rescuing Alice because Alice is not making any attempt to improve her situation but rather is wallowing in self-pity. In essence, there is no verbal agreement from Alice to engage in therapy. The leader would want to get such an agreement from her; otherwise, Alice might simply manipulate the group with her "poor me" routine.

. . . .

Hints and Cautions about Cutting Off

Timing

The first and perhaps most important hint for cutting off effectively pertains to the proper timing of the skill. The leader should *stop members quickly*, before they ramble too long, argue for an extended period, or offer unrequested and unhelpful advice. On the other hand, leaders will want to make sure they are not cutting short a legitimate and worthwhile comment; this can anger and frustrate members if practiced to an extreme, and will diminish sharing due to the anticipation of being cut off. Unfortunately, there is no way to spell out exactly when the leader should cut someone off, since each situation is different. Experience and feedback from members will probably be the leader's best teacher.

Use of Voice

A second hint concerns the leader's use of voice. Voice tone, pitch, and inflection while cutting off have a lot to do with how the leader comes across to the members. If the leader seems critical, gruff, or angry, members are likely to react in a negative way. When cutting off, the goal is not to criticize any one member but rather to stop something that is not helpful to the group or to an individual member. Leaders who feel frustration or irritation toward one or more members will more than likely communicate this through the voice unless they are careful. It is important to remember that members are usually not consciously giving the leader or other members a hard time; rather, they don't understand or have not yet learned how to be productive group members.

Clarifying

A third hint is to explain to the members why you are stopping what is happening. Explaining is a good practice because confusion and anxiety can result if someone is cut off for no apparent reason. Lacking a true knowledge of why they are being cut off, members will contrive reasons in their minds. Some may think it is because the leader does not like them, or that their opinions don't matter. Others may gather that they should not speak unless asked to do so. To prevent members from making up reasons for being cut off, the leader can offer an explanation. In many of the examples presented in the previous pages, the leader gave a brief explanation. Of course, there will be many instances in which the leader will choose not to offer an immediate explanation for cutting someone off—for example, if the leader feels it is important to move on immediately or that the reason is obvious.

Use of Eyes

A fourth hint concerns the use of the leader's eyes. The leader can let a member know that he wants the member to stop simply by avoiding eye contact with her while she is talking. The member will most likely "wrap it up" once she notices this.

Nonverbal Signals

Another hint for the leader is to signal the member with his hand that he would like the member to stop. Just a slight gesture, such as would be used by a traffic officer, is sometimes enough to cue the member to "wind down."

New Focus

The sixth and final hint is that the leader should know in what direction he will refocus the group after cutting a member off; that is, on what topic, person, or exercise he wants to focus. The leader should decide this *before* actually cutting anyone off. Sometimes the only alternative the leader can think of is a minilecture on a topic, and this may not be any better than what is happening.

One other way to conceptualize cutting off is that it is possible for the leader to cut off a member and yet stay with that member. He can do this by getting others to give the member feedback. He can ask the member to be more personal or more specific about her issue of concern. Also, the leader can cut off the member but hold the focus on the topic she was discussing; or the leader can shift to a new person or a new topic. To further illustrate the cutting-off skill and to help clarify the hints above, two examples are presented below in which a member is skillfully cut off.

EXAMPLES . . . .

Ron is a member of a group for high school dropouts. He has been rambling for several minutes about his mother and has repeated himself a couple of times about problems he is having with her.

Ron: *(In a shaky voice)* And then she said, "Why don't you get out and get a job?" I told her where to get off, because nobody talks to me like that. She started crying to make me feel sorry for her, but I wasn't going to give in for a second. She has got to stop treating me like a baby and let me make my own decisions. Heck, she always cries when she brings up that job stuff. She says you gotta get out and get a job if you're not going to go to school, and I always tell her to shut up because I hate being talked to that way.

Leader: (*Realizes that Ron is rambling and repeating himself but feels he is asking for help; also observes that members are losing interest*) Ron, let me stop you. The reason I am doing so is because I think you are trying to get some help on this issue with your mom, but you're getting lost in your words. I wonder if you could state in a sentence or two what you want help on. I do think we can be of help if you can pinpoint exactly what the issue is.

.   .   .   .

This group is composed of first-year college students in a residence hall. They are meeting as part of an outreach program of the counseling center. The purpose is to share concerns about school and other personal matters. The issue of their families has been the focus during this session. Mary begins to cry as she relates her family problems to the group. Some of the members become uncomfortable as Mary speaks, and they attempt to shift the focus away from this emotion-laden topic.

Mary: (*Sobbing*) Dad used to drink a lot. I hated it when he drank, because he called Mom and me all sorts of names. I just hated him!

Jim: (*Shifting about*) My uncle was an alcoholic, but he seems to have it under control since going to AA.

Betty: In one of my classes, I wrote a paper on alcoholism. It sure seems to affect a lot of people, and it's not always skid row bums. Have any of you studied alcoholism?

Leader: Let me stop you all here, because I don't want us to get away from Mary. Let's back up to her for a moment. Mary, if you can, tell us some more about your feelings toward your father.

Cutting off is often intermixed with other skills. The leader's response above is actually a combination of cutting off, shifting the focus, holding the focus, and drawing out (discussed later in this chapter). The need to mix techniques in your response is evident when comparing a pure cutting-off response to a mixture of cutting off and something else. Let's look at the first example, in which Ron was talking about his mother. A pure cutting-off response would have been something like, "Ron, stop" or "Ron, let me stop you" with nothing following. As you can imagine, the group's reaction would probably be silence, since the leader would have stopped the current action but provided no stimulus for further comments or discussion. Combined with another technique such as drawing out, cutting off becomes more functional. For example, the leader could also have said to Ron, "Ron, let me stop you. Try to put into a short phrase what you are attempting to say." This response is more effective because it stops the rambling and provides the stimulus for further comments.

. . . .

Practice

In this section you will have the opportunity to practice what you've learned. Five examples follow, to which you may respond in your own words. Read each one and think about what you would say and why; you may want to write out your responses. Each example is discussed after it is presented.

EXAMPLES . . . .

The group is composed of prisoners, all of whom have committed violent acts against others. The purpose of the group is to help members overcome their inability to control their anger. The members are talking about events during the past month that have triggered their anger. Don has been talking for the past 90 seconds, and as he ruminates about an event he becomes angrier and angrier. He says:

Don: And then that @!*#!* just looked at me and grinned, and I knew I couldn't do a thing about it. If he'd been out on the street I would have fixed him. The next time that @*#!* pulls that on me I'm—

Think about what you would say if you were the leader. Your goal would be to stop Don from continuing to speak, since he seems to be escalating his anger. In addition, the other group members have probably experienced the same feelings as Don and may be identifying with what he is saying. Therefore, cutting Don off and seeking other members' comments could be a mistake, since they may be just as angry and frustrated. The leader may want to cut Don off and talk for a short time until members "cool off."

Leader: Don, let me break in here if I may. (*Looks at all members*) I want to talk about something I am sensing in the group. I think many of you have short fuses like Don's; when the fuse goes there is an explosion, and that explosion gets you into trouble—namely, prison. I hope we can lengthen those fuses so that you can stay out of trouble and not hurt anyone unnecessarily. How could Don have stayed calmer in that situation?

The important thing to note in this example is that the member was getting more and more agitated and his comments were not helpful to himself or to other members. This would be a definite signal that some form of cutting off was needed.

. . . .

The group is composed of middle school students whose parents are divorced. The group, for support and therapy, encourages members to share any feelings they have about their family situation.

Sarah: I've just been hoping that Mom and Dad will get back together. Mom is seeing another guy named Dave, and I just can't stand him. He always kisses me and it just makes me sick. Sometimes when Dave is there I sit in my room and cry, wishing that my dad would come back.

Mike: (*Making crying faces at Sarah and the group*) Boo-hoo! So Sarah cries for her daddy. Isn't that too bad. I don't even want my dad to come back, and even if I did, I wouldn't cry about it.

What would you say if you were the leader? The leader would certainly want to cut Mike off, since he is making fun of another member. The leader could use the incident as a way to talk about not making fun of others in the group:

Leader: Mike, please stop and let me say something to you as well as to everyone else here. The purpose of this group is to give everyone the opportunity to share openly with each other the problems and frustrations they are having. To do so, everyone must feel that what they say will be taken seriously, and certainly, Sarah, I think what you are saying is serious. Now, what again are your feelings?

The important thing is that Mike be stopped. The sooner he is cut off, the better. Some leaders might mistakenly get angry at Mike and hold the focus on him and his behavior, thus leaving Sarah, who is in pain. The leader may at some point want to focus on Mike's inappropriate behavior, but not right at this moment.

. . . .

This is a weekend growth group composed of married couples whose goal is to discuss and eliminate problem areas in their marriages. Couples have been sharing about their hobbies and vacations. One couple, Mary and Tom, are now arguing about how they take their vacations.

Tom: Why do we have this insurmountable difference over where to go on vacations? You always demand that we see your parents.

Mary: That's because we only see my parents once a year, but we practically live with yours. Besides, all you want to do on vacation is fish or camp, and you know I hate that! You are so uncaring and unfair! Why don't you care about *me*?

Tom: Don't start that again. You always do this!

What would you do if you were leading this group? Some leaders might make the mistake of allowing the argument to continue. It is apparent that the couple has fought over this issue a number of times. There are several things the leader could say:

• Let me stop you, because I don't think you are hearing each other (*To the group*) What do some of you think is going on with Tom and Mary? (This holds the focus on Tom and Mary but gets others involved and stops the useless arguing.)

• I want you to stop, since it doesn't seem that you are getting anywhere. I want the two of you to listen to others who have probably had similar problems. Have any of you had problems like this? (The leader is second-guessing that other couples have had problems over vacations.)

• I want to ask you something. Why do the two of you get nowhere with this argument? Think about it. What is happening to each of you as you talk? (This holds the focus on them and will probably involve other members, because the focus has shifted to communication patterns.)

• I want to try something here that I think may help you see what you do to each other. I need someone to play Tom and someone to play Mary, and I want you to act out this argument. Tom, you and Mary just watch. I think you'll learn something. Who can play either Tom or Mary? (This cutting off stops the arguing and shifts to a role-play that should generate more involvement for all members. Tom and Mary should especially benefit.)

. . . .

The group is composed of high school seniors. Its purpose is to discuss various situations that young adults face once they leave high school.

Leader: (*To start the session*) What did you find out about loans and credit? Did any of you ask your parents or friends about this?

Larry: I did. I found out a lot about loans and interest and how that all works. (*Larry goes on for a couple of minutes*)

Leader: How about others of you? What did you find out about the different places to borrow money?

Larry: Oh, I found out that there were a number of places. They are—

Leader: (*Notices that there is silence when Larry finishes*) Let's talk about buying a house. From talking to some of you before we started this afternoon, I know you found out some interesting things regarding home buying. Who would like to share what they learned?

Larry: I would.

How would you respond if you were the leader? It is a good bet that Larry's constant replies are affecting the other members. Any time a leader allows a member to dominate a group, the other members usually share less and feel less involved. This is especially true when the dominant member is not saying particularly interesting things but rather seems to be talking due to anxiety or a need for attention. Some of the options available to the leader are the following:

• Larry, let me cut in and stop you in order to give other members a chance to speak. Others of you, what reactions do you have?

• Larry, I want you to hold off on your comments until others have shared.

• Larry, I notice that you are always ready to speak first. I'm wondering if that has any significance and I'm also wondering if you'd like some feedback from the group on how they feel about your always commenting. (This shifts the focus to Larry, and the leader would only want to do this if he or she thought Larry would benefit from feedback. Often the leader can tell by the members' nonverbal reactions how they are feeling about the "talker.")

• • • • • • • • • • • • • • • • • • • •

The members of this group are all about to be married. The purpose is to help couples communicate better.

Leader: Jenny, what about you? Do you have any fears about getting married and living with Gary?

Jenny: Well, I—

Gary: Jenny thinks we're going to have a tremendous marriage. She believes that if any two people are well matched, we are.

Leader: Is that right, Jenny?

Jenny: Well, uh—

Gary: Yes, and another thing that we're excited about is that we don't have the same problems as our married friends.

How would you handle this situation if you were the leader? A cardinal rule to follow when leading groups is to not let members speak for other members because it prevents the "spoken-for" member from fully learning from and experiencing the group; it also discounts that person's ability to think and speak. The leader could simply stop Gary or could clarify what he was doing by saying:

Leader: Gary, let me stop you. I don't know if you realize it or not, but you often speak for Jenny. Jenny, is this frustrating to you?

Note that the leader's response focuses on Gary's and Jenny's interaction pattern and not on the question that was asked about fears of marriage. The leader must decide whether to focus on the question or the pattern. If she wants to focus on the original question, she could say something like the following:

Leader: Gary, I want to point something out to you that I'd like you to think about. Just now I asked Jenny a question and you answered for her. From observing Jenny, my hunch is that she probably doesn't like that. (*Jenny nods*) Think about it. Jenny, I would like to hear your answer to that question.

. . . .

DRAWING OUT

Drawing out is the name we have given to the skill of eliciting group members' comments. Throughout this section, we will discuss various reasons for drawing members out and how to accomplish this effectively.

Reasons for Drawing Members Out

One of the main reasons for using the drawing-out skill is to get greater involvement from the group members. Group interaction is usually beneficial in discussion, support, and task groups, whose primary goal is hearing different ideas from the members. The verbal give-and-take and the sharing of ideas and feelings are the fuel that make the group go.

Another major reason for drawing out is to help members who have a difficult time sharing in a group. In most groups, there is usually a member who has trouble talking in front of others. By drawing out those members, you benefit both the member and the group. The member benefits by talking and gaining some sense of confidence about speaking up, and the members benefit by hearing other ideas.

A third reason for drawing out is to probe for greater depth. Some members will share but not really explore a problem in depth; that is, they stay on the surface. Getting a member to go deeper is a form of drawing out that is very helpful to members in support, growth, and therapy groups. People usually gain more when they explore "uncharted waters."

E X A M P L E . . . .

Carlos has been talking for approximately five minutes about his problems in school. He has mentioned that he cannot concentrate and that he daydreams and worries a lot about the future.

Carlos: (*In a worried, storytelling voice*) . . . and some days I just sit and stare. It is important to me since I am the first to go to college. My family is counting on me. Maybe I am not college material. I think—

Leader: Carlos, I'd like you to take a few seconds and think about what you are saying. There is more to it than you are telling us, but I'm not sure what it is. I think you will help yourself out by sharing those inner thoughts and feelings.

Carlos: Well, I don't know, uh, well, you see my mom has been having a lot of trouble with my dad since I left home and I worry about her and my sister. I sometimes feel that I should be at home.

. . . .

Other reasons for drawing out are to shift the focus, to hold the focus, and to cut off some other member. That is, the leader may decide that the focus needs to shift because she knows that some members have an interest in a certain topic. She can bring up the topic and then draw out members on the new topic, thus shifting the focus. On the other hand, the leader may want to hold the focus on a topic that a member has just brought up. She can do this by simply drawing out the same member, which would hold the focus on that topic. In other cases, the leader may feel that a certain member needs to be cut off; when another member makes a brief comment, the leader can draw that member out, thus cutting off the first member.

E X A M P L E . . . .

Shannon is a member who loves to tell stories about her past. The leader has talked to her about this, but Shannon has just begun another story. Members listen because the stories are entertaining, but they take up too much time and are not relevant to the purpose of the group. Shannon has been talking for a minute or so when a member comments. The leader draws out the other members as a way of cutting off Shannon.

Bonni: Shannon, that's similar to how my parents were. They were always on the go.

Leader: Bonni, when you say they were on the go, what do you mean, and more importantly, how do you think that affected you?

Bonni: I think it affected me in many ways. I. . . .

The leader may now choose whether to focus on Bonni or shift to another topic or person.

. . . .

Causes of Silence

Most leaders consider using drawing-out skills when members are silent. Understanding the reasons for silence is necessary, because drawing out is not warranted for all types of silence. Knowing the reasons a member is silent will help the leader decide if drawing out is needed and, if it is, the kind of drawing out that would be most effective. The following is a list of reasons why members are silent. Members may be any one or more of these:

- Afraid
- Thinking or processing
- Quiet by nature
- Not mentally present
- Not prepared
- Confused
- Bored
- Not committed to the group
- Lacking in trust
- Intimidated by a dominant member or leader

Fear

Even when members desperately want to speak, they sometimes do not because they are afraid of what other members might think. They conjure up images of people laughing at them, turning away in disgust, or thinking "What a stupid fool." Drawing out these individuals is very important and at the same time very difficult. It is important because such members need to realize they are, in fact, inventing how the group will respond. It is difficult because the members may feel "picked on" unless the leader is careful.

EXAMPLE . . . .

In this example, the leader of an ongoing therapy group knows why Frank is in the group (from the intake interview) and knows that he is afraid to speak.

Leader: Frank, you have not shared why you are here. My hunch is that you are afraid of what others are going to think of you. All I can say is that we are not here to judge you or anyone else; rather, we are here to help. Would all of you agree? (*Members nod*) Also, Frank, the way you are going to help yourself is by talking about it.

Frank: It's hard to face anyone. I don't know why I did it.

Leader: I know you don't, and I hope that by sharing here and in individual counseling you will come to understand yourself better.

Frank: Well, I'll try. I know that all of you will think this is horrible, but I exposed myself to these teenage girls last month.

Leader: (*After glancing at the members' faces and seeing that they are concerned for Frank*) Frank, if you will look up you will see that no one here is thinking you are the scum of the earth like you seem to think.

In this example the leader felt confident about how the members would react because he had been meeting with the group for a number of weeks. Even in a situation like this one, however, the leader cannot absolutely guarantee how the members will react and should be prepared for a negative reaction. If this leader felt Frank could not handle negative feedback he would have wanted to avoid drawing him out—or at least have been fully prepared to deal with the various comments himself.

. . . .

Thinking or Processing

A second reason for silence is that members are thinking about or processing the group interaction. This occurs most frequently immediately following the use of an exercise, a dyad, a round, or some intense work on the part of a member. Usually the leader can, by scanning the room, pick up on the facial expressions of members who seem to be really thinking or experiencing something. This kind of silence is productive, in that the members need time to reflect and think. However, such silences can become prolonged and sometimes a member who is ready to speak is a little hesitant to do so. Usually the leader can sense when members are on the verge of speaking and can often eilcit their comments through a simple head nod or hand gesture. The leader also has a number of possible drawing-out statements that could be used:

- Go ahead.
- It looks as though you are thinking. Would you like to share your thoughts?

- You seem to be reacting to something. Is there anything you would like to share?

- It seems that you were relating to our discussion on _____ .

Naturally Quiet Members

A third reason for silence is that some members are simply quiet people. They grew up listening more than speaking and are not in the habit of saying much even to family and friends. It is important for the leader to assess this and not attempt drawing out when that member is uncomfortable, which may cause the member to withdraw further into silence. However, it is important to realize that, if it is done with caution and forethought, drawing out may help this type of member say more in the group.

EXAMPLE . . . .

In this example the leader decides to try to draw out Lucinda, who has contributed very little during the first three sessions of an educational group on improving communications.

Leader: I'd like to get a number of you to share your reactions to the model, and then we will practice some. Speaking up does seem to be difficult, and knowing these different categories can be helpful. (*In a gentle, caring voice*) Lucinda, I realize that you are a rather quiet person. Did the model give you any additional understanding of yourself?

Lucinda: It is true that I am rather quiet. I am the quietest in my family. It was interesting to hear about a model that allowed for people to be quiet. I do think I will say things when I think I have something to say. In this group I have been a little quieter than usual, but I really have not wanted to say more. I. . . .

. . . .

Mental "Absence"

Some members are not always mentally present. Their thoughts are on things outside the group, such as their term paper, financial worries, or children. Allowing these members a couple of minutes to talk about what is on their minds can help them get focused on the group.

EXAMPLE . . . .

The leader has noticed that Phil has been silent for the first 20 minutes of the group. She decides to draw him out.

Leader: Phil, you have been quiet. Is there something on your mind?

Phil: Well, yes, I guess I am not with it today. My father is at the doctor's right now because he has a spot on his lung, and they are supposed to tell him what it is.

Leader: Even though this is not really in line with our purpose, if you would like to take five minutes or so to talk about that, we could. Obviously it is a major concern.

Phil: But this group is about career planning and job interviewing.

Leader: I realize that, and I think we can spare five minutes. Also, if we allow you some time, then you may be able to focus a little more on what we are talking about here.

. . . .

Lack of Preparation

In certain groups, members may simply not be prepared. In discussion, education, and task groups in particular, there are often out-of-group assignments to complete before the next session. A member who has not completed the assignment will probably not be as involved. Drawing out these members in an effort to combat their silence will be largely unsuccessful. What is needed instead is a way to motivate the members to do the assigned work.

Confusion

Members may also be silent because they are confused. Rather than speaking up or asking for clarification when they are unsure about what is going on in the group, some members will remain silent. It is good for the leader to be aware of this kind of silence, because when members are confused they often withdraw or get annoyed with the leader. If the leader thinks the members are being silent for this reason, the following might be an appropriate comment:

Leader: I have noticed that some of you have been quieter than usual. I was wondering—is it because you might be confused, since things have kind of jumped around?

Boredom

Another reason for silence is that the members are bored. Boredom results when the focus is not interesting or when the focus has been held for too long on one person or topic.

Lack of Commitment to the Group

Members are often silent if they don't want to be in the group and have no commitment to what is happening. This lack of commitment is common in nonvolunteer groups, such as groups for drunk drivers, prisoners, or youth in group homes.

Lack of Trust

Another reason for silence is that members don't trust the leader or some of the other members in the group. That is, the tone of the group does not feel right, so the member or members are relatively silent.

Intimidation by a Dominant Member or Leader

A final reason for members' silence is that the leader or one of the members tends to dominate, causing others to sit back and listen rather than contribute. Also, in situations in which one person dominates, members may have found that when they have tried to speak they were interrupted by the dominating person.

In summary, there are many reasons for silence on the part of one or more members. The skill of drawing out can be effective in getting these members to respond and comment when they fall into the first three categories of our list on "Causes of Silence." On the other hand, drawing out may not be the skill of choice for involving members when they belong to the other categories. In those situations the leader may want to try some energizers or exercises; initiate discussion about the purpose, trust, or commitment; or possibly get either verbal or written feedback about the group to use in revamping it.

Of course, there will be many instances in which one or more members are silent, and the leader has no idea why. In these cases, the leader might choose to discover the reason by asking directly, by putting himself in a dyad with the silent member and then asking, or by waiting until the break or the end of the session to ask.

How to Draw Out Members

Skillfully drawing out members is a real art. The skilled leader is able to get a member to talk, share, or express herself without feeling forced or pressured. The challenge is to be able to invite members to share but at the same time give them a number of ways to decline. The idea is to give the member *permission* to speak, possibly even gently encouraging her to do so, without alienating her. Beginning leaders often make the mistake of putting people on the spot when they are trying to get them to speak. For example, such a leader might say, "Marvin, what do you think?" or "Cheryl, you have been quiet—why don't you share your ideas?" In certain situations this type of probe would be totally acceptable, but if Marvin and Cheryl were not ready to speak, they would certainly feel put on the spot.

The art of drawing out is evident when one is able to allow "outs" for the members while getting most of them to join in and share. One way to provide an out is to call on two or three members instead of just one. Then the leader may use her eyes to see if one of those members seems willing to speak. Focusing one's eyes for too long on a member can make him feel as though he were under a spotlight, so the leader will not want to gaze at just one member for any length of time. By looking at the member for a brief moment, the leader can let her eyes invite the member to speak. By shifting her eyes, the leader gives the member an out and relieves him of any pressure beyond that caused by having his name mentioned. (This slight pressure would be intentional, since the leader would be trying to draw the member out.)

Two other components of drawing out are the leader's voice and attitude. At no time should the leader use a tone of voice that could be interpreted as condescending. The leader should never ridicule or embarrass a member for not being an active participant but rather should try to understand that member and then, if it seems appropriate, try to draw him out.

Two examples follow. The first one illustrates how *not* to draw out; the leader puts a member on the spot and does not give her an easy way out. The second example illustrates a more effective way to use the skill.

E X A M P L E S . . . .

The group is composed of high school seniors who are about to graduate. They have been discussing career objectives. It is near the end of the session, and one of the members, Jackie, has not spoken.

Leader: (*In a demanding tone*) Jackie, why haven't you said anything? Would you like to comment on something or tell us about your career goals? (*The leader maintains eye contact with Jackie. All members of the group have their eyes on her*)

. . . .

This is the same group and situation as in the preceding example.

Leader: (*Tentatively*) Jackie, I've noticed that you have been silent this session. I am not sure if you would like to comment or not. Certainly we'd like to hear from you if you feel comfortable. (*Shifts his eyes to scan the group*) Who would like to comment on anything that they are thinking about? (*The leader watches to see whether Jackie seems to want to talk*)

In the first example, the leader comes on too strong. Also, the leader puts Jackie on the spot by maintaining eye contact and directing the group's attention to her. If Jackie is quiet because of discomfort, the leader's behavior can only increase that discomfort. Another error lies in not giving Jackie a choice whether or not to participate.

The second example is quite different: in it the leader is tentative in his approach and does not focus the group on Jackie. In fact, the leader simply acknowledges that Jackie has not spoken, invites her to do so if she wishes, and then moves on. Because of this, Jackie feels no unnecessary pressure to speak.

. . . .

Another component of drawing out that we have alluded to in the preceding examples is the use of the leader's eyes. It is often possible to elicit comments from members simply by establishing eye contact with them and holding that contact for a few seconds. The leader's eyes are especially useful in drawing out members who are waiting to talk. By acknowledging people with the eyes and possibly a slight nod, the leader can often get them to comment. Or, if someone else is talking, the leader can cue others with the eyes and a slight nod that they will be next to speak.

Although the leader's eyes can be very helpful in drawing out members, he has to be careful how he uses them. One way to draw out a member while at the same time giving her an out is by maintaining a lot of eye contact with that member while speaking to the entire group.

EXAMPLE . . . .

Leader: (*Looking mainly at Carol*) Is there anyone else who wants to comment on his or her relationship? (*Scans the group, then looks again to Carol. If Carol does not seem to be ready to respond, the leader shifts his eyes to other group members*)

If approached skillfully, Carol would feel gentle pressure to speak, but the leader's broad request for comments allows Carol to refrain if she chooses. The leader has to believe in Carol's right not to speak. That is, if the leader is really trying to force Carol to talk, staring at her will cause her to feel singled out, and she will not hear the leader's words but rather the intent, which would sound to her like "Carol, speak!"

. . . .

The Direct Method

Obviously, the most direct method of drawing out members is simply to ask them if they would like to comment or if they have any reactions to what is taking place.

E X A M P L E S . . . .

The group is composed of high school teachers who are discussing the ineffectiveness of current guidelines for handling behavior problems in the classroom. Ron, who is usually very verbal, has not spoken.

Leader: Ron, we've discussed many new procedures, and several ideas have been offered. Is there anything that you would like to offer at this time?

Ron: Well, yes. I have one idea that I think could work. It deals with. . . .

. . . .

The group is composed of the officers of the junior and senior classes, who are planning the spring prom. Donna, the junior class vice president, has been nodding in agreement with some of the decisions being made.

Leader: Donna, you seem to have been reacting positively to some of the decisions today. Would you like to comment?

Donna: I like the ideas! I do have one suggestion. I think we. . . .

. . . .

The group is composed of members who have AIDS. One member has died recently, and John, his close friend, has been very quiet.

Leader: (*Very calmly and supportively*) John, you have been very quiet this session. I can only guess that it may have to do with Ted's death. Is there any way we can help?

John: Well, yeah, I really do think about Ted a lot—especially on group night. I. . . .

. . . .

Indirect Methods

There are also several indirect ways of drawing members out, which include using dyads, rounds, and written exercises.

Dyads.   Dyads, as we have seen, have many uses; one use can be to draw out members. When members are paired and given directions to discuss something of interest, the inevitable result is that the two individuals will talk to each other. The energy generated in the pairs is often sufficient to stimulate comments in the large group from members who might otherwise be silent. When the dyad is completed and the members are back in the group, the leader may use any of the following responses to draw out members:

- Who would like to comment on what you discussed?

- What are your reactions to discussing _____ ?

- What did you learn by discussing _____
  with your partner?
- Please comment on any thoughts or feelings you may be having.
- Joe, what did the two of you discuss?
- Jane, what did you learn from doing the dyad?

These questions are usually nonthreatening because the members are warmed up as a result of the dyads. Also, the members will usually have something to say, since they were just discussing the issue.

Another way the dyad can be used to draw out a member is for the leader to pair herself with the member she wants to draw out. By talking and sharing with this member, the leader can often encourage him to share in the larger group, or, at the least, the leader can find out why the member has been silent. It is, by the way, acceptable to ask a member why he or she does not talk much. However, it is usually best to do so privately.

Rounds.   Rounds are another very useful technique for getting silent members to say something, because in a round the leader is asking everyone to comment without singling out any one member. If, when doing a round, the leader comes to someone who seems very hesitant or anxious, she can skip that person for the moment; that is, the leader wants to be careful not to spotlight the member.

Besides being helpful in getting a shy member to briefly participate, the round can be used as a way to try to focus on a member whom the leader feels needs to be drawn out. At the end of the round, the leader can ask the group if anyone has questions about what has been said, hoping that someone will ask the quiet member a question. If not, the leader can ask a couple of members questions about their responses and then do the same with the shy member. By not immediately focusing on the silent member, the leader prevents the member from feeling singled out.

Another way to draw out a member through a round is to end the round on that person; that is, the leader can start the round with the member sitting next to the person with whom he wants to end. In this way, the leader can more easily ask the member questions because she was the last to comment in the round, the focus must shift from the round now that it is complete.

E X A M P L E . . . .

The group is a support/therapy group composed of women who are single parents. All group members have been actively involved in the discussion except Beth. Interest in the current topic is beginning to wane, so the leader decides to shift the focus to a new topic that may add energy and get Beth involved.

Leader: OK, if we're finished with this issue, I'd like to shift the focus. In a word or a phrase, what is the hardest thing about being a single parent? Think about that for a moment; then I'm going to get everyone to comment. (*After about 20 seconds*) Jamie, in a word or a short phrase, what is toughest for you? (*Jamie is seated next to Beth*)

Jamie: It's finding time for myself.

Sally: (*Seated next to Jamie*) Being both parents!

Jane: Money—making ends meet.

Molly: Dating and not feeling guilty.

Beth: Not feeling appreciated by anyone.

Leader: What exactly do you mean by not being appreciated?

Beth: My teenage daughter doesn't appreciate any of my sacrifices or efforts. She blames me for the divorce.

Leader: I believe others here struggle with that. Could you say a little more about your feelings and your daughter's feelings?

Beth: Well, my daughter. . . .

In this example, the leader chooses to focus directly on Beth and uses the method of having the round end on her. The leader might also have chosen to let the group ask questions about the various comments in the hope that someone would ask Beth a question. Or the leader could have asked a few other members about their word or phrase and then asked Beth about hers, with the intention of holding the focus on Beth if she seemed comfortable.

. . . .

Written exercises. Another method of drawing out members is by having them complete a writing task. Drawing out in this manner is indirect and nonthreatening because the leader merely asks members what they wrote—that is, the leader asks the members to report their answers. Writing tasks can be such activities as making lists or completing sentences.

Sentence completions can consist of anything you wish, depending on the purpose of the group. When using a sentence completion, the leader has a number of options. After members have completed the sentences (usually no more than five), the leader can ask members to share their answers on a particular sentence. This type of invitation to share is usually effective in getting members involved. Or the leader can start with the first question and call on different members to give their answers. With the answers in front of them, members usually do not mind being asked to share their responses. Also, when the leader calls on members, it does not seem like the spotlight is on them, but simply that the leader wants them to share their written answers.

EXAMPLE . . . .

The group is an educational group on crisis intervention for volunteers at the mental-health center. The first week dealt with drug overdoses. This week the topic is suicide. The six members are still somewhat hesitant to speak. The leader feels that more participation is needed, so he says the following:

Leader: I want you to respond to the three items on this sheet I'm handing out. They are: (1) List three questions you have regarding suicide, (2) List two or three fears you have about dealing with suicide, and (3) What are your beliefs about why people want to kill themselves?

When the members are finished, the leader has two options: he can ask them to read aloud their answers to the first question, or he can start with the second or third question to get some involvement and sharing within the group. The point is that by having the members write down some things, the leader gains a number of ways to draw them out.

. . . .

Additional Hints for Drawing Out

First, if possible, draw out *all* of the members during the early stage of the group—ideally during the first session. Getting members to talk early in the life of the group can ease some of their anxiety, much the same as a tennis player in a tournament needs that first volley in order to relax. The longer a shy or silent person waits to make his first verbal contribution, the harder it will be. In addition, involving members during the first session reduces tension in another way—if a member remains quiet for an extended period, the other members usually begin to wonder why. Because the quiet member offers no explanation for his silence, others formulate reasons in their minds. They sometimes imagine that the quiet member doesn't like the group or that he feels superior. By drawing out all members, the leader can often prevent members from making up what others are thinking and feeling.

A second hint is to assess how much a particular individual needs to talk. Sometimes leaders mistakenly believe that it is important for all members to speak up equally. Some members find it comfortable and beneficial to participate verbally at only a minimal level, yet they learn a great deal. The rule is *Don't draw out unless it seems needed.*

A third hint involves the atmosphere of the group. Before drawing out a reluctant or scared member, think about the kind of response she will get from other members. If the tone of the group is such that the leader feels a negative response is possible, he may not want to draw out the member.

Another hint concerns what to do with uncommitted members. Drawing these members out is one option; however, it is usually not the best option. Very often when drawn out, uncommitted members will resist the efforts of the leader and the other members.

One final hint: if the group has one or two members who do not seem focused at the beginning of the session, the leader may choose to run the group as planned; that is, she may choose *not* to draw them out. Frequently, the interaction and comments of the other members will help get those members "aboard," which means that no drawing out is necessary.

Practice

As in the previous section on cutting off, you now have an opportunity to practice. Think of various drawing-out responses to the following three examples. You may want to write down your responses and then compare them to ours, which follow each example.

E X A M P L E S .   .   .   .

The group is composed of seven women who are patients in the mental-health unit of a community hospital. The group meets daily and is open to all the women in the unit. All the members have been there for at least a week except for Jane, who has been in the hospital only three days. Jane has only commented when asked, and each time she has said very little. She is in the hospital because she attempted suicide. How would you try to draw her out if you were the leader?

There are several ways to draw Jane out. The leader could focus on Jane by simply asking her if she would like to share her story.

Leader: Jane, you have not said too much yet in the group. I think you would probably find it helpful to share some of your thoughts, feelings, and reactions to being here in the hospital. I do think we can be of help to you if you will just open up to us.

In this method, the leader asks Jane directly if she wants to share. It is important to note that the leader keeps commenting after he initially urges Jane to talk. These additional comments let him observe Jane's reaction; if it seems too intense, the leader may take Jane off the spot by saying something like, "Well, Jane, do think about sharing. Right now it seems like that would be too uncomfortable." A second way to draw Jane out would be to use a round that ends on her. The leader could ask the members to comment in a word or phrase on how they feel they are progressing.

Mary: I'm doing better. My family was here yesterday.
Dot: I understand why I am so depressed. The group and talking to the staff has really helped.
Jane: I am doing OK.
Leader: What do you mean when you say you are doing OK?
Jane: Things don't seem as bad as they did.
Leader: Maybe you can tell us a little about how it was.
Jane: I think I would like to. The reason I am here is because. . . .

Still another way the leader might get Jane to participate would be to focus on the topic of suicide, since Jane has attempted suicide.

Leader: A number of you have mentioned that you were depressed or lonely. I'd like us to talk about how you have chosen to handle those feelings. I know for some of you suicide may have been considered or even attempted.
Mary: I have never thought of suicide, but I sometimes feel that life really stinks. I didn't know how to deal with my feelings, but things are getting better.
Leader: Jane, what about you? I know a little about your history, although I do not know many of the details.
Jane: Well, uh, I tried suicide because I have been so lonely since my husband left me. The feelings are. . . .

·   ·   ·   ·   ·   ·   ·   ·   ·   ·   ·   ·   ·   ·   ·   ·   ·

The group is composed of six ministers who are on a weekend retreat for the purpose of discussing the stresses and strains of being a minister. During a discussion about the effects that being a minister has on families, both Mike and Jake have been exceptionally quiet. How would you, as the leader, try to draw these people out?

In this situation, the leader might guess that the ministers who are quiet are having problems at home. He will need to decide whether to draw both out at the same time or just one of them. To draw both out, the leader could say something like this to Mike: "I can't help but notice that both you and Jake have been quiet since we started the discussion about families. Would either of you like to comment?"

If the leader wanted to draw out only one of them, he could address that person directly: "Jake, you seem to be thinking about what we are saying. My guess is you are thinking about your family situation." The leader would choose to draw out only one member if it appeared that one were in greater need or if the other did not seem ready to share. By focusing on the one member, the leader could later draw out the other when he seemed more warmed up to sharing.

The leader could also use an exercise that would get at the ministers' feelings about their families. The leader could say, "On a 1-to-10 scale, with 10 being very stressful and 1 being not stressful, how would each of you rate the stress that the ministry has caused your family?" After members did this exercise, the leader could ask the quiet ones about their responses.

.   .   .   .

The group is composed of five college women who are discussing values as part of Mental Health Week. The discussion is about premarital sex. Helen has been quiet the entire session. Carolyn has shared with the group that she is not a virgin and now has her head down as April talks about how she plans to save herself for her husband because it is God's way. Susan and Janice have shared some of their thoughts but have not commented personally on their feelings about premarital sex. (How would you continue the discussion if you were the leader?)

The leader probably would want to stop April from talking, since other members seem to be reacting to what she is saying. The leader would then need to decide whether or not to draw out Carolyn, who is obviously feeling bad. If the leader decides to do so, she could say something like this:

Leader: Carolyn, it is important for you to realize that what April is saying is her opinion. Other members feel differently. When she was talking I could not help but notice your reaction. What were you thinking or feeling?

The leader could also choose to draw out Janice and Susan, since their opinions might differ from April's. Drawing them out first could make it easier to later draw out Helen and Carolyn. If the leader sensed that Carolyn was feeling quite bad, she would probably shift the focus to Carolyn.

If the leader felt that the other members differed with April, she could use a brief exercise to elicit comments from others. This would also serve as a way to cut off April. The leader could say, "I want each of you to complete this sentence: 'For me, being a virgin is _____.' "
This exercise would enable the leader to hear from Helen, Janice, Susan, and Carolyn and would make it easier to draw out those members since the leader can simply ask them about their written responses.

.   .   .   .

CONCLUDING COMMENTS

Drawing out and cutting off are absolutely essential skills. Knowing how and when to draw out and cut off members improves the quality of the group because the leader is able to get more involvement from the members. In the first part of this chapter we discussed the situations calling for cutting off as well as how to cut members off. In the latter half of the chapter we enumerated why members are silent and when and how to draw them out. We suggest you review this chapter periodically for various guidelines and hints.

Rounds and Dyads

ROUNDS

The round is an acitvity in which every member is asked to respond to some stimulus posed by the leader. The value of rounds cannot be overemphasized—no skill, technique, or exercise mentioned in this book is more valuable than the use of rounds. In task, education, and discussion groups rounds are extremely helpful in gathering information and involving members. In support and therapy groups, rounds can serve a variety of therapeutic functions. This section is designed to help you better understand the kinds and uses of rounds.

Kinds of Rounds

Basically, there are three kinds of rounds with which the group leader should be familiar. These are (1) the designated-word or designated-number round, (2) the word-or-phrase round, and (3) the comment round.

Designated-Word or Designated-Number Rounds

These kinds of rounds can be done quickly, since the members respond with either a single designated word or a number on a scale, usually from 1 to 10. By designated word we mean that the leader asks the members to use one, two, or three possible choices when responding to a question or issue, such as "yes" or "no" or perhaps "very helpful," "helpful," or "not helpful."

EXAMPLES . . . .

Leader: I want you to think about the film you just saw and give your reaction using one of three descriptions: "very valuable,"

"valuable," or "not valuable." (*The leader gives members a moment to decide, then goes around the group, hearing from everyone*)

In this way the leader knows how each person reacted and thus can plan the discussion accordingly.

. . . .

Leader: Who has something they would like to talk about tonight? We'll do a simple yes-or-no round. If you have something you'd like to discuss, just say "yes"; if not, say "no."

In this round, the leader is trying to assess who wants to talk. This kind of round is an especially useful one in therapy groups, since the leader has no way of knowing which and how many members have concerns they want to bring up. It is also helpful in discussion and support groups in determining where the "energy" is.

. . . .

Another designated-word round is "here/getting here/not here." This round is usually done at the beginning of a session as a way of assessing if the members' attention is on the group or if it is focused on something else. This round serves two purposes: it helps the leader know who is ready to begin, and it serves as a signal to the members to turn their attention to the group. The following example of a weight-loss group illustrates this round.

E X A M P L E . . . .

Leader: Let's start with a round of "here/getting here/not here"— that is, are you focused on what we are trying to do and what you can contribute and learn from the group, or are your thoughts somewhere else? If you are focused on the group, say "here"; if you are somewhere else, say "not here." And don't be afraid to say "not here." If you feel you are getting here, you can say that.

Rudy: Here.
Julie: Here.
Alice: Getting here.
Merv: Not here.
Carol: Here.
Kelly: Here.
Mel: Not here.

Leader: Is there anything we can do to get you more here?

Merv: I'm getting here—I've got a job interview at 4:00 today, and I am nervous.

Mel: I'm tired. Also, I didn't eat lunch. I'll get here.

Leader: OK, then we'll begin. Merv, would you want to take five minutes to discuss your job interview before we get into the topics for today, which are what to do when you slip from your diet and how to handle holiday feasts?

In this situation, the leader chooses to invite Merv to talk about his interview even though it is not related to the purpose of the group in order to help him reduce his anxiety enough to refocus on the topic of the day.

. . . .

The here/not here round allows the leader to determine which members are ready and gives the leader the option of drawing out those who answered "not here." There will also be times when a member will report a concern about something that is related to the group topic; then the leader can begin the group with that member's concern or issue.

1-to-10 Rounds

The 1-to-10 round can serve many purposes. For example, it can encourage members to think more specifically about the topic. A 1-to-10 round usually generates interest because members are curious about how their rating compares to that of other members. The round can also serve as a quick way for the leader to gather information that he can use. Here are some examples.

- On a 1-to-10 scale, how comfortable are you being in the group?—10 is very comfortable.
- On a 1-to-10 scale, with 10 being "very much," how much did you like the article you read for this week?
- On a 1-to-10 scale, with 10 being "very valuable," how would you rate tonight's group?
- On a 1-to-10 scale, with 10 being a lot, how would you rate the amount of fighting, arguing, and tension in your early home environment?

The value of the 1-to-10 scale (or a 1-to-3 or a 1-to-100 scale) is that you can gather information quickly from everyone. More will be said in a later section on the different ways to use the information obtained from such a round.

Word-or-Phrase Rounds

Another kind of round a leader can use is the word-or-phrase round. In this kind of round the members are asked to respond with only a word or a short phrase because the leader wants members to keep their comments brief. Here are some examples of word-or-phrase rounds; try to imagine these examples in context. You may find it helpful to think of situations in which you might use these rounds or rounds similar to these.

- In a word or phrase, how are you feeling about being in this group?
- In a word or phrase, how would you describe your feelings about school?
- In a word or phrase, how would you describe our task as you see it?
- How often would you like to make love in a week—think of the number and we'll do a round.
- I'd like to hear from everyone, so I want you to think of a word or phrase that describes your reaction to the proposal.
- How would you describe your current exercise habits?—answer in a word or phrase. You may say "none" or "daily" or "don't like to exercise" or whatever.

As you can see, there are an infinite number of words or phrases that a leader can use, and as you start to use rounds you will learn how valuable they really are for quickly gathering information and focusing the members. By using a word-or-phrase round, the skilled leader identifies a number of possible directions in which to lead the group.

Comment Rounds

In this kind of round, the leader asks an open-ended question and gives the members the option to comment. The comment round is used when the leader wants members to say more than just a few words, either because the leader thinks they will benefit from hearing comments or because the question does not lend itself to a word-or-phrase answer. The examples below are taken from different types of groups and should give you some idea of this kind of round.

- Let's do a round of progress reports—how has the week been? What have you tried?
- I'd like to get a brief reaction from each of you regarding how you think we should approach the task.
- What stood out to you about the group today? We'll do a round and hear from everyone.

- When you think of remarriage, what feelings or thoughts do you have? Take a moment and think about this, and then we'll do a round.
- When you think of parenting, what is hardest for you?

From these examples the difference between this round and the other two should be evident. In the designated-word round and the word-or-phrase round, the leader controlled the content and length much more than in the comment round. In comment rounds, members may talk for two or three minutes. As each member comments, other members are able to gather their thoughts so that they too can comment effectively. All three types of rounds, however, share the benefit of providing useful content with which the leader can work.

Uses of Rounds

The skilled leader uses rounds in many different ways. They help the leader gather information, thoughts, and feelings from each member. To give you some idea of the number of uses of rounds, we have listed them below. The leader uses rounds to do the following:

1. Get members focused
2. Deepen the intensity
3. Shift the focus to involve all members
4. Gather information and locate energy
5. Build comfort, trust, and cohesion
6. Process exercises
7. Draw out quiet members
8. Summarize

Getting Members Focused

The round gets members to focus on an issue or topic in two ways: first, they have to think of what they are going to say, and second, they listen to others comment on the subject at hand. Any of the three kinds of rounds can be used to focus the group. If members are jumping from topic to topic, the leader can pick one topic to focus on and can ask each member to comment on that topic. The leader can also focus the group by using a 1-to-10 scale or a word-or-phrase round.

E X A M P L E S . . . .

The group is made up of first-year college students who are having difficulty adjusting to college. To get the group focused, the leader might say one of the following:

Leader: On a 1-to-10 scale, with 10 being very well, how well did the week go for you?

or

Leader: In a word or phrase, how would you describe your week?

This kind of round gets members focused quickly at the beginning of the session on the purpose of the group, adjusting to college.

.   .   .   .

The group is a task group in a human-resources agency, discussing program improvements. The members are having difficulty focusing on one particular issue. The leader might say this:

Leader: I want us to talk just about the staffing of the program. Let's leave the location, the hours, and the publicity until later. Think of how many staff members we'll need. In a minute we'll go around and I'll get each of you to state that number. Then we'll discuss your rationale and so forth.

Deepening the Intensity of the Experience

In support, growth, and therapy groups, rounds can be used to get members to delve deeper into their thoughts and feelings. For instance, if the topic being discussed deals with personal worth, and the members are sharing their beliefs about how they "get" their worth, the leader might suggest the following word-or-phrase round:

Leader: I want each of you to think for a minute—what do you believe affects your feelings of personal worth the most? Now really think about this—think of a person or situation in your daily life that would describe this. It may be "Mom," "work," "my weight," or something else. What would it be? We'll go around and get each of you to comment.

Such a round encourages most members to think more deeply about the issues. They know they are going to share their comments out loud and they want to find a term that reflects their feelings accurately. Also, providing time for members to think about the issue encourages them to focus more intently on it.

A comment round can also be used to deepen the focus. For example, the leader could say to members of a group for widows:

Leader: Now that we have shared how each of you came to be a widow, let's go a step further and talk about your feelings and fears. In a couple of sentences, how would you describe what you have been feeling since your husband's death?

Shifting the Focus to Involve All Members

Rounds can be used to shift the focus from a person to a topic. If one person has been talking for a while and you decide to involve other members more, you may use a round that spins off from what the member has been saying. A comment round is a good way to shift from a person because it involves the entire group. Members who have been drifting away from the group may get reinvolved.

E X A M P L E . . . .

The group is a support and therapy group for teenage boys; it is the second meeting. The leader wants to focus on the topic of relationships at home. Andre has been talking for a couple of minutes about how bad his home life is.

Andre: . . . and it really is unbelievable how strict it is.

Leader: Andre, I want to get everyone in on this. Each of you think for a minute of a word or phrase that describes your home life, then we'll do a round in which all of you will comment. (*Leader waits a few seconds and scans the room to see when people seem ready*) OK, let's start here on my left, with Gary.

Gary: Well, my dad, you see they are divorced and, uh, it all started.

Leader: Gary, let's do this for now—tell with whom you live, like mom, brother, sister, and then add the word or phrase that best describes your home life. (*The leader changes the round a little, realizing that the group would benefit by hearing with whom each member lives*)

Gary: OK, my mom, my grandmother, and my two older sisters. As for a description—lousy—everyone is always bossing me around.

Leader: Tim?

Tim: My mom, my stepdad, my little sister, who is 2. My other brother lives with my dad on the farm. As for how it is at home—bad. My stepdad and I hate each other! Just last week—

Leader: Hang on, Tim. Let's get everyone to comment, then we'll come back to you and others.

Al: I live with my mom and dad. They are real old, though—in their fifties. They just don't understand how things have changed.

Rick: I live with my grandparents—my mom can't handle me along with her three other kids. My real dad—well, I don't know where he is; I think he's in Georgia—he left when I was 2. As for things with my grandparents, well, they are OK, I guess. Boring, but my grandparents let me do what I want. (*The leader lets Rick speak a little longer than the others because up to now he has not said very much in the group*).

Joe: I live with my uncle—my dad was killed in a car accident, and my mom is in the, uh, well, the hospital. Nerves and stuff. It's bad—my uncle really doesn't want me there. (*Joe is the last person*)

Leader: Let's talk about how your home life affects your behavior; that is, how the environment you live in may be contributing to some of your problems in school and on the streets.

After the above round the leader has much more information and a much clearer idea of the kinds of home conditions members are experiencing. The leader can relate members' comments and life experiences, thanks to the additional background information. Communicating such similarities among members acts to build a feeling of cohesion in the group. The leader knows that some members are missing parents, some are fighting at home, and that Joe may have some strong feelings about his mom being in a mental hospital. The round opens up options and aids the leader in deciding where to focus. Also, the members are now more involved in the topic.

. . . .

In the preceding example, the leader, wanting to focus the entire group on the topic of home environment, spun off from what Andre was saying. There will be other instances in which the leader will want to involve all the members simply because the member talking needs to be cut off. For example, in the following group, business executives are discussing how to bring more enjoyment to their lives. One member has been talking on and on about his summer vacation plans, and the leader interrupts him:

Leader: Let me jump in and pick up on what you were saying about summer plans not being fun-oriented. Think about your summer; I want to get each of you to briefly say what your plans are and if they are fun-oriented.

In this example, the leader stayed with the speaker's topic and simply expanded it to include the entire group. The leader can also use a round to shift the focus away from a narrow topic to another to which every member can relate.

EXAMPLE . . . .

The members are in a group at a hospital. One has been talking about how bad the food is. He has talked about breakfasts and is now on the topic of lunches.

Dale: As for lunches, well, they are even worse.

Leader: Dale, I want to pick up on your point about being dissatisfied. I'd like each of you to think of things that you would like to see be different here at the hospital—let's omit meals, since Dale has covered that one. We'll do a round of one or two things you'd like to see done differently here.

· ·

Gathering Information and Locating Energy

At various times the leader will want to know how members are thinking and feeling about some issue, topic, or assignment. The round is an excellent way to do this in a quick, controlled manner. By asking members to rate something on a 1-to-10 scale or to express their feelings in a word or phrase, the leader can quickly assess how much interest or "work" potential there is in a topic and who is most interested in working on or engaging in that particular discussion. Also, once the leader knows the members' feelings and thoughts, she can have the group delve into areas that are in line with members' interests. It is much easier to lead when you have some idea of how the members view a topic or issue. The two examples below further illustrate the value of rounds with respect to focusing, gathering information, building interest, and locating the energy in members.

EXAMPLES · · · · · · · · · · · · · · · · ·

The group consists of four students who work at the mental-health center as part of their coursework. The leader is conducting an educational group and the topic for the session is therapeutic drugs. The leader decides to start with a round because he has no idea how much the students know about medications.

Leader: I want to get some idea of what you know about drugs. On a 1-to-10 scale, with 10 being quite a bit and 1 being very little, how would you rate your current knowledge?

Jan: Uh, about a 2.

Mary: 1.

Eddie: 2.

Art: 8 or 9.

Leader: Art, why an 8 or 9?

Art: I did a three-hour independent study course on medications and wrote a 25-page paper on the subject. I'm willing to be here, though—I want to learn more!

Leader: Good, and certainly feel free to comment. Let's do another round; then we'll get started. How do you feel about using drugs as a form of therapy? Respond with "believe in them," "don't believe in them," or "not sure."

Jan: Not sure.

Mary: Believe in them.

Eddie: Don't believe in them. My brother has had all kinds of medications, and he is still not any better after three years.

Art: I started out a nonbeliever, but after doing the paper and talking to different therapists, I see some value in medications in certain situations.

.   .   .   .

The group is a discussion and education group for parents. The members have been assigned a reading in a book that the leader plans to discuss.

Leader: Let's do a word-or-phrase round on your reaction to the chapters on mealtimes and fighting.

Sandy: I liked them very much.

Pat: Helpful but hard.

Robin: I don't know if I agree with the idea of letting kids settle their own fights. My kids differ in age by four years, and—

Leader: Can you hold that?

Robin: Oh, sure.

Leader: Bill, what about you?

Bill: Mealtimes still have been bad—I've got some questions.

Dania: I tried to get my husband to read it so he'd understand, but he wouldn't. (*She starts to tear up a little*)

Leader: (*To the whole group*) Not getting cooperation from a partner can be very frustrating. Dania, let's talk after the group about your situation, OK? (*The leader purposely chooses not to go into Dania's pain*)

Dania: Yeah, I do need to talk to someone.

Leader: (*Decides to do a second round to focus the group*) What is hardest for you at mealtimes? I'd like each of you to briefly comment on mealtime problems.

Pat: Getting them to eat what I fix!

Bill: Getting them to the table, to not fight at the table, you name it!

Leader: Sandy, what about you?

Sandy: Dealing with the baby while trying to give my 3-year-old some attention.

Robin: Mine is similar to Sandy's—how do you do it?!

Leader: Looks like tonight should be interesting and helpful. We'll start with mealtimes. Your comments and questions are helpful to me in knowing where to start. Let's begin by. . . .

.   .   .   .

Building Comfort, Trust, and Cohesion

Rounds provide an easy way for members to talk, and thus often help them feel more comfortable. Simple and specific information rounds during the first and second sessions, when members are still getting to know each other, can be useful in building comfort and trust. Members are curious about each other and rounds can satisfy some of that curiosity. For instance, in a group for war veterans, members would probably want to know in which war each member fought, in which branch of the service they were, and what they did in the war. In a group for teenagers at a mental-health center, the kids would probably want to know where other members lived, why they were at the center, and how old they were.

The skilled leader is always thinking of possible rounds that will ease members' discomfort and help them get to know more about each other. Also, information rounds help members feel linked to each other when they hear that their situations are similar. Remember, rounds get members to share about themselves, which usually results in their feeling more involved.

Processing Exercises

After a group exercise the leader may want to get a sense of how all the members are feeling and thinking. A good way to do this is by using a round. Sometimes a quick word-or-phrase round will provide a lot of information.

E X A M P L E . . . .

The group has just completed an exercise on their fears about being in the group.

Leader: Now that you've done the exercise, how do you feel? In a word or phrase, how would you describe your feelings now?
Wayne: Better!
Akira: A little more comfortable, but still scared.
Sarah: Much better.
Tom: I still have my fears of being laughed at.
Tandy: It was helpful to hear that others were afraid. I still am hesitant to share a couple of things. I guess I want someone else to go first as far as sharing "heavy" stuff.

. . . .

In the example above a quick round was used, but there will be times when the leader will want to use comment rounds to process an exercise. Keep in mind that often after an exercise members have thoughts they want to share with the group. The round allows people to make some comments, which may be all they need. That is, they may not have a lot to say, yet they do want to say something. The round also gives the leader a chance to hear what is on their minds.

Drawing Out Quiet Members

In Chapter Seven, we detailed a number of ways in which rounds can be used to draw out members. By definition, a round gets everyone to respond, thus giving the leader greater opportunity to encourage or draw out any member. If the leader wishes to encourage a certain member to share more, she can start the round so that it ends with that member. When the round ends, the leader can naturally focus on the last person who talked, which would be the one the leader intended to draw out.

Summarizing

At different points in a group, it is beneficial to summarize the session or even the series of sessions. When doing so, it is valuable to both members and leader to hear comments from everyone. The round, since it gets everyone to participate, serves as a good vehicle. The leader can simply do a comment round asking members to summarize what they learned or what stood out to them. At other times the leader may want to use the 1-to-10 round or a word round summary. The leader could then gear the summary to address some of the comments heard during the round. A quick round will give you a chance to hear the important things that members experienced.

Additional Comments about Rounds

Several issues pertaining to rounds remain to be discussed. You will need to know the following:

1. How to set up rounds
2. Where to start rounds
3. Stopping in the middle
4. What to do if someone does not want to talk
5. How to process a round
6. How to avoid overusing rounds

How to Set Up a Round

Rounds, like any other group activity, have to be set up properly. The leader has to think about when a round would be useful and then introduce it in such a way that the members understand what is being asked for, that is, what the round is about. The leader also needs to allow enough time for members to formulate their answers, and not let an eager member start before the others are ready. Further, the leader wants to be sure to specify the kind of round: a word-or-phrase round, a 1-to-10 scale only, a scale with comments to follow, or a comment round.

Where to Start a Round

The leader chooses where to start a round. Many times, where the round starts does not matter, but the leader will not always want to start with the same member; for instance, always with the member on his left. It is a good practice to vary the starting point so that different members get to speak first and last.

At times, the leader will want to start a round with a certain member, for a number of reasons. First, a member may seem very eager to talk, so the leader lets that member start the round. This gets the round going with energy and enthusiasm, in addition to helping out that member.

Second, the leader always wants to set a positive tone for the round. In some groups there will be members who always tend to be negative. One way to keep those members from setting a negative tone is to start rounds with the more positive ones. The leader would also not want to end the round on the negative person, because the focus of the group could easily shift to that person's negative comments. By arranging the round so that the negative members are neither the first nor last to speak, the leader gains some control over the tone.

Third, on occasion the leader will want to end a round with a certain member in order to draw out that member's comments. When the round ends, the leader can focus on the last speaker's comments without spotlighting her.

It is important to think about where you start and end your rounds. Some members are not helpful to begin with because they are long-winded or always confused about what you are trying to do. If a member tends to ramble, it is easier to cut her off if she is not the last person in the round.

Stopping in the Middle of a Round

Sometimes a member says something in the round that seems important enough to focus on at that moment. Normally, however, it is best to finish any round begun, to allow all members to share their thoughts or feelings. Especially in a serious round in which members have had to give much thought to their answers, the leader probably would always try to finish the round because the members could feel "stranded" if they didn't get to share. But the leader must be flexible; if she is doing an information round that is not of a personal nature, stopping in the middle of the round can be fine. During an information round, a good topic may be raised, and the leader can spin off from it into a group exercise or minilecture that is more beneficial than completing the round. If the leader does stop a round in the middle, it is best for her to acknowledge that she is aware of doing so. The leader can quickly scan the group to see if any member seems upset at stopping.

When doing a serious, personal round, there will be times when a member will begin to cry or in some other way indicate the need for immediate attention. The leader will then have to decide whether to continue the round or work with the member. The decision is a difficult one; the leader has several options from which to choose:

- The leader can work with the member, stating that she will try to get back to the round.
- The leader can explain to the member that she will come back to him or her but that she feels it is important to let everyone share first.
- The leader can ask the members how they feel about stopping the round so that the group can help the troubled member.
- The leader can ask a member in whom she has confidence to step out with the troubled member while she finishes the round. This is appropriate only if the round will take considerable time.

You can see from these options that there is no one rule to follow. With experience, you will learn when to choose which option.

Handling Members Who Refuse to Talk

When doing rounds there will be times when a member either refuses to comment or can't comment because of fear, confusion, or lack of anything to say. If the refusal is based on fear, skipping that member is usually the best policy. Some beginning leaders make the mistake of focusing on that member, which often makes the individual feel even more uncomfortable. If the refusal is based on a negative attitude, the best policy would again be to move on to the next person, making a mental note about the problem with that member. Although the purpose of rounds is to hear from everyone, the leader should rarely push someone into commenting. If a member is not ready to comment when her turn comes, simply tell her you will come back to her at the end. And be sure to do so!

How to Process a Round

Most rounds need to be "processed." Processing involves discussing the responses in a focused, conscious manner. If a leader does a 1-to-10 round or a word-or-phrase round, he has many options for following up:

- He can ask different members questions about their word or rating—why it was low or high, for example.
- He can pair up the members according to their answers or ratings and have them discuss the topic further.
- He can focus on one member specifically.
- He can use the different answers to introduce a topic.
- He can do a follow-up round for further information.

EXAMPLES . . . .

The leader has just completed a round asking, "Is there someone in your life right now with whom you are angry?" Everyone has responded "yes." The leader then does a follow-up round:

Leader: We'll do a second round—I want you to state who this person is; that is, mom, friend, boss, and so on; then in a sentence or two state what your anger is about.

After this round, the leader can focus either on a member or the topic. Doing both of these rounds gives the leader a lot of information to work with and gets the members focused on the topic.

. . . .

The leader has just done a round asking how each member sees his or her present love relationship. The round has just ended and the leader decides to focus on one member.

Leader: I want to go back to what Melba said. Melba, what exactly did you mean by "distant"? Did you mean you feel distant or that the relationship is distant?

. . . .

The leader has just completed a word-or-phrase round on the members' reactions to three chapters in a book and decides to focus on a topic.

Leader: It seems like many of you got something out of the three chapters. Let's start with the first chapter—some of you said this was the best reading for you so far. Nelly, you mentioned that the chapter made you think about how change is possible. Let's talk about change. What do you think about changing?

. . . .

The leader has just completed a round on adjusting to the group home. Members have had a variety of comments and reactions to being at the home. The leader decides that there is a lot of energy for the topic and that members are still trying to get comfortable with being in the group. Based on this information, the leader follows up the round.

Leader: All of you have heard the different reactions to being here at the home. Now, I'd like you to pair up with someone you feel you don't know too well and continue talking about how you feel and what you heard others say.

.   .   .   .

Overusing Rounds

Even though rounds are very valuable, beware of overusing them. Some leaders do one round right after the other. This misuse of rounds can cause members to become bored, confused, or resentful of what they may view as a gimmick. Use the rounds to get members focused and thinking, not just to fill time. Remember, rounds can help you get the group focused on its purpose—however, they should not *be* the purpose!

DYADS

A dyad is an activity in which members are paired with each other to discuss issues or to complete a task. Dyads are immensely valuable because they can be used in so many ways and for so many different reasons. In general, dyads are helpful because they provide an opportunity for members to have more personal contact with each other, give members a chance to generate ideas, and vary the format of the group. As the group leader, you will need to decide when to use dyads, how to pair up the members, and the length of time dyads should last.

Uses of Dyads

Eight different uses of dyads will be discussed here:

1. Developing comfort
2. Warming up members and building energy
3. Processing information and group exercises
4. Finishing a topic
5. Getting certain members together
6. Providing leader/member interaction
7. Changing the format
8. Providing time for the leader to think

Developing Comfort

In any group you lead, there will be occasions when you will want to focus on building the comfort level among the members. A dyad can be a helpful exercise, as people are often more comfortable talking to one other person than to an entire group. Two occasions in which using dyads to build comfort is particularly important are during the beginning stages of the group and when members are exploring a new topic or issue that is personal.

In the first or second session of a group, members are often uncomfortable at the prospect of sitting around and talking in front of other people. They may be concerned about not having anything important to say or about how they will be viewed by others. One of your tasks as a group leader is to help members become more comfortable so there will be an open exchange of thoughts and ideas. By placing members in dyads during the early stage of the group, the leader accomplishes several things. First, members who are feeling uneasy about speaking to the whole group will get a chance to talk to just one person. Second, dyads provide for better contact between members: they experience each other as individuals rather than as faces in the group. Finally, as members spend time in dyads, information and ideas get shared, and members become better acquainted and more knowledgeable about each other.

For all these reasons, a leader conducting a group meeting for a number of sessions should consider using at least two or three different dyads during the first session. Below are a few examples of dyads for first sessions. These examples could occur at almost any time during the first session, the purpose being to increase the comfort of the members.

- So you can get a little more comfortable with some of the other members, I would like each of you to pair up with someone whom you don't know very well and simply share why you decided to be in this group.
- We are going to do something a little different now. I am going to ask you to get into pairs and talk for a few minutes, and then we'll come back to the group and share your various thoughts. This way you'll get to know one other member a little better and you'll get a chance to share your ideas. I'd like you to share your ideas about _____ .
- I would like you to get into pairs and discuss how you are feeling about being here. Discuss your excitement and fears.

Dyads can also be used to develop comfort when the topic is more sensitive or personal. Topics such as sex, marital problems, or fears often can be shared more easily in a dyad than in a large group. When members have a chance to share in pairs, they often begin to feel more comfortable and will share when the large group reconvenes. One way to introduce this kind of dyad follows:

Leader: We've agreed that sex is an important issue to discuss. Let's begin by pairing up and talking about some of the things you'd like to explore. Talk about any topics you think would be good to bring up and any concerns you have about discussing sex.

Warming Up and Building Energy

A use for dyads that is related to developing comfort in the group is that of warming up and building energy. While this may sound more like a health-club goal than one of group leadership, in reality there are some similarities. Just as you would stretch and run in place to get physically warmed up and energized, it is likewise important that your members go through a warm-up and energizing phase. Warming up and energizing are often needed when a group begins and when a new topic is introduced. Although there are other ways to warm up members, dyads are one of the easiest.

Of the many ways to use dyads to energize the group, one option is to begin a session by having the members get into dyads: the leader simply asks the members to pair up and talk about such things as their week, the assignment, their hopes for the session, or their progress on a project. By starting with a dyad the leader can get members focused and ready to share their thoughts and feelings.

E X A M P L E . . . .

This career-awareness group for 11th-graders is beginning its third session. The leader opens the session:

Leader: Let's get started. (*Pauses until members become quiet*) To get warmed up, I am going to pair you up and have you discuss some of the things you have thought about as a result of our last meeting. As you recall, we spent a lot of time talking about the pros and cons of college and technical school. What have you thought about? We'll take just a couple of minutes to do this. Joe, you and Hector pair up. . . .

. . . .

The use of dyads to energize is not restricted to the beginning of the group, of course. Any time the leader or a member is introducing a new topic, the leader may choose to use dyads as a way to get members focused on the topic. If, for example, the group were going to begin a discussion of siblings, friends, causes for their divorce, or ways they have tried to diet, the leader could start the discussion by letting members first share in dyads. In the example below dyads are used to prepare a group of parents for a discussion of their feelings about having a handicapped child.

Leader: During the next few minutes you are going to get a chance to share your feelings about your child. To start with, I'm going to ask you to pair up with a person next to you and share for about three minutes some of the struggles and tough times you have had; then we'll come back to the large group and continue that sharing.

Processing Information and Group Exercises

Two other points during a group at which members can benefit from talking in dyads are when they have just received some information or have just completed a group exercise. The advantage of using the dyad is that it provides each member with the opportunity to give reactions, share ideas, or raise questions. If the leader processed the exercise or information in the large group, more time would be needed and also considerable time would elapse before the last few members got to speak. The dyad allows for everyone to share immediately. Of the two examples below, the first uses a dyad to process information and the second to process a short exercise.

EXAMPLES. . . . .

The group is an assertiveness-training group and the leader has just presented information about the differences between being assertive, nonassertive, and aggressive. The leader says to the group:

Leader: To give you a chance to process what I have been saying, I want you to pair up with someone with whom you have never been paired before and discuss what we have just been talking about. Try to relate the information to yourself; that is, how you are assertive, nonassertive, or aggressive. We'll do this for about five minutes.

. . . .

The group is made up of parents with stepfamilies; the leader has just had members react on paper to three common situations that occur in stepfamilies. As the members complete the exercise, the leader says:

Leader: I'd like you to pair up and discuss your reactions to the situations. From your vigorous writing, it appears that many of you were able to relate to them. I'd like you to pick partners. Matt, who would you like to be with? . . .

. . . .

Finishing a Topic

Dyads can be helpful in ending a discussion about a topic. If the group has been discussing an issue or topic for some time, the leader may feel that it has triggered some thoughts in most of the members and may choose to close off the discussion by using dyads. This gets members to share their final thoughts but not necessarily with the entire group, since the group needs to move on to another issue.

EXAMPLE. . . . .

This group had been discussing ways of improving their relationships with their parents; the leader feels that things are winding down and that the group needs a break soon. To set up a dyad for finishing the topic, the leader says the following:

Leader: I think this discussion has given each of you food for thought. Before taking a break, I'd like you to get into pairs and talk about what the last 30 minutes have stirred up in you and what you are going to do differently, if anything. We'll go for about five minutes and then take a break. Be sure to focus on your relationship with your parents.

. . . .

Getting Certain Members Together

In some group situations the leader may want to get certain members talking to each other. This may be because they have something in common, such as both being single parents or both recently having had a parent die; or it may be because they don't feel comfortable with each other and the leader thinks that if they get a few minutes together some of the discomfort might dissipate. Another reason for wanting certain members to pair up could be because they have differing points of view on an issue. The point here is that as the leader gets to know the members and as issues come up in the group, the leader may see the usefulness of dividing the group into pairs to give certain members a chance to interact with one another.

Providing Leader/Member Interaction

Whenever a leader wants to spend more time with a member—helping him finish something, encouraging him, or helping him get clearer on something—she can use dyads. That is, she can put all the members into dyads and pair herself with that member. The leader can also use the leader/member dyad simply to get to know the members better.

Changing the Format

So far in our discussion of dyads, we have mentioned various situations in which dyads can facilitate specific aspects of the group: improving the comfort level, energizing the members, and so forth. Another use for dyads is when the leader simply feels a change of format is needed. Dyads can provide a refreshing change from sitting in the group, and are useful whenever the leader senses that members are restless and in need of a change.

Providing Time for the Leader to Think

Because groups are so unpredictable, there may be times when the leader needs some time just to think. This may be necessary if the leader finds that the energy for a topic has waned sooner than expected or if the interests of the group have moved it in an unexpected direction. Another such time might be when a group activity simply has not worked well and a new focus is needed. By placing members in dyads, the leader obtains a "time-out" period without the group actually taking a break and losing momentum. The leader gives the members something to talk about in their dyads while thinking about what to do next.

Pairing Members for Dyads

In the examples given so far, we have for the most part implied that when members pair up they choose each other without any specific instructions from the leader. Often this system works fine. However, on many occasions the leader will choose to facilitate the pairing, either to make the process go more smoothly or because the leader has a particular goal in mind for the group or for individual members. In this section we discuss techniques for pairing members and the rationale for using each technique.

Member's Choice

The simplest and most obvious approach to pairing is allowing members to choose whomever they wish to be with in a dyad. As demonstrated in many of the examples in this chapter, the leader can merely say, "Pair up with someone" or "Choose a partner." The members are then left to themselves to make a choice. Their individual rationales for making a choice will vary greatly. Friends may choose each other or a member may identify with another member based on something that was said in the group. If there is an age spread in the group, older members may pair with each other, as might members of a similar racial background or members who are married or divorced or who have children. Usually members will pair in the most comfortable way possible.

For this reason, allowing members to make their own independent choices usually is a less threatening experience. A word of caution here: while this method usually goes smoothly, the leader should be on the lookout for any negative reactions stemming from having members choose a dyad partner. There may be some who feel uncomfortable with this method such as those who find it reminiscent of childhood games and feeling left out when not chosen for a team.

A disadvantage of allowing members to choose on their own is that they will often continue to choose those people with whom they perceive themselves to be most comfortable and therefore will not get acquainted with other members of the group. Since the purpose of the dyad may be for members to have contact with those they don't know, the leader might say the following:

- Pair up with someone you would like to know better.
- Pair up with someone who seems to be different from you.
- Pair up with someone with whom you don't feel comfortable.

A variation on having members choose at random is for the leader to choose a member who in turn picks a partner. For example:

Leader: Tim, pick a partner to be with.
Tim: James.
Leader: OK, Carol, you pick someone.
Carol: Ralph.

This is usually a fairly smooth process and has the advantage of enabling the leader to select those who don't usually speak up to pick their partners.

Leader's Choice

By seating. Of the ways in which the leader can assign dyad partners, the easiest is by seating arrangement. The leader simply says, while pointing at two members sitting next to each other and then moving to the next pair: "The two of you pair up; the two of you; and the two of you." Even in this situation the leader may want to exercise some control over who pairs up with whom. This can be done by starting the pairs at any point in the circle. Suppose a group of six are sitting in a circle in this order: Joe, Bill, Bob, Sam, Roy, and Ed. If the leader starts the pairing with Joe and Bill, the other two pairs would be Bob with Sam and Roy with Ed. But if the leader wanted to split up Bob and Sam, he could start pairing with Bill and Bob, thus leaving Sam with Roy and Ed with Joe. The quickest and easiest way to pair people is by seating, but the leader can start the pairing at any point in a circle, with the idea of splitting up certain members.

One common mistake that beginning leaders make is to say to the group, "Turn to the person on your left and talk about . . ." This seems as if it would work; however, if everyone tried to talk to the person on her left, no one would, in fact, talk to anyone!

By leader's discretion.   Sometimes the leader will think that some member would benefit by being in a dyad with some other member. In this case, the leader can simply assign the dyads by saying something like "We are going to spend the next few minutes processing what has happened here: Tom, you and Carl pair up; Jana, you and Phil; Mike, you and Sharon. Take about five minutes to talk about what you have experienced during this last half-hour."

Sometimes in the group the leader may simply pair people on the basis of similarities or differences. For example, the leader may decide to pair those who feel religion is very important in their lives either with each other or with those who do not feel religion is important. The pairing would depend on the leader's purpose. In addition, the leader may want to avoid pairing certain people, such as those who do not like each other or those who have a strong relationship outside the group.

Another point to keep in mind is that the leader can choose whether or not to be in a dyad. At times the leader will want to talk with one member in particular: when setting up the dyads, the leader simply pairs up with that person. If there are two members the leader wants to be with, the two of them can be put together and the leader joins them.

Additional Thoughts about Dyads

How Much Time to Allow

Dyads can last anywhere from 2 to 20 minutes, depending on their purpose. If the time is too short, members may get frustrated. On the other hand, if it is too long, they may get bored and wander from the topic. In an educational group to help clients at a rehabilitation center learn how to get a job, dyads to discuss techniques for greeting a receptionist may need only a couple of minutes. By contrast, dyads to discuss their feelings about going out and applying for a job could take 5 to 10 minutes; practicing talking to a potential employer could take up to 20 minutes. The leader will always want to give thought to the appropriate amount of time for the dyad.

At times leaders will want to allow all members to finish their assigned task, while at others they will want to bring the members back to the large group before the energy has dissipated. That is, when leaders are using dyads to build energy, they will want to end the dyads before the discussion has peaked, so that the members bring that energy back to the group. However, if the members are working on a task, the leader will want to give them ample time to finish. Keep in mind that some pairs may move at a very slow pace, and the leader would not often want to wait until the very last pair finished, since the others' focus and/or energy would be lost.

Leaders should always tell the members in advance the approximate amount of time that the dyad will last. Sometimes the leader will see that either more or less time is needed once the members have been talking for a while. In that case, asking the members how much more time they need is a good way to judge the amount to allow. It is also helpful to give members some warning before bringing the dyad to a close. For example, the leader might loudly say one of the following:

- We'll go for another two minutes.
- Please wind down in the next 30 seconds or so and then come back to the large group.

Time warnings are very helpful when there are a number of subjects the leader wants the members to cover in dyads, such as the answers to five questions, or feelings about school, work, and friends. Often people will get stuck on one topic or one person; the time warnings help keep them moving. Also, time warnings and the proper allotment of time help bring dyads to a smooth rather than an abrupt end. Abrupt endings can cause members to become frustrated and angry with the leader.

Giving Clear, Simple Instructions

If the leader gives lengthy or confusing instructions for the dyad, members may misunderstand, ask many questions, or fail to do what was asked. The best policy is to make the instructions easy to understand and to make sure that everyone does understand them. Usually the directions are given before the members pair up. However, if the instructions are somewhat complex, it is often better to have members get into pairs first and then tell them what to do.

Making Sure Members Stay on Task

Often members may be slow getting to the task, or may stray from the intended purpose of the dyad. The leader may want to remind members of the purpose about 30 seconds or a minute after the dyad has started. Another way to ensure that the dyads are on target is to listen in on each of them for half a minute or so to hear if they are in fact doing what was asked. If not, the leader can urge the members back to the topic. Another advantage of listening in for brief moments is that the leader gets some ideas for discussion in the large group.

The Leader's Role during Dyads

The leader has many options during the time that members are in dyads. It is up to the leader to decide whether or not to participate. In any case, the leader should first make sure that everyone understands the dyad's purpose. If the leader decides not to be involved in the dyads, the time can be used to plan the remainder of the group. A leader who is participating may work with a partner, "float" from dyad to dyad, or join one dyad for the entire time. It is important to remember that while participating in a dyad the leader still needs to be aware of the time, give time warnings, and end the dyad at an appropriate point.

Some reasons why the leader might want to form part of a dyad include getting to know the members better, allowing the members to get to know the leader better, having a chance to work with one or two members, or making up an even number if the group has an odd number of members. If the leader does not want to be in a dyad even though the group has an odd number of members, she can simply make one of the dyads a triad instead.

The Physical Arrangement for Dyads

Usually the dyads take place in the area where the group is meeting. However, at times the leader may want them to meet in other parts of the room or even in other parts of the building. This would be appropriate when the dyads are going to last for a relatively long time (10 to 20 minutes) or the leader feels that the members can benefit from being in a more private, less noisy situation.

Using Triads Instead of Dyads

Although this section is about the use of dyads, there are times when grouping members in threes instead of twos can be valuable. With three people, more ideas or points of view are presented, which may be what the leader wants. For this reason triads are often used in educational, discussion, and task groups. Another advantage is that even if one person is not involved, the other two people can interact. A disadvantage is that quiet members may be able to "hide" more easily while the other two members carry the conversation. Also, more time is usually needed for a triad than for a dyad, since more people need time to express themselves.

CONCLUDING COMMENTS

In this chapter, we have discussed two very useful tools: the round and the dyad. We emphasized the use of these tools to provide information for the leader, energize the group, help members share with each other, and vary the format of the group. We also pointed out situations in which rounds and dyads can be used and how they help the leader in both gathering and processing information. In our opinion learning to use these two tools effectively is a must for any group leader.

Exercises

The term *exercise* is used among group leaders to refer to activities that the group does for a specific purpose. An exercise can be as simple as having members get into dyads to discuss a topic or as involved as the "Blind Trust Walk," which entails one member leading around another, blindfolded member. Other examples of exercises include having members read a poem or a saying and then discuss it, having members complete sentence stems, having them draw pictures to represent their situations or feelings, or having them complete a certain task. In other words, when the leader directs the behaviors, discussion, or attention of the group members by using a specific activity, it is an exercise. In this chapter we discuss the reasons for using exercises and the kinds of exercises available for use in groups. In Chapter 10 we will continue our discussion in terms of introducing, conducting, and processing exercises of all types. Before discussing the reasons for using exercises in groups, we want to briefly review the various theoretical viewpoints on the use of exercises in groups.

According to Yalom (1985), structured exercises were first described for group work in the T-groups of the 1950s. Since then the use of exercises in groups has been described in great detail by a number of authors. In fact, a number of books that contain nothing but group exercises have been written (Lewis & Streitfeld, 1972; Morganett, 1990; Pfeiffer & Jones, 1972–1980; Simon, Howe, & Kirschenbaum, 1978; Stevens, 1972).

There are differences of opinion among the experts on whether or not exercises should be used in groups. Carl Rogers (1970), in his definitive text on groups, emphasizes the unstructured role of the group leader; he feels that the leader should take little responsibility for directing the group and should not employ exercises. In fact, Rogers states, "I try to avoid using any procedure that is planned" (p. 56). Rogers refers to group therapists as "facilitators," and advocates that they play a role akin to those of other members of the group rather than attempting to be viewed as the leader. Rogers, who coined the term *encounter group*, argues that the leader's act of prescribing members' behavior robs them of the opportunity to formulate their own group and experience the process or stages that groups typically go through in their development. Other authors have not agreed. Yalom (1985), Corey, Corey, Callanan, and Russell (1988), Trotzer (1989), and Dyer and Vriend (1980) all advocate the use of exercises when needed and view their use as an invaluable aid to the leader, members, and process of the group.

Our position is that group exercises are very valuable and that they can play an important role in making a group meaningful and interesting. Exercises that are well thought-out and used properly can be of great benefit in almost all groups. The exercises described in this and the following chapter come from a variety of sources. Some appeared initially in the excellent resource volumes of Pfeiffer and Jones (1972–1980). Others originated in Stevens's (1972) and Simon, Howe, and Kirschenbaum's (1978) work. Many of these exercises have been modified over time and passed along through workshops or by word of mouth. It is important for the beginning leader to adapt exercises both to the needs of the group and to the skill level, age level, and sophistication of the members.

WHY USE EXERCISES?

There are at least seven reasons for using exercises in a group. The leader may choose exercises to do the following:

1. Generate discussion and participation
2. Focus the group
3. Shift the focus
4. Provide an opportunity for experiential learning
5. Provide the leader with useful information
6. Increase the comfort level
7. Provide fun and relaxation

Generating Discussion and Participation

In most group situations, interaction among members is one of the most important components of the group process; the use of group exercises often increases member participation by providing them with a common experience. Also, exercises serve as a way to stimulate members' interest and energy.

Focusing the Group

An exercise can be used to get members focused on a common issue or topic. For example, if the leader wanted to focus the group on the benefits of good study skills, she could say, "On a piece of paper, I'd like each of you to list three benefits of planning your study time." Or if the leader wanted to focus the group on the topic of sexual satisfaction, she could say, "On a 1-to-10 scale, with 10 being very satisfied, how would you rate your satisfaction with your present sex life?"

Shifting the Focus

A leader may want to use an exercise to shift the focus when she feels a new topic is needed. For example, in a group for adolescents, if the leader wanted to shift from discussing anger at parents to feelings about themselves, she could say the following:

Leader: It seems like you have a wide variety of feelings of anger toward your parents. Hopefully our discussion here has given you some new ways to look at your relationship with them. I would like us to shift to a different topic now: how you feel about yourself. I want you to think of three things that you like about yourself and three things you don't like about yourself.

Providing an Opportunity for Experiential Learning

A fourth reason for using exercises is to provide an alternative approach to exploring issues, other than through simple discussion. Sometimes it is helpful to get members to act out themes being expressed in the group rather than just talk about them. For instance, let's say the group discussion centers around not being accepted by peers. To focus on this theme other than through verbal sharing, the leader could have all members except one gather in a tight circle with arms interlocked. The member outside the circle would then be instructed to attempt to break into the circle by whatever means possible while the members tried to prevent the individual from entering. This exercise usually gets at feelings of loneliness and members' methods of attempting to gain the acceptance of others.

Providing the Leader with Useful Information

Exercises may be used to get information from the members that the leader will use in the discussion to follow. Rounds are often used in this way. For instance, the leader might ask members to use a single word to describe their home environment when they were growing up. In describing their home environment, members might use words such as "playful," "warm," "hostile," "cold," "competitive," "abusive," and "healthy." By hearing how each member describes his early environment, the leader obtains information that can help her to focus the group. Another round to help the leader might be "On a 1-to-10 scale, how valuable do you find this group?" This round would quickly give her some idea of how different members feel about the group.

Increasing the Comfort Level

Exercises may be used to increase the comfort level of the members. Many members experience some degree of anxiety during the first couple of group sessions. Getting-acquainted exercises often increase comfort among members. The use of dyads can also be helpful in increasing comfort during the early sessions, as well as when a very personal topic is about to be discussed.

Providing Fun and Relaxation

Certain exercises can loosen up the group through laughter or relaxation. Using these kinds of exercises may be quite helpful when the group seems to need a change of pace. One fun exercise is called "Pass the Mask." In it one member makes some kind of face at the next member and that member tries to make the same face back; then, the second member turns to the next member and makes a new face. The third member copies the mask and then creates a new one for the fourth member. This takes place rapidly and usually results in fun and laughter.

There are a number of relaxation exercises. A popular one calls for the leader to simply take a few minutes and go through a series of relaxation steps. The leader asks members to close their eyes and, starting with their head, try to relax their muscles. They proceed to the neck, shoulders, and so on, until the entire body is relaxed. Another relaxation exercise is a group massage. In this exercise, one person lies on the floor and is massaged gently by all the other members.

In summary, exercises may be used to increase interest and energy, generate a focus for the group, heighten members' awareness, gather information, reduce anxiety, and have fun. In addition to these general uses, there are particular instances during any group in which the leader may wish to use an exercise to accomplish a goal that is specific to what is happening in the group at the moment.

WHEN TO USE EXERCISES

Starting a Group or Session

An opening name exercise, as you know, is often helpful when beginning a new group. Exercises may also be used when opening any of the subsequent group sessions. During the first several minutes of a group session, members often are not focused on the task at hand. They may be nervous and unsure of what will take place, or they may be thinking about something that happened just before coming to the group or something that concerns them at work or at home. Using an exercise to structure the first several minutes often helps members get focused on being in the group.

For example, in the first moments of a session the leader might say, "I would like each of you to think of a word that describes how you are feeling right now." Another good exercise for the beginning of a session is to get members to report on significant events since the last meeting. The leader might simply say, "I want each of you to think about what has happened in your life since our last meeting, and I'm going to ask you to share the one or two most significant events." Or, "I think we'll start with progress reports. Each of you will have a minute or two to share what progress you feel you are making."

The opportunity always exists at the beginning of a session to use an exercise; however, it is certainly not necessary—or always advisable—to use an exercise every time you begin a group or session.

At the End of a Session

Exercises may also be used to bring a session to a close. By using an exercise the leader helps members summarize and bring a sense of closure to what has been discussed during the session. Without bringing the session to an appropriate end, members may leave feeling frustrated or "unfinished." Rounds are often helpful for this purpose: the leader might say, "Think of a word or phrase that sums up what you have learned in this session." Dyads can also help members to summarize. The leader may pair up members and direct them to discuss what they learned in the session, how the session was helpful, or what points or issues they plan to think about between now and the next session.

During the Middle Stage

Of course, exercises may be used anytime during the session, for any of the reasons listed in the section titled "Why Use Exercises?" As the leader develops a plan for a particular group session, it will be helpful if she also considers what exercises might be useful. If she plans to focus on members' relationships with their parents in the third session of a growth group, she should come to that session with some relevant exercises in mind. They may involve an activity, such as having members role-play communication problems with parents, or a written task, such as having members complete a checklist of parent-relationship problems.

Remember that exercises are usually not in and of themselves help-ful; rather, it is the time spent personalizing and processing the exer-cise that is the helpful component. Another important thing to consider when choosing an exercise is whether or not it is appropriate for the members of your group. Many inexperienced leaders choose exercises that merely fill up time rather than meet the needs of the members. With so many exercises to choose from, tailoring them to the group should not be that difficult.

KINDS OF EXERCISES

There are at least 14 kinds of exercises. The advantage of having a vari-ety of types of exercises available is that, depending on the kind of group you are leading, the ages and needs of your members, and the topics or issues to be dealt with, certain kinds of exercises will be more useful and relevant than others. Your understanding of the value and uses of each type of exercise will help you make appropriate choices. In some instances these exercises are interchangeable in terms of their purpose and utility, but there are times when a certain kind of exercise is better than another. We discuss each kind in some detail:

1. Written
2. Movement
3. Dyads and triads
4. Rounds
5. Creative props
6. Arts and crafts
7. Fantasy
8. Common reading
9. Feedback
10. Trust
11. Experiential
12. Moral dilemma
13. Group decision
14. Touching

Written Exercises

Written exercises are structured written activities in which members write lists, answer questions, fill in sentence-completion items, write down their reactions, or mark checklists relating to an issue or topic. Written exercises are one of the most versatile and useful of all the exer-cise types. Their major advantages are that members become focused while completing the writing task and they have their ideas or responses in front of them when they are finished. Drawing out members tends to be easier when they have answers or reactions readily available. This eliminates the pressure of having to create responses on the spot.

Sentence-Completion Exercises

One of the most useful types of written exercises is the sentence completion. A sentence completion is a written statement with a portion left blank for the member to fill in. For example:

When I enter a new group I feel _____ .

I am most afraid of _____ .

Sentence completions are useful because they trigger a number of ideas and thoughts as well as serve to focus the attention and discussion of the group. Sentence completions also generate interest and energy among members because they are usually curious about how other members have responded to the same sentence stems. Sentence completions are flexible; they can be devised for any topic or issue. For example, if the topic of discussion is divorce, the following sentence completions could be developed to help generate discussion:

Being divorced means _____ .

The hardest thing about being divorced is _____ .

When I think of future relationships, I _____ .

The thing I would most like help with from the group is _____

_____ .

There are only four sentence stems here but a leader can develop as many as she likes. The length and kind of sentence completion should depend on the kind of group, the purpose of the group, and the depth of answers desired. Usually a leader will not want more than 5 or 6 sentence stems, although there may be times when as many as 10 or 15 are used.

The following are three additional examples of helpful sentence-completion forms. The first example is an excellent one to use in the beginning of many kinds of therapy, growth, and support groups. It could be used right after any introduction exercise or later on in the first session. The questions give members a chance to share many thoughts and feelings about being in the group and about themselves. Also, the questions are worded so that the leader can use the responses to comment on how the group will be conducted and what will happen in the group.

When I enter a new group, I feel _____ .

When people first meet me, they _____ .

When I am in a new group, I feel most comfortable when ⎯⎯

⎯⎯⎯⎯⎯⎯⎯⎯⎯⎯⎯⎯⎯⎯⎯⎯⎯⎯⎯⎯ .

When people remain silent, I feel ⎯⎯⎯⎯⎯⎯⎯⎯⎯⎯ ·

I feel annoyed when the leader ⎯⎯⎯⎯⎯⎯⎯⎯⎯⎯ ·

In a group, I am most afraid of ⎯⎯⎯⎯⎯⎯⎯⎯⎯⎯ ·

Those who really know me think I am ⎯⎯⎯⎯⎯⎯⎯ ·

I trust those who ⎯⎯⎯⎯⎯⎯⎯⎯⎯⎯⎯⎯⎯⎯⎯ ·

I feel closest to others when ⎯⎯⎯⎯⎯⎯⎯⎯⎯⎯⎯ ·

People like me when I ⎯⎯⎯⎯⎯⎯⎯⎯⎯⎯⎯⎯⎯ ·

My greatest strength is ⎯⎯⎯⎯⎯⎯⎯⎯⎯⎯⎯⎯ ·

I am ⎯⎯⎯⎯⎯⎯⎯⎯⎯⎯⎯⎯⎯⎯⎯⎯⎯⎯⎯⎯ ·

The second sentence-completion form is intended to generate discussion about how individuals view themselves.

I am ⎯⎯⎯⎯⎯⎯⎯⎯⎯⎯⎯⎯⎯⎯⎯⎯⎯⎯⎯ ·

Those who really know me think I am ⎯⎯⎯⎯⎯⎯⎯ ·

My greatest asset is ⎯⎯⎯⎯⎯⎯⎯⎯⎯⎯⎯⎯⎯ ·

I need to improve ⎯⎯⎯⎯⎯⎯⎯⎯⎯⎯⎯⎯⎯⎯ ·

I regret ⎯⎯⎯⎯⎯⎯⎯⎯⎯⎯⎯⎯⎯⎯⎯⎯⎯⎯ ·

If I had it to do all over again, I would ⎯⎯⎯⎯⎯⎯ ·

My best accomplishment is ⎯⎯⎯⎯⎯⎯⎯⎯⎯⎯⎯ ·

I get my kicks out of ⎯⎯⎯⎯⎯⎯⎯⎯⎯⎯⎯⎯⎯ ·

Compared to others, I think I am ⎯⎯⎯⎯⎯⎯⎯⎯ ·

I want most out of life to ⎯⎯⎯⎯⎯⎯⎯⎯⎯⎯⎯ ·

Five years from now ⎯⎯⎯⎯⎯⎯⎯⎯⎯⎯⎯⎯⎯ ·

My biggest fear is ⎯⎯⎯⎯⎯⎯⎯⎯⎯⎯⎯⎯⎯⎯ ·

I need ⎯⎯⎯⎯⎯⎯⎯⎯⎯⎯⎯⎯⎯⎯⎯⎯⎯⎯⎯ ·

The third sentence-completion form would be used to focus discussion on members' thoughts and feelings about sex.

I think sex is ⎯⎯⎯⎯⎯⎯⎯⎯⎯⎯⎯⎯⎯⎯⎯ ·

Many of my feelings about sex come from ⎯⎯⎯⎯ ·

Discussing sex in this group is ⎯⎯⎯⎯⎯⎯⎯⎯⎯ ·

I would like to have sex ⎯⎯⎯⎯⎯⎯⎯⎯⎯ times a week.

The sexual topic I would most like us to discuss would be _____

_____ .

Devising sentence completions that are consistent is very important. If you are devising your own sentence-completion forms, be sure that the sentences do focus the members in the areas that you desire. For instance, in the third example above, the leader wants to focus on issues pertaining to sexual activity. An inappropriate sentence stem would be "I enjoy being the sex I am because _____." It would be inappropriate because it would generate discussion about gender and sex roles rather than sex and sexual behavior.

Listing Exercises

Having members make a list is another very useful written exercise. Lists can be done quickly and can easily be geared to the level and needs of the group members. Some examples of lists include the characteristics of friendship, hobbies the members enjoy, the most important people in their lives, positive personal qualities, traits desired in a love partner, or characteristics inherent in the ideal job. The list is useful to members because it allows them to summarize their thoughts in a succinct fashion; it also helps them to remain focused. Once the list is complete, it can be used in a variety of ways. The leader can simply ask members to share a portion or the entirety of their list, or have them share lists in dyads, triads, or small groups. For example, in an education/growth group about stress, the leader might ask members to list things that are stressful to them. Once the members have done so, the leader could ask them to get into triads and discuss their lists, starting first with work stressors, then home stressors, then other stressors.

Written-Response Exercises

The third type of written exercise we call the "response" exercise, since it calls on members to respond in various ways to problems or questions posed by the leader. Some examples are as follows:

- Members write their own epitaph or obituary.
- Members write short responses to questions such as "What is the role of a school counselor?" or "How does having children change one's life?"
- Members write reaction papers after viewing movies or TV shows or reading books or poems. For example the leader, knowing that a certain movie will be on TV, might ask the members to watch it and afterward write a personal reaction reflecting what the movie meant to them. The members would bring their reactions to the group.
- Members complete multiple-choice, preferences, or one-word answers to different questions.

In each case, members would have their reactions or answers in front of them, thus allowing the leader to ask different members to share their responses.

Diaries

A fourth type of written exercise uses diaries both during the session and at home. Within the session, members write personal reactions to what had taken place in that particular session. Often this is done at the end of the session; the leader allots the last five or ten minutes for members to write. She would say something like, "I want you to spend the last ten minutes writing in your diaries about what stood out for you tonight. Please include any thoughts, feelings, or reactions to the session."

The diaries are usually left for the leader to read; this gives her both immediate feedback about the session and the opportunity to write comments in the diaries. The leader gets an idea of what the members are gaining from the group and what might need to be addressed in future sessions. The leader's written comments can be encouraging statements, clarifying comments, suggestions, or any other remark she feels might be helpful. On the other hand, if the leader fears that members will not respond honestly or deeply because they know she will read the diaries, she may choose not to have members turn them in. The obvious disadvantage to this is that the leader then has less information about how the members are experiencing the group.

Diaries can also be used at home. Members take their diaries home and write their reactions to the group and/or to anything that happens to them during the week that is relevant. These journals or diaries would periodically be given to the leader. This tells the leader what is helpful in the group and also how members are reacting and feeling about things that happen to them during the week. An advantage of jotting down thoughts or events throughout the week is that members focus on themselves at all times and not just during the hour or two each week that the group meets. Writing also helps members remember what happened to them and ensures that they will report to the group important happenings in their lives. With the member's permission, comments from a diary may also be shared with other members if the leader feels something has been mentioned that would be helpful to the whole group.

Movement Exercises

Movement exercises require members to do something of a physical nature; that is, the members move around. The movements can be as simple as standing up and moving about in order to stretch or as complex as the "Trust Lift" (in which four or five members collectively take turns lifting one member above their heads) or "Breaking In" (in which the group, standing up and holding hands, tries to keep a member outside the circle from breaking in). Some additional examples of movement exercises are described below.

Changing Seats

This involves members simply standing and then finding a different seat in which to sit. The purpose is to allow members to stretch and move around and also to sit next to different members and to face different members by virtue of changing location. The leader might introduce this exercise by saying, "I'd like you to stand up and take a minute to stretch, then find a seat other than the one you had. Try to seat yourselves next to some different members."

Milling Around

This involves having the members walk around. There are a number of activities that the members may be doing while milling, such as experiencing or avoiding eye contact or touching another member gently on the shoulder or elbow. The specifics of what to do while milling will depend on the purpose of the exercise. The milling would last for no more than two minutes. To begin, the leader might say the following:

Leader: I want you to stand up. (*Members stand*) We are going to do a nonverbal milling exercise. The first thing I want you to do is to move about the room with your head down, avoiding eye contact with anyone. (*Members do this for about one minute*) Now I want you to mill around, but this time make eye contact for as long as you desire.

This exercise gets members in touch with their comfort level with others. It can be used in groups that are exploring their feelings about interacting with others.

Values Continuum

Members position themselves according to how they think and feel about an issue. The leader designates certain locations in the room as symbolic of a viewpoint. One side of the room might represent one point of view and the other the opposite point of view. The members are asked to stand in the middle of the room and then move to the position on the continuum between the two designated spots.

EXAMPLE . . . .

Leader: I want everyone to stand up and line up here in the middle of the room behind Jim. OK, now on the count of 3, I am going to ask you to position yourself where you feel you are on the continuum that I am about to mention. The continuum is from the wall on your right, which will be "high risk taker," to the wall on your left, which will be "play it very safe." Everyone understand? OK—on 3, position yourselves. Ready? 1, 2, 3.

Possible continuums include saver/spender, happy/unhappy, at peace with religion/experiencing turmoil with religion; the list is endless.

. . . .

The benefit of having members walk to a designated area is that all the members have to declare their position at the same time and everyone can visually see how others feel about a given issue. It also offers a change in the format; instead of stating their position, this exercise gives members the opportunity to move and to view others' "positions."

Goals Walk

In this exercise, the members line up across from each other with about 3 to 4 feet between the two lines. Each member will take a turn walking through the area between the members. The members act as obstacles in the walker's path toward his or her goal, which is at the other end.

Leader: I want everyone to stand up and make two lines with three on one side and four on the other. Stand a few feet apart, making sort of a "road." What we are going to do is have each of you walk down the road. Let me have a volunteer. (*Hilda volunteers and steps to the front of the road where the leader is standing*) Hilda, I'd like you to envision reaching your goals and life being fairly smooth as being at the other end. OK, now what I want you to do is tell us how difficult you perceive it will be to reach that end. If you see it as hard at first, then, Jane, you and Sandy will want to sort of block her and make it hard since you are in front here. If it is going to be hard in the middle, then Kevin and Karen will make it hard. I know some of you have some pretty tough things ahead of you. What we want to do is give each person a chance to experience physically some of the bumps in the road toward his or her goals. You'll make it hard by blocking, holding, or whatever, but it is important to not make it impossible and also not to laugh since that will take away from the person's experience. OK, Hilda, tell us how you see the road ahead.

If done right, this exercise can be very thought-provoking. If members know each other well, certain members in the line can play certain characters in the person's life, such as drinking buddies, old lover, ex-spouse, mother, or the "bottle." The leader has to pay close attention to make sure it does not get too physical or turn into a joking kind of activity. We have used this in many different ways and found it to have great impact.

How Far Have You Come?

In this exercise, the leader has the members stand side by side and think about how far they have come during the group in terms of reaching their goals.

Leader: I think this exercise can be of help in getting you to see where you are in the group. Everyone stand up and line up next to each other. (*The leader stands about 8 feet away*) If the imaginary line that I'm drawing represents your reaching the goals that we talked about in our first session, how far have you come toward reaching them? Some of you have come pretty far; others, not so far, but I want each of you to position yourself in terms of your progress. On 3—1, 2, 3.

After people position themselves, there usually is much interaction and discussion. The leader can also have them put one foot forward, symbolizing a step toward their goal and have each person talk about what that step would be.

Sculpt Your Feeling about the Group

This is an exercise in which the leader has the members stand in a circle and "sculpt" how they feel about the group, using their body and hands.

Leader: I want everyone to stand and make a large circle. In a minute, I am going to ask you to indicate how you are feeling about this group by using your body language and position. If you are really into the group and open for it, you would come to the center and have your arms open. If you are against the group, you would turn your back to the group and have your arms closed around you. Everyone understand? OK, on 3—1, 2, 3.

This is an excellent exercise if the group is not going well but the leader believes it has some potential. The exercise can tap that potential.

Family Sculpture

In this exercise the leader has members "sculpt" their families as they see them now or when they were growing up. This exercise is usually very revealing, and members find it interesting to sculpt their own family and to see how other members sculpt theirs. It is used to generate discussion about family relationships.

EXAMPLE . . . .

The group is composed of male teenagers.

Leader: Today we are going to focus on our families. To do this, we are going to do an exercise called "Family Sculpture." What this entails is that each of you will "sculpt" your family by picking other members to play your parents or the adults you live with, your siblings, and any other significant person in your family and positioning them to show how they relate to one another. For example, the parents may be holding hands or they may be far apart with their fists raised. The kids may be close together or very far apart. Some may be close to dad but not mom, or they may even have their backs to their parents. Who will volunteer to go first? I'll explain more as you go along.

Tony: I will. What do I do?

Leader: Stand here in the center. Who lives at home with you?

Tony: My mom, my dad, and my little sister.

Leader: Pick a member to be each one of these, and pick someone to be you.

Tony: Bob, you be my dad. Sam, you be me. Don, I guess you will have to be my mom, and Bill, you be my sister.

Leader: Now position these people as you see them. Are your mom and dad close?

Tony: No, they hardly speak. They would be at the opposite ends of the room. Can I put them there?

Leader: Sure. Where would you put you and your sister?

Tony: My sister is real close to my mom, so I would put her over there with her. I am not close to anyone, so I would be way over in the other corner away from everyone. Gee, this is heavy!

The leader will usually spend two or three minutes discussing the sculpture as each member designs it. When everyone has had a turn, a long discussion usually takes place on family issues.

. . . .

Home Spot

In this exercise, members stand in a circle holding hands. Each one picks a spot in the room toward which to try to maneuver the group. Since most members will have a different spot and all are holding hands, many different dynamics occur. The leader might use this for a change of pace and for focusing members on how they try to get what they want, how persistent they are, and how protective they are of other people.

EXAMPLE . . . .

> **Leader:** Let's try something different. We've been discussing how many of you do not always go after what you want and need. There is an exercise that I think you'll find interesting. I want you to stand up and move your chairs all the way against the wall. (*Members do this*) Now come to the center and form a circle, holding hands. Not too tight of a circle. Now I'd like each of you to look around and pick a spot in the room. In a minute, I am going to ask you, while still holding hands, to try to move to that spot. This is to be done without any talking or laughter. Your main goal is to get to your spot, without letting go of the other members' hands. Get ready. OK, try to move to your spot.

Members will pull, push, give up, kneel on the floor, and so on. The leader will stop the exercise after a minute or so and then process the various reactions.

. . . .

Personal Space

This exercise consists of members standing in a circle not too close to each other—almost at arms' distance. The leader then instructs them to close their eyes and to feel the space around them, exploring around their head and in front, to the sides, and in back of them. The leader will then instruct them to venture out of "their space" by using their arms, which usually results in members touching each other. Discussion often centers around the comfort level of their own space and feelings about venturing out. Members will usually discuss how they feel about their "space" as they live their daily lives.

Become a Statue

This exercise requires members to stand at some distance from each other; on the count of three they all become "statues" of how they see themselves, either in the group or in their lives outside the group (depending on the purpose of the exercise). This exercise is good for giving members the chance to visually represent themselves. Discussion and questions that follow center on their self-images and how they see others.

Opening Up

In this exercise, members get into pairs; one person sits on the floor and curls up in a ball. The other then takes hold of the partner's arms and gently but somewhat firmly tries to "open him or her up." The exercise usually arouses feelings of control, resistance, fear of being open, or liking being opened up by another.

Trust

There are a number of trust exercises, many of which involve movement. These will be discussed later in the chapter, in the longer section titled "Trust Exercises."

Reasons for Using Movement Exercises

There are at least five good reasons for using movement exercises.

1. They give members a chance to stretch and move around. This can be good for young people and for members who have been sitting for a long while. It is important to remember that members can become bored and fatigued if seated too long or if the format remains unchanged for extended periods.

2. They provide a change in the format and this in turn can serve to keep the group interesting and may boost energy.

3. They give group members a chance to *experience* something rather than simply discuss it. For example, if the topic of the session is the desire to belong, the breaking-in exercise mentioned earlier may be used to let members physically experience exclusion by being kept out of the circle.

4. The drama of movement exercises may cause members to remember what took place in the group more readily in the days or weeks following than might otherwise occur after simply discussing an issue.

5. Movement exercises usually involve all the members. That is, all members are up and doing something, whereas in discussion exercises some members may not be involved.

Cautions for Using Movement Exercises

Various situations and/or client populations may not be conducive to using movement activities. For example, leaders should not attempt strenuous movement activities with persons with significant health problems or the very elderly. Any time the exercise calls for vigorous movement, make sure that objects such as chairs, desks, or tables are well out of the way. Also make sure that members remove eyeglasses or any other items that may be damaged or that may injure others.

Dyads and Triads

Placing members in dyads or triads is a group activity that can be considered an exercise. It is mainly intended to give members a chance to (1) interact with one or two other individuals, (2) practice some skill, or (3) do an activity that calls for two people to interact in some prescribed manner. Since we have discussed the use of dyads extensively in Chapter Eight, we will not discuss their use or value here in any detail. Here are three examples.

One exercise is called "I Have To—I Choose To." In this exercise, members pair up and take turns saying aloud their list of things that they feel they "have" to do. Then they go back and change the recitation from "I have to" to "I choose to." A variation of this would be a list beginning "I need," which would change to "I want." These kinds of exercises give members a chance to hear how they can change some of their demands or needs. Saying statements out loud, to another, makes more of an impact than saying them to themselves.

Another dyad exercise is one in which a member says to the partner "I should. . . . " and the partner firmly responds "No, you shouldn't!" Each partner would go through the list of "shoulds" and experience being told "no." This exercise helps members think through what really are and are not "shoulds" in their lives.

Another dyad or triad exercise that can prove to be very enlightening to members is to have them pair up and each assume the role of one of their parents. Then the "parents" talk about their son or daughter. This exercise can help members experience how they perceive their parents' opinions of them and is a valuable exercise for all age groups. Stevens (1972) calls this exercise "Parents' Chat."

Rounds

As we said in Chapter Eight, rounds are probably the most valuable exercises to which a leader has access. They are quick and can help gather considerable information. One kind of round not mentioned in Chapter Eight is the forced-choice round. This consists of the leader reading a statement and the members stating how they feel about the statement. The members would usually respond with "strongly agree," "agree," "disagree," or "strongly disagree." The following are some examples of statements that could be used:

Blacks and whites should never marry each other.
Extramarital affairs are always harmful.
Divorce means failure.
One should love one's parents no matter what.
Being married is essential for happiness.

As you can see, responses to these kinds of sentences have the potential to generate a lot of discussion. The leader's skill comes in choosing appropriate statements for the members to react to. Forced-choice sentences can serve as a simple yet effective way to stimulate interaction in a group.

Exercises Using Creative Props

Different counseling props can be used for interesting and engaging group exercises (Jacobs, 1992). Items such as rubber bands, styrofoam cups, a small child's chair, and an empty beer bottle all can be used. For a full discussion of these and other creative techniques, see *Creative Counseling Techniques: An Illustrated Guide* (Jacobs, 1992). The following examples show how leaders can use props effectively in group exercises.*

Rubber Bands

E X A M P L E S . . . .

> **Leader:** I want each of you to take one of these thick rubber bands and stretch it until you feel the tension. Hold your hands out and experience the stress. Since this group is on stress management, I thought that rubber bands may help you to see how you are doing. Since our meeting last week, is the stress greater or worse? I want you to either increase the tension, or loosen it. Also think about ways you can reduce your stress and note that for the tension on the rubber band to decrease, you have to do something! Think about this for a minute, and then I'll ask you to share your feelings and thoughts.

. . . .

> **Leader:** This is now the third meeting of our couples group, so I thought we would take a look at the tension you have in your relationship. I want each of you to get with your partner and take a rubber band. (*Some playfully act as though they are going to "pop" their partner*) I see some of you already are kind of acting out parts of your marriage. I want you to think about how you can use the rubber band in various ways to symbolize your relationship and interactions. I'll give you about three minutes to talk about how you would use the rubber band.

*Adapted and reproduced by special permission of Psychological Assessment Resources, Inc., 16204 North Florida Avenue, Lutz, Florida 33549, from *Creative Counseling Techniques: An Illustrated Guide*, by Ed Jacobs, Ph.D. Copyright 1992, by Psychological Assessment Resources, Inc. Further reproduction is prohibited without prior permission from PAR, Inc.

Jane: We each did exactly the same thing. We pulled until it nearly broke and then we sort of looked at each other. Neither one of us gave in, though, so here we sit with the tension at its maximum.

Carl: Ours was very different. We played with it, and then we each popped each other sort of hard. It made us realize that we do hurt each other sometimes.

. . . .

Styrofoam Cups

E X A M P L E S . . . .

Leader: I want each of you to take a cup and a pencil. I want you to think of the cup as representing your personal worth and then I want you to punch holes in the cup as you think about the things that cause you not to like yourself. A hole may represent your appearance, not having friends, your parents' reactions to you, your intelligence, or anything else you can think of. When you are done, each of you will get a chance to share your cup. Some of you may have some holes that you don't want to share yet with the group and you can just say something like, "There are two more big ones that I am not ready to share yet." The point of the holes is to help you see what you may want to work on in the group.

. . . .

Leader: I want everyone to look at this cup I am holding, and think of it as your own self-worth. (*The leader now stands on the chair*) As I stand and start to squeeze the cup, I want you to think of whom you give your worth to—whom you have on the chair that you allow to hurt or squeeze you. (*Everyone looks up and seems to be in deep thought*) Any comments or reactions?

. . . .

Small Chair

E X A M P L E . . . .

Leader: We have been talking about having fun, so I want you to focus on the whole idea of having fun. To help you, I want you to look at this small chair and think about the fun little boy or girl inside you. I want you to think about what happened to him or her as you have grown up. Since many of you said you don't have fun, we need to hear from the child part of you. (*All stare intensely at the chair. A couple of members start to cry*)

Cathy: This is very powerful for me. I stopped having fun when I was 4 because of something that happened. (*Cries*)

Matt: I used to have fun, but when my mom died, I felt that I had to help out, and I have been doing that ever since.

. . . .

Beer Bottle

E X A M P L E . . . .

Leader: I want each of you to look at this beer bottle and this string. I want you to let the string represent either your life, your ability to control your mood, or your tolerance for not getting angry. Now watch what happens to the long string as I put it into the bottle. What do you see?

Carlos: It gets shorter.

Danie: It gets gobbled up. Disappears.

Leader: Now, what do you take this to mean for you? (*The leader places the bottle in the center of the group. Everyone stares at it*)

. . . .

These are just some of the props a leader can use to focus the group on a topic. Some other useful props are shields, old cassette tapes, playing cards, and furnace filters (Jacobs, 1992).

Arts-and-Crafts Exercises

Arts-and-crafts exercises require that members draw, cut, paste, paint, or create something with a variety of materials. These exercises, like the others discussed here, can generate interest, provide fun, focus the group, create energy, and trigger discussion. Arts-and-crafts exercises allow members to express themselves in a different way. That is, they can put their thoughts and feelings into a project before they share verbally with others. This is especially helpful for members who have difficulty identifying or expressing feelings directly. For this reason, arts-and-crafts exercises are useful with younger children, but they are also useful for all ages. Having members draw their dream house or their imaginary coat of arms can stimulate very interesting discussions.

One example of an arts-and-crafts exercise involves the use of paper bags, magazines, scissors, and tape or glue. All these materials are passed out to each member. Members are then told to look through their magazine and cut out any word, phrase, or picture that describes them right now. Those aspects they are willing to share with the group are to be pasted on the outside of the bag. Those they are not willing to share are placed inside the bag. When it comes time for discussion, members hold up their bags and tell the group about themselves. This exercise is particularly useful in helping members become acquainted with each other and making sharing about themselves easier. The leader can also choose to focus on what is in the bag by discussing why people tend not to want to share parts of themselves.

A second purpose of arts-and-crafts exercises is to serve as projective devices for the members' thoughts, feelings, and experiences. That is, current problems members experience may be represented in a creative project. For example, the leader might ask members to draw a picture of themselves and their family engaging in a typical interaction. Often, much is revealed by such drawings.

A third purpose is sharing: members seem to enjoy seeing what other members have drawn, painted, or built. Thus, sharing oneself and listening to others becomes more interesting when members can see what is being talked about.

Fantasy Exercises

Fantasy exercises are most often used in growth and therapy groups, employing group members' imagination and visual imagery. Fantasies help members become more aware of their feelings, wishes, doubts, and fears. An example of a fantasy exercise is the "common object" fantasy, in which the leader directs the members to imagine themselves as an object that is in the room (a book, wastebasket, cup, purse, window, pencil, chair, and so forth). The leader guides the members through the fantasy by asking what it feels like to be the object, what life is like being that object, their role in life, and so forth.

EXAMPLES . . . .

> **Leader:** (*Very slowly and softly*) I want you to look at this brief-case, and I want you to become this briefcase. Think about what your life is like as a briefcase. How does it feel? (*Pause*) What happens to you as a briefcase? (*Pause*) What is it like being a briefcase? (*Pause*) In a few seconds I am going to

ask you to share your experience of being a briefcase. I would like you to start by saying, "I am a briefcase, and as a briefcase, . . .

. . . .

Leader: I want each of you to close your eyes and get comfortable. (*Pause*) (*Using a soothing voice with a slow pace*) Now I want you to imagine that you are a tree. (*Pause*) What kind of tree are you? (*Pause*) What are your surroundings? (*Pause*) What is life like as a tree? (*Pause*) How does it feel being the tree that you are? (*Pause*) OK, who wants to go first and share what he or she experienced?

. . . .

Other examples of fantasy exercises include the "stump/cabin/ stream" fantasy (members imagine themselves as each of these objects, describing their relationship with each other as well as their differences); the "rosebush" fantasy (members imagine themselves as a rosebush); the "wise man" fantasy (members imagine taking a trip up a mountain to visit an old wise man and to get an answer to a most important question); and the "funeral" fantasy (members imagine their own funeral and the reactions of people attending it).

When members discuss their fantasy the leader encourages them to determine if the feelings attributed to the object or fantasy do, in fact, apply to their daily lives. Because certain kinds of fantasy exercises may cause members to explore thoughts or feelings that have been denied to their conscious awareness, leaders who use fantasy exercises should be prepared for members to get in touch with some painful material.

Common-Reading Exercises

Common-reading exercises require that members read a short passage, poem, or story. Such readings often serve the purpose of triggering ideas and thoughts and of deepening the focus on some topic or issue. For example, in growth groups the "Gestalt Prayer" (Perls, 1969) may serve as a stimulating common reading:

I do my thing, and you do your thing.
I am not in this world to live up to your expectations
And you are not in this world to live up to mine.
You are you and I am I,
And if by chance we find each other, it's beautiful;
If not, it can't be helped.

Although members have a variety of reactions to this passage, it usually triggers discussion about demands and expectations placed on others as well as the need for approval and acceptance. Other passages and poems that have proven effective have come from *The Prophet* by Kahlil Gibran or poems by T. S. Eliot or Robert Frost. An example of a passage by Frost, from his poem "The Road Not Taken," follows:

Two roads diverged in a wood, and I—
I took the one less traveled by,
And that has made all the difference.

This is a very inspiring passage and often gives members permission to be different and not follow the crowd. As members read the passage they are reminded of incidents in their own lives concerning choices they have made. Some may have taken the less-traveled road, while others did not. Usually a good discussion follows the reading of this passage.

The key factor to keep in mind when using common-reading exercises is the purpose of the group. Make sure that the material will trigger thoughts related to the purpose. Another consideration is the intellectual capabilities of the members when asking them to read and react to a poem or written verse. Obviously, the preceding examples would not be appropriate for elementary schoolchildren. There are interesting materials written for all educational levels. Common readings should address common themes to which most group members can relate.

Feedback Exercises

One potential benefit of being in groups is the opportunity to hear what others think of you. Listed below are a number of feedback exercises that may be valuable to members. Feedback exercises allow the members and the leader to share their feelings and thoughts about each other. Leaders should not do a feedback exercise unless they feel the members have enough goodwill to try to be helpful rather than cruel or insensitive. It would be a major mistake to do a feedback exercise with members who want to hurt other members and who have no desire to be helpful or to listen to feedback that they might receive from others.

"First Impressions"

This is an exercise in which members share their first impressions of other members. This can be done in the first session or can be used in later sessions when the members have had a chance to revise their first impressions. If used in a later session, members get a chance to hear how they are perceived now and how they were perceived when others first met them.

Adjective Checklist

Members are given a written list of 15 to 20 adjectives that describe people. They then take turns being the focus of the group, while other members pick three to five adjectives that describe the spotlighted member. Using the adjectives gives members a structured way to respond to each other.

Talk about the Members

Each member in turn can be the focus of a group discussion. The leader would have members talk about the member, mentioning strengths and weaknesses. When doing this, the leader may have the member being discussed close his or her eyes, turn around so as not to face the group, or simply sit quietly as the members talk about him or her. This will depend on the kind of group and the kind of feedback that is about to be given. If the leader feels the members will speak more openly if the member of focus is not watching, the leader may have that member turn around. Also, many people have said they can listen better when they are not looking at the others while they are talking.

"Strength Bombardment"

This is similar to the exercise above in that the members talk about the member of focus, but it is done in a more organized fashion. That is, the leader directs the group to first describe the strengths of the designated member. The leader appoints one member to keep a list of all the strengths, so that the member can have the list when the exercise is over. A variation would be to also list weaknesses or areas needing improvement.

Wishes

A very nonthreatening way to give feedback is by using wishes. The leader sets this exercise up by asking members to verbalize any wishes that they have for a given member. The leader would say something like, "What I would like you to do is think of wishes that you have for various members. We'll focus on one person at a time and anyone who has a wish for that person will say, 'My wish for you is . . .'" This is a good exercise for members who are concerned for each other and who have various things to say to each other. It would be good in support groups and in some growth and therapy groups.

Metaphorical Feedback

The leader asks members to think of an animal; a character in real life, in the movies, or on TV; or an inanimate object, such as a sunset or a babbling brook, that reminds them of a designated member. Each member gets to hear how others see her in a different way.

Written Feedback

Members are asked to write out feedback for each member of the group. This is usually done between sessions, since it takes quite a bit of time. The value of this kind of feedback is that members experience reading about themselves from the point of view of a number of other people. This kind of feedback activity can only be used with members who are basically stable. The leader would provide members with instructions on what kinds of feedback to write.

Most/Least Feedback

This kind of feedback involves members sharing how they feel about other members by using a "most" and "least" designation. For example, the leader may ask members to designate the following:

- To whom they feel most similar and least similar
- With whom they feel most comfortable and least comfortable
- Whom they trust most and whom they trust least
- Who they feel is working hardest in the group and who they feel is working the least

This kind of exercise can create extensive interaction and must be used with care. The leader will want to be sure that this is the best kind of feedback exercise to use. The leader may also want to do just the "most" and "least" category rather than both.

When deciding which feedback to use, the leader should consider the level of trust, the purpose of the group, and the type of feedback desired. Different kinds of feedback exercises will elicit different kinds of responses.

Trust Exercises

Because groups involve sharing to some degree, the amount of trust that members have in each other is a group dynamic that the leader must assess. If the leader finds that members do not trust one another or that more trust seems to be needed in the group, she may choose to have the members participate in trust exercises. Each exercise is intended to focus members' attention on the issue of trust and specifically on trust in one another.

Rounds

A number of rounds let the leader focus on trust. For example, the leader might say the following:

- On a 1-to-10 scale, with 10 being a person who can trust others easily and 1 being someone for whom it is difficult to trust, how would you rate yourself?
- In this group, do you feel that there is a lot of trust, moderate trust, or little trust? I want each of you to think how you would respond to that question, and we will go around the group and hear from each of you.
- When you were growing up, would you say your environment was very trusting, moderately trusting, or not trusting at all?

In each of these rounds, the issue of trust would be the focus. The first two could relate directly to the group, whereas the last one would reflect what members learned about trusting at an early age. Certainly some of what they learned is probably affecting them in the group.

"Trust Lift"

In this exercise, members stand in a tight circle with one person in the center. The members gently move that person around by the shoulders for about a minute to set the tone. During this time, the member's eyes are closed, his feet are stationary if possible, and everyone is silent. Then, gently, the members take the person by the feet, waist, shoulders, and head and gradually lift him over their heads. Then they slowly rock the person while bringing him gently to the floor. A member willing to do this would be trusting the group not to drop him. The group's working together to lift another member often creates bonding or trust, as well. The leader should focus discussion both on being lifted and on being responsible for lifting.

The obvious caution for this exercise is that the members must be capable of lifting the person. Also, the leader should be prepared for one or two members to choose not to participate as the person lifted due to their fear of being dropped or perhaps even of being touched. During this exercise the leader must make sure that someone holds the person's head and neck; otherwise it would be uncomfortable.

"Trust Fall"

This exercise is done in pairs or threes. It consists of one person standing, with one or two members right behind her. The person in front falls backward, and the others catch her at a safe distance above the floor.

The cautions mentioned in the "Trust Lift" would also apply to this exercise.

"Blind Trust Walk"

This exercise is done in pairs, with one person blindfolded and the other serving as a guide. During the exercise there should be no talking except for directions, such as "Step down." The purpose of the exercise is to experience trusting another person to lead you. When doing this exercise, the leader would want to be in a setting that would accommodate members walking around without interference. It probably would not work in an agency or school unless there were a very large room or if it were after hours. Each member should be led around for about five minutes to get the effect; ideally, the walk should be such that the blindfolded member experiences more than walking around in a circle. That is, it is good to have members walk where there are doors, chairs, steps, tables, and so on to maneuver around. In addition, most of the time should be spent discussing trust, although some time will be spent on discussing the experience of the walk.

Some of the exercises in the next section can also be used to build trust.

Experiential Exercises

Several group exercises could be classified as experiential because the members are involved in some kind of individual or group experience that is active and often challenging. Probably the most well known exercise of this kind is the "Ropes Course," which is "a blend of activities designed to take individuals and groups beyond their own expectations, or perceived willingness to try" (Project Adventure, 1992). The activities are done outdoors on a carefully designed course made up of ropes. Some of the activities are very challenging and seem dangerous, which force individuals to come face to face with themselves (Project Adventure, 1992). Other activities on the ropes course depend on members cooperating with each other; thus, it is good for team building. Some group leaders use the ropes course as one part of their group, whereas other leaders just lead groups through the ropes course or some other kind of experiential activity.

When thinking about experiential exercises, the leader will want to make sure that the exercise fits the purpose. There are many outdoor activities that are fun and interesting, but they may not be appropriate for the group that is being led.

Moral-Dilemma Exercises

Several group exercises could be considered "moral dilemmas"; that is, a story is read or passed out to the members and each one has to decide how she would handle the situation. Some of these stories involve stealing food to sustain life, deciding whom to let stay in a lifeboat, or deciding whether to tell the authorities about a crime. Simon, Howe, and Kirschenbaum (1978) describe one involving a fallout shelter and whom to let in; another involves a cave-in and who should be at the front of the line as the survivors walk out. Probably the most popular moral-dilemma exercise is called "Alligator/River." It is a story about a woman needing to cross a river to obtain a lifesaving medicine. She must decide whether to give in to the demands of the riverboat captain in order to get across. You may wish to use these exercises or contrive your own stories. Moral-dilemma exercises have been found to be very helpful in facilitating discussion among adolescents.

E X A M P L E . . . .

> You are on a ship when it shipwrecks. Seven people want to get into the life raft, and it only holds five. The people are you, a 12-year-old hoodlum-type kid, a 69-year-old retired teacher, a 35-year-old star baseball player, a 22-year-old auto mechanic, a 52-year-old preacher, and a pregnant, 39-year-old homemaker. Who would you think should *not* be allowed on the life raft?

. . . .

This kind of exercise is useful in that it helps members to realize that people have different values. These exercises usually generate a discussion about values, justice, and fairness. They can be used at the beginning of a session and become the focus of the entire session, or they may be used as an exercise that takes about 30 minutes to discuss and process.

Group-Decision Exercises

Other kinds of exercises that can be used in groups are group-decision activities. These involve members working together to solve some sort of problem, such as being lost on the moon with certain supplies: the group would be asked to determine the best way to use the supplies. Depending on the size of the group, the entire group may work together as one unit or be divided into two or three groups of four members each.

Another activity calls for sharing resources such as rulers, scissors, tape, paper, string, and pencils to complete a project. This one would usually be done nonverbally. Members would be given different resources and a task to complete; they would be told that they can share or do anything they like except talk in order to complete the task. It would either be stated or would quickly become apparent that they do not have all the resources themselves, and that other members of the group have different resources than they do. This kind of activity is interesting and, depending on how it is used, can generate discussion about competition, sharing, and cooperation.

Johnson and Johnson (1991) describe a number of different kinds of group-decision activities. Two examples are: (1) having members try to figure out the right supplies to take ("Winter Survival") and (2) having members try to complete a complicated puzzle through cooperation ("Hollow Squares Exercise").

Touching Exercises

A number of exercises involve touching. Some are done with the entire group, such as a group massage or milling and touching; others are done in pairs, such as members lightly touching each other's hands or faces. Also, many of the trust exercises involve touching in some manner. We cover touching exercises as a separate category because there are some cautions to consider when doing them.

First, be aware that some members may not be comfortable with physical contact. If an exercise involves any form of touching, be sure members understand what will happen and then allow anyone who wishes to opt out of the exercise. Second, in almost all situations it is best to avoid touching exercises that may have a sexual connotation. Some massage exercises, for example, may be interpreted as sexual unless properly conducted. The only possible reason for using such exercises would be if the leader were planning to focus on the issue of sex and touching. In this situation you would want to be *very* careful to explain the exercise and its purpose, and to allow members to choose not to participate. Exercises that tend to arouse sexual feelings usually serve no useful purpose, may frighten members, and may inappropriately arouse feelings between two members.

CONCLUDING COMMENTS

As we have stated throughout this book, using exercises can be very beneficial, especially when the proper ones are chosen. In this chapter, we discussed seven reasons that leaders should use exercises as well as when to use them. We concluded with the discussion of 14 kinds of group exercises, giving examples of each type. Once a leader has decided to use an exercise, it is his or her responsibility to consider how to make it most effective; this will be covered in the next chapter.

Introducing, Conducting, and Processing Exercises

For exercises to be productive and useful, they must be introduced properly, conducted properly, and processed in a way that is helpful for the members. In this chapter, we address each of these important skills.

INTRODUCING AN EXERCISE

Proper introduction means, among other things, giving clear instructions to members on how to carry out an exercise. This is as important as the exercise itself. Leaders often give ample thought to the exercise, but if their instructions are not clearly presented and if certain cautions are not expressed, the likely result will be confusion and the exercise will be almost meaningless.

A second introductory consideration is that skilled leaders use their voices to set the right tone for the exercise. If the exercise is to be a serious or thought-provoking one, leaders will want to slow their delivery down, using pauses and a quieter voice. If it is to be an energizing, fun exercise, the leader would probably want to speed up the delivery, using a very enthusiastic voice. Too often, leaders fail to use their voices effectively and the exercise in turn does not produce the kinds of responses that are desired.

When introducing an exercise, it is also important to gain the cooperation and goodwill of the members. Therefore, members should not be made to feel the leader is doing something to them or that they are being forced to participate. It should be made clear that they have the right not to participate if they so desire. There is greater likelihood that the exercise will be beneficial if the members are participating of their own free will. Discussed in this chapter are other considerations with regard to introducing an exercise.

General Considerations

Inform Members of the Purpose and Procedure

When introducing most exercises, the leader will want to inform the members of the purpose and how the exercise will be carried out. A straightforward introduction will cause members to have more understanding of and, be more cooperative in the exercise.

E X A M P L E S . . . .

EFFECTIVE INTRODUCTION

Leader: Today I am going to show you some pictures I cut out of a magazine. I am going to ask you to make up a story about one scene. One purpose of this exercise is to help you realize that each of us has our own way of seeing things. There are no right answers, and I think you will find this really interesting.

In this example, the leader tells the members what the purpose is and that there are no right or wrong answers in the hope of relieving any uncomfortable feelings that members might have about sharing their stories. In the following example, the leader is less effective because he does not tell the members why they are being asked to make up stories about the various pictures.

. . . .

INEFFECTIVE INTRODUCTION

Leader: I want you to look at this picture and tell me what you see. Who wants to go first?

. . . .

In some exercises it will not be desirable to inform the members fully of the purpose, because telling them the specific purpose could interfere with the effect. When introducing such exercises it is a good idea simply to tell the members that the purpose will be explained following the exercise. Again, the leader's attitude as reflected in tone of voice, gestures, and related cues will be a major factor in ensuring cooperation.

Avoid Confusing Directions

When introducing an exercise, the leader must clearly present what the members are to do. If the instructions on how to complete the exercise are not clearly presented, members will become confused and will not fully participate. The directions should be as simple as possible. If the exercise is a complex one in which members are going to be asked to do a number of things, you might practice by giving the directions to colleagues or friends before trying them in the group. In the following ineffective example, the leader would have seen that the directions were too vague had he practiced them with someone first.

EXAMPLES. . . . .

The exercise involves members cooperating with each other in order to complete a given task. The members may actually share materials and work together to complete the task, but the leader fails to point this out.

INEFFECTIVE INTRODUCTION

Leader: Each of you will receive an envelope that has a task described in it and some materials. You are to try to complete the task without talking to others. The tasks are different. The goal is to try to finish before anyone else.

By failing to tell them that they may share, this leader causes some members to become frustrated and think that pieces were omitted or that others were given more items and that the exercise is unfair.

. . . .

EFFECTIVE INTRODUCTION

Leader: Each of you will receive an envelope that has a number of things in it such as tape, a pencil, or a ruler. Also included is the description of a task to complete. The task will be something like making a 3-by-6-inch red rectangle and taping it on a white circle. In order to complete the task you will need to share with others, since your envelope will not include all the materials necessary for completing the task. You can negotiate with other members, but you can do this only nonverbally—that is, no talking. The goal is to try to finish before anyone else.

. . . .

When giving directions for an exercise, the leader should be watching members' reactions. Nonverbal cues will often tell him if the members understand the directions. If the directions are not clarified at the beginning, members will interpret how to do the exercise in many different ways, causing the leader to have a difficult time processing it effectively. Also, members find it very frustrating when they do not understand directions.

Another mistake occurs when the leader comments on how the exercise will help the members focus on some topic when in fact it does not do so. Members start thinking in one direction and then, when the actual directions are given, they experience confusion.

EXAMPLES. . . . .

> **Leader:** Today we are going to focus on how you have fun in your life. I think it is something to which not enough thought is given. I want you to pair up and, with your partner, discuss how you and your family spent weekends, vacations, and summers when you were young.

Here the leader makes two mistakes. The leader implies that the discussion about fun will relate to the present, but then focuses the members on the past. Second, the leader assumes that "fun" means recreational time, weekends, and vacations. This may be the leader's frame of reference, but it overlooks the fact that people can have fun completing a difficult task, playing with children, cooking dinner, and so forth.

. . . .

> **Leader:** In a minute, I'm going to ask you to do an exercise that should get you in touch with your thoughts about the difficulties of having a disabled child. There are many difficulties, and I think this exercise will help you get in touch with them. Get out a sheet of paper and a pencil. (*Pause*) I want you to write down the first thing that comes to mind when I say these key words: *anger, guilt, failure.*

Again, the leader is operating from his own frame of reference. Of the many difficulties that parents of a disabled child may encounter, feelings of guilt or anger may be one, but others have to do with financial problems, baby-sitting and day care, obtaining public services for their child, handling their own fatigue, and so on. This leader may unwittingly anger the group members by his insensitivity to the range of issues.

. . . .

> **Leader:** Today we are going to talk about your family of origin and what life was like in your home. I want you to think of the different feelings you had growing up: how you felt about your mom, dad, and any siblings. Maybe there were other significant people in your life such as a grandparent, neighbor, or

teacher. On the paper in front of you, I'd like you to draw a rough sketch of the house you grew up in. You can fill in the area around the house—really, anything you want.

As you can see, the leader switched the focus from feelings about family members to a visualization of the house in which members grew up. The two are totally unrelated.

. . . .

In each of these examples, the leader gets the members to travel along one line of thought and then does an exercise that is only slightly related or not related at all. Time and time again, it seems that beginning leaders introduce a topic and then do an exercise that does not relate to that topic. This causes the members to be quite confused. Beginning leaders make this mistake primarily because they have not thought through the issue sufficiently. For instance, in the third example the leader apparently jumped to the conclusion that focusing on the houses members grew up in would stimulate them to think of their families. After considering this more thoroughly, the leader would have realized that the drawing exercise would probably get members in touch with feelings about themselves or events that occurred rather than with feelings about family members. Obviously, there is a major difference in these two topics. A leader should make sure that the introduction fits the exercise *and* that the exercise is relevant to the topic being discussed.

Avoid Lengthy Directions

A common mistake group leaders make when introducing exercises is giving directions that are too long or complex. If the instructions are necessarily long or complicated, it may be best to give them in stages. For example, if the leader wants members to form triads and each play a certain role for the exercise, he should have them form triads and determine who is playing which role before proceeding to the next stage of the instructions.

EXAMPLES. . . . .

INEFFECTIVE INTRODUCTION

Leader: I want you to get into threes; one of you will be the mother, one will be the child, and one will be the father who is returning the child from a visit with him on the weekend. Each of you should be upset about something—the mom can be upset about how the dad is always late in bringing the child back. The child is upset about a number of things—he wanted to stay with the dad longer and wanted to go with his dad next weekend, but the dad had to say "no." The dad is upset about not being able to keep his son longer and because he could not have his son next weekend for a special occasion.

. . . .

EFFECTIVE INTRODUCTION
Leader: I want you to get into threes. (*Pause while they do this*) Now I want you to decide who will be the mother, the dad, and the child. (*Pause—leader checks to make sure everyone is doing this*) OK, now all those who are playing mom, here's the role I want you to play. . . . All those playing dad, here's the role I want you to play. . . . And all those who are playing the child, here's the role. . . .

By presenting the instructions in stages, this leader minimizes the confusion.

. . . .

Other Common Errors

Leaders sometimes assume that the members are prepared to discuss some article, movie, or task assigned from the last session. Instead, the leader should first ask the members if they have completed the assignment. At times the leader might want to go ahead with the exercise even if one or two members are not prepared, telling them to observe or participate as best they can. An alternative plan is always needed, however, in case the majority is unprepared.

Failure to tell members how long an exercise will last is another mistake typical of beginning leaders. Without guidelines concerning time, members may either rush in order to finish or procrastinate and be halfway through when it is time to stop. Something direct, like "We'll spend five minutes on this exercise," is sufficient.

Exercise-Specific Considerations

Written Exercises

When introducing a written exercise the leader should distribute or ask members to get the necessary materials (usually paper and pencil), let them get settled back into the group, and then give the instructions.

If the leader fails to do this and the members have to search for materials, one or more will forget the instructions.

A leader should always be prepared to provide the necessary writing materials such as pens, pencils, and paper. Even if the leader is certain that members will bring materials with them it is a good idea to have extra materials on hand in case pencil leads get broken or ink runs out. When passing out any forms that are going to be completed, it is a good idea to turn them face down and ask members not to look at them until the instructions have been given completely.

Movement Exercises

While introducing movement exercises it is often best to have members stand and move into the designated starting position before giving the instructions. It is also important that the leader not give the instructions while the members are moving around, since they will not be paying attention.

EXAMPLES . . . .

INEFFECTIVE INTRODUCTION
Leader: We are going to do a movement exercise involving milling. Each of you is to start out in a spot in the room that is far from the center. I am going to ask you to walk around, moving to different parts of the room with your eyes looking downward; then I am going to have you mill around while glancing at each other. Then you will make steady eye contact. OK, move to a spot that is away from the center. (*Members move to various spots; a couple have to find new spots because another member is there already*)
James: Now what do we do first? I forgot. Do we glance at each other?

. . . .

EFFECTIVE INTRODUCTION
Leader: We are going to do a movement exercise involving milling. First, I want each of you to find a spot in the room that is far from the center. (*Pause while members do this*) I want you to look down. (*Checks to see that this is happening*) In a minute, I am going to ask you to mill around while looking down, then I will have you do some additional things. OK, please start milling around, but continue to keep your heads down.

. . . .

Arts-and-Crafts Exercises

Introducing arts-and-crafts exercises is very similar to introducing written exercises, in that materials should be in front of the members before directions are given. Of course, arts-and-crafts exercises may require many more materials, such as paste, scissors, paint, crayons, and rulers. It is important to provide the space necessary for members to participate in the exercise in a comfortable manner.

Common-Reading Exercises

When introducing common readings the leader might choose to give the instructions before handing out the reading, or he might want to hand out the reading first, face down. Usually it is a good idea to tell members to mark the sentence or paragraphs that stand out to them as they read. Also, the leader will often want to give a very brief introduction to the reading in order to help the members become focused.

Fantasy Exercises

When conducting a fantasy exercise, leaders should speak slowly and give members time to allow the fantasy to develop. Since fantasy exercises employ members' imagery and feelings, it is very important for the leader to use a deliberate tone in order to evoke the feelings and images necessary. It is also important to mention that members may close their eyes during the exercise, or leave them open. Giving members such a choice can help them feel more comfortable with the fantasy exercise.

Although most members will feel more comfortable closing their eyes during a fantasy exercise, it is important for the leader to keep her eyes open and observe the reactions of the members. Some members may not "get into" the fantasy. If the leader observes that this is happening, she can anticipate a different reaction from those members than from the others. Observing the members also helps the leader pace the exercise.

Feedback Exercises

When introducing a feedback exercise, the leader should allow members enough time to think about what they are going to say before they give feedback to other members. The leader will also want to take a minute or two to explain the value of giving helpful feedback. She might want to give examples of what would be helpful and what would not. If the leader is not careful in the instructions, the members may give only superficial and meaningless feedback.

CONDUCTING AN EXERCISE

There are at least six considerations of which the leader needs to be aware when conducting an exercise:

1. Making sure members are following instructions
2. Allowing members not to share
3. Handling emotional reactions
4. Changing or stopping the exercise
5. Keeping members informed of the time
6. Choosing whether or not to participate

Each of these considerations is discussed in this section.

Making Sure Members Are Following Instructions

Once members begin the exercise the leader should observe whether they are following through as expected. For example, when members are talking in pairs, they may discuss or share about an issue unrelated to the purpose of the exercise. If the leader observes this, she may move quietly to those members and clarify what they should be doing. If a number of members seem confused, the leader may want to go through the instructions again.

Allowing Members Not to Share

In many exercises, such as in rounds or sentence completions, members are asked to respond with a number, a word, or a short answer. The leader needs to be prepared for a member to ask to be passed by, either because the member feels uncomfortable sharing or because she has not formed a response. If this situation arises, the leader should be sure to not cause the member discomfort by focusing attention on her. When everyone has commented, the leader may or may not want to bring the focus back to that member. This will depend on how uncomfortable the member seems and what the purpose of the group and exercise is. Some leaders make the mistake of waiting for a member to respond; this usually causes that member to become more uncomfortable.

E X A M P L E S . . . .

The leader is doing a round in which members describe in a word or phrase their early home environment.

Mike: Loving, but strict.
Carlos: Confusing.

Marty: Good, steady.
Rosa: Can you skip me?—I just don't want to say.
Leader: Fine. Bill?
Bill: Happy.
Sam: Good with my mom, hell when Dad was home.
Leader: Rosa, is it hard to share because it hurts too much?
Rosa: Yes, and I would rather not discuss it right now. Maybe later.
Leader: Sure. What we are going to discuss is how your upbring-
　　ing affects you today.

. . . .

The leader has asked members to get into pairs to discuss their feelings about their marriages. The dyads have been in progress for about 45 seconds when one member gets up and walks toward the leader.

Peggy: I don't feel like talking about this; can I be excused?
Leader: (*To Peggy's partner*) Dan, why don't you join Jim and
　　Gloria? Peggy, let's you and I talk for a minute so that I know
　　what is going on.

. . . .

If a member chooses not to participate at all in an exercise, the leader will want to do everything he can to make that member and the others as comfortable as possible with that decision. Depending on the exercise, the member may simply sit and observe or be asked to leave the room temporarily. If possible, the leader will want to determine why the member does not want to participate and, if appropriate, the members should know why. In most instances the leader would not want to take too much time determining the reason, because it would detract from the exercise. Doing so is a common mistake and a damaging one when the leader has already introduced the exercise, which will presumably benefit the other members of the group. As a general rule, unless a member is experiencing a major psychological crisis, it is best not to let one member's needs determine the entire group process.

Handling Emotional Reactions

When doing an exercise that focuses members on personal issues, the leader must be prepared for one or more members to react emotionally. Fantasy exercises, feedback exercises, and some movement exercises tend to do this more than others, but any exercise can stir up intense feelings. If the leader sees that a member is experiencing a strong emotional reaction, she has several options. Which option she uses will depend on the intensity of the situation, the kind of exercise, and the purpose of the group. The leader can stop the exercise and focus on the member; form dyads, pairing up with the member to discuss his or her reaction; or acknowledge the member's discomfort and continue the exercise, allowing the member simply to listen and learn from the discussion among the other members. If the leader feels the member's reaction is too intense to be handled then, the leader might choose to have the member take a break until the exercise is over or to have another member take a break with that member.

EXAMPLES . . . .

The group has completed giving feedback to two of five members in a group.

Leader: OK, let's move to Kathy next. Each of you look over the list of 25 adjectives and think of those that best describe Kathy.

Joe: Quiet, reserved, caring.

Miguel: Quiet, warm, sensitive.

Betty: Caring, quiet, nice.

Leader: (*Noticing that Kathy is starting to tear up*) Kathy, would you like to talk about what you are feeling?

Kathy: I don't like it that I am quiet. I wanted so much for someone to say "intelligent" or "strong." All I have ever been seen as is *quiet!* I hate it!

Leader: Would you like to discuss this some more? (*Kathy nods*) OK. Let's talk about how you can change that. Before we start, because our time is limited, I'd like to ask Joe if we can postpone his feedback till next week. (*Joe nods*) Kathy, tell us how you would like to be different.

. . . .

The group is discussing a sentence-completion form. The questions pertain to attitudes about sex. The sentence they are discussing is "I feel _____ about my early sexual experiences."

Leader: This question is one that may get you in touch with some guilt or pain. I hope you will be willing to share what you wrote, and perhaps more.

Diane: I said mostly OK.

Don: Guilty about one thing—good about the rest.

Leader: Sharon, what did you answer?

Sharon: (*Starting to cry*) I don't want to talk about this right now.

Leader: OK, we'll skip you. (*Looking around the group as he talks*) I do want to say that no matter what any of you did, you do not have to feel guilty about it. Hopefully we can focus on how to let go of guilt. Sharon, if it gets too uncomfortable, let me know; otherwise, I hope that you will listen and maybe later join in. Carol, what did you answer?

Carol: I said that I feel I learned a lot from those early sexual experiences.

. . . .

Changing or Stopping an Exercise

When doing an exercise, the leader sometimes decides to change it or to stop. He might do this either because he feels that it is not producing the kinds of responses he had anticipated or because a good topic for discussion has emerged that is more in line with the members' immediate needs.

E X A M P L E . . . . .

The members of a growth group were asked to list three significant people in their lives. Two of the five members have already shared their lists.

Bobbi: My dad is the most significant person in my life. Last week he went into the hospital with cancer.

Jud: (*Abruptly*) My mom has cancer, too. I didn't put her down as one of my most significant people, but I'm really scared she might die.

Leader: What we might do for a few minutes, if Bobbi and Jud would find it helpful, is to talk about this.

Bobbi: I think that it would help me.

Jud: It would definitely help me.

Leader: OK, let's focus on Bobbi and Jud now, and then we may come back to your lists a little later.

In this example it seems appropriate to stop the exercise and focus on Bobbi and Jud, who both have immediate needs in common. The topic of loss may also be one that other members can relate to, so that the work with Bobbi and Jud may eventually involve others. The leader can return to the exercise if it seems that to continue will help the other members.

. . . .

Keeping Members Informed of the Time

Leaders should keep members informed about how much time is left to complete the exercise. A statement such as "Take about two more minutes to complete the exercise" is usually a sufficient cue to let members know the amount of time left. Informing members of the time remaining gives them some idea of how to pace themselves so as to be able to complete the exercise or wind down discussion. Members are then better prepared to return to the large group to process or discuss material from the exercise. Also, by observing members' reactions to an exercise, the leader may want to lengthen or shorten the amount of time that was originally allotted to it. For instance, if the leader sees that members are actively sharing in their dyads, he might choose to let them continue for a couple of minutes longer than originally planned.

Choosing Whether or Not to Participate

A leader has the option of participating or not participating in an exercise. As a nonparticipant, the leader can closely monitor group members' activities. For example, if members are talking in dyads and their discussion is not on task, the leader can intervene and help them focus by reiterating the purpose. Another benefit of listening and watching rather than joining in is that the leader can hear what members are saying and see what they are doing. During the processing of the exercise, he may even use what he heard by saying something like, "I was listening to John and Eileen, and Eileen brought up a very important point about . . ."

Another reason for the leader not to participate is that the members may focus too much on the leader's opinions or comments. Often in certain rounds or sentence-completion exercises, the leader may choose not to do the exercise in order to avoid that focus; in other words, the leader should only participate when his participation can be of value to the members.

A third reason for not participating is that the leader can more easily get a sense of when the energy for the exercise is waning or when members have neared completion of the task. In certain kinds of exercises, the participating leader can get so involved that he loses track of time, loses the energy of the group, or both.

As a rule, the leader should not participate in an exercise that could cause him to focus on his own thoughts, feelings, or "unfinished business." A leader should not do personal work in a group he is leading; it is a good idea, however, for him to have previously done or given considerable thought to any exercise that he uses in a group.

Participating in the activity also has its benefits. For example, it can help members get to know the leader. Members are usually very interested in the leader's opinions, ideas, reactions, and feedback. If members view the leader as distant and nondisclosing, they may be less likely to share personally relevant material in the group.

The leader may also wish to participate in order to create a certain effect. For example, in certain kinds of groups, the leader may want to play devil's advocate in order to get the members to see both sides of some dilemma. Participation may also be helpful in a dyad exercise if the leader sees the need to give feedback or to help out a particular member. For example, if at some point in the group a member needs help beyond the immediate time frame or purpose of the group, the leader may divide members into dyads and pair up with the member in need. During this time the leader may do some brief counseling with that member or give information on how the member can get help.

The leader might also participate in an exercise when there is an odd number of participants and an even number is needed.

PROCESSING AN EXERCISE

Exercises merely act as catalysts for initiating interaction among members by triggering thoughts and feelings. *Understanding the processing of exercises is essential* since it is by far the most important phase of any exercise. By *processing*, we mean spending time discussing thoughts, feelings, and ideas that result from doing the exercise. Many books on exercises tell the potential leader what materials to use and how to conduct the exercise, but spend very little time discussing how to process the exercise. In this section we address not only how to process an exercise but also a number of considerations regarding the processing of exercises.

Although some exercises do not need processing because they are used for warm-up or for fun, most exercises will be of little value unless they are processed. For many exercises, the processing and the conducting of the exercise overlap in that the discussion is a part of the exercise. This would be true for some feedback, sentence-completion, and experiential exercises in which the leader asks processing questions while conducting the exercise. For other exercises, such as a trust walk or completing the ropes courses, the processing comes when the exercise is completed.

The leader will want to keep in mind several questions regarding the processing:

1. What is the goal of the processing?
2. How much time is needed for adequate processing?
3. What ways of processing should be used?
4. What kinds of processing questions should be used?
5. How much time should be spent discussing the actual exercise?

6. Should the focus be on the entire group or on one individual?
7. When should the focus be held, and when should it be shifted?
8. Is the exercise present-centered or past-centered? Do I want to focus on the past or present?

Goals of Processing

The first consideration regarding the processing of an exercise would be the goal or purpose. There are three possible goals when processing an exercise, each having a slightly different focus.

1. *To stimulate sharing and discussion related to the group dynamics and group process.* For example, a trust walk exercise can lead to a discussion about trust and then specifically about trust within the group. An exercise in which members rate how they feel about the group will usually lead to a discussion about the group dynamics and group process. Group decision exercises and experiential exercises often lead to processing that focuses on what is happening within the group.

2. *To stimulate sharing and discussion about topics or issues.* This is the goal of most exercises. Sentence completions and other written exercises are used to get members talking about different subjects. Often movement, experiential, common-reading, and moral dilemma exercises lead to beneficial discussions.

3. *To stimulate members to delve deeper into thoughts and feelings that were stirred up by the exercise.* Leaders often use fantasy exercises, certain common readings, creative exercises, and many other kinds of exercises to get members in touch with their feelings. By being clear that the goal is to get members sharing at a deep, personal level, the leader will not spend too much time on the discussion of the exercise itself or on topics.

Time Needed for Adequate Processing

A leader should always make sure there is enough time to process the exercise to the depth level desired. Many exercises are designed to take members to a very deep, personal level. Unfortunately a number of group leaders fail to allow enough time for processing. They either begin the exercise when there is not adequate time to discuss members' reactions or they move on to another activity too soon. Both of these mistakes can lead to frustration, confusion, and a shallow, meaningless experience.

EXAMPLE. . . . .
INEFFECTIVE PROCESSING
Leader: I want you to think of an animal that you would like to be if you could be any animal in the world. What would it be? (*Pause*) Who wants to go first?

Frank: A cat.
Dannie: A tiger.
Mel: A big black bear.
Sharon: A bird.
Dave: An alligator.
Leader: Any comments?
Sharon: Dave reminds me of an alligator.
Dannie: I agree, he does. He sort of sits and waits.
Leader: Any other comments? (*Pause*) Now what I'd like you to do is think of where you would like to live if you could live anywhere you wanted.

In this example, the leader does not spend time discussing the members' choices before going on to a second exercise. Therefore, very little, if anything, is gained from the exercise. The skilled leader would have a purpose for doing the animal-fantasy exercise: usually to allow members to project thoughts and feelings upon their fantasy animal. The leader would spend a few minutes having members share why they chose their particular animal. This often leads to members' having some insight about themselves that they are willing to explore further.

.   .   .   .

Another way leaders make a mistake regarding time is by letting the exercise take up too much time, leaving only a few minutes for processing. In most cases, the majority of time allotted to an exercise should be for processing the exercise and not for conducting it.

Ways of Processing

When an exercise has been conducted and completed, it can be processed in several ways:

1. In dyads or triads
2. Through writing
3. Through rounds
4. In the entire group
5. In any combination of the preceding four ways

A leader may want to use dyads or triads when there seems to be a lot of energy and members could benefit from sharing their thoughts and feelings. The use of dyads or triads gives everyone a chance to talk. Writing can be used after exercises in which members have many thoughts and feelings they might want to express but not want to say to anyone else. Exercises that are very thought-provoking and emotional, such as family sculpture or certain fantasy exercises, might lend themselves to this kind of processing.

The round is a good way to start the processing. The leader can say something like, "In a sentence or two, what stood out to you about the exercise?" or "Let's go around the group and hear from each of you as to what you thought of the reading."

Even if the first three ways are used, most often the majority of the processing will occur among the entire group. The first three ways listed often serve as a way to start the processing. Once the group is warmed up, the leader will use certain questions to stimulate the discussion such as, "Does anyone want to share thoughts or feelings?" or "What was triggered for you?" or "Let's talk about your reactions." The leader can also use these questions at the beginning of the processing if she feels that no warm-up is necessary.

E X A M P L E S . . . .

Members have just completed an exercise in which they drew three egograms (a transactional analysis diagram) of themselves at home, work, and with their family of origin.

Leader: This activity usually stirs up a lot of thoughts and feelings. First, I am going to get you to pair up and share your egograms and any thoughts that you have. Let me have the two of you to pair up, and the two of you, and the two of you. . . .

Leader: (*After allowing five minutes for sharing*) Let's come back to the large group. What have you learned from doing this exercise? Do you see some changes that you want to make?

In the preceding example, the leader uses dyads and then the whole group for processing the exercise. In the next example, the leader uses a round and then opens the discussion to the entire group with questions that will deepen the focus.

Leader: Let's do a quick round on your reaction to the exercise on a 1-to-10 scale, with 10 being "has you really thinking" and 1 being "the exercise had no impact." Who wants to start?

Ramos: 10.

Clyde: 8.

Marlene: 9.

Paulette: 8.

Tray: 8.

Leader: So everyone is really thinking. We should be able to have a very interesting session. What hit you? What are you thinking about?

Kinds of Processing Questions

The skilled leader will always consider the kind of processing questions to be asked because the questions will direct the focus of the processing (Kees & Jacobs, 1990). The questions can cause members to focus on the exercise, the group, issues or topics, or on individuals. Questions such as "What happened?" "What did you write?" "What did you draw?" and "What part of the reading stood out?" are the kinds of questions that will get the members to talk about the exercise. These questions often are used at the beginning of the processing phase but some leaders make the mistake of using only these questions, which can lead to a shallow group.

If the leader wants the members to go deeper, she should use other kinds of questions, such as the following:

- What insights did you get from doing this?
- What feelings were stirred up for you?
- How can you use this exercise to help you in your life?

Leaders will always want to make sure that their questions are congruent with the goal of the exercise. The biggest mistake leaders make is asking questions that do not foster any in-depth exploration—questions that generate discussion at the 10 or 9 level instead of at the deeper 8, 7, or 6 levels. Very often, the processing questions can help funnel the group to a deeper level.

Time Spent Discussing the Actual Exercise

Often, the leader will have to decide how long to discuss the actual exercise. For instance, if the group has just engaged in a fantasy exercise, the leader would want to let members tell their fantasy but the main purpose of processing would be to get them to talk about what feelings they got in touch with. The same would be true of a movement exercise in which people struggled to reach their goals. The processing would initially be on what it felt like when they had to struggle, but the leader would want to get the discussion to center on the struggles they are having in their lives, not the struggle in the exercise. It is very easy to allow members to share at a superficial level about the exercise itself and thus not maximize the benefit of the exercise. Many, many leaders make the mistake of having members merely talk about the exercise and do not try to take the discussion to a deeper, more meaningful level. Good, thought-provoking questions that tap into the emotions and feelings of the members can eliminate this mistake.

EXAMPLES . . . .

The leader has just completed a movement exercise in which the members were told to form a circle, hold hands, and then silently pick a spot in the room toward which they were to try to pull the rest of the group. The purpose of this exercise is to see how determined and persistent members are and to see how they attempt to get what they want.

Leader: What was that like? What happened?

Jose: Boy, that was tough. I really got into that exercise. Sandy, you should have seen the look on your face as you tried to pull away from the group!

Sandy: Yeah, I was surprised at how strong you were, Jose. All I could think to do was to free myself from your grip.

Donald: I had no idea that you girls could pull as strongly as you did. . . .

It is evident here that the discussion is conversational. No real learning is taking place, since the members are merely discussing their actions during the exercise itself. To effectively process the exercise so that they learn from it and apply this learning to their lives, the leader might say something like "Think for just a moment not so much about what happened during the exercise but about what this exercise meant to you. What did you learn that you can apply to your current life situations?" The leader could also say, "Did the exercise we just finished have any meaning for you in terms of your lives outside this group?" Group discussion following such leader prompts might sound something like the following:

Angie: Yes, I think I learned something. The thing that stood out to me about this exercise is that I tend to fear competition. I've always shunned opportunities to compete and, as a result, I think I've been missing out on some potentially rewarding experiences.

Donald: That's interesting, Angie. I feel almost the opposite, in that I always compete and have a difficult time just enjoying life without always comparing myself to others. I often come up short when I play the comparing game.

In this second dialogue the group members are applying their reactions to their lives, and the exercise acts to trigger thoughts. Keep in mind that the exercise usually only stimulates members' reactions. It is the leader's guiding statements that will often cause members to personalize the experience.

. . . .

The following examples illustrate ineffective and effective ways of processing exercises in groups.

EXAMPLES . . . .

The group has just completed a fantasy exercise that involved having the members visualize themselves on a journey to see an old wise man.

INEFFECTIVE PROCESSING

Leader: What was it like seeing the wise man?

Jerry: My wise man had a long, gray beard.

Ted: Mine was dressed in a long, white robe and carried a cane.

Cristina: When we met each other, I gave him a hug.

Janet: He never said a word to me, but I know that he was glad to see me because he smiled.

Leader: What else happened when you saw the wise man?

Joey: I was frightened. I thought he had too much on his mind to see me.

Tammy: It felt good. He was glad to see me and I wanted to stay longer.

Leader: Did the wise man give any of you an answer to your question?

Ted: Yes.

Janet: He just smiled when I asked him my question.

Leader: What about when you left? How did you feel?

The discussion could continue like this all session, with members recounting what they thought and imagined during the exercise. The discussion would remain on a surface level, with no significant learning taking place. The members are not applying the exercise to their lives.

. . . .

In the next example, the leader's comments stimulate the members to think about how their reaction to the exercise could apply outside the group.

. . . .

EFFECTIVE PROCESSING

Leader: Did any of the thoughts, feelings, and images you had as you went to see the wise man relate, in any way, to your own personal life?

Cristina: It did for me. Seeing the wise man was just like going to see my grandfather. I'm always glad to see him and we always hug.

Joey: I was really scared as I walked up that mountain. I was afraid that he wouldn't be glad to see me or wouldn't have time for me. I sometimes feel that way when I'm at home. I have four brothers and sisters and sometimes I feel like Mom and Dad don't have time for me.

Leader: Maybe that's something we can talk about in a minute. It seems important.

Ted: I felt like the wise man was telling me not to worry about school and home so much. I worry a lot about those things sometimes, and it makes me sad.

Leader: I never thought of you as worrying about your home life. Would you like to talk about that?

Ted: Yes, I think I would.

Leader: OK, we'll do that sometime before the session is over. I want to get a few more comments about the experience of seeing the wise man. Janet?

Janet: When I asked the wise man my question, he just smiled. Then I realized that I have the answer inside me, and I don't always have to rely on other people to make decisions for me.

In this example, the members are relating in a personal manner. The exercise opens avenues for discussion and allows members to share their thoughts and feelings as well as to hear the reactions of others. Because the processing of the exercise has caused members to share personal information, several concerns have emerged. The leader might now choose to focus more intently on Ted's or Joey's concerns.

．　．　．　．　．　．　．　．　．　．　．　．　．　．　．　．　．　．　．

Focusing on One Member or on the Entire Group

When processing exercises for personal growth, support, and therapy groups, the leader will sometimes have to decide whether to focus on one person or on the group. It is usually best at the beginning of the processing phase to hear from all the members who feel like sharing in order to get a sense of what is going on with the members. This can be done by using rounds or by just asking for some brief comments about their reactions to an exercise. If there are members who would like to work on something, the leader will have to make a decision if individual work is better than continuing the discussion with the entire group. (We discuss working with individuals in Chapter Twelve.) The last scenario above is a good example of the leader having to decide whether to go with a group discussion or an individual focus on either Ted or Joey.

It is difficult to give specific guidelines as to when the leader should focus on individuals. If the group is a growth group, you may not want to hold the focus too long on one individual. If the group is a support or therapy group, it often is very beneficial to let the focus be on one person for 10 to 20 minutes, especially if that person is willing to work at a deep personal level (6 or below on the scale).

Holding and Shifting the Focus

An error commonly made by inexperienced group leaders when processing an exercise is to focus the group for too long on the first person who talks. It is usually best to give all or most of the members a chance to talk before holding the focus on any one person or issue. Exercises should create energy and interest among all the members. Focusing prematurely on one member may result in losing the interest and attention of others who have not had a chance to react to the exercise.

Also, be aware that the first person who speaks following the group leader's request for reactions may be speaking out of anxiety or a need for attention or a desire to please the leader. This member's response may therefore be a function of those needs rather than a reflection of genuine feelings about the issue.

E X A M P L E S .   .   .   .

INEFFECTIVE PROCESSING

Leader: (*Following a sentence-completion exercise*) Who would like to share an answer with the group?

Tod: (*Appearing anxious to respond*) I would. On that question concerning my thoughts on divorce, I thought about what different reactions people have. My uncle was depressed for months and hardly left his house except to go to work. My aunt, however, seemed to be happier as a result and went on about her life as though nothing had happened. What do you suppose was the difference?

Leader: I don't know. What do you think the difference could have been?

Tod: (*In a storytelling voice*) Well, one difference could have been the length of time that they were married or the fact that my uncle had been divorced once before. He told me. . . .

In this example, Tod is the first to speak, and his response is not relevant to the group. His voice indicates he is not speaking introspectively but rather with a storytelling intent. The leader makes an error in continuing to focus on him. It is more than likely that other members will become bored and restless.

.   .   .   .

The following example shows the same leader helping members process the same exercise appropriately by not focusing on the first member to speak.

EFFECTIVE PROCESSING

Leader: Who would like to share an answer with the group?

Tod: (*Appearing anxious to respond*) I would. On that question concerning my thoughts on divorce, I thought about what different reactions people have. My uncle was depressed for months and hardly left the house except to go to work. My aunt, however, seemed to be happier as a result and went on about her life as though nothing had happened. What do you suppose was the difference?

Leader: I'm not too sure in their particular cases, Tod. If you are interested in exploring this, you and I can do it after the group adjourns. Right now, however, I guess I would like others to share their specific answers with the group.

Tim: OK. For number 1, I said divorce does not always mean failure.

Leader: What did others answer for number 1?

In this example, the leader chooses not to focus on Tod, even though there seems to be some energy. Many novice leaders are so relieved that someone is speaking that they will focus on the first person to speak rather than give others a chance to comment briefly. Also, the leader realizes that it would be a mistake to hold the focus on Tod because there is much energy in the group for processing the sentences rather than discussing Tod's aunt and uncle.

. . . .

Present-Centered or Past-Centered Exercises

Although most exercises focus on the present, many are designed to get members to reflect on their past. Members may be asked to draw the house they lived in when they were young or to describe how they felt when they were 10 years old. A very powerful exercise that focuses on the past is "Family Sculpture," in which members "sculpt" their families as they saw them when they were growing up.

There is no right or wrong about where exercises should focus, although we feel that in most cases focusing in the present about the past is usually more productive than just focusing on the past. The reason for this is that group members cannot change their past but rather they can change how they are affected by it. It is good to focus on the past to get at various hidden and possibly painful material, but then it is usually important to bring the discussion to the present. This can be done by such questions as "How do you think your past affects you to-day?" or "What can you learn from looking at those past relationships?" The leader can also say something like, "It is important to take a look at how our past experiences affect us today. What did you learn?" "Does this stir up some unfinished business that you may want to work on?" or "What are your carried feelings from your childhood that you need to sort out?"

We stress the point about past- and present-centered exercises because we have seen too many group leaders focus on the past and not have members consider what they need to do in the present to change their feelings or thoughts. Too often, leaders process a past-centered exercise by just having the members describe past experiences. This can lead to members getting "unzipped" and left "opened up."

CONCLUDING COMMENTS

This concludes our discussion of exercises. We hope the last two chapters have given you a better understanding of the kinds of exercises, when to use them, how to introduce them, and how to conduct and process them. Throughout this chapter, we have pointed out a number of common mistakes made by leaders when using exercises. The following is a review of some of the main points to consider when using an exercise in your group.

- Choose the kind of exercise that is best for what you are trying to accomplish.
- Make sure the exercise is relevant to members' needs and the group's purpose.
- Make sure directions are clearly stated.
- Try to clear up any confusion before the exercise actually begins.
- Keep directions short and simple.
- Make sure all necessary materials are present and in front of members before introducing the exercise.
- Place handouts or sentence completions face down before starting, to avoid distraction.
- Generally, have members stand up and get situated before giving directions for movement exercises.
- Give directions that include enough information for completing the exercise successfully.
- Allow more materials and more space for arts-and-crafts exercises.
- Allow members to refrain from participating.
- Explain the purpose of an exercise before beginning it.
- Explain how long the exercise will last.

- Remember that exercises are means, not ends. Learning comes through processing.
- Open processing discussions with thought-provoking, open-ended questions.
- When processing an exercise, make it relevant to group members' lives.
- Do not use exercises one right after another without processing sufficiently in between.

Leading the Middle Sessions of a Group

As you learned in Chapter Two, any group that lasts for several sessions can be divided into three stages: the beginning, the middle or working stage, and the end. The middle stage encompasses the discussing, the sharing, and the working on problems or tasks. The emphasis here will be on groups that meet for a number of sessions; however, the information will also be useful for groups that meet only once or twice, since they too will have a middle stage. In this chapter we discuss the planning and assessment tasks that leaders face during the working stage as well as some essential leadership techniques and activities they can employ. Also in this chapter we offer outlines for covering common topics, discuss the mistakes that leaders often make during the middle sessions, and mention roles and strategies especially useful to certain types of groups.

As a group moves into the middle stage, a number of group dynamics will need to be considered and observed, such as the members' feelings about each other, the leader, and the group. Although it is important that the leader observe these interaction developments and other group dynamics during the beginning stage, it is even more important to do so during the middle stage.

PLANNING AND ASSESSMENT

In Chapter Three, we pointed out that some planning is necessary for every group. Certain kinds of groups, such as education and discussion groups or groups for elementary schoolchildren or the severely disturbed, may require considerable planning in that the content or members require more structure. Others, such as certain therapy or support groups, require only a minimum of planning because the members come ready to share and disclose. Other therapy and support groups will require considerable planning—it really depends on the members. During the middle stage, the leader will have to decide how much planning is needed based on the purpose of the group, the personalities and needs of the members, and the levels of trust, interest, and commitment. Some leaders plan the entire series of sessions before the group begins and make the mistake of failing to modify those plans according to the evolution of the group. It is important to realize that session plans that were conceived well in advance or that were used for a previous group may not work for the current situation. To plan the middle sessions, the leader must take into consideration how the members are feeling about the group.

Assessing the Benefits

Periodically during the middle stage, the leader will want to assess the group's value to its members. This is essential in planning because if the group is not beneficial, she will want to make adjustments. To assess the benefits to the group, the leader can use any of the following activities:

- A 1-to-10 round on how valuable the group has been. The leader can say something like, "I want each of you to think about how valuable this group has been for you. If 10 means very valuable and 1 means not valuable at all, what rating would you give it?" The leader would follow up with a discussion of the ratings.
- A round in which the leader asks each member to comment on the value of the group.
- Turning the group's attention to the topic of the value of the group by saying something like, "For the next half hour or so, I'd like people to comment on how this group is being helpful." This differs from the activity just described in that it is not a round; therefore, not everyone need comment and the discussion will be more extensive.
- A more detailed evaluation, obtained by taking time at the end of a session to have members write for five to ten minutes on what they have gained from the group up to that point. Good stimulus questions include the following:

    How is this group helping you?
    What activities are most beneficial to you?
    How do you feel about the group?
    What things do you dislike about the group?
    What would make the group better for you?

- Having the members write, between sessions, a one- to three-page summary and evaluation of the group. Certainly a leader would not want to do this unless the members seemed to be willing to do an outside activity.

- Having members in education and discussion groups review each topic discussed. Getting members to comment on what has stood out to them can help the leader evaluate the effectiveness of the group experience. If the members are not remembering the main points or if they have little to say, there is a good chance the group is not as beneficial as it could be.

Although it is the leader's responsibility to try to make the group a meaningful experience for everyone, it is important to remember that this is not always possible, due to the personalities of the members. Some individuals may lack the personal resources, such as attention span or communication skills, to benefit from certain kinds of groups. Likewise, the leader should not be overwhelmed or feel defensive if members have various criticisms. It is important that leaders remember that not everyone will always like everything that takes place in the group. By engaging in one of the preceding activities, the leader should have a better understanding of how the members feel the group is benefiting them, which in turn will help improve future sessions.

Assessing Members' Interest and Commitment

Another kind of assessment important for the leader to make during the middle stage is that of the members' interest and commitment levels. If interest and commitment are low, the leader will probably need to plan more carefully because he will not be able to count on the members for ideas and topics. To assess the interest and commitment of the members, the leader will want to observe the frequency of absences and late arrivals, which is often one indication. Also, she will want to observe the energy at the beginning of and throughout the session. If the members seem "dead," this may indicate that they have lost interest. The leader will want to look for patterns of disinterest over a period of two or three sessions rather than in a single session, since outside stresses and concerns can easily affect a member's level of commitment for any given session.

When the members' interest seems to be declining, the leader first has to assess whether the loss of interest applies to everyone or just a few of the members. If every member has lost interest, the leader can (1) decide that the group has served its purpose and end it; (2) plan the group differently in the hope that a change of format will generate new interest and commitment; (3) bring up the issue for discussion in the group; or (4) meet with members individually or in pairs and discuss the group. If only some of the members have lost interest, the leader will want to understand why. In some situations, the leader may already know why. It may be that their interest was low from the very beginning due to being forced to be in the group. It could also be that some members do not feel the group is relevant to them. Other reasons that members may not be committed to the group include not finding the content interesting, not feeling their needs are being met, and not being ready to make changes in their lives. No matter what the reason is, the leader will want to try to remedy the situation, possibly by using one of the options suggested below.

 • *Bring up the issue with the entire group,* keeping in mind that there will be differences of opinion. The discussion may prove helpful in clarifying the purpose of the group and in revealing why certain members are not interested. Depending on what is said, the leader may or may not be able to make changes that will increase some members' interest.

 • *Give members permission to drop out* of the group. This can be done in two ways: (1) mention that some may want to drop out and that this would be a good time; or (2) have a closing session for the current group, letting members know they have the option to join a second group that will be starting immediately.

 • *Meet with those whose interest seems low,* and talk to them about how they could be more involved. If they are really no longer committed to the group, the leader may choose to ask them not to return. This option should not be used often but it should be considered, since no group can go well when a number of members lack commitment to its purpose.

Assessing Each Member's Participation

During the middle sessions of any group, the leader will want to consider each member's frequency and style of participation. While there is no "correct" way to participate in a group, active verbal participation is usually better for most members than merely observing or occasionally commenting. However, for some members, observing with little verbal participation is the best or only way for them to experience the group. In certain kinds of groups, such as education, discussion, and task groups, active participation is usually desired. In growth or therapy groups, equal verbal participation is not necessary because members' needs vary. The important thing for the leader to do is assess how each member is participating and then try to determine if that way is best for that member. The leader may feel the need to get members to participate more.

A number of exercises that help to increase participation are available to the leader. The round can be used to get members to share more. Written exercises, such as lists or sentence completions, usually make it easier for the leader to elicit reactions from the members, since they simply have to read what they have written. As a rule it is desirable to try to get quiet members to share their thoughts and feelings in the hope that they will become more comfortable sharing in the group, but there will be times when getting them to share more is either not possible or not desirable.

A related member-participation problem arises when the leader feels that members are only making superficial comments. To change the level of participation, the leader can use a variety of skills and techniques:

- He can change his voice so that it reflects the tone he desires—a quiet, deliberate voice usually indicates a more serious tone, and members tend to respond more seriously.
- He can mention his observation of what is happening and suggest that the level of participation change.
- He can shift to an exercise or activity that has the potential for generating more serious discussion.
- He can shift to a topic that will generate more personal discussion.

Assessing Members' Level of Trust and the Group's Cohesion

In almost all groups the leader needs to be aware of the level of trust that the members are feeling in one another. Certainly in support, growth, and therapy groups, where personal sharing is emphasized, trust is crucial. The development of trust begins with the first session and should be continually promoted for members to believe that the group is a safe place to share feelings and thoughts. Trust develops best when there is a positive environment, which the leader provides by stopping members from attacking or criticizing others and by encouraging members to express support and concern for and interest in others in the group. In such an atmosphere members feel respected and cared for and feel they will not be attacked or ridiculed for what they say. Unfortunately, sometimes the leader does not pay enough attention to the continued development of trust, which leads to members feeling uncomfortable in the group.

If a leader finds herself in a situation in which the group's trust level is low, she will want to focus on the issue of trust, either by bringing it up for discussion or by using one of the several trust exercises such as the Trust Walk, Trust Lift, and Trust Fall (see Chapter Nine).

LEADERSHIP SKILLS AND TECHNIQUES FOR THE MIDDLE SESSIONS

Several skills and techniques are especially appropriate for the middle sessions. Many of them have already been mentioned in previous chapters, so only brief descriptions will be given here.

Stimulating Members' Thoughts

Leaders need to be prepared to stimulate discussion, since they cannot always count on the members to be ready to share their ideas. To do this, leaders may use exercises and various activities. The leader may also use some general questions or comments that encourage and facilitate sharing and discussion. Below are a few examples:

- What are the one or two points that stood out to you?
- Does anyone else feel that way?
- Would anyone like to react to that comment?
- I would imagine that not everyone feels the same way. Who has a different point of view?
- In listening to the comments, I felt that many of you were holding back your true feelings. For this group to be truly helpful, I urge you to share how you really feel. (*Pause*) Any comments on what I just said?
- We have covered a variety of issues, but no one has mentioned _____ , which is probably the most important one. It also may be the hardest one to talk about, yet I think it is essential that we do so. What are your thoughts on _____ ?

It is important for a leader to have a number of ways to stimulate interaction. Sometimes all the leader needs to do is ask a general question. At other times, the leader will want to make a brief statement and then ask a question, such as in the last three examples above. Many leaders use questions only and do not realize the value of sometimes prefacing their question with a brief comment.

Using One's Voice to Get Members to Think

As noted in Chapter Five, the leader's voice quality and pace of speech can influence the tone of the group. Softer or modulated voice tones coupled with a slow, deliberate pace tend to help members focus more deeply on their thoughts. Below is an example of how the leader might use voice when asking a question. While you cannot hear the voice quality, we will try to give you a sense of this.

E X A M P L E . . . .

The group is dealing with career choices. The leader speaks at a regular rate of speech, then in a soft, slow voice.

Leader: Now that we have a list of why people work, (*Slowly*) I want you to think about the following question: With regard to your work needs, (*Pause, then slowly*) what would you say is your greatest need?

. . . .

A question posed this way can get members thinking, not merely coming up with a general or superficial answer. The more personal thought they give the question, the greater energy they will generate when they share.

Introducing Topics for Discussion

In order to keep interest high, the leader must continually be listening for new slants or themes as members discuss various subjects. When the leader sees that the energy is starting to wane, he will want to introduce new topics for discussion. The leader can accomplish this by spinning off what has been said; that is, shift the focus to a topic that has emerged from the ongoing discussion.

E X A M P L E . . . .

The members have been discussing communication with their spouses and how to handle trouble areas, such as children, in-laws, and money.

Jane: We do OK in most of these areas. Money problems we now seem to have under control. We still have problems over sex and religion. We cannot discuss those at all. I really do feel at a loss. Last Easter was really a bad scene. He refused to go to church!

Leader: Let's take a look at communication with regard to religion. For some couples, this is a major source of friction. One of the main reasons is that each person usually has a belief about religion and often those beliefs clash. Anyone want to comment?

In this example, the leader took a topic that one of the members mentioned and introduced it to the group by making a brief comment.

. . . .

The leader can always choose to introduce a new topic as the need arises. The skilled leader is sufficiently aware of the members' needs to be able to introduce topics that are relevant and interesting. For instance, in the preceding example, if the group seemed to be losing interest in the topic of religion, the leader could shift the focus to a new topic, saying something like "Another topic that's important to talk about in regard to communication with your spouse is sex. Let's spend the rest of the time discussing how you and your partner communicate about sex." The leader can also ask the members if they have an issue or subject they would like to discuss.

Varying the Format

In some groups, the format for each session stays the same because the members seem to like and benefit from it. For example, a group may always start with introduction of new members, move to a review of study questions, and follow up with a film and discussion. In other groups, the leader will want to vary the format when he sees that the group members are bored with the same agenda. Chapter Nine covered in detail the kinds of exercises a leader can use to vary the format. Other devices include speakers, films, or reading materials.

Using Outside Materials and Assignments

Some groups lend themselves to homework assignments. Homework can be in the form of reading assignments, writing assignments, or *doing* assignments. By *doing*, we mean such things as calling someone, talking to a certain number of people, signing up for some kind of lessons, varying the morning routine, and so forth. For many groups, outside reading materials, TV shows, and other forms of homework can serve as a way of keeping members involved in the group between sessions and as a stimulus for discussion during the group meeting.

Using Progress Reports

In therapy, growth, and support groups members often will share aspects of their lives that need to be followed up on during the session. An excellent way to do this is by starting each session with progress reports from various members. Not only is this helpful to the members who share their progress, but this kind of sharing also helps build cohesion in the group. Some leaders make the mistake of letting progress reports take up too much time. Five to ten minutes should be sufficient.

Meeting with Members Individually

In certain kinds of groups, during the middle stage, the leader may want to meet with each member individually to discuss feelings about the group. Such a meeting gives the member a chance to share his opinions and reactions to the group with the leader's undivided attention. It also gives the leader a chance to discuss various things with the member for which there has been no previous opportunity.

Changing Leadership Style, If Warranted

Sometimes during the middle stage of the group the leader may feel there is a need to change style of leadership. Often this takes the form of doing less leading and encouraging the members to take more responsibility. Other situations may dictate that the leader take a more active role, especially if the group has evolved into a therapy group.

Informing Members in Advance When the Group Is Ending

Since members usually have some feelings about the ending of the group, it is essential that the leader tell the members if and when it is ending. Members should have at least three to five weeks advance notice that the group is going to end. Usually the ending of a group is determined during its beginning stage, although there will be occasions when no ending time has been set. Even when the ending time is set, it is a good idea for the leader to remind the members that the group will be ending in a few weeks.

Changing the Structure of the Group, If Warranted

There may be times during the middle stage of the group that the leader will see the need for a change in structure. Changes may take the form of adding new members, meeting less often, or having an extended meeting, perhaps over a weekend. Before deciding on any of these changes, the leader would usually want to introduce the idea for discussion.

In certain kinds of groups, some members will want the purpose of the group to be one thing while others will want the group to serve an entirely different purpose. It is important that the leader recognize this situation when it exists, even though there really is no easy solution to the problem. There are a number of options for dealing with such a situation.

- The leader can divide the group into two subgroups. (This often is not possible due to size, time considerations, and so on, but it is an option to be considered.)
- The leader can divide the time in half—that is, half the time the group will do one thing, and half the time it will do another. (This

will only work if the members can be cooperative when the group is doing the half in which they are not interested.)

- The leader can let the members decide how to handle their differences of opinion about what the group should be doing.
- The leader can inform the group that there are no options, since the group has a specific purpose to which they must adhere.

It would be helpful to be more specific about what to do when members want two or more different structures or purposes, but each situation is unique. If you find yourself in this situation and you take some action, it is important to realize that some members may be upset with you or with the group, creating a dynamic that will need to be monitored.

MIDDLE-SESSION TOPIC OUTLINES

It may be helpful to take a number of topics common to many kinds of groups and outline the key issues that might be covered, introductory exercises, and other exercises. Too often an important topic is brought up in the group but wasted because the leader does not know how to develop it so that it is meaningful to the members. That is, the leader has not given thought to the various key issues regarding that topic, nor to exercises that might facilitate discussion and sharing. The outlines that follow should give the reader some awareness of possible ways to focus on the topic and to deepen the focus so that the discussion is meaningful.

We chose to outline four topics: religion, the need for approval, sex, and self-esteem. These were selected from a list of common topics that emerge as focal points during the life of a group. We could have chosen several other topics, such as worry, love relationships, divorce, death, or parents—all are major topics. For each topic, we list several key issues (there are more) and possible exercises that would help members focus on the issues. It is important that you realize that the choice of when to use which exercise is your own. Much thought must be given to the appropriateness of any of the exercises described in these outlines.

Topic 1: Religion

Key Issues

1. Early messages/parental messages
2. Religious history of members
3. Benefits in your life
4. Restrictions in your life
5. Religion as a personal choice versus a "should" for everyone

6. Effects of religion on
   a. guilt
   b. sexual issues
   c. marriage and divorce
   d. abortion/birth control
7. Determinism versus free will
8. Life after death
9. Degree of importance of religion in your life
10. Belief in God

It would be important for the leader to realize that the members would more than likely be coming from many different points of view and that the leader and the group must be tolerant of almost any viewpoint held by a member. The leader would want to be aware that the discussion of religion can become very emotional and heated, which in most instances would not be to the purpose. Rather, the usual purpose of a discussion about religion is to help members feel comfortable with their beliefs and behavior and to be tolerant of others.

Introductory Rounds, Dyads, and Other Exercises

- Round: What issues regarding religion would you like to discuss?
- Round: Briefly introduce your religious background and tell where you currently stand with regard to organized religion (church member? nonmember? nonbeliever?)
- Round: How much influence does religion have in your life? (1 to 10)
- Round: Does religion cause any problems in your life? (yes/no)
- Round: Are you bothered by any current issues concerning religion? If not, what were some past issues?
- Round: Do you profess a particular religion? How do you practice your religion?

These introductory rounds would be useful to the leader in gathering information about how the members feel about religion. The introductory rounds would also get the members focused on the topic. The exercises below would be used only as appropriate and usually would not be used as beginning rounds to introduce the topic of religion.

Deepening Rounds, Dyads, and Exercises

- Round: If you are currently in a relationship, do you and your partner agree or disagree about religion?
- Dyads or triads: Discuss briefly what is the most disturbing aspect of religion in your life.
- Dyads or round: What do you find the most helpful and the most difficult about your religious beliefs?

- Triads or round: What would you do differently with your children concerning religious training than your parents did with you?
- Respond to the following statements with "strongly agree," "agree," "neutral," "disagree," or "strongly disagree":

Religion is the opiate of the masses.
We all have free will.
There is life after death.

- Written exercise: List early messages about religion.

Topic 2: The Need for Approval

Key Issues

1. Sources of approval: parents, lover, boss, children, friends
2. Where does need for approval come from?
3. How people seek approval
4. How strong is the need for approval?
5. Positive and negative ways that people seek approval
6. Trusting oneself
7. Dependence/independence
8. Difference between needing and wanting approval
9. How to reduce approval-seeking behavior

Introductory Exercises

- Round: How important to you is the approval of others? (1 to 10)
- Dyads: Discuss early experiences in your family. Did you feel you were approved of? How does that affect your current functioning?
- Rounds or dyads: Whose approval do you seek and how do you seek it?
- Written exercise: List people whose approval is important to you. Arrange in order of importance. Then discuss in dyads, triads, or in the group.
- Sentence completion or rounds:

If my parents did not approve of me, I would _____ .

If my supervisor did not approve of me, I would _____ .

If my spouse/lover did not approve of me, I would _____ .

I approve of myself _____ percent of the time.

If I sense disapproval, I _____ .

Deepening Rounds, Dyads, and Exercises

- Round: The need for approval is a desire, a necessity, or a burden. (Choose one.)
- Written exercise: Make a list of gains and losses resulting from your approval-seeking behavior.
- Dyads: Discuss ways you attempt to gain approval from others and classify each as effective or ineffective.
- Round: Respond with "strongly agree," "agree," "neutral," "disagree," or "strongly disagree" to the following statement: "Approval from others is more important to me than my own self-approval."

Topic 3: Sex

Key Issues

1. How you learned about sex
2. Satisfaction with sex life
3. Guilt
4. Early experiences
5. Difficulties and inhibitions regarding sex
6. Preferences, frequency
7. Sex without love
8. Sex and religious beliefs and early messages about sex
9. Communication with partner
10. Orgasm
11. Masturbation, fantasy
12. Extramarital sex
13. Homosexuality

It would be important for any leader discussing sex to be clear about the many different issues, since the members, more than likely, will not be. Ideally, the leader would not be judgmental but, rather, tolerant of various sexual attitudes, beliefs, and behaviors. The leader would also want to be prepared to deal with members' negative reactions to such issues as homosexuality, affairs, or unorthodox sexual practices.

Introductory Exercises

- Round: If 10 is very comfortable, how comfortable are you with discussing sex in this group? (1 to 10)
- Round: How much importance do you place on sex in your love relationship? (1 to 10)
- Dyads: What are some issues related to sex that might be discussed in the group? (Have pairs report back to the entire group some topics they discussed.)

- Round: Complete the following sentences:

  I think sex is _____ .
  Discussing sex in this group is _____ .
  Many of my current feelings about sex come from _____ .
- Round: In a word or phrase, how would you describe your present sex life?

Deepening Rounds, Dyads, and Other Exercises

- Reaction sentences (Have members give their reaction to any of the following sentences. Reactions could be given in writing, in a round, or by having members locate their opinion along a continuum from "strongly agree" to "strongly disagree.")

  Masturbation is a bad thing.
  It is my obligation to make sure my partner has a satisfying experience.
  If either party fails to have an orgasm, the encounter is a failure.
  Everyone should have sex before marriage.
  To have a good sexual relationship, you must be in love.
  I should have sex even when I don't feel like it.
- Round: I would like to have sex _____ times a week.
- Triads: What is your greatest concern or fear regarding sex?
- Round: Do you have any "leftover" or current guilt regarding sex? (yes/no) (If there are "yes's," the leader could ask if the members want to work on their guilt. Or the leader could introduce a helpful discussion about sex and guilt.)
- Round: In a word or phrase, how would you describe your comfort communicating with a partner when having sex?
- Written exercise: List your expectations in a sexual relationship.
- Round: If my partner had an affair, I would _____ .
- Written exercise: Write on a 3-by-6-inch card anything pertaining to sex that you would like to talk about. (The exercise is anonymous so that members can write such things as "having been sexually abused," "having an affair," "having certain sexual fantasies.") The leader would then collect the cards and lead a discussion about the various written comments. (This can be a very powerful and helpful exercise if conducted properly.)

Topic 4: Self-Esteem

Key issues

1. What is self-esteem?
2. Where does it come from?

3. How to raise self-esteem
4. Can a person change his or her feelings of self-esteem?
5. Parents' roles
6. Siblings' and friends' roles
7. Spouse's or lover's role
8. School, grades, intelligence, and self-esteem
9. Appearance and self-esteem
10. Sports and self-esteem
11. Work and self-esteem
12. TA, I'm OK, You're OK; the not-OK child ego state
13. RET, self-talk, and self-esteem
14. What is a winner and what is a loser?
15. Guilt, shame, and self-esteem

It would be important for any leader who is leading a group on self-esteem to have a theoretical understanding of self-esteem. We mentioned TA and RET, but certainly there are other theories that are useful when working with self-esteem. We have had very good results with school-age children when using these theories.

Introductory Exercises

- Round : If 10 is liking yourself a whole lot and 1 is hating yourself, what rating would you give yourself?
- Round: What one or two things affect your self-esteem—that is, affect how you feel about yourself?
- Written: Using a 1-to-10 scale, with 10 being very good, list how you feel about yourself on the following: appearance, intelligence, personality.
- Written: In a sentence or two, define self-esteem. Then write down your ideas regarding it: can it change, and if so, how? If not, why not?
- Dyads: Pair up and discuss how you feel about yourself and why.
- Sentence completion: My self-esteem goes up and down when

——————————————————————————————— .

Deepening Rounds, Dyads, and Other Exercises

- Round: What is one thing you need to do to improve how you feel about yourself?
- Round: What negative sentences do you tell yourself that cause you to feel "less than" others?
- Dyads: Pair up and talk about what you were told about yourself by significant others when you were growing up.
- Creative-props exercise: I want each of you to take a styrofoam cup and think of it as your self-esteem or self-worth cup. Now

I want you to take a pencil and punch holes in the cup, with the holes representing the holes you have in your self-esteem. Many of you have big holes from childhood, parents, school, and various other relationships and incidents. Take a minute or so to think, and then punch your holes.

- Movement: I want everyone to stand and line up side by side, facing me (about 8 feet away). I am going to draw an imaginary line here in front of me that represents your feeling really good about yourself. In a minute, I am going to have you move toward the line to where you see yourself. Where you are standing now is feeling very "not OK" about yourself . . . .On 3, move—ready, 1, 2, 3. (*Everyone moves*) What can you do today to help you move closer to this line?

As we said in the beginning of this section, the examples above are just some of the possible exercises for the chosen topics. There are many more exercises that could be outlined. Our intent is to encourage you to thoroughly think through a topic before you lead a group on it.

COMMON MISTAKES MADE DURING THE MIDDLE SESSIONS

There are many mistakes that leaders can easily make during the middle stage of a group. It may be helpful to discuss some of them in detail.

Letting the Focus Shift Too Often

Throughout the book, we have talked about holding the focus and taking it deeper. One of the tasks of the leader during the middle sessions is to try to make sure that the focus is held long enough to have some impact on the members. In any group situation, it is very easy for the focus to move from 10 to 9 to 8, then back up to 10-9-8, and then back again to 10-9-8 unless the leader holds the focus. In many situations, the leader will want the members to assume more responsibility for the process of the group and to share more during the middle sessions, but the leader cannot relax regarding the focus. Very often members will shift to other topics, thus minimizing the benefits of the session. We feel that the leader should always be aware of the focus and the depth of the focus. During the working stage the leader should try to get the focus to at least a 7.

Focusing on Only One or Two Members of the Group

It is important for leaders to remember they are leading a group in which most if not all of the members have needs to be met. It is therefore a mistake to devote too much time to trying to help any one member. Yet some beginning leaders will devote week after week to the same member. This practice is very easy to fall into, since groups frequently have a member who is very talkative or very "needy."

To ensure that each member's needs are assessed and addressed, the leader might think about how each member would answer the following questions.

- How do I feel about coming to the group?
- What would I like to learn from the group?
- What things would I like to talk about?
- What do I need to talk about but am afraid to bring up?

By trying to answer these questions, the leader should be able to get some sense of what each member wants or needs from the group. The answers help a great deal in planning the session and also enable the leader to go into a session with a number of possible options and topics.

Planning Only One or Two Exercises or Activities

Another mistake is to put all the leader's eggs in one basket; that is, to plan for only one exercise or topic. There will be times when a topic or an exercise simply does not generate discussion or interest. In such a situation, if the leader has mistakenly planned just one or two exercises for the entire session, the leader and the group will be floundering. It is always wise to have backup plans, because there are times when your plans don't generate much group energy.

Underleading or Overleading the Group

One major goal during the middle sessions is to make the group interesting and valuable. The way to accomplish this is by knowing members' needs and then providing activities that meet those needs. For this reason, it is risky to turn the group over to the members unless there is a good indication that they will make it interesting and beneficial. The skilled leader is usually the pivotal person in the success of a group, seeing to it that interesting discussions and interactions happen. On the other hand, it is possible for beginning leaders to overlead; that is, not to let the members have enough input into the group. The skilled leader leads to the degree that members gain from his guidance; beginners often lead too much or too little.

Failing to Allow Time to Process a Film or Activity

It is important to allow enough time to discuss and process any film, guest lecture, or group exercise. Films that last the entire session should not be used. Speakers should be told in advance how long they have to speak and should be interrupted if they exceed the allotted time or if the leader sees there is not going to be sufficient time to share and discuss the talk. Usually the majority of the time should be for sharing and processing rather than for viewing the film, listening to the speaker, or doing the exercise.

Choosing Uninteresting Speakers

When using a guest speaker, the leader should make every effort to ensure that the talk is relevant for the members and that the presentation is interesting and stimulating. It is helpful to meet with the speaker in advance, clarifying the group's purpose and eliciting a general idea of the talk the speaker has planned.

Focusing Too Long on a Member Who Does Not Understand the Content

Focusing on a member who does not understand the content of the group primarily occurs in education or discussion groups, but may occur in any kind of group. For example, in a parent-education group in which a member is just not able to understand the difference between two methods of responding to a child when the child seeks attention, the leader has a number of options for handling the situation. This is important to realize, because most leaders think they have only one option: to spend as much time as is necessary to get the member to understand. This option is often not the best, because too much time can be lost, and frequently other members get very bored. Here are some of the options available if a member does not seem to understand the content:

- Take time to explain, if it can be done in a relatively short time.
- Have members try to explain or clarify the issue.
- Tell the member you will explain after the session or at a break.
- Tell the member you will meet with him at another time to go over the material.
- Arrange for another member to meet with that member to go over the material.
- Ask another member to go to another part of the room with that member and explain the material. You would not want to do this often, because the helpful member would be missing the group.

If a member continually has difficulty understanding material in the group, the leader may ask that person not to remain in the group. Again, this is an option that you would probably not use very often, but it is an option.

MIDDLE-SESSION LEADERSHIP
TACTICS FOR SPECIFIC GROUPS

Besides the skills and techniques already discussed, specific kinds of groups call for particular leadership tactics. Here we'll cover three kinds of groups: the discussion group, the education group, and the task group. In the next chapter we will discuss leadership skills that are useful for the working stage of growth groups, support groups, and therapy groups.

The Discussion Group

The leader of a discussion group has two main functions: to stimulate thought and to facilitate discussion. The discussion group leader's first task is to get the members thinking about a topic or issue. To accomplish this, she will use many of the skills discussed in this and previous chapters. Once the discussion is engaged, the leader's task is to facilitate and encourage discussion by using basic leadership skills, including clarification, summarizing, reflection, tying together, cutting off, and drawing out. The leader's other tasks are to keep the members focused on the topic, provide a chance for all members to participate, keep members from monopolizing the discussion, and shift the focus when needed. The leader must continually be listening for new slants or themes as they emerge, in order to keep the interest high.

The Education Group

The education group is designed to educate and inform members about a topic. It differs from the typical classroom learning experience in that much of the learning takes place through group interaction. The leader will shift from giving information to facilitating the discussion and back again to giving more information. This sequencing keeps the group flowing and increases the chances of achieving the goals of helping members learn and understand the material presented and helping them apply this new learning to their lives.

In an education group in which members are learning a skill, it is helpful to give members a chance to practice. Practice may be included in groups dealing with such topics as assertiveness or interviewing for a job. Practice gives members a chance to try out the particular behaviors that make up the skill. The leader can serve as a model as well as have members model these behaviors for one another. Role playing will be the primary technique used in the group to carry out the practice.

The Task Group

There are many different kinds of task groups. In this section we focus on the task group meeting to make decisions about some issue or to resolve some problem. In the middle phase of a task group the leader will always want to keep in mind how the members feel about each other and about the task they are working on. The leader will also want to consider who are the more influential members of the group and what type of pressure they are likely to exert on other members. Also, the leader should be aware of any private expectations or goals of the members.

The task group leader performs three main roles during the middle phase or stage of a task group. The first role is to help the members formulate or clarify the goals for the group. The other two roles are to help members generate options and to help them move toward a decision. The need may also arise for the additional role of mediator.

Helping Members Formulate or Clarify Goals

The first function of the task group leader during the middle phase is to help members clarify and formulate more specific goals. If there are strong differences of opinion regarding the goals, the leader will want to encourage free expression and bring out diverse points of view. The leader will be drawing out and cutting off members as well as clarifying and looking for common points to tie together and summarize.

Helping Members Generate Ideas and Options

Once goals are agreed on, the next step for the leader is to help members generate ideas and options for accomplishing those goals. The discussion of various options is sometimes difficult because members become emotionally identified with their own ideas and find it hard to discuss others. The skill required here is to be able to get members to discuss and exchange ideas in a productive manner. The leader's choice of any of the strategies listed below will depend on the number of members in the group, the kind of goals the group is working toward, the level of agreement among members, and their overall attitude of cooperation.

Brainstorming.   Brainstorming is the technique of having members generate as many ideas as possible without regard to practical limitations. The theory behind brainstorming is that people often impose unnecessary limitations on their creativity by assuming constraints that may in fact not exist or that may be possible to change. Once ideas are out in the open, others may come up with creative changes that eliminate the constraints. The basic rule for brainstorming is that no idea is too wild or crazy to at least be brought up. Brainstorming may be done by the entire group or by small groups of three or four. A time limit helps the group stay focused. Brainstorming is a good way to get members to throw their pet ideas into the ring along with other ideas they may have. The fact that ideas are not evaluated or censured during brainstorming also reduces the members' feelings of defensiveness.

Once ideas have been brainstormed, duplicate or overlapping ideas should be eliminated or consolidated and the advantages and disadvantages of the remaining ideas listed and ranked. Several of the better ideas can then be examined in greater detail and elaborated on as needed. If the leader uses the brainstorming technique effectively, every member should feel he or she has had the opportunity to provide some input.

The fishbowl.   The fishbowl is a technique that can be used with a variety of groups; it works especially well with larger groups. The group is divided, with half the members forming an inner circle and the other half an outer circle. While the inner group discusses an issue or idea, the outer group listens. (People often can listen better when they know they are not going to speak for a while.) After a given time period the groups may switch places, with the new inner group sharing its reactions to the previous group's discussion. The new inner group may provide constructive criticism or build on the ideas already generated.

Small-group variations.   Small-group interaction can almost always be useful, in that members have the opportunity to discuss ideas in greater detail and more people get to talk since the group is smaller. Members in small groups may all work on the same task or on different phases of the task. The results of the small-group discussions are then shared in the larger group.

Guided fantasy.   In a task group, the guided fantasy provides a chance for members to picture, think about, or get a feeling for the outcome of various solutions generated by the group. Also members may fantasize the outcome and then construct what must happen for that outcome to be realized, thus generating various solutions. Below is an example of how a guided fantasy could be used.

EXAMPLE . . . .

A school counselor is leading a task group consisting of parents. The task is to develop a drug-education program for junior high school students. The leader introduces a guided fantasy by saying the following:

Leader: At this point, let's think about the outcome of the program you might each envision for yourself and your children. You might want to close your eyes to try this. Picture an uncomfortable conversation between you and your child regarding drugs. Now envision a program in which your child is learning about drugs. What are some of the things that are happening? When you are ready with your ideas, write them down.

. . . .

This technique helps establish goals, which in turn aid the leader in developing and maintaining the focus.

Hypothetical crisis. An exercise used for certain kinds of task groups is the hypothetical crisis. This exercise requires members to imagine being faced with a crisis such as being lost together (in a cave, on the moon, and so on); they are then required to make decisions about how to use the provisions they have. Such exercises cause members to work together. Beware, however; while such exercises can be useful under the proper circumstances, they can also divert members from their real task and create frustration in those who are ready to work on the real issues. Exercises of this nature should not be used unless they are needed.

In summary, the task group leader has three basic functions: helping members formulate the issues, tasks, and goals; helping members generate options; and helping members move toward a decision that can be implemented. Since the task group involves a group goal rather than individual goals, members may be committed to the extent that an outcome affects their professional or personal lives. Members may take strong stands on issues they feel will have an impact on them. There are a number of ways to deal with these strong feelings, such as brainstorming, having members work in small groups, giving all members a chance to have their ideas discussed, having ideas presented anonymously, and having ideas presented using the fishbowl technique.

CONCLUDING COMMENTS

In this chapter, we have outlined skills, techniques, and roles that the leader will want to use during the middle sessions. When planning the group, the leader will want to assess the benefit of the group and the members' interest, commitment, and trust level. When leading the middle sessions, the leader should stimulate thought; introduce new topics, use her voice effectively; vary the format when necessary; and change leadership styles, the structure of the group, or both, if necessary. The leader will also want to keep in mind the kind of group she is leading because different strategies are needed for the various kinds of groups.

Therapy in Groups

In this chapter, we discuss therapy groups and the skills needed for leading such groups. Counseling and therapy groups are conducted in many different settings, such as psychiatric units, mental-health centers, hospitals, college counseling centers, schools, child guidance centers, rehabilitation centers, youth crisis centers, child abuse centers, women's shelters, and juvenile training schools. Therapy groups may focus on personal problems in general or on specific topics, such as anxiety, depression, cancer, AIDS, panic attacks, recovery, shyness, divorce, or relapse. We are using the term *therapy* to mean helpful insight into one's behavior.

GOALS OF THERAPY GROUPS

Behavioral researchers have identified two types of therapeutic goals for groups: process and outcome. The term *process goals* refers to goals that are related to the group process. For example, the leader can help members improve their comfort level in the group. *Outcome goals* are goals that occur outside the dynamics of the specific group. Examples of outcome goals include obtaining employment, improving an interpersonal relationship, maintaining sobriety, or experiencing a feeling of greater self-esteem. Although we think process goals are important, we strongly believe that outcome goals are more important.

SETTING UP THERAPY GROUPS

The ideal therapy group is composed of five to ten members. The membership remains constant once the group has begun. In the ideal group, the members attend voluntarily and share at a very personal level.

In private practice, groups are often like this. Unfortunately, in many other settings, groups are not at all like this. The membership is ever-changing, and many of the members have not volunteered to be in the group. Groups with such limitations are often found in youth crisis centers, residential treatment centers, prisons, and psychiatric hospitals. In these settings, leaders may be asked to lead groups with anywhere from 15 to 20 members. The leader regularly has to devote group time to introducing a new member or saying goodbye to a member who is leaving. In such large groups, there is less chance that individual atten-tion will be given to the members, and it is difficult to involve all the members in any discussion. Sharing might be less personal because members might not feel the sense of cohesion and trust that exists in groups that are more similar to the ideal group.

Large groups and nonvoluntary groups are much more difficult to lead and are usually only minimally effective. In settings in which a large group (12 or more members) is mandated by agency policy, the leader may want to try leading an education/discussion group for all the residents and then a smaller therapy group for those who seem to have some commitment to personal change.

When establishing a therapy group, the leader should screen the members if possible. Depending on the therapeutic purpose of the group, the leader may or may not want members with the same kind of con-cerns. Groups are usually easier to conduct when there is a common problem such as drug abuse, child abuse, depression, or agoraphobia. There are several advantages to a homogeneous group. In such groups, the purpose of the group is usually clarified more quickly and it is easier for the members to focus on the issues. However, when selecting members for a homogeneous group, it is important that the leader con-sider at what stage the various members are with their problems. If a group were composed only of severely depressed persons, the energy to work therapeutically on personal issues would probably be low. If substance abuse clients who were all in the denial stage of their illness were together in a group, the leader would have a difficult time getting the members to accept the need for personal change. Screening the members gives the leader a chance to include members at various stages of their problem.

It is possible to form a heterogeneous therapy group; that is, one composed of members with different problems. In such a group, one member may express concerns about getting or keeping employment because of aggressive behavior; another, about her marital troubles; another about his lack of assertiveness; and another about the anxiety that prevents her from going more than three miles from home. The skill-ful leader will need to be able to work with each of these problems while keeping the interest of the other members. One way to accomplish this is to define the issue more broadly so that many of the members can relate to it. For example, the issue of aggressive behavior can be defined more broadly as an issue of how the members express their anger and dissatisfaction as well as how they go about getting what they want. Most, if not all, of the members will have some interest in this broader issue. In this way, the leader can work with the aggressive member while involving most of the other members.

There really is no specific number of times that a therapy group should meet. Some groups meet on a daily basis for one or more hours while others meet once or twice a week for one to three hours. For different populations and settings, the leader should try various meeting schedules to determine the optimal number of meetings per week or month.

FIVE ASPECTS OF THERAPY GROUPS

Experts have set forth their ideas about therapy groups based on five aspects:

1. The role of the leader
2. The therapeutic paths in a group
3. The responsibility for the therapy
4. The focus of the therapy
5. The theoretical approach to group therapy

In forming your view of therapy groups, you will want to think through each of the five aspects. There is a wide range of opinions about each of these aspects. It is important that the reader be aware that therapy group leaders can have completely different views of how therapy groups should be led and what should happen. Co-leading can be almost impossible if the leaders hold two distinctly different views.

The Role of the Leader

The leader should be actively involved in the planning, setting up, screening, and conducting of any therapy group. It is the leader's responsibility to create an atmosphere for the group in which members feel safe to share their thoughts and feelings. The members should feel that they will not be attacked or judged if they choose to speak. Many beginning leaders make the mistake of letting the members have most of the responsibility for the group. This results in confusion, boredom, and frustration. Some leaders even allow members to attack each other. This rarely is productive and often is damaging because of the negative tone that is set for the group. Establishing a productive, positive working tone is the responsibility of the leader.

The Therapeutic Paths in a Group

There are many ways that groups can be therapeutic for the members. Members can benefit by the following:

- Trying new behaviors
- Discussing topics that cause them to think differently
- Helping others work on their problems
- Focusing on their own issues and receiving help from the members and leader

The leader of any therapy group will decide which of these to emphasize. For some groups, trying new behaviors may be the emphasis, whereas in other groups, focusing on problems will be the main emphasis. Some leaders approach therapy in groups using only one of the above avenues for growth and change. This is very limiting, especially since therapy groups are so diverse. Members in most therapy groups will experience some therapeutic gain from each of the paths mentioned in the preceding list. However, it is important to realize that how the therapy group develops will be a function of what the leader sees as the best way to provide therapy for the members.

Trying New Behavior

For some people, talking and sharing with others will be both new and therapeutic. Members get the chance to try new behavior, such as saying what they are feeling, asking for what they want, or practicing something that would be hard for them, such as talking to their boss. It is important for the leader to realize that for certain groups, the therapy does not have to be on problem solving per se. The group experience in itself is therapeutic because the members are engaging in new behavior simply by being in the group and talking. Groups in psychiatric units often emphasize this therapeutic process.

Discussing Topics That Cause Members to Think Differently

Therapy can take place when members share thoughts, feelings, and ideas about various issues. For instance, a good discussion about how to cope with guilt, anger, or the loss of a spouse can be quite therapeutic. The leader's role is to take the discussion to a depth that achieves therapeutic impact. Some leaders make the mistake of letting the discussion go in whatever direction the members take it rather than focusing the discussion so that it is valuable. A skilled leader who knows how to lead therapeutic discussions can provide much therapy in groups.

Helping Other Members Work on Their Issues

Members often will find it therapeutic to help other members. People often feel better about themselves when they help others. Also when helping others, members will be thinking about themselves; this can be beneficial. Further, by being involved in helping others, members have a chance to practice problem solving; this can be quite therapeutic.

Focusing on Their Issues and Receiving Help

For most therapy groups, much of the therapeutic benefit will come from members sharing a personal issue and being the focus of the group for a period of time. Our approach to group therapy emphasizes focusing on individuals; we believe this is usually the most beneficial because it incorporates the other paths to therapeutic change.

The Responsibility for the Therapy

The leader is the primary orchestrator of change within a group. The members are very important, but it is the leader who creates the therapeutic climate and is responsible for the focusing of the group. This does not mean that the leader does all the talking or counsels one member while the other members passively watch. It means the leader is in charge. He makes sure the focus is held long enough on a person or a topic so as to have impact. He also tries to funnel the therapy group's interactions down to a meaningful level (below 7 on the 10-to-1 depth chart).

Although we see the leader as the main agent of change, some experts maintain that the members are the primary agents of change in groups (Casriel, 1963; Glasser, 1965; Rogers, 1970; Vorrath, 1974; Yalom, 1985). In their view, the members serve in a supportive or confrontive capacity, or both, and are responsible for the therapeutic outcome.

The Focus of the Therapy

In most therapy groups, the focus should be on the issues that the members have in their lives. For instance, members who have trouble with relationships should have the chance to discuss these concerns with the group. Those struggling with alcohol should be able to discuss their problems. The goal is to get members deeply into their issues by either using focused discussions and powerful exercises or by allowing members to bring up their concerns and then focusing on them in ways that take the group to a depth level of 6 or below. Therapy groups that primarily focus on the concerns of the members are usually much more beneficial than groups that focus primarily on the interactions among the members.

In our approach to therapy groups, the leader will occasionally hold the focus on one member for 10 to 20 minutes (sometimes longer), helping that member explore his or her problem in depth. When holding the focus, the skilled leader usually involves the other members in an active way, but there may be times when the leader chooses to conduct a few minutes of individual counseling. In order to do this the leader needs to have the skills to take the session deep enough so that the members are very much involved even though they may just be watching. The leader uses theories and a variety of techniques such as drama, psychodrama, rounds, questions, empty chairs, and feedback from members. For leaders who do not yet have the ability to conduct engaging counseling while the members watch, we suggest relying more on the members to help with the counseling.

Some educators teach that the content of the group should relate only to what is happening in the group in the "here and now" and that outside concerns are less important. We see this approach as limited. Member feedback, interaction, and confrontation can be valuable, but this should not be the primary focus for any therapy group.

The Theoretical Approach to Group Therapy

No leader should lead counseling groups without an in-depth knowledge of counseling theories. Unfortunately, many people who lead therapy groups do not have much experience in individual counseling or a background in counseling theories. Some leaders believe that all they need to know is information about group process and group dynamics and that the members will be the agent of change. This simply is not true for many therapy groups that exist, such as sexual abuse victims, agoraphobics, suicide patients, sex offenders, drug abusers, children of alcoholics, and codependents. The members in these groups and many other therapy groups have no theoretical understanding of their problems and they need a leader who has a complex understanding of their pain. The leader who knows one or more theories can help members by using the theories during the sessions. We often teach our group members the basic tenets of the rational emotive and transactional analysis theories because members can learn these models rather quickly. Members can use the concepts to understand their own problems and those of other members, and the concepts give everyone a theoretical way to view the concerns presented. We also use Gestalt therapy because of its emphasis on the present and on experiential learning.

As educators, we are not as concerned with which theory a leader uses as we are that he is able to use one or two theories in a therapy group. Therapy groups that do not have theoretical foundation will usually be shallow and not very beneficial.

THE LEADER'S RESPONSIBILITIES IN THERAPY GROUPS

Knowing the Subject or Topic

It is the leader's ethical responsibility to have a good grasp of the issues that may arise in a therapy group. For instance, in an Adult Children of Alcoholics (ACOA) group, the leader would need to know about trust, intimacy, and relationships. In a group for members who are depressed, the leader would expect them to express issues such as low self-esteem, lack of friends, fear of failure, and hopelessness. Not only do leaders need to know what to expect, but they need to know how to help members through their painful issues. Knowing the issues enables the leader to introduce topics that are relevant and use exercises that are designed to get members to explore their inner thoughts and feelings. Too often we hear of therapy groups being led by someone who does not know the issues nor what to do with them if they are brought up in group.

Directing the Focus

The therapy group leader should be constantly aware of where the focus is and whether it should be held or shifted. If the group is focused on helping a member with a concern, the leader must assess if the concern being discussed has relevance for the other members and if the members can get involved in helping the member with her problem. For example, in a group for recently divorced women, it would be quite appropriate to discuss such issues as fears about dating or anger at the ex-spouse. If, however, a member wanted to discuss the problems she was having with her neighbor over a new fence, the leader would probably want to shift the focus to something more relevant. She could offer to discuss the fence issue with the member after the session.

Being Aware of Individual Members

Another responsibility of the leader is to pay close attention to each person in the group, because at any moment a member may react strongly to something being discussed. For example, one member may be discussing her parents' recent divorce, when another member may nod his head and begin to cry silently. By watching all the members, not just the one who is speaking, the leader will observe different reactions and draw out certain members who seem ready to share.

Watching the Clock

Another responsibility is making sure that enough time remains in the session to cover an issue adequately. Sometimes leaders make the mistake of introducing a topic or allowing a member to begin discussing a very personal issue with only a few minutes left. Examples would be the topic of death or a client sharing that she was raped when she was young. Much time would be needed to cover these topics adequately.

Apportioning "Air Time"

A final responsibility is to be aware of the amount of time that each member has had to bring up problems. Members should not necessarily have equal time, but it is important not to devote an inordinate amount of time to one or two members. If a member seems to need a lot of the group's time, it may be best to see that member individually or, in extreme cases, request that the member not remain in the group. The leader must realize that the group should not be dominated by one person's therapy needs. Some group leaders prefer to have one person be the focus for an entire session. Our position is that in most kinds of therapy groups, a number of members should have the opportunity to share and that one member's problem should not take the entire session unless the issue is one that is meaningful for most of the others.

To avoid spending too much time on one person, the leader should reflect on the following questions:

- How long has the group been focused on the member?
- Is the discussion relevant for most of the other members?
- Do members seem annoyed at the amount of time being spent on the person?
- How much time in past sessions has been spent on this person?

We usually do not spend more than 10 to 30 minutes on any one person. Naturally there are exceptions that depend on the issue, the members, and the purpose of the group. If the discussion is not relevant for most members, we usually will shift the focus unless, perhaps, this is the first time the member has chosen to talk about anything in the group. If members seem annoyed, we either shift the focus, try to draw members in, or explain why the focus is being held on the member. We try to be careful not to let one member have the focus week after week.

INDIVIDUAL THERAPY IN A GROUP

As mentioned earlier, any leader of therapy groups must give thought to the different ways that groups can be therapeutic. One of the main leadership decisions that the leader makes is how much time should be spent on group interaction and exercises, and how much time should be spent on individuals working on specific problems. Our approach to most therapy groups is a combination of focusing on topics relevant to the purpose of the group and focusing on individual concerns. By focusing on individual concerns, two valuable things occur: (1) the person who is working on the concern gets some help at a meaningful level and (2) the other members can hear, see, and be involved in how an important concern can be dealt with. In any given session of most of our therapy groups, as many as three or four members may be the focus of the group for 10 to 20 minutes. Early in the development of the group, the leader will want to explain to the members that much of the time will be spent working with various individuals on their concerns. The leader could say something like this:

Leader: Periodically in the group, a member will bring up a concern, and I will hold the focus on the member and the problem by using various techniques and theories. I will also involve the rest of you in many different ways. I may ask you to act out part of the problem or be involved in other ways. I may ask members to give feedback or offer suggestions. I may even do some brief individual counseling while you mainly observe.

Our experience has been that groups are not very beneficial for the members when the focus is never held on an individual's issues or when the focus is held too long. We have heard of many situations in which one member has been the focus for the entire group. This should rarely be the case.

Focusing on an Individual

In most therapy groups, a primary goal should be to get members to focus on themselves. By *focusing on themselves,* we mean more than just commenting and sharing. We mean the member asks for time in the group to work through a problem or concern. Following are five ways in which members may be moved to work on themselves.

1. Spontaneously
2. As a result of an exercise
3. As a result of hearing someone else work
4. As a result of the leader asking
5. As a result of a round

Spontaneously

At nearly any time a member may be moved to work on an issue. Simply asking members about their week may stimulate emotions which would lead to a member wanting to work on something. For example, a member may begin telling a story about his children and then break into tears. The leader would probably ask the member if he wanted to explore his pain further, since this came up spontaneously; that is, the leader would get a contract first rather than immediately launching into helping. Members may ask for help as a result of intense thoughts and feelings that are triggered by discussions of topics such as relationships, death, parents, or drinking.

As a Result of an Exercise

One of the main reasons for doing exercises is to get members in touch with certain concerns that they have so that they will see the need to focus on them. During the processing phase of an exercise, members may make comments that indicate they want or need to work on some issue in greater depth. The member may ask for time in group, or the leader may ask if the member wants to work further on something. Too often, leaders discuss the exercise in general and then move to another exercise or topic rather than focus on one or two members' concerns that were triggered by the exercise.

As a Result of Hearing Someone Else Work

Often, when a member is discussing personal concerns and is the focus of the group, it will cause other members to want to discuss their own personal issues.

EXAMPLE . . . .

Mandy has just finished doing some work on not feeling good about herself when she was a little girl.

Leader: Mandy, do you feel that we have done enough for today?
Mandy: Yes, this has been really helpful. I have lots to think about.
Leader: How about others of you? Did Mandy's work trigger anything that you would like to work on?

Kim: I got in touch with some unfinished business with my mom that I'd like to talk about.

Mike: I'd like to talk about me and my feeling about being dumb.

Leader: Anyone else? (*No other indications*) Why don't we start with you, Kim? I think we'll have time to do your issue, Mike. If not, we'll be sure to talk about it next week.

In this example, the leader selected Kim because she does not tend to say much in group, and Mike had worked on something last week.

. . . .

As a Result of the Leader Asking

There will be times when the leader feels that a member would benefit from doing some personal work. When this occurs, the leader may simply ask if the member would like help on a particular issue or concern. While it is valuable to try to draw out members, the leader will want to be careful not to create undue pressure to respond. Often members will appreciate the leader's drawing them out.

As a Result of a Round

The leader can use a round to find out if members want to work on issues. This is the easiest and most efficient way to assess who wants to work that day in group. The leader says, "Who has something they want to work on today?" We suggest using this round in groups in which several members usually come wanting help.

EXAMPLE. . . . .

Leader: To get a sense of who has something they would like to talk about, we'll do a yes/no round. Simply answer "yes" or "no" if there is something you would like to work on or talk about. (*Pause*) Steve, let's start with you.

Steve: Yes.

Jeff: No.

Angela: No.

Ellen: Yes.

Kathy: No.

The leader could then ask both Steve and Ellen to explain very briefly what they would like to talk about. After the round and the follow-up, the leader has a good idea of who wants to talk and about what topics. If there are a number of "yes" responses, the leader will then need to decide on which person to focus. The leader can pick the person who appears to have the most pressing concern or whose concern seems most interesting and relevant to the members. The leader could also pick the person who has not said much or who has not been the group focus in a while. Or the leader can let those who said "yes" decide who goes first, although in most cases the other three options are better. It should be noted that even if some members answered with a "no," they in fact often later share that they do have something about which they would like to talk.

. . . .

SKILLS FOR GROUP THERAPY

Many of the skills used in therapy groups are the same as those used in any other group. These include drawing out; cutting off; use of eyes; holding, shifting, and deepening the focus; and self-disclosure. Discussed below are four additional skills that are especially relevant for use in therapy groups.

1. Providing the right atmosphere
2. Leading therapeutic discussions
3. Getting a contract
4. Spinning off

Providing the Right Atmosphere

To be effective the leader of any therapy group must be able to get members to want to share in the group; that is, the members have to feel comfortable and/or experience the group as a place to get help. The leader provides the right atmosphere by creating a positive environment in which trust and respect are communicated and modeled. This requires cutting off comments that are negative, hostile, or that in any way suggest that personal statements can be the target of ridicule. The leader will use certain phrases that serve to remind members they are there to help each other. Some good phrases to use are the following:

- What ideas do you have that might be helpful?
- What is something you can say that may help?
- Do others of you feel similarly?
- We are here to help and support each other. Does anyone have a suggestion, thought, or reaction that they think may be helpful?

Leading Therapeutic Discussions

Much therapeutic benefit can be derived in groups when the members have a meaningful discussion on a given topic such as guilt, blame, getting along with parents, or overcoming fears. It is the leader's responsibility to make sure that the members stay focused on the subject and that the sharing is at a level that is thought-provoking and helpful. The leader should know the topic being discussed and ask questions or conduct exercises that cause the members to share and explore the topic in a meaningful manner. Members sharing their thoughts and feelings on a subject can be of great value to all the members if the leader makes sure the discussion is not superficial. With an unskilled leader, discussions may wander from topic to topic, or members may be allowed to tell stories and "chatter" about the topic. These discussions are of little value.

Obtaining a Contract

The leader always needs to get a "contract" from an individual when the focus is going to be held on that person for any length of time. By a *contract*, we simply mean that the member agrees to be the focus of the group's attention and to attempt to better understand and resolve some concern. For example, in a group composed of children whose parents are divorced, a young boy may start crying as he relates that he has to move to another state and may not get to see his father very often. When asked if he would like to spend some time getting help with those feelings, he indicates that he would. In this example, the leader has asked for the contract. There will be other situations in which the contract is merely implied. The point is, one needs to be sure that there is a contract, because on many occasions leaders make the mistake of focusing on a person when that person is not ready and/or willing to work on the issue in the group. When leaders sense that a member may benefit from being the focus, they might ask something like:

- Would you like to work on that?
- Would you like to discuss that for a few minutes?
- Would you like to understand that better?
- How can the group be of help to you?
- If we work with you on this issue for 20 minutes, what would you like to receive help with?

There will be many times during a group that a member will describe a problem or concern that appears to be severe enough to warrant help from the group. For example, a member may recount his recent divorce in angry tones or another may tell of how, as a child, she was abused by her parents. Still another member may state how guilty he feels over some past action or behavior. Often, the stories told by these members are dramatic and capture the attention of the others. Much group time could be spent in focusing on these members and their problems. The mistake that some leaders make is to assume that because members tell dramatic stories and appear to need support from others, they want to work on their problems. The severity of the problem or the observed emotional state of members as they share with the group is not necessarily an indication of a desire to receive help. We have observed leaders who forego getting a contract from such members and dive right into trying to help by offering suggestions and intently focusing the group's attention on that one person. As a result, suggestions and advice are often met with a "Yes, but" response or resentment. The group members in turn become frustrated and the leader begins to view the focused-on member as resistant.

There are several reasons for members to give an account of their problems yet not want help. First, some members have a history of blaming or externalizing their problems. These individuals have little desire to take charge of their own lives. Second, some members are frightened by the efforts of the group and of committing themselves to a plan of action in front of others. Third, some members tell a story in order to gain the sympathy of the group or to have others reinforce their position on some issue. Sometimes, if such members' stories seem pertinent to the others, these individuals should be allowed to tell their stories— not to offer them direct help, but to trigger thoughts and sharing among the other members. Instead of getting the group to focus specifically on them you can spin off by getting other members to share similar experiences from their own lives. By spinning off and not focusing on a member who does not accept the group's help, the leader ensures that other group members will not become frustrated. Finally, some apparently reluctant members may have worked through their concerns and do not need additional help from the group. The leader must be aware of when a member is recounting an experience in order to receive help and when the member is simply sharing a past experience for whatever it is worth. The point is that there are many instances in which seemingly interested members do not want to receive the help of the group. Without gaining a contract from a member, the group will be wasting its time.

Spinning Off

When the focus is being held on one member, the leader needs to periodically spin off to the other members. The leader should always be thinking about ways to get everyone involved in either the member's work or in their own work. To get members involved in their own work, the leader will periodically seek comments from other members while putting the working member on hold. To do this, the leader might say the following:

Leader: David, I want you to think about what you have said in the last few minutes while I hear from others. (*Looking at the other members*) What has this made you think about?

This question serves a number of purposes: (1) members get to share what is on their minds (at this time the leader would not focus on a new person because he has the other member on hold), (2) the leader gains information about how many others are ready or almost ready to work, (3) the sharing can be helpful to the working member, and (4) the working member gets some time to collect his or her thoughts.

Another way that the leader spins off is by making a few comments to the group about what the working member is saying:

Leader: Let me comment on what you are saying, Joe. Joe is talking about his part in weekly fights over household chores. Each of you may want to think about any routine fights that you have and the part that you play in those fights. It is really important that you understand your part in a fight. If I can get each of you and Joe to see how you contribute to any fight, then I think many of you can change some of those fights. Joe, let's get back to you.

Spinning off to the members is *essential* for good leading. By making thought-provoking comments to the others and eliciting their comments about themselves, the leader can cause more members to be thinking about themselves and thus be ready to share when the current person's work is completed.

Techniques for Group Therapy

As we have said throughout this chapter, a major goal when leading a therapy group is to have members focus on themselves. When this happens, the leader will need to know how to be helpful. The leader will direct the personal work by using theories and other techniques to help the member gain insight and understanding about his problem. The leader may conduct briefly some individual counseling or may enlist the help of the other members to facilitate the member's work. Described below are a number of techniques that can be used to involve the other members when one member is focusing on a problem.

Techniques That Involve the Members

Members ask questions.   Once a member has talked for a few minutes about the specific concern, the leader can use the technique of having the members ask the working member questions.

Leader: I want you to think of a question that would be helpful for Ralph to answer. Who has one?

Judy: If your wife lost weight, would you feel more attracted to her? (*Ralph answers*)

Carlos: Why do you think you can't develop a long-term relationship with the other woman? (*Ralph answers*)

Sarah: If you rid yourself of the notion that divorce is wrong, would that help you make a decision? (*Ralph answers*)

There are a number of benefits of using this technique:

- It gets the members involved and prevents them from becoming bored or disinterested.
- Questions that need to be asked get asked.
- Questions that the leader might not produce get asked.
- The questions cause the member to think.
- While the members ask questions, the leader has time to think about the direction he believes the therapy needs to go.

Members make guesses about what the problem is.   Another way to involve members and to cause the working member to stop and think is to have the members guess what the problem is. The leader would use this technique when the member is being vague or confused.

Leader: I want you each to try to guess what Ralph's problem is. I am not sure, and I don't think Ralph is, so perhaps our guessing will help.

Judy: I think Ralph would really like to be divorced but is afraid of his parents' disapproval.

Carlos: I sense that Ralph is afraid to get divorced because he fears he will be left with nothing.

Sarah: I think Ralph is feeling guilty about the thought of leaving his kids and wife of 15 years.

The benefits of having members guess what the specific concern might be are as follows:

- It gets the members involved.
- It breaks up the member's storytelling (many times, members will ramble without really concentrating on what the specific problem might be).

- It causes the member to listen and think about what he or she is saying.
- A member of the group may identify the problem.

It is important that the leader closely monitor the guesses made by members because these guesses are sometimes projections of how they would feel based upon their own values and past experiences.

Members role-play the working member. A technique that is sometimes effective and also causes the members to be involved is to have the members role-play the working member. By *role-playing the working member*, we mean that another member acts as the working member. Here is how this may occur.

Leader: I would like each of you to put yourself in Ralph's place and attempt to relate what the specific concern is. Be sure to speak in the first person singular, just as if you were Ralph. Try to feel what he is feeling based on what you have heard him say. (*After giving the members about a minute to think, the leader begins*) Sarah, would you like to go first?

Sarah: I think that Ralph—

Leader: (*Cuts in*) Sarah, see if you can speak as if you were Ralph.

Sarah: OK. I'm real confused about what to do. I feel torn. Also, I feel guilty when I think about leaving my family. I'm not sure if this desire for a divorce will pass or not.

Carlos: I'm feeling like a real jerk. My wife has been nothing but good to me, and here I am fooling around on her.

Judy: I just wonder how I will feel once I make a decision. Will I miss my wife if I divorce her? Will I miss the other woman if I decide to stay with my wife?

The advantages of having members play other members are as follows:

- The working member gets to hear what other members might be feeling if they were in a similar situation.
- The working member gets to hear how he might be feeling. This is especially true if some of the members are very good at pinpointing what the working member is feeling.
- The working member gets to feel understood if the other members are on target.

Some other techniques involving members follow:

- All the members are asked to stand in front of the working member, who sits on the floor and looks up at the standing members. This activity would be used when a member expresses feelings of "less than" or insignificance in comparison with others. By seeing the other members standing, the seated member experiences visually what he is expressing. This often stimulates further discussion.

• One or two members are asked to stand on chairs beside the working member. They would represent the enormous size of the parent or child ego states, or both. This activity would be appropriate when the working member has expressed a feeling of being dominated by either the parent or child ego state or by both.

• Members are asked to talk about the working member in a kind, caring way while the member listens. (If the leader feels it would be helpful, the member may be told to close his or her eyes or face away from the group to facilitate listening.) This gives the member a chance to hear how others see him or her or the problem. To facilitate this, the leader would say, "Jeff, I want you to close your eyes and just listen as we talk about your situation. (*To the others*) What do you think of the situation and how he is handling it?"

• Members are asked to gather around and touch a working member in a caring way. This technique would be used when the leader feels a member is struggling and may benefit from feeling the support of the group. This is especially helpful when the issue is feeling low self-worth. It would be accomplished by the leader saying something like, "Linda, I want you to come to the center of the group. I want the rest of you to form a circle and reach out and gently touch Linda in a way that communicates that you care."

• Members are asked to participate in various therapeutic rounds (discussed in a later section).

• Members are asked to pull on the working member's arms to symbolize feelings of being pulled in two directions. The following dialogue illustrates this example.

Dan: I just feel pulled, you know? A part of me wants to get married because. . . . (*States the reasons*) Another part of me doesn't. (*States the reasons*) I just can't seem to make up my mind.

Leader: Bill, you and Tom stand up. Dan, you stand too. Bill, I want you to stand on one side of Dan and take his arm, and in a minute I want you to tug on his arm, saying all the reasons why Dan wants to marry. Do this as if you were Dan—that is, in the first person. Tom, you get on the other side and pull on the other arm, saying all the reasons why Dan does not want to marry. OK, begin.

What happens is that Bill and Tom talk and pull Dan's arms simultaneously. Thus, Dan feels pulled in both directions. Dan is merely instructed to listen to each side and pay attention to the sensation of feeling pulled. He is also instructed to pay particular attention to whether one side of the issue emerges as more powerful or persuasive than the other side.

Note that using techniques such as the one just described requires that the leader make sure that everyone knows his or her part. The working member must not experience merely two people pulling on his arms but rather the mental struggle between two sides of an issue. This technique may also seem like a gimmick or a slapstick routine if the leader does not set the tone properly. The leader must explain the purpose of the technique and remain serious about carrying it out, even if the members laugh or snicker.

• Members can play various ego states of the working member. This technique assumes that the members have been taught the theory of transactional analysis. For example, if the working member appears afraid to take risks, the leader might appoint another member to play the working member's not-OK child ego state. In essence, the other members act as different ego states of the member.

In this section, we discussed many ways the leader can involve the members when the focus is being held on an individual. Too often leaders just conduct individual counseling and do not take advantage of all the possible ways that the members can be helpful. By using the members, the working member may be able to more quickly or more profoundly experience or visualize his concern. Also, the leader has a much greater chance of keeping the members' interest when they are involved. Too, there can be much vicarious learning when the members are part of the helping process. Even though we have stressed how the leader may engage the members, we want to point out that much of the help that members give each other is through the sharing, caring, supporting, and challenging that takes place during all phases of the group.

Techniques That Involve the Leader

If the leader sees that a member wants to work on a particular issue, the leader can involve herself in the therapy in several ways. As we have said, the leader can hold the focus on the member who wants to work and get the other members involved, or she can take charge and basically conduct an individual session. The leader can also participate in the therapy in several ways so that it impacts the other members as well as the working member.

Sometimes the leader role-plays the member. The advantage of the leader playing the different parts rather than having the other members do it is that the leader may be able to play the part more accurately due to past experiences working with people. The following are techniques the leader might use.

• Sit across from the working member and play the self-defeating part while the member plays the healthy part. This gives the member practice in developing the healthy part.

• Sit across from the working member and play the healthy part while the working member plays the self-defeating part. The leader models healthy responses.

• The leader and another member play out a dialogue that the member has been describing.

• The leader may conduct individual counseling for 10 to 20 minutes, using counseling skills while continuing to pay attention to the other members. Ideally the leader will use an approach that the other members can also relate to, such as behavioral, TA, Gestalt, or RET.

• The leader may direct a psychodrama in which he helps the working member act out some aspect of his or her life. This often is highly emotional.

These are just some of the ways the leader can involve himself in a therapy group. We want to emphasize that the leader can, and usually should, be active during a therapy group. The reason is that in most therapy groups, the members are limited in their ability to be helpful. They can share and offer good suggestions or insights, but if the therapeutic process goes deep enough, the members will not know how to be helpful. This is where the leader must take an active, therapeutic role. The two examples that follow illustrate how therapy can be conducted in a group.

E X A M P L E S . . . .

Fred: I don't believe I am a worthwhile person because I don't have a job.

Leader: Let's examine that. It is true you do not have a job, but how does that make you a worthless person?

Fred: It just does. Look, if a man can't feed his family, he's worthless. I've worked since I was 16, and now look at me. I'm 42 and have no job!

Leader: Let me ask the group—do you think Fred is worthless because he doesn't have a job? (*Members shake their heads "no"*) Fred, no one here thinks you are worthless. Is it really a fact that you are worthless?

Fred: I feel worthless.

Leader: I know that, but are you worthless or are you a man without a job? I want each of you to think about that for Fred, and Fred, you think about it too. (*Pause*) Which is it, is it that Fred has no job or is worthless?

Angelo: There's no way in the world he's worthless.

Leader: Do you realize how Fred and probably many of you tell yourselves self-defeating, illogical sentences that you then believe?

Fred: What can I tell myself?

Leader: That's a good question. Let's all think about what Fred could tell himself.

Malcolm: I think Fred needs to realize that he is worthwhile no matter what.

In this example, the leader involves the members by getting them to comment while he continues to work with Fred, using principles of rational emotive therapy. The leader may work with Fred for another 10 to 15 minutes, trying to help him give up his irrational sentences. During this time, the leader would more than likely involve the members in ways similar to those in the preceding dialogue. Teaching Fred about his irrational beliefs would be a good strategy because most of the members can reflect on their own irrational beliefs. Thus the leader can use Fred's situation to teach how to apply rational emotive therapy to a problem.

. . . .

Ivan: I can't stand the way my parents fight and I feel in the middle. I thought when they divorced, it would get better but now I have to work that much harder to keep the peace. It's awful! I hate it! Why can't they stop?

Leader: Let's try to help. What were your reactions to what Ivan said?

Chris: Why do you feel you have to stop them? Why not stay out of it? I know my parents still fight but I have learned, mostly from the group, that it is not my problem. I don't like their fighting, but now I walk away.

Ivan: But they drag me into it and then claim I am taking sides! The other day, Dad pumped me for 30 minutes about what Mom has been doing and what she has been saying about him.

Carla: I used to get that all the time until I finally said to each of them, "I will not tolerate you talking about the other one." This worked pretty well. They still do it some, but not nearly as much.

Ivan: I can't do that. I just think I should be able to help them.

Chris: Heck, you're just 15 years old! You're not a shrink.

Ivan: Yes, but I just feel—

Leader: Let me jump in here. (*In a kind, caring voice*) Ivan, do you really want help from us, or do you just want to talk about it and play sort of the "yes-but" game?

Ivan: I think so, but—

Leader: Do you hear Ivan's "yes-but"? Often when faced with a problem, many people play the "yes-but" game. Each of you can think about this for yourself. Many of you are playing the "yes-but" game with yourself. Ivan, let me ask you again, do you want help?

Ivan: (*With tears in his eyes*) Yes, I do. I don't know what to do.

Leader: I'm glad you want help. What do you think Ivan can do to feel better about his situation?

Andra: I would think he has to let go of the idea that he should be the one to fix his parents. They are grown-ups.

Ivan: But they are my parents. I can't stand to see them crying.

Leader: (*Realizing that to take Ivan deeper, she will need to take charge and use some counseling theory because the members don't know how to help*) Ivan, I think you can really benefit from hearing what everyone here is saying. It is not your job to fix your parents' situation, nor does it seem possible, given how you describe their behavior. Remember the TA model about the Parent, Adult, and Child? What we want to do is help you get an Adult perspective on the situation. Right now I think most of what is happening to you is coming from your Child, the little boy that wants to please. (*Turning to the group*) I think most of you can see how Ivan is contaminated by his Child ego state. You may want to think about yourself and see where your Child gives you trouble.

Carla: My Child is in the way big time when it comes to my brother. Can I tell you what happened?

Leader: Let's stay with Ivan for now, and then, Carla, you and others can comment on your insights. Let me use two chairs to represent the Adult and the Child.

The leader would then do some work with Ivan, using the TA theory, the chairs, and the other members.

.   .   .   .

The Use of Therapeutic Rounds

A therapeutic round differs from the rounds described in Chapter Eight in that in a therapeutic round the working member is the one completing the round. The descriptions of therapeutic rounds below should make this clear to you.

The stationary round. This is a round in which the working member says something to each member of the group while remaining in one place. The first type of stationary round is one in which the working member makes the same statement to each member.

Using our example of Ralph, let's assume that Ralph has been talking for about 10 minutes and one of his concerns is his parents' reaction to a divorce. In this stationary round the members mainly serve as a sounding board for Ralph.

EXAMPLE . . . .

> **Leader:** Ralph, I would like you to turn to each member, starting with Sarah on your immediate left, and say, "I'm afraid to get a divorce because of what my parents will think."
>
> **Ralph:** *(To Sarah)* I'm afraid to get a divorce because of what my parents will think. *(Ralph then repeats this sentence to the other members)*

> By saying the same thing over and over, Ralph gets a chance to listen to himself. It is important to note that in this type of round the members do not say anything. They merely act as listeners. By repeating something a working member is usually able to gain some insight and understanding about his conflict.

. . . .

The second type of stationary round is one in which the working member turns to each member but has no specific sentence to say.

EXAMPLE . . . .

The leader asks Ralph to look at each member and say, "If I get divorced, it means _____ ."

> **Ralph:** *(To Sarah)* If I get divorced, it means that I am a miserable failure.
> **Ralph:** *(To Carl)* If I get divorced, it means that I've let my parents down.
> **Ralph:** *(To Judy)* If I get divorced, it means that my children will be harmed.
> **Ralph:** *(To Liz)* If I get divorced, it does mean that I'm a failure.

> By having the member do this type of stationary round, the leader comes to better understand how Ralph is thinking and feeling about getting divorced. More important, when a member does this type of round, he often recognizes some of his self-defeating beliefs.

. . . .

The third type of stationary round is one in which the working member responds to a repeated question from the other members.

EXAMPLE . . . .

The leader might say to the group, "I want each of you to ask Ralph the following question: 'Ralph, does getting a divorce make you a failure, or does it make you a man who no longer loves his wife?' Sarah, you go first and ask Ralph that question. Ralph, you look at Sarah and respond to the question."

Sarah: Ralph, does getting a divorce make you a failure, or does it make you a man who no longer loves his wife?

Ralph: Well, I took marriage vows and promised to love until death do us part.

Carl: Ralph, are you a failure for getting a divorce, or are you just someone who is not in love anymore?

Ralph: Well, that's right. I'm certainly not in love. I've tried to get the love back, but I just can't seem to do it. Maybe I'm not a failure. (*Each member asks Ralph this question, and Ralph responds to each*)

Responding to a repeated question causes the member to examine his thinking about a given issue.

. . . .

A fourth type of stationary round is one in which each member asks a different question of the working member, using the round format.

EXAMPLE . . . .

The leader might ask the members to do the following:

Leader: I want each of you to think of one question that you want to ask Ralph in terms of what he is saying about divorce. Try to make the question one that will cause him to really think about what he is saying and feeling. Who has a question that he or she would like to ask Ralph?

Judy: Ralph, do you believe that everyone who gets divorced is a failure? (*Ralph answers*)

Liz: Ralph, could you tell me a little more about why you don't think you love your wife? (*Ralph answers*)

. . . .

Often members will ask good questions that cause the working member to explore the concern in greater depth. In addition, this allows the other members to be more involved.

The in-depth round. In contrast to the stationary round, in which the working member remains in a stationary position, the in-depth round requires the member to move in front of each of the other members, thus intensifying the experience.

E X A M P L E S . . . .

Sherry has been talking about not liking herself but has been vague.

Leader: Sherry, I want you to sit in front of each member and say, "I don't like myself because. . . ."

Sherry: (*Moves in front of Pam*) I don't like myself because I am fat.

Sherry: (*Moves in front of Kate*) I don't like myself because my teeth are ugly.

Sherry: (*Moves in front of Beth*) I don't like myself because my parents never liked me. (*Starts to cry. Beth starts to reach out and take her hand, but the leader shakes his head "no," because he believes Beth would be trying to "rescue" Sherry from her pain*)

Sherry: (*Moves in front of Patty*) I don't like myself, oh, I don't know if I can say it. (*Cries more*) I don't like myself because of what my father did to me when I was growing up.

Leader: Was it sexual?

Sherry: (*Sobbing, looking down*) Yes!

Leader: (*In a calm, firm voice*) Sherry, I want you to look up and see the others' faces. No one here thinks less of you. Look up— don't watch that movie that says "Sherry's a horrible person." (*Sherry slowly looks up*)

In this example, the round serves as a way to get the member into her feelings. The leader also used a couple of other skills. First, he did not let the member's work be interrupted by her crying. Often in groups when a member cries, the other members and leader make the mistake of rushing to support the member, causing the work to cease. There are times when a person in pain needs to be shown that the group is there with her, but some of the time it is best to let the member struggle with her pain.

The second skill was having Sherry look up right after she disclosed the sexual abuse. By doing this, the leader did not allow Sherry to reinforce her negative feelings by watching negative images in her mind. Also, by seeing the faces of concerned, caring members, Sherry could experience that they did not think less of her. This latter technique obviously requires that members in the group be empathic and sensitive.

. . . .

In the following example, the leader thought it would benefit Ralph to focus on his belief that divorce means failure.

Leader: Ralph, I want you to move your chair and sit in front of each person and say, "If I get a divorce, it means I am a failure as a human being."

Ralph: (*Moves his chair in front of Liz*) If I get a divorce, it means I am a failure as a human being.

Ralph: (*Moves his chair in front of Carl*) If I get a divorce, it definitely means that I am a failure, but I'm not sure why.

Ralph: (*Moves his chair in front of Sarah*) If I get a divorce, it— but wait, I've got to be able to have a choice in my life!

. . . .

This kind of round is one of the most powerful techniques for producing intense, in-depth exploration. Moving in front of the other members creates a potent atmosphere that often causes the working member to gain insight. During these rounds, there will be times when the leader will ask the members to sit silently as the person makes the round. Other times, the leader will instruct the members to ask a certain question or to respond in a specific way, such as "No, it doesn't mean that." The role of the members will depend on the content of the specific round and the purpose that it is serving.

EXAMPLE . . . .

Skip has been talking about how he feels worthless because he was put up for adoption when he was 4. The leader has been challenging Skip's irrational, self-defeating belief and thinks that Skip may be about to give up this belief.

Leader: Skip, I want you to sit in front of each member and answer the question "How does being adopted make you worthless?" Each of you ask Skip that question. Skip, start with Bonnie.

Bonnie: Skip, how does being adopted make you worthless?

Skip: Well, if they loved me, they would have kept me.

Leader: Skip, move to Donna. Donna, ask him the same question, and if he does not answer the question, try to get him to be more specific.

Donna: Skip, how does being adopted make you worthless?

Skip: If your parents give you away, you are worthless.

Donna: You said that they gave you away because they just could not handle their own lives and they had no money! Now how does that make you worthless?

Skip: I don't know. I feel it.

Leader: Go to the next person. Calvin, try to say something that will challenge Skip's thinking.

Calvin: I don't believe being adopted makes you less of a person. My closest friend is adopted, and he certainly doesn't feel worthless, and I don't think he's worthless.

Skip: Well, uh, maybe I've been seeing this all wrong. I think I'm getting the point.

.   .   .   .

Another variation of the in-depth round has the members ask the working member a question of their choice as the member sits in front of each of them.

To reiterate, the use of in-depth rounds can be very beneficial when they are used at the right time and with the right kind of problem. A leader should only use the in-depth round when she is trying to get a member in touch with some intense feelings or to give up some self-defeating beliefs.

The working member moves about in a predetermined manner. At times situations will arise in which a member may benefit from some experiential activity. For instance, if the member does not feel part of the group, the leader may have the group stand in a circle holding hands and have the member walk around the outside of the circle with the option of asking or "fighting" to break into the circle. This can be very effective if the issue is feeling left out or not knowing how to be a productive member of the group. An experiential technique could also be used with a member who feels held down by all of his obligations and responsibilities. To help the member experience this, the leader might have the member sit on the floor, with four or five other members holding him down. The leader instructs the member to experience the feeling and then decide on a course of action. Some members do nothing; others fight very hard to break free. The experience usually proves valuable to the member and often to other members as well.

Another effective way for experientially helping a member is to use drama. The member may act out a scene that she is worried about, such as a job interview or a conversation with one of her parents (other members or the leader would play the other roles). The person can get feedback and then try the scene again. In some cases, the leader may get another member to play the working member's role to give the individual a chance to view how the conversation could be handled more effectively.

Gestalt therapy places emphasis on the present moment. One powerful way to get members into the "here and now" is to set up a dialogue with either the different "parts" of the person or with the person with whom the member is in conflict, such as a spouse or boss. Two chairs are used for this activity. The member plays both parts by changing seats. The changing of chairs and the development of the dialogue can be very enlightening for all the members (Perls, 1969; Passons, 1975).

Techniques for Helping More Than One Member at Once

There will be occasions in therapy groups or even growth and support groups in which two members will be in need of help at the same time, often concerning the same issue. For example, let's say the members of a therapy group are sharing in a personal way on the issue of abortion. One of the members, Susan, gets in touch with some old feelings of guilt. As she begins to talk about her abortion and her sense of guilt another member, Donna, identifies with what Susan is saying. She too indicates a desire to receive help from the group. At this point the leader has several options and can do any of the following:

- Ask Donna if she can wait until the work is completed with Susan.
- Ask Susan if it is OK to shift to Donna, since her pain seems greater.
- Work with both of them at the same time.
- Ask a co-leader or another member to go to another area of the room with one of the two members.

The first and second options require that the leader hold the focus on one member until her concerns have been alleviated enough to switch the focus to the other. In the example above there may be no need to do this since their problems are similar, but in an instance in which one person is talking about guilt over an abortion and another brings up guilt over her husband's suicide, the leader may find it extremely difficult to deal with these issues simultaneously. The leadership skill that is required in this situation is knowing how to put one member on hold. This is done by being straightforward with the two members and asking if one can wait. If the leader feels both members need immediate attention, she may use the last option in the preceding list.

In many instances, the concerns are so similar that it would save time and benefit the two members for the leader to work with both of them simultaneously. Instead of only one member being the main focus of the group there are two. Sometimes the leader will have one or both of the working members complete an in-depth round and then have them talk about each other's round. Or the leader may have the two members give advice or suggestions to one another. At other times the leader will do a stationary round by having the members ask each working member in turn the same question, such as "Why does having an abortion make you less of a person?" or having both of them complete a sentence stem, such as "Because I had an abortion, it means I am _____," addressing the other members or each other. The benefit of working with two members simultaneously is that each member sees another person in the same situation and will most likely identify with the therapy being done.

Techniques for Working with Individuals Indirectly

At times in therapy groups the leader will do therapy in an indirect manner with one or more members. Indirect therapy may suit a member who does not feel comfortable being the focus of the group. Sometimes this occurs with the leader's knowledge; at other times the leader may have no idea that the work with one member—or simply a discussion of an issue—is indirectly helpful to another member.

Let's assume that one of a group's members, Sarah, had a friend who died tragically two years ago. Although Sarah has never mentioned this in the group, she did write about it briefly one time in the journal that she keeps for the group. Sarah has not participated much verbally and has never been the focus of the group. To help Sarah, the leader has a number of options.

- She can bring up the issue of death and grieving in order to get a discussion going and hope that this will prompt Sarah to speak.
- She can talk to Sarah privately before the session begins and suggest that receiving help on this issue might be beneficial. The help could then come in the form of either group or individual counseling.
- She can work with another member who has a grief issue, knowing that the work will probably be beneficial to Sarah.
- She can forego pursuing the issue in the hope that Sarah will bring it up herself.

If the leader chooses the third option, the group will focus on a member's pain over a death. While working with that member, the leader would scan the group in an effort to observe any reactions from Sarah. In some cases the work being done will trigger the silently working member to open up and request help.

The leader can also attempt to draw out the silently working member. The leader could ask members to comment on whether or not the work done had any meaning for them and, if so, what. This will sometimes cause the silent member to open up. Or, using dyads, the leader could pair the working member with the silently working member. Both of these methods may be successful in getting the silently working member to share.

If these methods are not successful in drawing out comments from the targeted silent member, the leader should keep in mind that members benefit from hearing others whether or not they actively discuss their own personal concerns. Hearing the concerns and coping strategies of the other members can help the indirectly working member feel that others have the same problem, and may provide some suggestions for how to cope with the concerns. Often members identify with the discussion to such an extent that they personalize the work as if the focus of the group were directly on them.

Techniques That Cause Members to Share on a More Personal Level

The goal of any therapy group is to have the members gain some insight into or help with various concerns in their lives. As stated earlier, therapeutic help happens for different members in different ways. For many, discussing their specific concern in front of the group is extremely helpful. For others, watching other members resolve certain problems is therapeutic. For still other members, being involved in an in-depth discussion about an issue can prove quite beneficial. Many leaders know how to introduce relevant topics but do not know how to engage the members in personal sharing that is meaningful. A very useful technique that increases the chances for more personal sharing is the use of ratings. A rating question would be something like this: "On a 1-to-10 scale, with 10 being very satisfied, how satisfied are you with your present love relationship? (your job? your life? your family? yourself as a parent?) (*Pause*) What stands between your number and a 10?" When asked questions like these, members usually will give thought to them and will often want to share their answers. These responses are usually both focused and personal.

Other techniques that are used to cause members to share more personally are the following:

- The leader uses rounds to get members to commit themselves out loud about their position. Members tend to then reflect on what they said.
- The leader discusses the concept or issue in a well-thought-out, thought-provoking way.
- The leader cuts off storytelling and directs members to more meaningful exploration.
- The leader points out the value of sharing.

The following are examples of deepening the focus of the group using the techniques mentioned in the preceding list.

EXAMPLES . . . .

The group consists of outpatients at a mental-health center. The leader has introduced the topic of guilt for discussion. One member has described how she felt guilty about leaving her dog at home by itself all day; another how he felt guilty about not going to visit his grandfather more often. Neither of these members seemed too bothered by their guilt, but the leader senses that many of the members are, in fact, very much bothered by their guilt feelings. The leader decides to deepen the focus.

Leader: I guess I am wondering if some of you have some guilt feelings that are hard to live with. That is, you feel bad about something you did or are doing and those actions cause you to think less of yourself. Guilt is often associated with doing something that runs counter to some value or expectation we hold for ourselves. Religion and sex are often involved in guilt. Let me ask this—is there something that you feel guilty about that would be hard to share? I'll ask you to say "yes" or "no," but you do not have to share what it is.

Troy: No.

Maria: Yes.

Bob: Yes.

Beth: No.

Cindy: Yes.

Ted: Yes.

Leader: What makes it hard to tell?

Cindy: I am afraid of what people would think of me.

Leader: I think that is true for many people. More important though is how you feel about what you did or what you are doing. How many of you answered "yes" because of things that you are doing currently? (*Maria, Ted, and Cindy indicate that they did*) How can a person quit feeling guilty?

Ted: I don't see how I can not feel guilty—it is wrong. I never thought it would go this far. (*Looks down*)

Leader: Ted, perhaps if you talk about it you will see it differently. I urge each of you to talk about what you are feeling guilty about because there are solutions to guilt. You do not have to continually beat up on yourself. How much longer do you want to punish yourself?

Ted: You're right about the punishment. I hate it, but I feel so rotten.

Leader: From what you said earlier, Ted, my hunch is that it has to do with your marriage and possibly an affair. Others of you may have guilt over something in your marriage or your past that pertains to sexual issues.

Ted: That's it—you see, at work. . . .

In this example, the leader asks members to be more specific and keeps gathering information. The leader also makes some comments and asks thought-provoking questions in order to get members to personalize the discussion. The leader keeps exploring the topic until one person indicates that he wants to work.

. . . .

The members are all women in an eating-disorder group. They are talking about their problems with food.

Sally: When I am bored or upset I eat, and when I start eating I can't stop.

Lori: That's true for me. I like all kinds of food, but cookies and candy are my real downfall.

Sara: My downfall is ice cream. My favorite is chocolate chip.

Najwa: Ice cream is one of my downfalls. Let's list our favorite downfalls. (*Everyone laughs*)

Leader: (*In a slow, deliberate voice*) Rather than focusing on what your downfall is, I'd like each of you to think of how you lose control over your food intake. When does it occur and how do you cause it to occur? Think about that for a minute. (*Pause*) Any thoughts on that?

In this example, the leader shifted the focus to a new, more personal topic because she saw that the group could get focused on a "surface" topic. As a result of the leader's question, each member has to think about herself. Too often leaders will get caught up in the flow of the discussion and not direct the members to more personal and meaningful dialogue.

. . . .

The group consists of members who all experience frequent panic attacks when they are out in public (agoraphobia). Three different members have shared stories about their intense fear.

Joe: (*Finishing his story*) And as a result of those attacks, I have not been out of the house for longer than an hour in the last five years. I get out maybe once every two months. It's hell!

Leader: I think Joe is right. It *is* hell, and since you are all here for the same reason, I know that most of you feel the same way. One goal in this group is to help you realize that you are not alone, and I think most of you can see that now from hearing others talk. The other goal is to get you over your fears. To do this we have to look at what causes panic attacks and what can be done about them. I want each of you to think about your panic attacks and the events and thoughts that occur right before they happen and during an attack. As you talk about your situation, please try to comment on this since your understanding of what happens to you right before the attacks and during the attacks will help you get over them.

In this example, the leader is introducing a meaningful topic rather than just letting the members relate incidents from their lives. By focusing on what happens right before an attack, the members are more likely to share personal information and to get to the pertinent issues.

. . . .

The members are sharing events of the week without giving much thought to what they are saying.

Leader: I'd like to say something that I think will be helpful to each of you. (*Using a soft, encouraging voice*) We have three sessions left, so I want to urge you to really give some thought to what you want to talk about tonight. In the past few weeks we have discussed a number of personal issues and I want to encourage you to look into yourself and see if there are other issues that you may need to talk about. What obstacles are in the way of having your life go the way you want it to? Are there some fears or unfinished business from the past that you need to talk about? Really stretch yourself in these last sessions. Are there some things that you would like to bring up in this session?

Sandi: (*After about 20 seconds*) There is something I would like to bring up. It has to do with me and my religion . . . .

. . . .

We hope these examples help you see how the leader can be very instrumental in deepening the focus, which in turn makes the group more personal, usually more interesting, and probably more therapeutic.

Intense Therapy

In this chapter, we have discussed therapy in many ways—from helpful insight to deep therapy. Many counseling groups, such as those in schools, are not aimed at deep therapy. However, many groups have as their goal deep, personal work; that is, the leader funnels the group to individual work at a level of 3 or below. In these groups, the leader usually directs much of the therapy because the members do not have the skill or insight to play a major part. For instance, in recovery groups from alcohol, incest, rape, or abuse, we use a variety of techniques, including Gestalt, psychodrama, or in-depth rounds, to get at the deep-seated emotions. We then use RET, TA, Gestalt, and some creative techniques to help the client work through the pain. Any leader who is getting members to look at their buried emotions has to know how to help the members get through their pain. Stated another way: *Do not unzip members unless you know how to zip them back up!*

Intense therapy requires that you have good individual counseling skills. If you plan to work in settings in which you will be doing some intensive group therapy, we strongly suggest that you become knowledgeable and skilled as an individual therapist. It is those skills, coupled with the ideas in this book, that will make you a good group therapist.

PROVIDING THERAPY
IN A NONTHERAPY GROUP

At the beginning of this chapter, we mentioned that therapy may take place in nontherapy groups. Quite often in groups in which the purpose is something other than therapy the opportunity will arise to focus on one member's concern. Topics discussed in a support group or even a discussion or education group can cause members to get in touch with unfinished and/or painful issues.

The first thing that a leader must do when the opportunity for therapy arises in a nontherapy group is to decide if therapy would be appropriate. If the leader decides it is appropriate to focus on one member's concern (that is, the topic is relevant to the other members and there is enough time), she should ask the member if he desires immediate help. She may also want to ask the other members if they are willing to spend some time focusing on one member's problem. Once the leader has consent from the member and the other members of the group, she will use many of the skills and techniques outlined in this chapter. The following are examples of when it might be appropriate to hold the focus on a member and do some brief therapeutic work.

- If a member of an education group for pregnant teenagers starts crying about how she hates being pregnant, the leader might choose to work with her for a few minutes because, more than likely, others are having similar feelings.
- If a member of an experiential group shares how he has gotten in touch with how bad he felt about himself when he was growing up, the leader might decide to funnel the group to a deeper level by focusing on this member.
- If a member of a parenting group discloses that she feels guilty about her baby because it was the result of an affair that her husband does not know about, the leader might want to take a few minutes and try to be helpful.

The benefits of conducting therapy in nontherapy groups are very much the same as for therapy groups. The main difference is that the therapy portion of the group is short-term. The focus is then brought back to the main purpose of the group.

COMMON MISTAKES MADE
WHEN LEADING THERAPY GROUPS

Several errors are common among leaders of therapy groups. These errors have been discussed earlier in the chapter or in other chapters, but because they are so important, we want to review them briefly.

Attempting to Conduct Therapy Without a Contract

Many leaders attempt to focus on a member of the group without getting agreement from that person. The result is that the member resists the leader's attempt to be helpful.

Spending Too Much Time on One Person

Some leaders make the mistake of spending week after week trying to help one member who is in pain, or spending too much of the session on one member. It is important for the leader to realize that some members seek and/or need inordinate attention from the group. The natural tendency of the leader is to focus on those individuals, especially if other members are not as talkative.

Spending Too Little Time on One Person

Many beginning leaders will be hesitant to hold the focus on one member when others also want to share. When this happens, one member shares for a minute or so, then another member, then another member. Sometimes this is helpful and valuable, but at other times this type of sharing is not as personal as when the focus is held on one member. Holding the focus on one member causes him to delve more deeply into his problem, which in turn often causes other members to look more closely at their own concerns.

Focusing on an Irrelevant Topic

Too often the leader will let a member ramble on about a personal experience, even if the story has no relevance to the group. The leader might even ask the member questions about the story or have other members ask questions. A similar mistake occurs when two or three members are focused on some irrelevant topic and the leader fails to shift the focus. It is important to realize that if the leader does not cut off certain topics and individuals, the session is likely to be much less meaningful for the majority of the members.

Letting Members Rescue Each Other

If a member begins to cry, it is often a mistake for another member or the entire group to immediately rush to the member's side, take his hand, and try to comfort him. The leader should discourage this type of behavior. Most of the time, the member needs to be with his pain, not to be "rescued" from it. The members should show support, care, and concern, but should not rescue. The leader prevents rescuing by saying something like "Let Mike be with his pain—I think he knows that we care. Mike, do realize that we care and want to help."

Letting the Session Become an Advice-Giving Session

Very often in groups, leaders make the mistake of turning the session into an advice-giving session. That is, a member will bring up a problem, then all the other members will try to solve it by giving advice. This is *not* what a therapy group is supposed to be. Sometimes advice is given and is helpful, but by and large each member should work on his or her own concerns with the help of the other members.

CONCLUDING COMMENTS

This chapter has shown that therapy groups are different from support and growth groups in that the leader focuses on the members in an in-depth manner. The main purpose of therapy groups is to help members alleviate personal concerns that inhibit them outside the group. Therapy may also take place in nontherapy groups, in short-term formats.

The approach we have described for leading therapy groups emphasizes the role of the leader as being responsible for the therapy that takes place, in contrast to some experts who believe that the members should be the agents of change. Our belief is that the leader of a therapy group should be in charge because she is more knowledgeable about the field of counseling and about therapeutic techniques.

When one member is exploring a problem in depth, the leader can use a variety of skills and techniques. He can use his individual counseling skills to help the member clarify and work through the problem. He can also use the other members to play various roles, or he can use himself to help dramatize the problem. It is the leader's responsibility to establish a positive tone for the members and to get a contract from a member before focusing intensely on him or her. Once there is an agreement to work on a concern, the leader may need to help the member clarify the problem, using any of a number of techniques such as having the member engage in a clarifying round or having the other members ask the working member questions. A very valuable technique when working with an individual on a concern is the therapeutic round, either stationary or in-depth.

When conducting individual therapy in a group, it is important to spin off to the group and hear members' personal reactions, to make sure they are involved in trying to help the working member, or both. It is also important to point out the theme of an individual's work, such as "how to deal with anger" or "how to finally let go of negative feelings from the past." By spinning off and pointing out the themes, the leader keeps members more involved and this usually causes them to be ready to share when the focus shifts from the working member.

In summary, we view the leader not as a counselor who does solely individual therapy in the group but rather as an orchestrator who may focus the group on one particular individual for a time while involving other members in the therapeutic process.

Closing a Session or Group

Two kinds of closings are discussed in this chapter: the closing of a session and the closing of the entire series of sessions. We refer to the first kind of closing as the *closing phase.* It is the period of a session during which the leader wraps things up until the next meeting. The second type of closing is referred to as the *closing stage.* The closing stage may be the last session of the group or the last several sessions, depending on the kind of group and the total number of sessions involved.

THE CLOSING PHASE

Every session should have a closing phase. The amount of time allowed will depend on both the length of the session and the kind of group being led. Usually the longer the session, the more time is required. For a 1-hour session, the leader may find 3 to 5 minutes sufficient; a 2- to 3-hour session may require 5 to 15 minutes to accomplish the closing phase. The closing phase of a discussion or task group may simply require summarizing the main ideas or decisions made; since this is fairly straightforward, less time will be required. In a support or therapy group in which members share a range of thoughts and feelings, more time will be required to pull together key points, clarify goals, check for unfinished business, and encourage reactions. With experience, the leader learns to judge the amount of time needed to bring closure to the session.

During the closing phase the leader has the opportunity to encourage members to share their thoughts and feelings about the session. In general, sharing during the closing phase can contribute to a greater sense of involvement with the group and cohesiveness among members. Members may share how they benefited from activities or discussions that took place during the session or from comments made by other members.

It is especially important for the leader to hear from those members who were less active in the session, for two reasons. First, the leader can benefit from hearing how they feel about what is taking place and if they are feeling comfortable. Second, less active members may be perceived negatively by other members as contributing less or playing an observing rather than a participating role.

It is important to inform the members that the session is being closed. This can be done by saying any of the following:

- We need to start winding down, so I want you to think about the session today and what it has meant to you.
- Since there are only a few minutes left in today's session, let's review what we have gone over today.
- I think we are at a good stopping point, so let's spend the next few minutes summarizing the session today, and then we'll talk briefly about next week's session.
- Let's begin the closing phase of the session, because we need to stop in about ten minutes. (This statement assumes that the leader has taught the group about the various phases of a session.)

Purposes and Goals of the Closing Phase

The closing phase may serve one or more of the following purposes: (1) summarizing and highlighting the main points; (2) reinforcing commitments made by individual members; and (3) checking for unfinished business from the session.

Summarizing and Highlighting the Main Points

One purpose of the closing phase is to pull the session together by highlighting and summarizing important points. For example, in discussion or task groups, key ideas or decisions can be highlighted. In education groups, members may focus on what they learned and what impact this new information may have on their lives. Members of support, growth, or therapy groups can look back on what experiences helped them feel more comfortable about an issue or recall what issue led them to some new personal awareness or decision about themselves. Pulling together salient points or experiences helps members remember them after the session has ended; the impact of the session can thus be increased.

By having the members summarize their reactions and thoughts, the leader is also better able to assess what each one has gained from the session. This allows her to plan the next session better. Having the group focus on key points also gives members a chance to hear what was important to others. This sharing often tends to build greater trust and cohesiveness among the members.

Reinforcing Commitments

In task, growth, or therapy groups, members may make commitments to some task or change in their behavior. The leader will want to review such commitments in the closing phase and try to encourage the members in whatever way possible. The two examples below show how a leader might clarify goals and strengthen commitments.

E X A M P L E S . . . .

It is the end of the second session of a task group made up of members who work at a mental-health agency. Their task is to develop a new residential program for adolescents.

Leader: Let's review who is to do what. Joe, what are you going to do before the next meeting?

Joe: I am going to call those two agencies that have residential programs and find out what problems they have had.

Leader: Good. See if they'll send you any material, too.

Pablo: I am going to draw up a tentative list of rules for the unit that the residents would have to live by.

Leader: Be sure to get input from us, especially from Cindy, since she worked in a residential program.

Cindy: I am going to devise a list of personnel that would be needed to staff such a unit.

Bill: I'm going to try to get funding for the unit.

Leader: Bill, I think what we decided was that you were to look into possible sources for funding and that you would bring that list to the group. Then we, as a group, would decide the best route to take to get the unit funded.

. . . .

It is the third session of a therapy group. Members have shared a variety of concerns during the session, and the leader wishes to clarify members' goals and reinforce their commitments to those goals.

Leader: Each of you in today's session has expressed a desire to change an aspect of your life. Three or four of you worked on specific goals you want to follow through on before our next meeting. As we close today, let's take a few minutes and briefly hear from each of you about your goals.

Chang: I want to go home this weekend and not fight with my mother. And I now think I've got some ways to avoid fighting.

Leader: You sound pretty committed to that, Chang. I'd like to suggest you keep notes and report back to us on how that works. (*Chang nods*) Who else feels they might try something different this week? (*Pause*)

John: (*Looks around at the group*) Well, I know I've got to do something about staying out so late.

Leader: What did you decide as a result of discussing it here today?

John: I am going to discuss with my wife which days are better for her to have me stay out late.

Leader: Didn't you also say that first you have to see if she will agree to let you stay out at least two nights and that you are going to ask her if she would like to come with you?

John: That's right! I forgot that part, and it's important.

Leader: You bet it is. You have it now, so what you are going to do?

John: I'll talk to her and really try to be open with her.

Leader: Fine; we'll look forward to hearing how it went at our next session.

. . . .

In both of these examples the leader increases the likelihood that the members will follow through on their commitments. A good closing phase is necessary in order to review and clarify decisions and plans made during the working phase of the session.

Sometimes members make commitments and plans that are unrealistic. Reviewing various members' commitments and plans during the closing phase allows such unrealistic goals to be clarified. The following are two examples of a leader helping a member modify an unrealistic goal.

EXAMPLES. . . . .

It is the third session of a personal growth group in a college counseling center. During the working phase of the session Frieda discussed her study problems and plans to change her study habits. During the closing phase of the session, the leader asks various members about their goals.

Leader: I think we've summarized what we covered today pretty well. In the next few minutes it might be helpful if people share specific goals that they are shooting for this week. Betty, I know you decided to try a different approach with your boyfriend when he's late.

Betty: Today I learned that yelling only gets us into a fight. When he is late, I'm going to calmly tell him that I'm disappointed and that I'm only willing to wait for 20 minutes. I feel better knowing I can be in control.

Leader: Frieda, how about you? You said you wanted to set up a study schedule. Have you come up with any thoughts about how you might do that?

Frieda: I decided I'm going to study six hours every night. That should really help me catch up.

Leader: (*Turning to the other members*) What do you think about Frieda's plan?

Will: That seems like a lot. I'd get burned out in one day. (*Other members nod agreement*)

Leader: What do you think, Frieda?

Frieda: Well, maybe that is a lot. I guess I'll start with an hour and see how that goes.

By helping the member develop a realistic goal, the leader has increased the likelihood of the member experiencing success.

. . . .

During the session, Al discussed his desire for a salary increase. With the help of the group, he role-played strategies for talking with his employer about the raise. Although he made progress, Al needed further assistance in increasing his assertiveness and in exploring ways to handle potential rebuffs and excuses from his boss. The group is now in the closing phase.

Leader: Who else learned something from today's session?

Al: Boy, I did. That role playing about asking for a raise really helped. Even though you think I am not ready, I do. I think I'll go in tomorrow and ask for the raise!

Leader: Al, if he says no, what are you going to say? We didn't get a chance to practice that.

Al: Oh, I didn't even think of that. All I was thinking about was how I now know what to say. You're right. I'm not prepared for a negative answer. I'll wait till we talk about it next week in group.

If the leader had not clarified the member's goal during the closing phase, Al would probably have asked for a raise even though he had not developed the resources to cope with the situation. By reviewing Al's reaction to the session, the leader was able to discover his unrealistic plan and caution him about moving ahead prematurely.

. . . .

Checking for Unresolved Issues
(Unfinished Business)

The closing phase is also the time to check with members for any unfinished business. *Unfinished business* means issues that are not fully resolved during the session. The leader may have found it unproductive to focus for too long a time on a particular member or issue and thus brought temporary closure to the discussion. The closing phase may be used to refocus on that previous issue or concern, providing an opportunity for a member to express new thoughts or for the leader to help the member agree to continue to work on the issue in the next session. Occasionally, a member may have unfinished business that cannot wait until the following session, either because a decision is imminent or because the issue is causing considerable discomfort for the member. The leader could ask the members if they would be willing to extend the session to work on the issue. If this cannot be done, the leader may see the member individually as soon after the session as possible.

To find out if members have unfinished business the leader could say something like this:

- Is there any unfinished business from the session that you think needs to be discussed for a few minutes?
- Does anyone have something that got "stirred up" during the session that they want to mention? We'll either deal with it now, if it won't take too long, or we will deal with it at the beginning of the next session.

Because there are time constraints during the closing phase, the leader may need to carry unfinished business into the next session. However, by having members mention their unfinished business, the leader is able to either help them finish the issue or assure them that they will be able to discuss the matter at the next session.

EXAMPLES . . . .

A counselor is leading a personal awareness group at a rehabilitation center. John expressed some angry feelings regarding his parents' not visiting him often enough, but he was not able to see how he was making himself upset by blaming his parents. After working with John for about 20 minutes, the leader chose to focus on another member. Now, during the closing phase, the leader wishes to see if John has had any additional thoughts about his anger toward his parents.

Leader: We'll spend the next few minutes bringing things to a close for today. I'd like each of you to think about what stood out for you. (*Pauses and scans the group. After a short silence,* *the leader makes eye contact with John)* John, I felt there were more feelings you had to express about your parents. While we don't have time to work a lot more with those feelings today, do you have additional thoughts you would like to share with the group?

John: I feel better for talking about it, but I still think they should visit more.

Leader: I guess I'd like you to keep thinking about this between now and our next session. We'll bring it up again and see if we can help you work on it more. *(John nods agreement)*

Here the leader contracts informally with the member to work on the issue during the next session. He wants to make it clear to the member and the entire group that he is not forgetting the issue and plans to come back to it. He also wants to make sure that if there are any pressing feelings, they are handled before the session ends.

. . . .

A group of divorced men and women are meeting for the fourth session in a personal growth group. One member, Ann, worked on guilt feelings about giving the custody of her two children to her husband. During the session, Ann came to the conclusion that she did not have to feel guilty about her actions. However, when the focus of the group shifted to another topic, Ann continued to think about her decision. Now the leader is bringing the group to a close and, among other things, is determining if there is unfinished business for any members.

Leader: Several of you worked on some pretty important issues today. It might be useful to review our session and see if you have additional thoughts about anything you discussed.

Sue: It was really helpful for me to see that even though my parents don't believe in divorce, that's their value and it's OK for me to have a different value.

Leader: I'm glad that helped, Sue. What about other people?

Ann: *(Looking down and speaking in a weak voice)* I've been sitting here thinking about my kids. I know being without them right now is best for me. Yet to be a good mother, I still feel I should be with them. I guess I'm confused all over again.

Leader: Ann, it's apparent there is more we need to do to help clear up your concerns. It sometimes happens that after we work on something, the old feelings can surface again. If you feel this can wait till our next session, we will work on it then.

Ann: I think it can wait and I really want to work on it.

Had the leader not checked for unfinished business, this member might have left the group feeling stranded with those feelings. Also, the leader could have finished the session thinking that this member had worked through a personal issue when in fact she was still struggling with it.

. . . .

In summary, sometimes unfinished business discovered during the closing phase can be finished quickly with some simple clarification. At other times, the leader and member jointly determine that the issue can wait until the next session. When a member is having strong feelings about an issue at the close of a session, and it is not possible to extend the session, the leader may wish to meet with the member to do some individual counseling following the session.

Formats for Closing a Session

There are several formats that can be used for closing a session. The choice of format for a particular session should depend on the kind of group, the purpose of the particular session, and what went on during the session. The leader may want to vary the closings of different sessions so that members do not get bored with the same kind, session after session. In a discussion, education, or task group, it may not be important for each member to speak during the closing phase since members have shared ideas and thoughts rather than personal feelings. In support, personal growth, and therapy groups, it is usually valuable for members to share their reactions and feelings about the session. Formats for closing a session include having the members summarize, having the leader summarize, using a round, using dyads, and getting written reactions.

Members' Summaries

A simple yet useful way to close the session is to have one or more members summarize what has transpired. The leader can ask for a volunteer to summarize or may select a member who would do a good job. If one member summarizes, other members may also be given the opportunity to add what they feel is important. The leader may also want to add any important events that were overlooked by the members. It is important that a summary during the closing phase not be long or boring. The purpose is to give the members a brief review. Following the summary, members may wish to comment on particular points that were especially important to them.

Leader's Summary

The leader may choose to summarize the session. The advantage of this method is that the leader can emphasize certain points and focus on certain members' comments. The disadvantage is that the leader may forget something that was important to one or two members; this may result in those members feeling hurt or resentful. To prevent this, the leader may find it helpful to let members contribute additional summaries following the leader's.

Rounds That Elicit Member Comments

Eliciting brief comments from members about what they learned from the session or what stood out as they think back on the session is an excellent way to close a session. The format we use most frequently is the round or series of rounds. This process would serve as a summary, since many different thoughts about the topic or session are expressed.

Leader: As we close tonight's session, I'd like each of you to take a minute to think about what you learned or what stood out to you. When you are ready, we'll go around the group and get comments.

A round provides a chance for every member to comment and may encourage those who have talked less during the session to share their reactions. A round also allows the leader to respond to certain members if feedback to them would be helpful. When setting up a round, the leader should instruct the members to limit their comments to a sentence or two. Longer responses defeat the purpose of the closing round, which is to highlight important points for each member.

EXAMPLE . . . .

Leader: In a sentence or two, what will you take away from the session today? (*Pause*) Tim, let's start with you.

Tim: I learned that I am more nonassertive than assertive.

Guillermo: I learned that it is hard for me to be assertive. I guess I'm chicken.

Leader: I wouldn't say chicken. You simply have not learned to be assertive.

Bill: I learned that my parents are the cause of my being so aggressive.

Leader: Bill, let me clarify that for you and everyone here. We learn things from what our parents do and say. Often we tend to act like them unless we pay attention to our behavior. (*Turns to Bill*) In your case, from what you described, your parents are very aggressive. However, this does not mean you have to be aggressive, but you probably will be unless you monitor yourself. I hope the group will be a big help to you.

. . . .

Dyads Followed by Comments to the Group

Starting the closing phase with dyads is a good way to involve all the members. Also, dyads can energize members, especially if the energy level is low toward the end of a session. To use dyads for closure, the leader would say something like the following:

Leader: Let's take the next few minutes to close. I'd like to form pairs composed of Phil and Pat; Roger and Paula; Ted and Ramón; Mike and Kay. What I'd like you to do is share with your partner one or two things that were particularly important to you about today's session. Then we'll come back to the large group and share any thoughts and feelings.

In this example, the leader decided to pair the members, but she could have allowed the members to select partners. If the leader decides to do the pairing, she should give special thought to anything that occurred during the session that might make it especially valuable for certain members to be together; for example, two members who expressed similar concerns or worked on similar problems could be paired.

In the following example, the leader decides to participate in a dyad to encourage a member to share during the closing phase.

E X A M P L E . . . .

It is the second session of a support group made up of spouses of alcoholics. One member, Sally, has spoken little during these first two sessions.

Leader: As we're closing tonight, I'd like to take a few minutes to see how each of you is feeling about the group so far, what you think has been helpful, and what other topics or issues you'd like to discuss. To do this, I'd like people to pair up for about two minutes and then come back to share your thoughts. (*The leader pairs up the members, pairing herself with Sally. She learns that Sally is worried about how other members might view her because she has continued to live with her abusive, alcoholic husband. The leader reassures Sally that she will not let the members attack her and that it might be helpful if Sally shared some of her concerns before the session ended. Sally agrees. The leader ends the dyads and brings the group* *together again.*) I'd like each of us to share our thoughts about the group.

Molly: The group has been good for me to just get things off my mind. I feel better knowing there is a place I can come to unload.

Bill: Jack and I talked about what it was like to have alcoholic wives. I feel relieved just knowing other people are in the same boat.

Leader: Sally shared some of her fear about talking about her family situation in the group. We both agreed it would be helpful for her to talk a little about that before we stop.

Sally: It's real scary for me to be here. I feel I contributed to my husband's drinking by trying to cover it up.

Molly: I didn't know you'd been thinking that all this time. I feel the same way—I hope we can talk about this at the next meeting.

The leader knew it was important for this quiet member to "break the ice" with the group before the end of this session so that she and the other members would begin to feel comfortable with one another. Because of its emphasis on sharing thoughts about the group experience, the closing phase was a good time to do this.

. . . .

Written Reactions

There are several ways in which the leader can use written reactions during the closing phase. The leader can begin the closing phase of a session by asking members to write their reactions to the session. The leader would say something like this:

Leader: It's about 8:45. Let's summarize and close the group. First, I'd like you to spend five minutes jotting down any reactions, thoughts, or feelings regarding the session tonight. We'll then share some of those thoughts and stop by 9:00.

Writing can be helpful for those members who respond more comfortably after having had a chance to put their ideas on paper. Some leaders may choose to begin the closing phase of each session this way or may use writing periodically for variety.

A different use of writing during the closing phase is to have the members write for five to ten minutes at the very end, when the group has completed the closing. This is usually done in a journal that the members leave with the leader, who then has an opportunity to read their reactions. The leader may choose to write encouraging or clarifying comments in the journals and then return them to the members at the next session. When journals are used, writing at the close of each session may become the standard format. Journals used to close a session provide a lasting chronicle of the entire group experience from the first to the final session.

Helpful Closing Skills

Several skills are particularly important to use during the closing phase. They include clarifying the purpose, cutting off, tying together, and drawing out.

Clarifying the Purpose

We have discussed clarifying the purpose as a group leadership skill earlier in this book, but it is especially important during the closing phase. A variety of issues and concerns can be raised by members during the closing phase that can take the group in unproductive directions. If the leader is unclear about the purpose of the closing phase, she can easily be drawn into a discussion of new material. Therefore, it is important that the leader avoid bringing up new business. Similarly, should one or more members wish to bring up new topics, the leader will want to explain to them the purpose of the closing phase of the group and offer the option of bringing the topics up again at the beginning of the next session. Occasionally a member may bring up a personal issue at the end of a session that he has been "sitting on" during the session. The leader can determine with the member if the issue can wait until the following session. If not, the leader may, with the agreement of the other members, decide to extend the session for a few minutes. If this is not possible, the leader may meet with the member after the session to work individually on the issue. The important thing to remember during the closing phase of a group session is that the leader is trying to bring the session to an end.

Cutting Off

To maintain the necessary focus on closing, the leader must be ready to use cutting-off skills. Members will not only bring up new material during the closing phase, but often will get into rehashing the session rather than highlighting or summarizing.

E X A M P L E S . . . .

Leader: What else did you learn from the session today?
Linda: I'd like to know from the other girls if they have to go to church every Sunday. I do, and I hate it!

Leader: (*In a warm, caring voice*) Linda, that seems like an important issue for you, but we really do not have time to get into a new topic right now. If you will bring that up at the next session, we'll certainly talk about it.

In this example the leader stops other members from answering by speaking first. She does so to make sure that a new topic does not get started during the closing phase.

. . . .

The next example is similar, but in this case the leader has to cut off a member who is rambling.

Leader: We seem to have a good list started. What else did we talk about that we are going to observe this week?

Frank: The thing we don't have there that we really need to talk about is getting some improvements in visiting hours. I'm so tired of visiting hours always getting changed around. My family can never get here—

Leader: Frank, I'm going to jump in here. Visiting hours may be a really important area to look at, but it will have to wait till next week. We want to summarize for the next few minutes the things we talked through today so we don't lose anything.

. . . .

Tying Together

The skill of tying together is especially beneficial during the closing phase of a session. By using this skill the leader can create a sense of interrelatedness of themes, issues, and personal experiences. It is important for the leader to identify those points that relate to one another and then share them in such a way that the members see how patterns, issues, and people are connected. This is something they are often unable to do themselves.

Drawing Out

Drawing out is also an important skill to use during the closing phase of a session because the leader usually likes to hear from as many members as possible. Several of the techniques for closing mentioned earlier—especially the use of dyads and rounds—will facilitate the drawing-out process. It is especially important for the leader to draw out members who are less active during the session, both to help them feel involved and to get their reactions to the session.

Helpful Techniques for the Closing Phase

Wishes

A useful technique for closing certain kinds of growth, support, and therapy sessions is the use of "wishes." This activity helps build positive and supportive feelings among members. The leader can use this technique as part of the closing phase, perhaps after a summary or after a round.

EXAMPLE . . . .

Leader: I think that pretty much summarizes the session. Any comments? (*Pause—no one seems ready to comment*) Let's do this. (*Speaking slowly*) Look around the room and see if there is anyone you would like to make a wish for. If there is someone, identify the person and then say "My wish for you is. . . . " For example, Joe, my wish for you is that you will call your parents and say those things that you want to say.

Max: Don, my wish for you is that you get out at least twice this week.

Joe: Cherry, my wish for you is that you will stop blaming yourself.

. . . .

Handling Criticism of the Session

An occurrence for which the leader should be prepared during the closing of the session is criticism about the session or the group itself. It is important that the leader not be defensive. In most cases the leader will not want the closing to be spent entirely on criticism unless he senses that the majority of the members are having the same feelings. The way the leader handles the criticism will depend on the kind of criticism, the merits of the criticism, and the amount of time needed for the actual closing. The following are several ways the leader can handle criticism during the closing phase.

EXAMPLES . . . .

Melvin is a member who has tried to dominate the group, and the leader on numerous occasions has had to cut him off. The leader has a strong sense from the members' nonverbal responses that they appreciate the fact that Melvin is not allowed to dominate.

Melvin: (*In a hostile voice*) I have something I want to say. I feel you lead too much. In other groups, the leader hardly said anything—this is more your group than our group!

Leader: (*To Melvin and the entire group*) I do hope you feel that this is your group. There are times when I direct what is happening simply because I am trained as a counselor and a group leader. And, as I said earlier, there will be times when I may cut you off in order to hold the focus on another issue or when it seems like you have gotten a little long-winded. Certainly I do not want you to feel that I am dominating the group. Does anyone else feel that way? (*No one responds*) Let's go back to summarizing the session. Other thoughts or reactions?

In this example, the leader briefly responded, got support from the members, and then went back to closing the group.

. . . .

James has been in the group for only two sessions.

Leader: Who else wants to comment on what stood out to them?
James: I feel like the group gets too personal. When Troy was talking, I felt you really pushed him too hard!
Leader: James, let me answer that. (*Looking at the entire group*) The group is personal, and I do push members hard because all of you have problems that need to be dealt with on more than a superficial level. Certainly I try not to push you *too* hard, but do realize that not dealing with your problems is what got you into the hospital.
Troy: I'm glad you pushed. I think I understand why I get so angry.

. . . .

The leader has been feeling that the group has not gone well the last couple of sessions.

José: I don't mean to be critical, but the group has not been very valuable for me lately.
Leader: How do others of you feel? I, too, think something is missing.
Rusty: I would like us to be more personal rather than just discussing things. Does anyone else feel that way?
Pam: I do. The discussions about legal issues, custody, and so on are all good, but there are personal things that I think I am ready to share.
Paul: I would like that better.
Leader: So what you are saying is that you would like this to be more of a sharing group than a discussion/education group. How about the rest of you, how do you feel?

In this example, the leader decided to focus on the criticism because he felt that the group did perhaps need a new emphasis.

. . . .

Acknowledging a New Member

The leader may want to vary the closing slightly when a member is present for the first time. (In "open" groups, members may enter the group after it has been meeting for a number of sessions.) The leader might want to focus on the new member if the member seems to feel comfortable enough being spotlighted. Focusing on the new member gives that member a chance to share, which can help her feel even more comfortable. It also gives members a chance to know a little more about her. By hearing from the new member, the leader also has a better idea of how that person is feeling about being in the group.

E X A M P L E . . . .

Two members have finished summarizing the session, and others have commented.

Leader: Connie, I hope this first session has been interesting and maybe even helpful.

Connie: Well, I was really nervous for the first ten minutes, but I did relax. I am sorry that I didn't say more, but I really don't like talking in front of groups. I hope it will get easier for me.

Leader: Was the session helpful?

Connie: Oh, yes. I already realize that others have feelings similar to mine. I really identified with what Patty was saying.

Leader: I hope that during the next session you will feel freer to share. Anyone else have any closing thoughts before we stop?

. . . .

Acknowledging Losing a Member

There are occasions when a member leaves a group even though the group continues. In a closed group, members might drop out for any variety of reasons. More often, the departure of one member occurs in an ongoing, open-membership group, such as residential treatment programs in substance abuse or physical rehabilitation centers. Those members leave the group because they are finished with their treatment.

When a member is leaving it is important that the leader allow enough time during the closing to focus on that member. Many of the same issues that would be covered when ending the entire group should be covered for the exiting member. For example, the leader may wish to review the member's goals upon entrance to the group and the progress he has made, provide encouragement to continue to work on personal growth, give feedback on other areas in which the member might consider working, handle good-byes, and so forth. Although the exiting member will be the major focal point, the leader may wish to use this experience to help other members think about when they will be leaving the group and what they still need to do to get themselves ready for this.

The amount of time that should be given to a member who is exiting will depend on the length of time the member has been in the group, the purpose of the group, and the length of the session. In open-ended groups, members may be exiting fairly often, so the time devoted to taking leave of a member will need to be monitored to avoid spending an inordinate amount of time saying good-bye. Five to fifteen minutes is usually sufficient to conclude this exiting process.

E X A M P L E S . . . .

> **Leader:** We have about 15 minutes left in the session, so what I would like to do is begin to summarize the session. Too, I want to leave the last few minutes free to focus on Walt, who will be leaving the group after today. I want each of you to think of the one thing that stood out for you today. (*Pause*) Mike, you seem ready.
>
> **Mike:** The discussion about the importance of not keeping our feelings inside was really helpful.
>
> **Andy:** The thing that stood out for me was. . . .
>
> **Leader:** (*After spending time completing the round and processing the session*) OK, let's spend a few minutes saying good-bye to Walt. Most of you have known Walt for awhile now. I want you to think of how you see Walt as different than when he first entered the group. We'll share that and then we'll share any wishes that we have for him. How is Walt different?
>
> **Mario:** He is really different. (*To Walt*) When you first came into the group, you didn't talk or even look up. I really do think the program has helped you.
>
> **Leader:** I agree. You really have changed. I see you as a lot more open, and that chip on your shoulder seems to be gone.
>
> **Carl:** That's right! You did have a chip on your shoulder those first two meetings. It's gone.
>
> **Leader:** (*After others have shared*) If you had a wish for Walt, what would that be?
>
> **Jeff:** My wish is that you have that conversation with your wife that you practiced in here.

Bruno: My wish is that you don't let that chip come back. The soft, gentle side is much nicer.

Leader: (*After two other members have shared wishes*) Walt, what thoughts or reaction or closing comments do you have for the group?

Walt: Well, I appreciate all your support. I also want to say. . . .

In this example, the exiting member had benefitted from the program and seemed ready to return to his life outside the group.

. . . .

There will be times when a departing member has not really used the group or the program that much. In this case, the leader may want to focus on feedback and wishes, in the hope that something might be said that will help.

Leader: In saying good-bye to Sharon, I want each of you to think of what you think will be the roughest thing for Sharon to handle when she goes home.

Paul: I really think that Sharon is going to have trouble.

Leader: Instead of talking to me, could you address Sharon?

Paul: Sure; Sharon, I think you are going to have trouble with a lot of things, because you still seem angry at your parents.

Biff: Sharon, I think you are fooling yourself when you say that you can make it without going to AA meetings. I hope your pride will not keep you from calling someone for help.

In this example, the leader wants to make sure that the member is not attacked, since she is leaving that afternoon, but at the same time he is hoping that something someone says will be helpful because Sharon really does not seem ready to leave the program.

. . . .

Final Thoughts on Closing a Session

The leader who does a good job bringing a group session to a close enhances the value of the session considerably. Without an effective closing, many important issues discussed during the session may become blurred or lost. The closing phase requires thought and planning. If done well, members come away with a sense of completeness. Effective closing of a session also helps build cohesiveness, since members get to hear others' reactions. Many of the goals, skills, and strategies that apply to the closing phase of a session are also relevant to the closing stage of the entire group experience.

THE CLOSING STAGE

Probably the most important point for the group leader to remember when preparing for the closing stage of a group is that the group is not an entity in itself, but a collection of individuals. Of whatever benefit the group has been, it has been so to each member. When the group is over, it is the individuals who go away, taking with them new information, decisions, or beliefs; a clearer view of their lives; or new behaviors that make everyday living happier and more productive. The leader's work during the closing stage is designed to focus on these benefits, and several pragmatic considerations will make it easier for her to do so.

Time Allowed for the Closing Stage

The amount of time allowed to complete the closing stage of a group will depend on the kind of group, its purpose, its number of sessions, and the needs of the members. As a general rule, the greater the number of sessions and the more personal the sharing, the longer the closing stage will be. For example, in a therapy group meeting for 2½ hours weekly for 15 sessions, the leader might begin the closing stage toward the middle of the fourteenth session, since there will be a considerable amount to cover in order to complete it. In contrast, a task group working on improving a residential treatment program for drug abusers, meeting an hour each week for four sessions, may require only 15 minutes of the last session for the closing stage. The closing stage of education and discussion groups would usually not take more than 20 to 30 minutes of the last session. Similarly, a children's self-concept group meeting for an hour a week for five sessions might take only 20 to 30 minutes of the last session for closing. Although it is possible that the closing stage could take two or more sessions, the next-to-last and last sessions usually allow plenty of time for closing.

Purpose and Goals of the Closing Stage

The purpose of the closing stage is to pull together the significant ideas, decisions, and personal changes experienced by the members during the group. This is a time for members to look at their progress in the group and to compare their goals at the start of the group with their accomplishments at the end. While the leader may focus to some extent on the dynamics of the group itself, such as how the members have interacted or how they have helped each other, the main focus will be on each individual member's growth and development.

The goals of the closing stage will vary depending on the kind of group. For example, in the closing stage of a discussion group, the leader may want to review and summarize the major points discussed and provide a chance for members to comment briefly on ideas and discussions generated. In the closing stage of a growth, support, or therapy group, there are several goals to achieve or tasks to complete. Some of the most important ones are as follows:

1. Reviewing and summarizing the group experience
2. Assessing members' growth and change
3. Finishing business
4. Applying change to everyday life (implementing decisions)
5. Providing feedback
6. Handling good-byes
7. Planning for continued problem resolution

Reviewing and Summarizing the Group Experience

One of the first tasks during the closing stage of most groups is to review and summarize the significant developments of the group. In a task group, this might include reviewing and highlighting decisions or changes made as a result of the group meetings. In an education group, this would include reviewing the major points covered. In growth or therapy groups, the progress of individual members would be reviewed.

There are a number of ways the leader can accomplish the task of review and summary: (1) summarize the entire group, (2) get members to summarize their experience, or (3) facilitate interaction that focuses on summarizing and reviewing. The first option can be used if there have not been many sessions and the leader remembers most of the significant events. If the group has been fairly large or has met for a number of sessions, this might not be the best option because the leader may not remember some important topics or discussions. The second option, having the members summarize their experiences, can be valuable if the group is small and the summaries can be kept to two to three minutes each. If the group is large (ten or more) this is not usually a good option, because it would probably take too much time and become repetitious. Most often the third option, which allows members to share what has stood out to them, is best.

E X A M P L E . . . .

It is the final session of a high school growth group.

Leader: Since this is the last session, I want to spend the remainder of our time reviewing the group experience and how it has affected you. First, I want you to think of three things that stood out to you during the sessions. What discussions, exercises, or comments do you remember the most? (*Pause*) Sandi, you seem ready.

Sandi: The discussion about my mom and how I can deal with her better than I do. Focusing on the difference between being assertive and being aggressive. A third thing would be the discussion about taking risks in order to get more out of life.

Phillipe: The discussion concerning risk taking was the highlight for me. I think about that every day.

Leader: Let me just ask—was that a major insight for some others of you?

Armand: It was number one on my list, too. Whenever I am bored or afraid, I think over what risks I can take or remember that it is OK to be afraid when I am trying something new.

In this example, the leader had members share things on their list and then held the focus on risk taking and got members to share their reactions. After reviewing that issue, the leader would then ask another member to share his or her list. Having members share what was important and periodically holding the focus on various topics let the leader review the group experience.

. . . .

Assessing Members' Growth and Change

This goal applies to groups such as therapy groups, in which the primary purpose is personal growth or change. In these groups members can compare their progress from the beginning of the group to the present. This assessment reinforces any changes and encourages members to pursue further growth and development. Here is an example of how a leader might begin the process of helping members assess their own growth.

EXAMPLE . . . .

The group is in the closing stage of a personal growth experience in a university counseling center. The leader introduces a retrospective assessment.

Leader: Since this is our last session, I think it might be helpful if each of you spent a few minutes looking at the changes you have brought about in your lives during these past ten weeks. Some of you are more aware of your values and what you want to get from your life; others of you brought problems or concerns that you resolved through the group, and so forth. Take a minute and think about the important changes you've experienced in the group. When you are ready, I'm going to ask you to share those thoughts with the group.

The members may then report the changes they feel they have made to the entire group. This sharing can lead to feedback from other members, encouragement, and plans for continued work on issues following the end of the group.

. . . .

Finishing Business

During the closing stage it is common to have a few loose ends that still need to be tied up before the members can comfortably leave the group. It is important for the leader to allow time for this, because unfinished business can interfere with the sense of closure and may leave one or more members with unresolved issues. Here are some examples of unfinished business that might come up during the closing stage:

- An issue or question that was brought up in a previous session but never dealt with
- Negative feelings about how the leader handled a particular situation during a session
- A question a member has for another member or for the leader
- A member needing to work on some unresolved personal issue

While it is important to assess and handle unfinished business, the leader must be careful not to generate new business. For example, if a member expresses some dissatisfaction with how the leader handled a particular situation during an earlier session, the leader may simply want to accept the statement rather than get into a lengthy explanation or discussion. Sometimes justifying one's leadership behavior can detract from the purpose of the closing stage. If a member wants or needs therapy on an unresolved issue, the leader may choose to refer the individual for counseling or to see the member after the session. Delving into new issues is seldom appropriate for the closing stage.

The following is an example of how a leader might introduce the topic of unfinished business.

Leader: One thing that is important to do during this closing is to allow some time for any unfinished group business that needs to be dealt with. I am not asking for personal work issues, since we are trying to close the group, but rather questions you want to ask or reactions that you feel the need to share. If there is something that you want to say or ask, please do so. I urge you not to leave thinking, "I wish I had said this or that."

Applying Change to Everyday Life

As we have said throughout this book, our basic belief about groups is that they should improve some aspect of each member's life. This would be as true of a task group in which conflicts are resolved as it would be of a therapy group in which the members are struggling to overcome their problems. In effective groups, members have been applying what they have learned from the group on a regular basis between sessions. By the closing stage, they will have experienced the implementation of some of these changes in their lives. One problem that members face is that when the meetings stop they may return to their former ways. It is important for the leader to highlight this potential problem for members and to reinforce their efforts to maintain positive change. This can be done in part by getting members to evaluate their success in making changes and by providing feedback that can be helpful and encouraging.

Providing Feedback

During the closing stage, some final feedback to members is often helpful. For example:

Leader: Let's spend a few minutes thinking of positive changes that you have seen in other members. I'd like you to pick three people who you feel have made some positive changes. I'll ask you to tell each person what the change is and how you think the change is helpful for the person. For example, Alan, I feel that you are much friendlier, and it is much easier to talk with you.

An alternative approach is simply to provide a chance for members to comment to one another about the changes each has made. Such reinforcement should be sincere and as specific as possible. The leader should monitor the type of feedback given to make sure it is on target.

Leader: I want you to think about feedback that you feel would be helpful to give other members. You may want to think about changes that you have seen in members or thank them for something they said or did during a session.

Feedback can also be given to confront members who are still denying problems or who have not taken responsibility for their behavior. Such feedback, when given honestly and without anger or disappointment, can have an impact on a member who seems unwilling to face certain unresolved issues. Such feedback may be given by the leader, the members, or both.

EXAMPLE . . . .

In a drug treatment group, a member who is still denying that his continued use of drugs is having a negative effect on his family life may benefit greatly from feedback sincerely given by the other members of the group.

Sam: Dave, even though you are fooling your family, your therapist, and even yourself by your continued use of drugs, you are not fooling us, because we've been there.

Ann: I agree, Dave, you really have to stop thinking that you don't have a problem. Face it, you have a drug problem! Even though this group is ending, I do hope you will decide to really get help.

In this example, the members can probably have more impact than the leader, since they are seen as peers who have struggled and dealt with a similar problem. In other situations, the leader is better able to give confrontive or negative feedback because he sees aspects of a member's behavior that the members do not see or because he knows the member better from having worked with him on an individual basis.

. . . .

Handling Good-byes

It is important for the leader to remember that for many members the ending of the group is the end of a very special event in their lives. The relationships formed in the group may be the closest relationships some members have ever experienced. Such members will have especially strong feelings about the ending of the group. The leader should provide some time for those feelings to be expressed and for members to make final comments to each other. Members sometimes wish to exchange telephone numbers and addresses.

Planning for Continued Problem Resolution

For members to continue to work on problems after the group ends, resources must be available. For some, the best solution is involvement in another group experience. For others, individual, marital, or family counseling will be most helpful. Certain members may benefit most from joining a support group such as Alcoholics Anonymous. During the closing stage, it is the leader's responsibility to provide guidance, information, and the names and phone numbers of referral sources for any member who needs to continue working on personal concerns.

In summary, the seven objectives discussed should serve as guidelines for the leader in planning the closing stage of the group. Once the leader is clear about his goals during the closing stage, he must think about how he will meet the objectives.

Exercises to Use during the Closing Stage

The following are exercises and activities that can be used during the closing stage.

Using the Chalkboard or Handouts

An excellent tool for reviewing, summarizing, and consolidating information is a chalkboard (newsprint can be substituted). The chalkboard can be used to list points during the review and can be referred to as those points are discussed. It also serves as an excellent focal point for the members in that they continually gaze at the chalkboard and thus stay focused on the review. Writing on the chalkboard also gives members a chance to have direct input into the review and summarizing process.

Handouts are a variation on the chalkboard technique. They differ primarily in that the leader has already summarized the key points. Members should be given a chance to add thoughts of their own before the discussion begins. The advantage of the handout is that it saves time and gets the members focused on the discussion immediately. A handout may be particularly useful with discussion, education, and task groups, because the leader can often easily summarize the various key points.

Members' Writing about Their Experience

The leader may provide a chance for members to write about some aspect of the group, either in their journals (if journals were used) or on paper provided. The members may write on a variety of topics: four or five things they learned, the most helpful experience for them during the group, personal goals at the beginning of the group and the extent to which each was achieved, and how decisions they made in the group will be applied outside the group. The leader may then have members share their written thoughts in pairs, small groups, or with the entire group. If the topic the members write about is lengthy or complex, the leader may ask each member to underline two or three key passages to share with the entire group in order to save time and maintain the focus. When using journals, members may also review their journal entries from all the previous sessions and write a summary paragraph that pulls together the key points of the group for them.

Rounds

The use of rounds has been discussed at length elsewhere in this book; they can be especially helpful during the closing stage. The round can be used to summarize key points, get overall reactions to the group or a particular experience, or check the degree to which members feel they accomplished personal goals. The leader might introduce closing rounds with one of the following questions:

- On a 1-to-10 scale, with 10 being very satisfied, how satisfied are you with your progress during this group?
- If you had to capture how you feel about your group experience in a sentence or two, what would you say? We'll do a round and hear from everyone.
- Since this is the last session, what is a word or phrase that expresses how you are feeling about the group ending?

Wishes

The wishes exercise provides a special type of feedback for members during the closing stage. The leader asks if anyone has a wish for another member regarding that member's goals for the future.

EXAMPLE . . . .

It is the last session of a support group for recently divorced persons.

Leader: Let's take the next few minutes and see if there are any wishes you might have for one another. You may or may not have a wish. It's OK either way. I have a wish for Darlene. My wish for you is that you will be able to let go of your angry feelings toward your husband and get on with your life.

Darlene: Thank you.

Bill: My wish for you, Jane, is that you realize your teenagers are old enough to help out around the house and that you can stop being their slave.

Josefa: I have a wish for you too, Jane. I also have a wish for Leigh. My wish for you is that you take a chance. You won't know if you can build a new relationship if you don't try.

. . . .

Members may or may not acknowledge the wish as it is given. Also, members will not have a wish for everyone in the group. Therefore, this exercise should not be done as a round, since that places pressure on members to devise wishes even if they don't have any and can result in insincerity. Wishes can be used at the end of each session because they help build good feelings among the members.

"Reunion Fantasy"

An excellent exercise to use in closing certain personal growth, support, and therapy groups is the Reunion Fantasy. The purpose of this exercise is to get members to project their lives into the future. Many members are startled to find that in their fantasies they have the power to bring about significant changes. They are encouraged by this imagining process and gain confidence that their lives can change for the better. Conversely, members are also surprised to find that they are unable to imagine some of the changes they have worked for in the group. They realize the need for a greater commitment to change and that they must take more responsibility for their lives if change is to come about.

When conducting the Reunion Fantasy, a projection into the future of three to five years is usually the most productive. Here is one variation of the Reunion Fantasy.

Leader: I'd like you to relax. Close your eyes if that is comfortable for you. I want you to imagine that the time is five years from now; you have just gone to the mailbox and have received a letter from me inviting you back for a group reunion. In the letter I explain that I have received a grant to cover all expenses. Now that you have decided to attend, I want you to think of what you will tell the other members about your life and any changes. Think about where you are living, with whom you are living, what you are doing, and any significant events that have occurred. (*The leader pauses to allow the members to experience the fantasy.*) What do you most want to say to the other members about your life now? In a minute I am going to ask you to stand up and act like you are just seeing these people for the first time in five years, unless you will have remained in contact with some of them. Try to get into the role of having been apart for five years. (*Pause*) OK, everyone stand and start milling and sharing.

This exercise can be very thought-provoking for growth, support, or therapy groups in which the members have come to know each other very well. As with all exercises, this one must be tailored to the kind of group, its purpose, and above all the needs of the members as they experience the group coming to an end. This exercise would be good to use during the beginning part of the closing stage, since it would get members to think about the group ending and the issues and changes they have talked about in the group.

Further Considerations for the Closing Stage

As the leader plans the closing stage of the group, there are a number of points to think about. Among the issues a leader must think about are the following seven:

1. Dealing with feelings of separation
2. Guarding against ending with strong emotions

3. Helping members in their transition
4. Conducting exit interviews
5. Holding follow-up sessions
6. Evaluating the group
7. Ending with a party

Not every kind of group will require consideration of all these factors. It is the leader's job to determine which of these considerations are relevant.

Dealing with Feelings of Separation

We have already discussed the need for some members to say their good-byes as the group comes to a close. For most members this will go smoothly. However, for some the ending of the group will elicit anxiety over separating from the others. The positive effect of the group may be lessened if those feelings are not identified and dealt with by the leader. Clues to such feelings might be found in statements from members like these:

- I couldn't sleep last night because I knew today would be our last meeting.
- I feel like this is my second family, and I don't want to leave it.
- I don't think I can make it without this group.

When the leader hears comments like this, the first task is to help members realize that these feelings are normal and allow them to express their feelings of sadness or loss. Second, the leader might want to point out that although the positive sharing may have been a new experience, the kind of sharing and closeness members feel toward one another need not be unique. Such relationships can be developed outside the group with the awareness and skills members have developed. Also, if the leader knows that some members are going to have a tough time with the ending of the group, he may allow additional time during the closing stage to work with those members.

Guarding against Ending with Strong Emotions

When closing a group in which members have gotten very close and personal, the leader may wish to pay close attention to the emotional tone during the closing stage. If the leader is not paying attention, the members may experience the ending as a very sad, intense, or extraspecial event. If possible, these kinds of feelings should be avoided. Members should ideally see the ending as a new beginning, feeling positive about the past experience and excited about their future.

Leaders are often aware that members may be feeling sad about the ending and can usually modify those feelings through discussion and group exercises. What many leaders fail to realize is that ending the group on an emotional "high" can be just as damaging as ending the group with members in tears. During the closing stage, members sometimes let down almost all of their defenses as they share personal struggles and take risks that they ordinarily don't take. This often feels good and members leave the group expecting that these feelings will continue. They may go home and want to experience the same thing with their spouse, parents, friends, or co-workers. When they do not experience the same level of sharing and intimacy that they experienced in the group, members sometimes become angry, frustrated, or resentful at the people in their lives and/or the leader of the group. In essence, leaders should be aware that during the closing stage a false "high" can be created, through which members may actually feel closer to other members of the group than a spouse, children, or long-term friends. We do not believe that this is the purpose of the group. While the group experience can generate strong feelings among members, the leader will want to keep this intensity in check and explain to the members that they will probably not experience the same intensity at home and that it is OK. Also, the leader will want to explain that the very good, almost "high" feelings will diminish after a few days. This will not mean that the experience was not real or valuable; it simply will mean that the group experience is over.

The first example that follows is of a leader talking about sad feelings regarding the ending of the group. The second is of a leader talking about the possibilities of ending on a "high."

EXAMPLES . . . .

    Leader: When we stop today, I do not want you to feel really sad or feel that this is the end. I hope you will realize that it is a begining for you to do the things you have learned in this group. I purposely will try to have us end with good feelings and not sadness because I feel the group really has been a good experience for all of us. It has served the purpose of members sharing and caring, and I hope you have already started to create the same kind of sharing with significant others in your life.

. . . .

    Leader: I want to say something now, and I will probably say it again at the very end of the session. Many of you are really opening up and sharing with the group, and I think it is great. Also, the way you are responding to what is being said is terrific. I think nearly everyone is experiencing good feelings as a result of being here. For many these feelings are unique, and I want to caution you about going home and trying to share like this with your spouse and friends. Remember, they have not been in this group and have not had this experience. If you want this kind of sharing, give them time. Don't expect them to be able to do this immediately. Too, realize that they may never be able to do exactly what we are doing here.

. . . .

By presenting this attitude rather than one that focuses on sad or emotional good-byes, the leader can prevent the false high phenomenon. Rather than ending with the emphasis on the "high" with much hugging and joyous crying, you might try to end groups that have been very close and personal by saying something like this:

Leader: (*In a soft, rather neutral voice*) We are going to stop now. I do think the whole experience has been good, and the closing has been very good. I think you have had enough time to say what you wanted and to start a new beginning for yourself. If I can ever be of help, please feel free to contact me. I certainly have found the experience to be a good one. Let's stop.

Helping Members in Their Transition

A third consideration during the closing stage is the importance of helping members make a transition back into the "real world." Members must learn to employ their new information and knowledge about themselves with people in their daily lives. This is especially important for group members who have been clients in a residential treatment program for a period of time. Some members, such as those who have had addiction problems, will need continued support and monitoring in the community. Many communities have a variety of support groups available either as independent organizations or through mental-health centers, hospitals, or rehabilitation programs. If members may benefit from such support groups the leader should include a discussion of the value of these groups during the closing stage.

In some types of groups, members may form support networks of their own to ensure continued reinforcement of one another, and they may plan "booster" meetings periodically to report on their progress. The need for this type of follow-up should be assessed by the leader in conjunction with the members. The entire group may be involved in the network or members may choose one or more persons with whom to network. For members who ordinarily have difficulty developing and maintaining relationships, networking is very beneficial. Networking may also be a temporary measure for members who are new to a community or who have simply lost social contacts because of addictions or other problems. In some groups, time may be provided during the closing stage to develop individual plans for each member.

Conducting Exit Interviews

Earlier in this book, we discussed the value of interviewing potential group members before the group began to establish rapport and exchange expectations about the group experience. There is also value in conducting exit interviews with members as the group enters the closing stage. Exit interviews need not be conducted in all groups; the leader must consider the value of such interviews with regard to the kind of group and the needs of individual members. Exit interviews need not be long and may last only 15 minutes. If exit interviews are conducted, we suggest that they take place before the final session of the group to maximize their value. The reason for this is that the leader can suggest how the member might use the closing stage to his or her benefit, such as requesting additional feedback from other members. The exit interview can also be a time for the leader to reinforce the gains a member has made, as well as to focus more individual attention on ways the member can apply those gains to everyday living. The interview further gives the leader a chance to ask for feedback about the group and various aspects of his leadership. Depending on the kind of group, some members may feel more comfortable giving the leader feedback on a one-to-one basis.

Exit interviews can also be conducted after the last session. The advantage of this is that the group experience is completed. The disadvantage is that the leader is not able to make suggestions on how best to use the closing stage.

Holding Follow-Up Sessions

The leader may wish to consider the possibility of holding a follow-up session of the group several weeks or months after the final regular session. The decision to have one or more follow-up meetings will depend, again, on the kind of group and the needs of the members. For example, members of a task group who work together in the same organization may wish to have a follow-up session to assess how things are going. With some support or counseling groups, follow-up sessions give members a chance to share how they are doing, and lessen the anxiety of separation. The leader may set up a formal follow-up program in which members are notified and encouraged to return for a meeting; or simply set aside a time for members to drop in periodically as they feel the need. Occasionally, members of a group will decide they want to plan for a reunion in six months. This decision usually arises from the good feelings members have toward one another during the closing stage and is similar to the desire for a reunion among any group sharing a unique experience. Experience suggests that these reunions are usually not very successful because the feelings fade as time passes and members become involved in their own lives. If a reunion is planned, the leader should not feel disappointed by a small turnout, and members should be prepared for the experience to be very different from when they were meeting regularly.

One unique follow-up procedure that we use is to have members write themselves letters in which they assess their goals, give themselves feedback, and list wishes or plans for the future. The letters are given to the leader in a self-addressed, stamped envelope and are then mailed several weeks or months after the group has ended. Members have reported that this technique is powerful. They say that writing the letter is thought-provoking, and knowing that it will come in the mail someday causes them to keep working even after the group has ended. Others have said that often their letter arrived at a good time, as they were needing a "booster shot." The letter exercise is designed for use in a personal growth, counseling, or therapy group, but could also be used with a task group as a way for members to check on the degree to which they have followed through on their decisions.

Evaluating the Group

When any group ends, the leader will need to decide how she will evaluate the experience. Groups can be evaluated formally, with a questionnaire, or informally, with the leader asking specific questions during the closing stage. No matter how the evaluation is done, the leader should seek answers to the following questions:

- How valuable was the experience? (The group could use a 1-to-10 scale.)
- What did you like about the group?
- What did you dislike about the group?
- What did you like about the way the leader led the group?
- What did you not like about the way the leader led the group?
- How could the group have been better?

These are just the basic questions that should be asked. Certainly a more elaborate questionnaire could be devised that asked about specific topics, exercises, and events that occurred during the group. We urge leaders, especially beginning leaders, to evaluate any group that they lead. The responses and comments from their members can be very helpful in leading future groups.

Ending with a Party

A final consideration that comes up frequently is that members want to end the group with a party. They may suggest meeting at someone's house or meeting for pizza. We suggest that the leader give a good deal of thought to such a request, because often when the group meets in another setting the session never really takes place and thus no real closing occurs. If the leader and the group decide to meet in a setting like this, the leader will want to tell members ahead of time that the first hour or so will be devoted to closing the group.

A variation of this is for the group to plan a party to be held after the group has officially ended. Sometimes this type of party works fine, and other times it does not work out very well. We suggest that the leader at least prepare members for the possibility that the party may not go well.

CONCLUDING COMMENTS

In this chapter, we discussed how to close both individual sessions and entire groups. The *closing phase* serves the purpose of reviewing a session and ensuring that members leave feeling "finished." Planning the *closing stage* of the entire group is as important as planning the sessions in the other stages of the group. Its purpose is to maximize the impact of the group experience and to bring closure to the experience.

Included within these discussions were various leadership skills, techniques, and special considerations for achieving satisfying closure. For both types of closure, pragmatic considerations such as time allotted to closure, useful exercises to employ, and methods of summarizing were covered. Goals such as assessing members' progress, evaluating the experience, and providing follow-up support were also discussed in detail.

CHAPTER FOURTEEN . . . .

Dealing with Problem Situations

When leading groups, a leader must be prepared to deal with any number of situations. In this chapter we identify many of the most common problems that arise in the group setting and provide examples to illustrate some skills and techniques for handling these situations. The 11 common problems we have identified are as follows:

1. The chronic talker
2. The rescuing member
3. The negative member
4. The resistant member
5. The member who tries to "get" the leader
6. Dealing with silence
7. Dealing with sexual feelings
8. Dealing with crying
9. Dealing with mutually hostile members
10. Asking a member to leave
11. Dealing with prejudiced, narrow-minded, or insensitive members

THE CHRONIC TALKER

It is not difficult to spot the member who attempts to dominate discussion. He is often characterized by persistent rambling and repetition. As a result, other members who have concerns that they would like to discuss are prevented from doing so. Soon the group members either tune out the chronic talker and lose interest in the proceedings or get frustrated and angry at both the talkative member and the leader, who they feel should cut him off. The chronic talker can be categorized into three different types depending on the reason underlying his talkativeness. These three types include the nervous member, the rambler, and the show-off.

The Nervous Member

The nervous member talks to hide his feelings of nervousness or as a means of self-control. Easily recognized, the nervous member is often the first one to answer questions posed by the leader and the first to volunteer for some task. Because the nervous member is talking to alleviate anxiety, he will talk frequently and for as long as the leader lets him.

The Rambler

Ramblers dominate discussions because they are simply talkative people and are unaware of the effect their rambling has on others. They too are easily recognized because they tell long, drawn-out stories and often repeat themselves. The stories are often trivial and are not usually meaningful to others.

The Show-Off

Show-offs are talkative because they are insecure and want to impress the group leader, other members, or both. The show-off seems to be attempting to show others what he knows. In doing so, he answers all questions, asks irrelevant questions in an effort to grab the leader's attention, and may offer unsolicited advice to other group members. The other members often resent this and grow to dislike this type of member. The problem with the show-off is that he can quickly sway the group from its intended purpose.

To determine whether or not a member should be seen as a chronic talker, the leader should consider the following questions:

- For how long has the member been talking?
- How many comments has the member made compared with other group members? Are the member's comments in line with the intended purpose of the group?
- Is this member preventing others from talking?
- Are others becoming bored or irritated with the member's comments?
- Does the member seem to be talking because of nervousness or a desire to impress others?

There are several ways to handle a talkative member. For example, upon recognizing such a member the leader could have members get into dyads, making sure she pairs herself with the talkative member. In the dyad, the leader could attempt to speak to the member about his "talkativeness." The advantage of this strategy is that the talkative member receives the message about his talkativeness from only one person, thus causing less embarrassment.

Another strategy is to address the whole group in the hope that the talkative member hears the message. In the following example, the leader recognizes that a member is rambling. It is early in the life of the group, and the leader wants to curb the rambler's talking but at the same time not behave in a critical fashion toward the member. Therefore, the leader decides to deliver the message to the entire group by looking at everyone as she speaks.

Leader: Keep in mind that the purpose of the group is for *everyone* to share thoughts and feelings. If any one member gets too long-winded, the focus of the group changes from sharing to listening to one member. Please be aware of how much you are talking and whether or not you are dominating the discussion.

Another simple, often effective technique to use if a member is going on and on is to say something like this: "Let me stop you for just a moment. I want to make sure everyone has a chance to talk."

If the leader is about to ask the group a question and is sure that a talkative member will again speak up and attempt to dominate the discussion, the leader might say something like, "I'm going to ask a question, and I would like to hear from some of you who haven't talked yet." The leader should say this while avoiding eye contact with the talkative member. These techniques may stop the dominating member as well as draw out comments from members who have been silent. At times the leader unknowingly perpetuates a particular member's talking by maintaining eye contact with him and nodding her head as that member speaks. Maintaining eye contact simply reinforces the member's talking.

A fourth strategy would be to speak to the talkative member immediately after the session or sometime before the next session.

E X A M P L E . . . .

Leader: (*Talking to a member during a break*) Wanda, tell me if I'm wrong, but you seemed a bit nervous during the first half of the group tonight. You were repeating yourself a lot as you talked, and you talked very rapidly.

Wanda: Yes, you're right. I was hoping that no one would notice. I just get uptight every time I'm around a new group of people. It is something that I definitely want to work on.

. . . .

Giving feedback to the talkative member concerning the behavior is another strategy that can be used. The leader might say something like the following:

Leader: As I stated in the beginning of this group, one of the most potentially helpful aspects of a group such as this is for members to receive feedback about themselves from other members of the group. In effect, this feedback acts as a mirror, letting you know how others in the group see and react to you. Is there anyone here who would like to give another member some feedback?

The leader would use this kind of opening to a feedback exercise only if confident there were members who wanted to share their feelings about a member's excessive talking. If the leader felt that members would not speak up unless the leader did, a feedback exercise could be devised in which the leader also could give feedback to the rambling member. Sometimes members will offer feedback without being prompted to do so. When this happens the leader merely needs to make sure that the member receiving the feedback doesn't feel attacked.

Another strategy that could be used if the leader were having the members turn in any kind of written reactions to the group would be to give the member feedback in writing. (In therapy and growth groups, members often write a brief reaction at the end of each session.) For example, the leader might write the following feedback at the bottom of the member's reaction:

Leader: Tom, I sense that you are uncomfortable, since you talked quite a bit and at a very rapid pace. I am hoping that you will be a little more comfortable and thus talk a little less. Let me know if there is anything that I can do to help you feel more comfortable.

Members usually receive this message very well and become more cognizant of their talkative behavior. In addition, a note such as this often helps members feel more comfortable about talking to the leader outside the group. This is a nonthreatening way to offer feedback; its disadvantage is that there is no guarantee that the member receiving the feedback will respond favorably to it, and if the member reads it somewhere other than in the group, no one will be there to help with processing the feedback.

THE RESCUING MEMBER

"Rescuing" is the attempt of a member to smooth over negative feelings experienced by another member of the group. When a member becomes upset, often other group members attempt to soothe the member with such statements as "Now, don't worry, it will be all right" or "Everything has a way of working itself out if you just give it time." This is usually not helpful, and further, such comments sound patronizing. The negative effect of rescuing is that it prevents the member in pain from problem solving.

EXAMPLE . . . .

One of the members, Judy, cries as she tells the group about her upcoming divorce. As she does so, another member, Karen, attempts to rescue her.

Karen: Don't worry, Judy, everything will be OK. I went through a divorce myself, and you just have to make the best of it. I think—

Leader: (*Interrupting Karen in midsentence*) Judy, you are in a lot of pain right now, and if you would like, we can listen and try to be of help. I think by sharing you will at least get some of your thoughts out, and I think that you will feel our support. (*Judy nods that she would like to*)

Leader: (*After Judy has discussed her divorce*) I'd like to say something to all of you here. Usually when a member is struggling with some issue like a divorce, they don't need our sympathy or advice as much as they need to be listened to and supported.

. . . .

Teaching members that group sharing is different that friendly conversation is important as the group progresses. In the early life of the group the leader may need to intervene quite often, because the group members are not aware of what constitutes helpful group behavior. However, later in the life of the group, the leader might be able to intervene less if she has properly trained members how to be therapeutic. In the preceding example, the leader decided to convey the message about sympathy being unhelpful to the entire group so that they could observe her modeling the correct method of being therapeutic in the group. Members often think they are being supportive when in fact they are trying to rescue the member.

EXAMPLE . . . .

This group is composed of individuals who are going through a divorce. One of the members, Vivian, has consistently blamed her husband for the state of her life. Another member hears this and gives her sympathy and pity.

Vivian: I wouldn't be in this fix if it weren't for him. He got me pregnant when I was just 18. I had plans to go to college and make something of myself. We were married for ten years, and all I did was play Navy wife. I wanted a life of my own, but he never gave it to me. Now he makes me feel guilty because I want a divorce.

Rose: I know what you mean. Men are so inconsiderate of our needs. If they would only open their eyes and see that we are capable of having our own life, maybe they would allow us to live as we choose. I know my husband does the same thing. He just won't allow me to be who I want to be!

Leader: (*Remembering that Rose has made similar comments in the past about her husband*) Rose, I'm not certain that what you are saying is helpful to Vivian. At this point what would probably be more helpful would be to help her believe that she has the right to take charge of her life and to stop living her life as a victim.

In this example the leader not only put a halt to what Rose was doing but was indirectly speaking to Vivian.

THE NEGATIVE MEMBER

A negative member is one who constantly complains about the group or disagrees with other members of the group. Negative members are particularly troublesome in the group because their attitudes and behavior run counter to the leader's goal of maintaining a positive working tone. If one or two members become negative and begin to complain, either in or outside the group, other members will sometimes join in and also appear to be negative. The result is that group sessions become gripe sessions, and very little is accomplished.

There are three possible strategies for dealing with the negative member:

- Talk to the person outside the group and attempt to establish why he is so negative. The leader can even ask for the member's cooperation and help in making the group productive. Sometimes such members simply want the leader's attention or a role to play in the group, and can be offered a positive role.
- Identify the allies (positive group members) in the group and direct questions and comments to them. Allowing these members to talk more than the negative members can help to establish a more positive tone in the group.
- When asking the group a question, avoid eye contact with the negative person so as not to draw her out.

The biggest potential mistake in dealing with the negative member is to confront him head on about his negativism in front of the other group members. This could turn into an argument between leader and negative member and could create resentment in the other members. If the leader finds herself in this situation, she should shift the focus to another person or another topic and then talk to the negative member at the end of the group.

It is important to remember that groups will at times have one or two negative members. This is especially true at the beginning of a group and particularly so if the group is a mandatory one. Many times negativism diminishes as the group develops; the members see the value of the group. However, there will be times that no matter what the leader does, a member will remain negative. In extreme cases it may be necessary to ask the member to leave the group or to sit quietly. Too often leaders devote far too much time trying to work with the negative member, while ignoring those members who are interested in the group.

THE RESISTANT MEMBER

Some members are resistant because they are forced to be in the group. Sometimes these members will work through their resistance if they are given a chance to express their anger. This situation is difficult for the leader, because he does not know whether allowing the member to express anger will be of benefit or if the member will merely complain and set a negative tone for the group. It is essential, however, for the leader to pay attention when a member is seemingly working through her resistance.

Four examples of resistant members would be the following:

- The member who, during the first meeting, says he does not know why he has to be at the meeting and does not see how the group can be helpful.
- The member who comes and sits with her arms crossed and does not contribute unless forced to—and then says as little as possible.
- The member who always tries to get the group to focus on topics not relevant to the group, such as movies, sports, or the latest fashions.
- The member who is not resisting the group but is resistant to changing something about himself.

Some members have negative expectations about the effectiveness of the group. These members believe that the group will not be helpful, and they therefore refuse to participate cooperatively. If the leader is faced with a resistant member, her two primary strategies are to let the member share his feelings in the group or to talk to him in a dyad or after the session and try to help him work through his resistance. If neither of these works and the member has to remain in the group due to the setting (such as a residential treatment center), the leader will want to be sure *not* to focus on that member. Often beginning leaders will devote as much as half of each session trying to break down the resistance.

Sometimes a resistant member appears to be opposed to the leader's attempt to be helpful but not to the members' attempts. If this seems to be the case, then another method of working with the resistant member might be to set up situations in which the member can share with other members of the group rather than be the direct focus of the leader. This can be done through the use of dyads, triads, and small-group discussions without the direct participation of the leader.

Conversely, the resistant member may be opposed to the attempts of the group to be helpful but not to the leader's. If this is the case, individual counseling help may be offered that member. This can be done outside the group or through a dyad composed of the leader and the resistant member.

It is important that the leader distinguish between the member who is resisting the group process and the member who is resistant because he does not want to change something about himself or his situation.

EXAMPLE . . . .

Angela has been discussing being a mother and having a career. She has stated that she wants to continue her career but doesn't know what to do with her children during the day.

Jackie: Could you leave them at a day care center?

Angela: Yes, but I'm not so sure that they are safe anymore.

Todd: Does your company have a program for taking care of employees' children?

Angela: Yes, but I don't like some of the children and workers there.

Frances: Do you have relatives nearby who would be willing to care for them?

Angela: Yes, but I hate to impose.

In a case like this, the leader should realize that the member is resistant or hesitant to hear suggestions. One way to deal with this resistance would be to say something like this:

Leader: Angela, I think we understand the concern, but I am not sure how we can be of help here in the group. What would be helpful to you?

. . . .

Another way to handle resistance in a therapy or growth group is to focus on the resistant member in an indirect manner, as described in Chapter Twelve. That is, the leader may work with a more willing member with the intent of helping the resistant member to learn something by watching. Conducting therapy in this manner takes the direct focus off the resistant member.

The important thing to remember is to not spend too much time with the resistant member if it is taking away productive time from the other group members.

THE MEMBER WHO TRIES TO "GET" THE LEADER

When leading a group, the leader needs to be prepared for what we call "get the leader." This can be defined as a member attempting to sabotage what the leader is saying or doing in the group. "Get the leader" can take the form of disagreeing with the leader, not following through with instructions given by the leader, asking unanswerable questions so as to make the leader look bad in front of other members, or talking to others while the leader is talking. "Get the leader" is different from negativism in that the member is in opposition to the leader only, whereas the negative member feels apathetic, disinterested, or angry in general.

There are a variety of possible causes for members to want to get the leader. Often the reasons can be traced to something said or done by the leader that caused the member to become irritated or embarrassed. The following is a list of some leader behaviors that might cause members to want to get the leader.

- Putting a member on the spot in front of the other members
- Cutting off a member inappropriately (or even appropriately)
- Not giving a member the chance to talk or failing to recognize when a member wants to speak
- Telling a member that the group will come back to his issue or concern and then failing to do so
- Allowing the group members to offer too much negative feedback to a particular member
- Not being skilled enough to control the group
- Allowing the group to be boring due to the leader's lack of skill

Although the leader is often the cause of get-the-leader behavior in the group, there are other possible causes. These reasons are as follows:

- Members who are not self-referred sometimes take out their frustrations and anger on the leader.
- Members sometimes project their fears about being in the group onto the leader.
- Members who have struggled in their relationships with authority figures might attempt to spoil the leader's efforts.
- Members sometimes want to be the leader's "favorite" and react angrily when they don't feel that they are.

Probably the first thing a leader should do when he realizes that a member is trying to "get him" is to shift the focus away from any power struggle between the member and himself.

EXAMPLES . . . .

> **Leader:** I'd like us to begin today's session by talking about how drinking has affected your family life.
>
> **Joe:** Why do you always have to start the group and pick the topics? I thought this was *our* group. Tell me!
>
> **Leader:** Let me explain to all of you how I decide on the topics. Also, be aware that if there is a topic or something that you would like to discuss, you can let me know. There are a number of topics that I feel we should cover . . . (*Makes eye contact with all of the members, with no extra contact with Joe. This is to try to discourage Joe from additional comments*)

. . . .

> **Leader:** I would like each of you to close your eyes and try to imagine that—
>
> **Lynn:** (*Interrupting*) Are you going to do another one of those stupid fantasy exercises? What good are they!?
>
> **Leader:** Lynn, feel free to sit quietly. (*To the other members*) I want you to close your eyes and imagine that you are an animal. . . .

. . . .

Once the leader has sidestepped the member's attempt to get him, he should try to understand why the member has targeted him. Often, the leader will know why it happened, and if the problem is correctable by such techniques as paying more attention to the member, going back to the member's issue, or making sure not to put the member on the spot, then the leader should make the correction. If the leader does not understand why the member has targeted him, he might choose to pair up in a dyad with the member or talk to the member at the end of the session to see if he can gain some information, saying something like, "Something seems to be going on between you and me. Is it something I said, or did that upset you?"

If the member does not want to share his thoughts, the leader might be able to gain some insight from talking to other members. That is, often a member will share disgruntled thoughts with a fellow member but not with the leader. If the leader seeks information from other members, he must be very careful to ensure that the members do not feel any pressure to share something they feel they should not share.

If the member persists in trying to sabotage the leader, and the leader has talked to the member to no avail, the leader may get help from the group by asking for feedback about the member's complaints or behavior. The leader would do this only if he knew he had the support and understanding of all, or nearly all, the other members. The leader could ask the entire group, "Do you like the way the group is going and the activities I ask you to do?" Or he could be more specific: "I would like some feedback. Whenever I suggest anything, Cleve always wants to argue with or question me. How do the rest of you feel about Cleve's doing that?"

Assuming a favorable response was obtained from either of these feedback questions, the member will see that he is alone in his attacks or that the other members are annoyed with his behavior.

We hope this discussion has alerted you to the existence of this phenomenon and has given you some ways of dealing with it. Too many beginning leaders fail to recognize it and misread it as resistance or negativism when in fact it is something that they either caused or can change with a slight adjustment. Then again, there will be times when there is almost nothing the leader can do to stop the member other than removing that member from the group.

DEALING WITH SILENCE

There is both productive and nonproductive silence in a group. Productive silence occurs when members are internally processing something that was said or done in the group. Nonproductive silence occurs when members are quiet because they are confused about what to say, fearful of talking, or bored. Silence can sometimes serve as a signal to the leader. When the group is silent, the leader should ask herself, "Is this silence productive?" The leader can usually tell by observing the members' reactions as they are sitting there and also by considering what has just occurred in the group. If the members seem deep in thought as a result of someone's intense work, the silence should be allowed. Sometimes the leader may want to let the silence last for two or three minutes or for as long as it appears to be productive. The leader may choose to wait until someone else breaks the silence, or she may choose to break the silence by saying something like "Many of you seem to really be thinking about what just happened. I'd like you to briefly share your thoughts." If, however, the members are silent because they are not interested, then the silence should be a signal to the leader to change the focus or to address the group about their lack of interest.

Sometimes members are silent at the beginning of a session because they are not yet warmed up to the session. It can be a mistake to let silence occur at the beginning of the session, because what the members really need is some discussion or activity to get them started. This goes back to what we have said about the importance of leading the group rather than waiting for the members to take charge. Sometimes the wait is very long and not productive.

If the members are sitting there with nervous looks on their faces wondering who will start, or are sitting there with blank looks, we suggest that the leader break the silence after 15 or 20 seconds in order to get the group started. Although some experts feel very differently about this and will let the group sit in silence for five to ten minutes in the belief that the members should be responsible for what happens in the group, we have found this, for the most part, to be counterproductive. In groups in which this has occurred, many members have reported that they were confused about what was going on and were bored sitting there waiting for something to happen. It can also promote verbal attacks among members. We feel that in situations in which the members are not really thinking, the group time usually can be better spent when the leader breaks the silence with a question, a round, or an exercise that is relevant and productive. The leader may say something like the following:

- Let's start by focusing on a new topic. Each of you think of the last time you were angry and then we'll each share briefly what the circumstances were.
- What would be helpful to talk about? Think of one topic that you would find interesting to talk about today. We'll share that in a round.

When the leader feels the silence is being very productive and a member starts to speak, the leader can say to the member, "Let's wait just a couple of minutes. People seem to really be thinking."

In conclusion, silence in a group can be productive thinking time or it can be a signal that the leader needs to shift the focus of the group.

DEALING WITH SEXUAL FEELINGS

Sometimes group members will feel sexually attracted to other members, especially in therapy, growth, and support groups in which members share on a personal level. Certain group dynamics may emerge when this occurs. Members may try to impress each other; they may hold back sharing because of another; they may become jealous, hurt, or angry at what another member is sharing. It goes without saying that these kinds of dynamics can be detrimental to the group process, but a leader must keep in mind that sexual attraction can and will occur almost anywhere irrespective of the context. There is simply nothing the leader can do about it, and, in fact, leaders will not want to act as moral legislators. Some leaders set a ground rule that members cannot relate to one another outside the group. Our feeling is that members are going to do this anyway regardless of the rule, so the better strategy is to talk about how this can become a problem.

At times members form relationships that do not interfere with the group; other times outside relationships do cause problems. If a situation has arisen that is hindering the group (such as two people dating or one person being interested in another member who is not reciprocating), the leader might talk privately to the person or persons involved about possible solutions to the problem. Other times the issue can be brought up in the group, especially if other members feel that the relationship is disrupting the group in some way. This kind of situation is not easy to handle, but the leader should not simply ignore members being attracted to or involved with one another. Sometimes having one of the members drop out of the group is the best solution.

DEALING WITH CRYING

Members may cry at any time during the group. They may cry when either they or someone else talks about topics such as the death of a loved one, a divorce of their own or of their parents, the loss of a job, an illness, or moving from one place to another. The tears may range from moisture in the eyes ("tearing up") to uncontrollable sobbing and may indicate a range of emotions from sadness to fear, anger, depression, emptiness, confusion, anxiety, and even happiness.

In some group situations, such as an orientation for new students or a task group for deciding on a drug education program, dealing for any length of time with a member in psychological pain would not be appropriate. If the leader observes that someone is beginning to cry, he may want to shift the focus away from that member and then seek her out after the group. Or the leader may want to say something like, "Ted, I can see that there is some pain going on. Let's talk after the group." Beginning leaders often make the mistake, when leading education, discussion, or task groups, of holding the focus on the person in pain, thus deviating from the intended purpose of the group.

Another mistake that leaders make when they notice a member tearing up is to focus on that member without considering how much time is left in the session. They then find themselves having to cut short the work with that person or extending the group, which sometimes can cause other members to become angry. Naturally, if someone is in pain, the leader will want to be sensitive to that person, but he also needs to be aware of the time. One strategy that the leader may use is to have members get into dyads and process what they are thinking. The leader would then pair up with the member in pain to find out more about the pain. Another strategy would be to acknowledge the pain and to suggest to the member that they talk after the group.

Some leaders, when they notice that a member is starting to cry, will immediately start trying to help the member with the pain before getting a contract to do so. Often, members are not ready to discuss what they are feeling, so when the leader tries to help, the member feels pressure, which may lead to resentment. The leader should always be sure that the member wants to work on the problem.

Another important consideration when a member is crying is whether the crying is a result of some struggle or painful event or is an attempt to gain sympathy. The natural reaction of most new group members is to feel sorry for the person or to reach out and touch the person who is crying. They are usually not aware of the difference between a member who is genuinely struggling with some painful issue and one who is wanting to be rescued. Occasionally, it is appropriate to ask a member not to touch or hug another member who simply wants sympathy. If the member is feeling sorry for himself or playing a "poor me" game, hugging or touching that member would not be therapeutic.

EXAMPLES . . . .

The group is composed of cancer patients. One of the members, Wanda, has been discussing her failing health.

Wanda: Some days are better than others. I try to keep a positive attitude about the whole thing, and I succeed if I feel good that day. Today I've felt bad. (*She begins to cry*) It's on these days that I wonder if I'm gonna make it.

Jerry: (*Sitting next to her, he puts his arm around her shoulders and attempts to comfort her*) Wanda, let it out if you need to. I don't think it helps to always try to keep up a positive image.

In this example, Wanda was genuinely struggling with a life-and-death issue. It was perfectly acceptable for Jerry to touch her.

. . . .

A member named Leslie is discussing her parents.

Leslie: They just never let me grow up. Just like this past Christmas. I wanted to go to the mountains to ski, but my mother said that I should come home since my grandparents were going to be there. They make me so mad. (*Starts to cry*) And they also hurt my feelings. My dad said that I was selfish and that I only think of myself. I just wish they would learn to accept me and stop trying to make me a clone of them. (*Carey starts to put her arm around Leslie*)

Leader: (*In a calm, soft voice*) Carey, don't do that. Leslie, I am wondering if we can get the adult part of you to deal with this issue? Right now, I sense that you are coming more from the child ego state.

. . . .

One of the biggest mistakes that leaders make when a member begins to cry over some painful issue is to allow the other group members to ask a series of irrelevant questions. In the example above, some members might have responded to Leslie's statement in the following ways:

- Where do your parents live?
- How many grandchildren do your grandparents have?
- How often do you visit?

Those of you who have led groups know how group members can divert the central focus of the group by asking such irrelevant and untimely questions, often out of discomfort and a desire to stop the crying. When this occurs the leader must simply step in and cut off the questions.

Another problem that can come up regarding crying is a member's starting to cry during the first or second session, before either the member or the group is ready to deal with an intense emotional concern. Many times a member will be ready to delve into his concern. However, the leader needs to be careful in this situation, because sometimes members who share intensely during the first session are afraid to return to the group, or other members become frightened by the emotional intensity and do not return. During the first and second sessions, leaders should be cautious about how much pain and emotion they let members express. If the entire group is ready, of course, certainly do not hold back.

DEALING WITH
MUTUALLY HOSTILE MEMBERS

In any kind of group there is the possibility of a member disliking another member. This dislike may manifest itself in arguments, disagreements, and silence between members. Sometimes members begin the group disliking each other because of something that happened before the group began. This might occur in a school setting, for instance, in which members know each other. If possible, this should be checked out by the leader during the screening interview by simply asking "Is there anyone whom you dislike and would not want to be in the group with you?" However, this is not a foolproof method for preventing members from disliking each other, because even members who do not know each other at the beginning of the group can quickly grow to dislike each other as the group progresses. When this occurs, the leader may want to bring the issue up in the group if she feels that such a discussion would be beneficial.

If the dislike is so great that it is interfering with the group, one or both members should be removed from the group if possible and placed in different groups. In addition, if this type of behavior seems to be a pattern for a particular member, perhaps the member is not ready for a group and would benefit more from individual counseling before becoming a member of a group.

This is not to say that leaders should never focus the group on members' dislike for each other. Often members' behavior within the group is indicative of their behavior outside the group, and focusing on the process whereby members come to dislike each other can be one of the most beneficial discussions for them in terms of helping them become more accepting of others in their daily lives. Helping members come to terms with each other can also potentially be one of the most productive processes for solidifying the group and building group cohesion. The point here, however, is that there will be times in which, no matter what happens in the group, members will not overcome their personal dislike for each other. In these cases the goal is not to get members to like each other but rather to do what is necessary to ensure that other members have a positive group experience.

If the leader decides to focus on a major conflict between two members during a group session, we suggest that the leader discuss this with each member individually prior to the session to identify the issue clearly and explain the reason for wishing to deal with it in the context of the group. This individual contact between the leader and each member should also be used to build additional rapport and enlist the cooperation of the members. Without getting a commitment from each member to work toward a resolution of the issue, the leader is setting the stage for a potential disaster. If the leader simply confronts the members, either or both members may feel angry at what they consider an intrusion by the leader and use the group as a major battleground.

EXAMPLE . . . .

Two members of a group in a residential treatment center for adolescents are in a power struggle over control issues in the center. The leader has the option of switching either member into another therapy group, but decides to try to help them work on their issues. The leader meets with each member individually and then opens the session as follows:

Leader: Today I'm hoping we can spend some time dealing with an issue that is important to all of us. As you know, Jack and Phillip have had some problems with each other since they've been here. I talked to each of them and got them to agree to try and work some things out in the group. (*The leader then turns to the two members to get confirmation*)

Jack: Yeah, I agree to try.

Phillip: It's OK with me.

Leader: OK. I guess I'd like to start by asking the rest of you how the group might be different if Jack and Phillip got along better.

Moe: It wouldn't be as much fun. Those guys really get things stirred up.

Leader: Good point. Maybe it wouldn't be as exciting. How about someone else?

Pete: Some people here don't talk much 'cause maybe they're scared. So they might talk more.

Leader: So maybe the tension between these two guys keeps some things from happening in the group that might help others. What are some other ideas?

. . . .

In this example, the leader chooses not to give the two members in conflict center stage because this might exacerbate the conflict. Instead, the leader allows the other members to provide feedback and will gradually involve these two members as the discussion continues. Instead of focusing on specific complaints, focusing on the general topic of conflict resolution and ways of dealing with anger may be the most productive direction. Later in the session, examples provided by the two members in conflict may be used to demonstrate how differences can be handled. The leader is not avoiding the conflict between these members by this approach. On the contrary, the leader is assuming they lack good techniques for resolving their power struggle and must be provided with such techniques before their efforts can be successful.

The group leader may be able to prevent any further growth of animosity between members by paying attention to how she uses dyads and exercises. Placing members who dislike each other in pairs or having them complete an exercise with each other may only serve as a battleground for their dislike toward one another. On the other hand, forcing antagonistic members to work together may promote their coming to terms with their differences. Sometimes pairing the two members who dislike each other and then joining the dyad to help them talk through their dislikes is very effective. This is a delicate situation that the leader needs to watch carefully.

ASKING A MEMBER TO LEAVE

Although asking a member to leave the group is rare, it is an option that warrants consideration. There are several reasons a leader would ask a member to leave; some we have already mentioned. Another reason for asking a member to leave the group is that a particular member's needs may be so contrary to the purpose of the group that she would receive no benefit from it. For example, if a member needed personal counseling on many problem areas in her life, including her self-concept, her marriage, and her weight problem, but the purpose of the group was for members to learn about childrearing, it would be best if that member were not a part of that group.

After determining that a member should not be a part of the group, the next consideration is how and when to tell that member not to return. Sometimes the task can be quite easy. For example, the leader could meet with the member at a break or after the group and say something like the following:

Leader: Tom, it seems that the things you really need from a group are not what this group is about. Maybe you have even wondered whether or not this group could be helpful to you. Given that your needs will not be served by this group, I think it might be best if we found you another alternative. Perhaps we could locate a more appropriate group for you or refer you to someone whom you could see on an individual basis.

Another reason for asking a member to leave is that the member has been so disruptive as to impede the functioning of the group. Such disruption might include arguing with another member, overtly threatening the leader, repeatedly attempting to "get" the leader, or being too negative toward other group members. Certainly there must be attempts to bring the disruptive member under control before asking the member to leave. However, if these methods have little or no effect and the member continues to disrupt and intrude on the rights of the other members, the leader should ask that member to leave the group. Ideally it is best to do so at the end of a session. This prevents a power struggle from occurring in front of the other members. For example, at the end of a session, the leader could say something like the following:

Leader: (*Calmly*) Patty, I must speak to you very frankly for a moment. Whether or not you are aware of it, you are disrupting the group to the point that I'm afraid the other members are not receiving any benefit. All other attempts to halt your disruption have been to no avail. I think it would be best if you did not return. It is my responsibility to refer you to another group or to an individual therapist, and I will do so.

If the disruption is so severe that waiting until a break or the end of the group is not possible, the leader must act immediately so that the session may resume and be of benefit to the other members. In this case the leader must explain the action to the entire group and then say something like, "Steve, I must ask you to leave," or "Steve, you have disrupted the group too much; please leave."

Of course, the strategies mentioned above apply to group situations in which the members are removable; that is, they are volunteers for the group or the setting gives the leader the freedom to remove a member if necessary. In settings in which the members must participate and there is no freedom to remove a member, the leader may ask that the member sit in silence or sit outside the circle of working members.

DEALING WITH PREJUDICED, NARROW-MINDED, OR INSENSITIVE MEMBERS

Every now and then a leader will be faced with the problem of dealing with a member with a very narrow or prejudiced view of the world who tries to act as a moralist or preacher. This is a difficult situation, since one purpose of most groups is to hear different points of view and learn to be tolerant of others. However, there is a point at which a member who cannot refrain from preaching and judging others may need to be removed from the group. It is not good leadership to always let members have their say. For instance, if a woman is talking about having an affair and another member starts in about how evil and wrong it is, the leader should quickly cut off that member. Another common occurrence is a member telling the other members that they are "sinners" for not going to church. In a case like this, the leader would have to ask the member politely to try to understand that others view religion differently. If this does not work, the leader may need to ask the member to leave the group. The leadership rule is to be tolerant of members' differences and only intervene when a member's comments are so prejudiced that they could be harmful. In the example below, the leader did not hesitate to quickly cut off the member who was not being sensitive.

E X A M P L E . . . .

Susan: (*Crying*) I have never told anyone this, but I do think it has a lot to do with my problems with men.

Leader: (*In a soft, caring voice*) I think it would be helpful to get it out.

Susan: (*Crying harder*) When I was 13, my uncle, whom I like a lot, talked me into having sex with him. I didn't know what I was doing, but I sort of liked it. Then I realized it was wrong and when I tried to quit, he threatened to tell my parents, so I kept doing it until I went away to college. (*Sobbing now*)

Donna: You're disgusting. How could you do—

Leader: (*Firmly*) Wait a minute. Donna, if you cannot tune into her pain, then you need to be quiet. Your moral judgments are not helpful. Susan, I want you to look at other members and realize that we do understand how hard this was for you. (*She looks around and sees very concerned faces; Donna is staring down*) I feel that we can help you to let go of that very painful experience. Are you willing to talk about it some more?

Susan: Yes.

In this example, the leader had to intervene quickly, since the member was being insensitive to the situation.

. . . .

When a member is sharing something that is somewhat out of the ordinary, the leader should always be alert to possible judgmental comments that could be harmful. Other examples that could produce prejudiced reactions are a person's disclosing that she is gay, that she is having sex with a relative, that she is going to have an abortion, or that she is a member of a very unusual religious cult.

CONCLUDING COMMENTS

In this chapter, we have described some of the more difficult situations that leaders face, such as the negative member, the resistant member, the crying member, or the member who is out to "get the leader." The discussion and examples were provided to give you a better understanding of the various situations and strategies for handling them. We hope that when faced with situations that we have described (and you will be faced with them if you lead groups), you will refer back to this chapter and not feel the problems are unique to your group or reflect on your leadership.

Working with Specific Populations

Often group leaders work with specific populations. For each population, there are some unique leadership considerations. In this chapter, we have selected nine populations that we feel present some special challenges. There are a number of other populations that we could have addressed but we thought these were among the most frequently led groups or populations. The purpose of this chapter is to touch on some of the group counseling issues concerning the nine selected populations, but by no means are we attempting to cover the topic thoroughly. We discuss mainly support, growth, and therapy groups within each population. (Many excellent education groups could also be outlined, but the dynamics of those groups are covered elsewhere.)

1. Children
2. Adolescents
3. Couples
4. Chemically dependent clients
5. Older clients
6. Clients with chronic diseases or disabilities
7. Survivors of sexual abuse
8. Divorce
9. Adult children of alcoholics

CHILDREN

Many kinds of groups can be conducted with young children. Groups valuable for almost any child are those that deal with values and self-concept. Some excellent resources are available if you are considering leading self-concept (Canfield & Wells, 1976) or values (Chase, 1975) groups with children; they offer specific group activities and exercises that are interesting and helpful for children.

Besides values and self-concept groups, groups with a specific theme or purpose can be formed. Many elementary school counselors conduct groups for children whose parents are going through or have recently gone through a divorce. Counselors also set up groups for children living in stepfamilies. These groups offer valuable support for these children, who get to hear that they are not alone in their feelings. Another common type of group is for children of alcoholic parents. These groups provide information, support, and therapy for kids living with an alcoholic. For each of these kinds of groups the leader would need not only group leadership skills but also knowledge of specific topics such as the effects of divorce, stepfamily living, or living with a chemically dependent person. Topic groups on anger, siblings, shyness, and friends are also excellent groups for children.

The skills needed for leading groups with children are basically the same as those needed for adult groups. One of the main differences is that the leader may need to take more responsibility for the group than in a group composed of adults. That is, children often do not come each time with something they want to talk about. Exercises, short stories or skits, and the use of puppets all are helpful tools for the leader. If the proper tone is established, children usually will be more than eager to talk. In fact, the leader may frequently need to cut off members in order to let others share.

The length of the sessions and the number of participants should be different than for adults. Depending on the age group, anywhere from 30 to 45 minutes is appropriate. The best number of participants for most groups for children seems to be 5 or 6 although classroom guidance can be effective with as many as 20.

In many workshops for elementary school counselors that we have conducted, participants have commented that they had too much "fluff" (fun and games) in their groups and not enough depth. Granted, with children it is sometimes hard to take the group deeper, but if the leader is clear about the group's purpose, she can have a productive session. By using props, creative ideas, and good leadership skills, the focus can be held and taken to a level that is meaningful for the members. Usually the counselor will not do individual work for any length of time because the other children would probably become restless, but the focus on a topic can go to a 7 or a 6 level. Often, a group session can lead to an individual follow-up session.

If you are planning to lead groups with children, we suggest that you read Chapter Nine in Corey and Corey (1992), which describes setting up and conducting groups with children. They discuss such aspects as working with principals and teachers, obtaining permission from parents, confidentiality, and how to prepare for the group. At the end of the chapter, they offer an excellent list of additional readings on group counseling.

ADOLESCENTS

Adolescence is a difficult period in a young person's life. Voluntary growth, discussion, education, and therapy groups can be quite valuable at this stage. Groups can help with identity problems, sexual concerns, and problems with parents and school. Groups for pregnant teenagers, drug users, teenage parents, potential school dropouts, and runaways can be extremely helpful. Other helpful groups are those for adolescents who are having problems due to their parents' divorce, remarriage, or alcohol abuse.

A group leader working with adolescents should like and respect teenagers, want to learn more about their immediate world, and understand the kinds of struggles they go through while trying to grow up. Teenagers are very aware of phony attempts by the leader to be one of them or of a one-up attitude that suggests an adult knows more. They will often test the leader's level of acceptance of their values. Unfortunately, it is common for group leaders of teens to sound like "parents." Hidden agendas, such as wanting the members to study harder in school, stop using drugs or drinking, or behave better in class, are quickly spotted, thus causing the members to lose respect for the leader. Leaders of adolescent groups often will be confronted if they are dishonest or not open about their intentions.

Any discussion of adolescent groups would be remiss if it did not touch on the nonvolunteer adolescent group. Many groups for adolescents are not voluntary. These groups may be school ordered, court ordered, or agency ordered. Many schools have mandatory groups for those caught with drugs, those with too many absences, those with poor grades, or those who want to quit school. Courts sometimes order teenagers to participate in group therapy with an agency. Many residential settings have mandatory group attendance. Leading any of these groups is extremely difficult. The leader will have to be creative and innovative to turn the negative energy around. With adolescents, especially in the initial sessions, the leader must plan interesting and relevant activities. The use of role-plays, moral dilemma exercises, sentence completions, and common readings are all helpful to get members interested and involved. Starting with a formal presentation of the rules is *not* the way to start a nonvolunteer group—this sets a negative tone for members who are already negative! During the first couple of sessions of a nonvolunteer group, the leader should expect negative behavior, both verbal and nonverbal. Sometimes it is a good strategy to allow members time to complain during the initial session. One counselor we know handled her after-school group for adolescent drug users by starting with dealing with the anger.

Leader: I know you do not want to be here, so we can take ten minutes to bitch about it, but after that we'll get focused on what we are doing here. If you want to bitch, I am going to put this trash can in the center of the group. In ten minutes, after you have dumped much of your anger, I'll remove it and we'll get started.

Problems with confidentiality can often occur in groups with adolescents. Sometimes the leader can avert these problems by carefully screening the members to avoid placing in the same group members who do not get along. Because confidentiality is so important, the leader must make clear to the members the consequences of breaking that confidence. The consequences may be discussed and agreed upon by the entire group, or the leader may simply state the consequences, such as removal from the group.

Sessions with adolescents should last between 60 and 90 minutes. The size of the group should probably be no more than eight members, with six being ideal. Depending on the group's purpose, the leader may want to lead all males, all females, or a mix of the two. The value of the coed group is that there is a lot to learn about the opposite sex during the adolescent years, and the group can be a very good place to do so.

COUPLES

Several kinds of groups involve couples: marital enrichment groups, groups for abusive relationships, premarital counseling groups, or group therapy for couples. Groups for gay couples have been found to be very valuable for the participants. Other groups that have involved couples include groups for parents of young children or teenagers, parents of children with special needs, parents of babies who died suddenly, and couples who are caring for a mentally ill person or someone with Alzheimer's disease. In this section we mainly focus on couples therapy groups.

Groups for couples offer some special challenges to the group leader. The leader is not only dealing with the dynamics among six or eight members but also with three or four relationships that have their own dynamics. Couples' groups, therefore, are very complex and usually are difficult to lead. In a therapy group for couples, members may have different agendas. One member of a couple may be coming to the group hoping that the relationship can be improved or saved, while the other is perfectly satisfied with the status quo or wishes to negotiate a divorce. Groups of this nature can become quite intense because the two members will often air their differences in the group. Sometimes this is very painful for the couple as well as for other members who are watching.

Because the needs of couples wishing to participate in a group experience can vary considerably, it is important for the leader to be clear about the purpose of the group. Through screening interviews, the leader can inform couples about the purpose and assess their individual and mutual needs. Meeting with the couple as well as with each partner individually provides a chance for the leader to get a broader perspective on the relationship. If one of the partners is not committed to working on the relationship, the leader may suggest couple counseling before or in addition to the group experience. Often, during screening, it will be evident that one of the partners needs some intensive therapy rather than a couples' group experience. Other problems that may arise during the screening or during the group itself include the following:

- One or both partners may be reluctant to share personal thoughts and feelings in front of the other.
- One partner may feel the need to conceal an affair.
- Couples may use the group to vent powerful negative feelings they have held in for a long time.
- One or both partners may try to use the group as a jury to vindicate their behavior in some way.
- One member in the relationship may try to enlist the group to change the partner's behavior.
- One partner may use the group to search for a new relationship.
- Members may compare themselves or their partner with others in the group and feel bad because he or she does not compare favorably.

The format for couples' groups can vary. Many enrichment groups are held on an extended basis, for a full day or a weekend, with the idea that this allows time for partners more fully to explore the dimensions of their relationships and to work more intensely on issues (Corey & Corey, 1992). Full-day or weekend sessions also allow more sharing with and learning from other couples. A drawback to this format is that couples may leave the session with a group "high," feeling renewed and excited about their relationship, only to reenter the real world of kids, work, traffic, and in-laws. Their enthusiasm and renewed commitment may carry them along for days or weeks, but long-standing, underlying problems can surface again for some couples under the pressure of everyday living. Many leaders who conduct such marathon couples' groups hold follow-up meetings to support the couples' changes and to help strengthen areas they have worked on.

A weekly or biweekly group session format can also be used with couples. One drawback to this format is that a couple, especially if they are parents, may have a problem getting free to attend a two-or three-hour group session on a regular basis for several weeks or months. If couples are willing to make this commitment, however, much can be done to help them look at their relationship in the light of everyday problems. Couples can work on interpersonal skills, such as communication, improving intimacy, handling disagreements, decision making, and so forth, as well as have the opportunity to discuss and handle daily issues that might arise for them, such as parenting, money, personal time scheduling, sex, in-laws, and vacations. Weekly or biweekly sessions allow couples to try out communication and problem-solving techniques over an extended period of time; if they run into snags, the group is there to help work them out. This format takes into consideration that personal change, especially when two people are involved, is often slow and erratic, requiring continued reinforcement to be lasting.

For some couples, a good format is a combination of the extended weekend group followed up by a series of regular, shorter sessions. This allows couples who have not had time to truly explore their relationship in depth the opportunity to do so and still work on daily issues that may be of importance to them.

There are many excellent exercises available for leaders working with couples' groups (Corey & Corey, 1992, Stevens, 1972). Such exercises are helpful because they encourage couples to look at the broader issues that many people in relationships share, rather than to focus only on their own specific disagreements. Exercises help couples examine such areas as sex-role problems in the relationship, dependency, the need for innovation to keep relationships interesting, the need for separate identities, games that interfere with intimacy, and the role of childhood experiences in shaping values about relationships and marriage. Sharing and listening can do much to generate awareness and to build a positive understanding of each partner's needs. Hearing other couples discuss their reactions to the exercises is very valuable for the members. Dr. Pat Love, of the Austin Family Institute in Austin, Texas, has conducted some outstanding weekend workshops with couples regarding sex and intimacy.

In summary, couples' groups are exciting, dynamic, and challenging. Couples' groups call for an in-depth understanding of relationships as well as the ability to handle complex dynamics that often arise. Group leaders working with couples need to have extensive experience in individual and couples counseling along with strong leadership skills.

CHEMICALLY DEPENDENT CLIENTS

Many groups are available to the addicted client. Education groups can provide valuable information. Support groups can be very helpful for those in recovery. Twelve-step support groups, such as Alcoholics Anonymous and Narcotics Anonymous, have benefitted millions of people. Therapy groups are beneficial for those who are in denial or are still struggling with their addiction and its consequences. In this section we mainly focus on therapy groups dealing with those who have problems with alcohol and drugs, although most of our discussion is also relevant for groups that are dealing with sex addiction, eating disorders, gambling addiction, and other addictions.

There are many voluntary and nonvoluntary groups for those who have some addiction that greatly affects their lives. Voluntary groups consist of those seeking help as an outpatient, those in an inpatient facility, and those in recovery and relapse prevention groups. The nonvoluntary groups consist of those who were caught driving under the influence, those who were ordered by the court to attend because of a drug or alcohol problem, those in a treatment center that mandates group work, and those who were mandated to attend by their employer, school, or some other outside force. The initial sessions of any nonvoluntary group for alcoholics are difficult to lead because the members are not attending by choice, and many of them are in the early or middle stage of alcoholism. The leader must be prepared to deal with the members' anger at being forced to be in the group and the anger members feel when the leader refers to the fact that alcohol and drugs are creating problems in their lives. There are no easy answers to the problems of working with nonvoluntary alcoholics whose symptoms include denial and manipulative behavior. Leaders must be patient and be clear that they will not see quick and dramatic results.

Nearly all groups dealing with chemically dependent people have to deal with their denial, which makes leading quite difficult. Besides having a thorough knowledge of addiction and group leadership, the leader has to have the courage to be confrontive in a constructive way, because part of the disease process appears to be a tendency both to deny the abuse and to attempt to manipulate others into believing that the abuse is not a significant factor in the member's life. The use of confrontation requires skill and sensitivity. The leader must always remember that effective confrontation involves the leader or another member confronting a member about inconsistencies, rather than a personal attack.

Leaders can easily become frustrated with members who deny their problem and may use confrontation in a punitive way. Punitive confrontation is confrontation that attacks, belittles, and humiliates the member. It is inappropriate, and if a leader finds herself feeling anger toward a member, she should examine her own expectations for the member and perhaps talk with a colleague about her frustration. Constructive confrontation is valuable and often necessary. It involves statements like this one: "You tell us you are going to go straight, yet you have no real plan for how you are going to do it. That's why none of us believes it will work."

Careful planning must be done for most groups of substance abusers. For any nonvolunteer group, the leader should realize that the members often are going to be defensive about their substance abuse and hesitant to talk about any of their issues. The leader has to plan relevant, interesting exercises and discussions to get members involved and committed to trying to benefit from the group.

One other skill that is absolutely essential when leading groups for addicted persons is cutting off. The leader will need to use cutoff skills because alcoholics often want to tell their "story" over and over again. Many leaders who have worked with alcoholics have said that cutting off the long-winded stories has proven very valuable in allowing them to get more sharing and interaction going and being able to focus on a topic in depth without having to listen to one story after another.

In summary, always keep in mind that this population is extremely difficult to work with. The success rate is not as high as group leaders might find with members who have other types of problems. We strongly urge group leaders in the substance-abuse area to recognize the limitations of the disease and not to expect rapid, large-scale behavioral change. Leaders should be especially careful to avoid burnout by not having unrealistic expectations, not leading an excessive number of groups in a given day or week, and not feeling personally unsuccessful when members return to the treatment program for the same abuse problem.

OLDER CLIENTS

As with other special populations discussed so far, there are some special considerations to be aware of when working with groups of older persons. Although we speak of "older persons" or "the elderly," these labels cannot possibly accurately describe those over a certain age, because many people in their eighties function in the same way as those in their fifties. As group leaders, we must be aware that the needs of the elderly are similar to the needs of us all; that is, they are very diverse. Older people have feelings of anger, guilt, and loneliness, along with the fear of dying and the grief they experience as their friends die. Older persons may feel they have less personal power and impact than they had formerly in their lives when they were employed, had children who sought their advice, or had friends who relied on them. This may lead to feelings of lowered self-esteem or alienation. Older people may have less contact with family members, siblings, or children than in former years. They may also have fewer social contacts, their friends having died or moved away. This can lead to feelings of isolation and depression. Older people, having realistic concerns about physical and mental infirmity and death, can benefit greatly by being in a group where they can talk about these feelings. The group leader must be comfortable with dealing with thoughts and feelings about death.

Older people are often preoccupied with past events. They tend to reminisce and tell stories of past adventures. Although such storytelling may become boring for other members, it is often a healthy way for people to process their lives and feel good about themselves. A very common activity in groups with older clients is reminiscing about different aspects of their life. For example, the leader might allow a certain number of minutes for each member to recall his or her most memorable holiday, a particularly happy moment with a spouse or friend, or the most rewarding experience he or she can recall. These exercises can elicit memories that might lead to the member's wanting to do some personal work.

Goals and Kinds of Groups for Older Persons

While older persons can benefit from personal growth and counseling groups, the leader may find as much interest and response among older members for task, support, and education groups. A recent development being tried is to bring older people together, teach them about computers, and show them how they can communicate with others around the country. So far, this has been very successful.

Five possible goals may be established for different groups. The first goal involves providing information about various matters such as finances, health and medicine, housing, or insurance. The leader can either present the information or arrange for guest speakers.

Another goal is what we call "making things happen." Older people, especially if they are living in a residential facility, often do not have the resources or the influence individually to make things happen, such as changing a schedule, planning a Christmas party, improving living conditions, and so forth. A task group may take on such goals to improve the general quality of life. Such a group can also provide an opportunity for members to learn or relearn effective assertiveness skills.

A third goal involves working through personal issues. A personal growth or counseling group could help members deal with unfinished business from the past, such as guilt about not being a better parent or spouse, anger at a former friend or employer, or sadness at not having accomplished something during their lifetime. Issues such as their treatment by children or other family members or their concerns about the future, infirmity, or death are also potential areas for personal work. Members also will benefit simply from sharing these concerns and finding support within the group.

A fourth goal for groups with older persons is developing and maintaining social contacts. As people grow older, family contacts may be less frequent because of distance or their family's preoccupation with their own lives. Friends move away or die, neighbors change, longtime neighborhood hangouts close, and the opportunity for continued social contact seems to diminish. Making new friends can seem difficult, and therefore some older people tend to become more introverted and preoccupied with themselves and the past. This can lead to diminished social skills and initiating behavior. A support group can provide a place for members to socialize; that is, to regain former social skills, as well as to meet others with whom they may form more lasting relationships.

Finally, we have found that groups can be very useful in helping older persons explore new goals in life. Such a group may have characteristics of an education group, a support group, and possibly even a growth group as members shift their preoccupation from the past and focus more on the present moment and the future. The leader and other members may provide information and ideas for specific projects such as arts-and-crafts work or community activities such as joining a foster grandparent program. New goals may involve writing to old friends, establishing closer ties with other family members, or pursuing goals formerly abandoned, such as writing or taking college courses. Members can learn that, whatever their medical or health restrictions, it is possible to generate a new and continuing interest in life.

Settings

There are four primary settings in which groups for older persons might be held: (1) the community, (2) minimum-care residences or retirement facilities, (3) nursing homes, and (4) institutions. We will discuss the implications for each of these settings briefly.

The Community

There are older persons in most communities who do not have contact with family or friends and who may live a rather isolated life. Some may be in touch with local social agencies. A group program may be developed for such persons to pursue any or all of the goals discussed above. Such groups may be sponsored by the community mental-health center, schools or colleges, local churches, or senior citizen centers. Transportation may be a problem to be foreseen for members who wish to attend such group sessions.

Minimum-Care Residences

Standard living facilities designed for older persons also provide a setting in which such groups might be run. While such facilities may have professional staff qualified to lead groups, it is more likely that a group leader from the community will need to provide this service.

Nursing Homes

Nursing homes need some kind of group program. The severity of a person's physical illness will obviously place some constraints on involvement; however, the need may be just as great. Members should be screened for both their physical ability to participate and their mental status.

Institutions

There is a great need for groups for older persons in institutional settings. Many of the goals discussed here can be pursued effectively in such a setting. Institutional living can be very difficult, and, coupled with medical and psychiatric problems, can lead patients to become depressed and socially isolated. A group program can go a long way toward helping with resocialization, developing a support network, and providing information and guidance. Corey and Corey (1992) provide a warm description of the contributions Marianne Corey made to a group of older residents in an institutional setting.

In summary, the leader working with older persons in groups must be sensitive to relevant issues such as concerns with aging and death as well as to real constraints such as waning physical health and vitality and fewer social outlets. The leader should develop a group program that will meet a wide range of member needs.

CLIENTS WITH CHRONIC DISEASES OR DISABILITIES

Groups for persons with chronic diseases or disabilities can be formed on a community basis or in hospitals or rehabilitation centers. Such groups are especially important in light of the stress generated by the onset of a disability or long-term illness. Clients are often uncertain of the course or prognosis of their condition. They must deal with a change in lifestyle, may feel out of control, and often are physically separated from the support of family and friends. The focus of their lives for many weeks or months shifts from the day-to-day business of making a living or attending school, socializing, and being involved with family and recreation, to medical examinations, treatments, and waiting with some degree of uncertainty.

Given the uncertainty of medical factors, the need for emotional support, and the struggle of working through lifestyle changes, there is an important place for different kinds of groups in this population. Groups can provide education and information on health-related issues and help clients deal with psychological issues such as loss of identity, anger, and the grieving process. Groups can also provide support and help with problem solving.

Two groups that deserve special mention are those dealing with AIDS and cancer patients. Many excellent support groups are being led with each of these populations. If you are planning to lead these kinds of groups, you should be aware that literature discussing different approaches to each is increasingly available. We suggest you consult any group journal and any medical journal that deals with either AIDS or cancer.

It is usually best to form homogeneous groups based on one particular illness or disability because the illness or disability is the common denominator about which patients have concerns. There will be times, however, when this is not possible or when it is helpful to involve group members with different medical concerns. The leader must give a great deal of thought to who is let into the group, and must be especially sensitive to the intense anxiety, the depression, and the anger that people may experience following the onset of a long-term illness or disabling condition. As people move from the acute medical stage to the rehabilitative stage, many begin a grieving process that has some generally predictable phases: (1) denial, (2) anger, (3) bargaining, (4) depression, and, finally, (5) acceptance. It is important for the group leader to understand the phases of this grieving process, both in terms of selecting members for a group as well as in terms of actually leading the group. Members who are dealing effectively with their medical condition can provide information, lend support, and serve as role models for those who are still in the angry or depressed stages.

Groups with members who have a chronic disease or disability are led both as open and as closed groups. Most hospital groups are open because they need to accommodate new people arriving in the unit who are suffering from the same illness or disability. Groups for family members of people with certain illnesses are also being conducted with great success.

Leaders of groups that deal with a disease·or disability need to be prepared for many different dynamics. Because of the sense of injustice members feel at the onset of a chronic illness or disability, they will often have a strong need to express powerful feelings—frustration and anger, in particular. For this reason, group leaders must feel comfortable handling hostility, some of which will be displaced onto them. The anger will often take the form of finding fault with the medical staff, nurses, schedules, and so forth. It is important for the group leader to recognize this anger as an important aspect of the grieving process and to help the member work through it.

Members often become intensely focused on their medical condition to the exclusion of other aspects of their life. They may need to be encouraged to look beyond their medical condition to the possibility of future employment, socializing again with friends, regaining a role in the family, and so forth. The leader may also find that this intense focusing of members on their own condition and anxiety about their prognosis may cause some to try to dominate the discussion, especially in support groups. Effective cutting-off skills are important to use, along with exercises that structure how the members share. For example, a sentence-completion exercise is helpful, since the leader can then call on any member in the group.

Leaders, especially beginners, need to understand that clients with a chronic disease or disability often become quite knowledgeable on the topic of their condition. Rather than be threatened by the members' knowledge, leaders should try to learn from them. Certain members may try to use their superior knowledge about their condition to manipulate the leader, attempting to dominate the discussion or discount the leader's effectiveness because of lesser knowledge. The leader may need to use confrontation skills to make sure that such members do not sabotage the purpose of the group.

Having as much knowledge as possible about the disease or disability is always helpful. A few illustrations may help to emphasize this importance. For example, when working with young men with spinal cord injuries, sexual dysfunction is frequently a major topic that members wish to discuss. Banik and Mendelson (1978) point out the high degree of misinformation that circulates among such patients about sexual problems. The leader will not only need to have—or make available through medical staff— sound information on disability and sexual dysfunction, but also to anticipate the anxiety surrounding this topic. Group members who have had a stroke may experience mood swings caused by their physical condition, depending on the nature and extent of brain damage. It is important for the leader to be aware of the cause of such mood swings, to make sure the affected member knows the cause, and to ensure the other group members understand. Stroke patients may also experience difficulty expressing themselves at times or fully comprehending others' ideas. A lot of support and encouragement must be given such members to keep them involved in the group. Cardiac patients may develop a preoccupation with death and a concern about how much physical energy they can expend safely. Again, misinformation is common; even accurate information is often not comprehended fully because of these patients' high anxiety levels. Education, along with support and encouragement, is important when working with cardiac patient groups.

A final consideration in working with group members with problems of chronic disease or disability in a residential treatment program is the effect the setting may have on members' outlook and behavior. Most hospitals and rehabilitation facilities regiment behavior and foster dependency. Patients are frequently told when to get up in the morning, when to eat, what activities to attend, when, if, and how often they may use a telephone, and so forth. Patients may even develop a belief that their lives are literally in the hands of the medical staff. Regimented thinking and dependency may lead to apathy on the part of such group members. Leaders may find the need to work with both staff and members in countering this apathy.

SURVIVORS OF SEXUAL ABUSE

Sexual abuse of children and adolescents is a significant mental-health problem. One way therapists are dealing with this problem is to form groups for survivors. Groups are currently being led for youngsters in many schools and mental-health centers. For adult survivors, both men's and women's groups are being conducted in such places as mental-health centers, abuse shelters, and drug and alcohol centers. Leaders of survivors' groups should have considerable knowledge of the issues surrounding incest and sexual abuse. Classes, readings, workshops, and leading under the supervision of a more experienced leader should be aspects of the leader's preparation. If the leader is also a survivor of sexual abuse, she should consider the progress she has made in her own healing. As is true in leading any group, personal issues that the leader has yet to resolve could interfere with the leader's role or effectiveness. In the remainder of this section, we focus mainly on working with therapy groups for survivors.

Survivors of sexual abuse are likely to benefit from one of two kinds of groups: support or therapy. Support groups provide an opportunity for survivors to speak of their pain, perhaps for the first time, with others who have also been victimized as children or adolescents. These discussions can be empowering because they validate the abusive experiences and cut through the veil of secrecy that most survivors were subjected to as children. The chance to speak openly in a supportive, confidential setting often helps survivors gain courage to work more productively in their individual therapy.

We usually recommend that a potential member become involved in individual counseling before joining a survivors therapy group. Individual therapy gives survivors a chance to gain an initial understanding of what happened to them. It is not unusual for survivors to deny or rationalize their abuse or to feel overwhelmed with shame. Survivors are likely to benefit more from a therapy group when they have passed beyond their denial and are firmly committed to exploring their abusive experiences.

Individual interviews with the leader before the first group session are especially important in a survivors' group. Members should be informed of the purpose of the group, its goals, the frequency and length of sessions, the ground rules, and the techniques that will be used to help members work therapeutically on their issues. The interview should serve as a time for potential members to decide whether they feel ready to be in a therapy group. A member who is not committed to open discussions or is ambivalent about being in the group may feel too vulnerable to participate.

Survivor work in groups may take many sessions. However, because of the pain and distress survivors may experience, it is important to keep members motivated to work on issues. We suggest setting up groups on a time-limited basis, such as in six- or eight-week blocks. Although the group will likely continue for many months, these benchmarks allow members to assess their progress and decide whether they wish to continue or take a break. We especially want leaders to avoid ongoing groups in which the members and the leader become comfortable with meeting but are not doing the work that is needed.

Therapy groups for survivors focus in depth on the pain of the individual members. However, this does not mean that the members must discuss details of their experiences in the group setting. The extent of detail discussed will depend on the skill of the leader, the comfort level of the members, and the therapeutic needs of each member. Members gain much from sharing about their early family life, relationships with their abusers and other family members, expectations of them as children, and so forth.

Because of the potentially intense reaction of individual members when exploring their abuse, we recommend that the group leader work with one member at a time rather than, as might be true in other kinds of therapy groups, attempt to take the entire group to a deeper level. Even the most skilled leader will be ineffective trying to deal with the severe pain of four or five group members simultaneously. Leaders will soon discover that most members of survivors' groups can benefit greatly from watching other members explore their issues.

We support the idea that those in a survivors' therapy group either remain in individual therapy while in the group or, at least, maintain periodic contact with their therapist. Should the group experience feel overwhelming, members should have a "safe person" with whom they can process their experiences. In many instances, the individual therapist will be the group leader.

In summary, groups designed for survivors of incest or sexual abuse are important in meeting the needs of clients in many settings. Such groups may be set up in mental-health centers, schools, shelters for battered partners, drug and alcohol programs, rehabilitation facilities, and college counseling centers. If they are to be effective, these groups require a well trained leader and the careful selection of members.

DIVORCE GROUPS

Recovery and "starting-over" groups are offered for those who are divorced or divorcing. When setting up a divorce group, the leader must be clear as to the group's type and purpose. If the leader is not clear, then the composition of members may be such that the group cannot be successful. Divorce recovery groups consist of members who are currently going through a divorce or are recently divorced and are still very much grieving the loss. For these groups, the leader will want to make sure the member is not in so much pain that he or she would not be ready for the group. Some people need time with an individual counselor before joining a recovery group. Starting-over groups are for people who have worked through the initial pain and loss on their own, with a therapist, or in a group but who are still looking for help and support in fully letting go and getting on with their new life.

Recovery groups are usually short-term, lasting six to eight weeks. Many people who complete a recovery group go on to a starting-over group. These groups can last for several months if they are closed, or they can be open and last indefinitely. Recovery groups can also be either open or closed. Ideally, they would be closed, but because clients at an agency may need such a group, having the group be open might work best for the population being served.

A leader of a recovery group must have a thorough knowledge of grief counseling and not be afraid of the emotional pain that will be exhibited. Also, the leader must be skilled at individual counseling because the leader often works with one member at a time. Working with one person at a time usually is quite effective if the leader uses theories that the other members can apply to their own situation. Rational emotive therapy is quite useful in recovery groups because members will often say that they don't think they can live without their partner or that they never will be happy again. Also, they feel much anger at and blame of either themselves or their partners that needs to be discussed and challenged. The leader must be strong in theory and must realize that he cannot rely heavily on the members for helpful input because they all are feeling many of the same things.

In starting-over groups, the leader needs to understand the feelings of people who see themselves as starting life again. The leader has many options in the way this kind of group is conducted. He can let the members direct the focus of the group by letting them bring up topics that are relevant for them, or he can use a format in which he brings up relevant topics at each session. Some leaders, preferring the latter model, use one of the many books or workbooks that have been published about divorce. One book we have found excellent is *Rebuilding* by Bruce Fisher (1992).

A starting-over group is a support group in which members help each other by sharing their attempts at new behavior. The leader's role is to make sure that the group does not stay just on the surface when an issue is brought up and that important issues, such as children, dealing with an ex-spouse, anger, meeting new people, dating again, and sex, are discussed.

ADULT CHILDREN OF ALCOHOLICS (ACOA) GROUPS

Many adults who seek counseling come from families in which alcohol was a problem when they were young. There are three basic kinds of groups for adult children of alcoholics: leaderless support groups, leader-led support groups, and therapy groups. All these groups are valuable and have helped millions who have been involved with one or more of them. Our discussion will focus on the leader-led support group and the therapy group.

Leaders of support groups for ACOAs will want to make sure the members are ready to be in such a group. If screening is not conducted, leaders may find they have members who actually should be in individual therapy rather than in a support group. A support group can come early in a person's recovery and can help the person become aware of the issues that he has, or it can come when the person is in a later stage of recovery. The leader would probably not want to mix these because the needs of the members would be vastly different.

Leaders definitely should screen for a therapy group to make sure the members are appropriate. The leader will want to make sure that any potential member is able to function in a group. In addition, a potential member should not be in such great need that individual therapy would be more helpful than group therapy.

Any leader of ACOA groups must have extensive knowledge about alcoholism and its effects on family members. A leader definitely needs to understand issues such as trust, intimacy, shame, guilt, and abandonment that plague most ACOAs. Many excellent books have been written on this subject, and many workshops are presented that deal with working with ACOAs in groups.

The leader of therapy groups for ACOAs must be prepared to deal with much emotional pain and anger. Gestalt techniques of talking to an empty chair that represents the alcoholic have proven very effective. Using transactional analysis to help members understand their different ego states seems to give the members a better understanding of themselves now and when they were living with an alcoholic. Activities such as family sculpture or psychodrama are extremely valuable if led by a skilled leader who can deal with the emotional material generated. Too often, we hear of mental-health workers leading ACOA groups when they do not have the knowledge, the individual counseling skills, or the group counseling skills essential for leading such groups. If you plan to lead these groups, first be sure to get the necessary skills and expertise.

This has been a very brief introduction to ACOA groups because our purpose is to point out the value of such groups and to warn potential leaders of the dangers of leading these groups without being prepared.

CONCLUDING COMMENTS

In this chapter, we discussed considerations and skills involved when leading groups for nine different client populations: children, adolescents, couples, addicts, the elderly, the disabled, survivors of sexual abuse, those who are divorced, and ACOAs. Leading groups for each of these populations requires specialized knowledge. Our comments here are meant to introduce you to the issues and considerations involved. If you are planning to lead groups with any of these populations, we urge you to do additional reading regarding their special needs. You would also want to seek out material that deals specifically with leading groups with that population.

Issues in Group Counseling

In this chapter, we discuss co-leading, ethical and legal issues, evaluation and research in group counseling, training of group counselors, and the future of group counseling.

CO-LEADING

As discussed earlier, leading groups with one or more colleagues can be very advantageous, especially for the beginner. There are several issues to consider when co-leading. A simple yet important concern is where co-leaders sit when leading a group. For maximum awareness of nonverbal cues, co-leaders should sit across from one another in the circle. This provides an opportunity for them to easily maintain eye contact with one another while having different views of the group. There are many reasons why co-leading should be considered when planning a group; some of them are discussed below.

Advantages of Co-leading

Ease

A major advantage of co-leading is that it is often easier than leading a group alone. A co-leader can provide additional ideas for planning the group and can share the responsibility for leading during the session. If one leader gets bogged down or has been involved in leading a discussion or working with a member, the other leader is available to shift to a new topic or person when necessary. Co-leaders can provide support and relief for one another, especially when working with difficult groups.

Peer Feedback

Co-leading can provide leaders with a chance to improve their skills by getting feedback from one another. Also, a lot can be learned if there is an opportunity to co-lead with a more experienced and skilled leader.

Interaction Modeling

Co-leaders can serve as models for members of the group. Effective interaction skills and cooperation are demonstrated by co-leaders who work well together. Opposite-sex co-leaders may serve as role models and may be particularly effective in working with couples groups or with marital concerns. In certain kinds of groups male and female teams can also serve as parental figures in helping members work through unresolved family issues. Perhaps it should be pointed out that it is not essential that co-leaders be of the opposite sex. Many groups are led successfully by same-sex teams.

Special Knowledge

There may be occasions when a co-leader with more specialized knowledge about a given population is needed. For example, in an educational group for pregnant teenagers, a co-leader with a thorough knowledge of prenatal care can add valuable, relevant information to the group.

Varied Points of View

Co-leaders often bring different points of view and varied life experiences to the group, providing members with alternative sources of opinion and information on issues. Differences in the interpersonal style of each co-leader can also create variations in the flow or tone of the group that make it more interesting.

Disadvantages and Problems of Co-leading

A number of disadvantages and problems may occur due to co-leading. One disadvantage is that for some agencies and settings the use of co-leaders puts a burden on other staff members or on the leaders themselves. Therefore, co-leading may not be feasible when there is a large population to be served.

Problems with co-leading groups arise mainly from differences in attitude, style, and goals of the leaders. Co-leading becomes a disadvantage when two leaders work at cross-purposes.

EXAMPLE . . . .

Leader 1: To get started this evening, we'd like to have each person report on how the week went. I think it is important to start with comments about your week so that everyone is aware of how you are progressing.

Leader 2: You might also have some questions from last week's session. We'll be glad to answer them, too.

Leader 1: John, you were going to visit your dad. How did that work out?

John: Great. When he asked me if I had decided if I was going to medical school, I just said I was still thinking about it instead of arguing with him.

Leader 2: That's something we talked about last week, not arguing with parents. Instead it is often better to simply acknowledge what they have said. Let's talk some more about arguing with parents.

Sally: What about teachers? Can we discuss them?

Leader 2: Sure.

In this example, Leader 2 is working at cross-purposes with Leader 1. While Leader 1 is looking for self-reports about significant events that occurred during the week, with the purpose of searching for some existing energy. Leader 2 shifts to teaching more about handling authority figures. Although the focus of Leader 2 is not necessarily wrong, it is poorly timed. The members were ready to share events of the week and then were forced to shift their thinking. Leader 1 has a difficult decision: whether to abandon the original goal and allow Leader 2 to pursue this new direction, or to try to get back to the opening goal and risk a power struggle with the co-leader in front of the group. These co-leaders are not working well together and will need to correct this problem if they are to continue to share the leading.

. . . .

Problems also arise in co-leading when the following happens:

- The two leaders each want to control and play the dominant role.
- The two leaders openly dislike each other.
- The two leaders view group leading in totally different ways.

If either or both co-leaders feel a need to compete or dominate, co-leading will be difficult and the members will suffer. Co-leaders must work as a team· the process of co-leading should add to rather than detract from th group experience. Co-leaders should be secure in their relative positions in the group and must like and respect each other in order to have a good working relationship.

When two leaders have distinctly different styles of leading or opposing views on how to proceed in the group, co-leading is not recommended. Differences can be valuable, but totally different styles usually will cause friction, frustration, or both between the two leaders.

Another necessary component of co-leading is that the co-leaders must be willing to set aside time to plan each session and share feedback. The best intentions of co-leaders will break down if they are unwilling to take the necessary time for planning. Experience suggests that co-leaders who try to "wing it," going to the sessions without having prepared jointly, run the risk of not "flowing" well together. This may lead to conflict and bad feelings. Co-leading requires the joint commitment of the leaders to work together for the benefit of the members.

Co-leading Models

Three models of co-leading are presented here. The model chosen should depend on the purpose and goals of the group, the experience of the two leaders, the individual styles of the co-leaders, and the degree to which the co-leaders feel they can coordinate their efforts. The three models examined are the alternate leading model, the shared leading model, and the apprentice model. Each of these models assumes that the co-leaders are committed to planning the group and to discussing goals and activities for each session.

Alternate Leading

The alternate leading model is one in which co-leaders alternate taking the primary leading role. Alternating role patterns are usually decided upon during the planning of a given session. For example, one co-leader may be responsible for this week's session and the other for next week's, or one co-leader may be responsible for the first half of the session and the second for the last half. With experience, co-leaders who work well together find that shifting roles goes smoothly.

The alternate co-leading model may be appropriate if co-leaders differ somewhat in their approaches and find themselves pulling the group in opposing directions. Alternate leading allows one co-leader to have primary responsibility for directing the group for a specific period of time without worrying about interruptions from the co-leader. This does not mean that the second co-leader is totally inactive. On the contrary, the co-leader may offer supporting comments, clarify, or summarize as it seems to be helpful to the group.

Shared Leading

The shared leading model is one in which co-leaders share the leadership, with neither designated as the leader during a specific time period, such as in the alternate leading model. Leaders "flow" with each other and lead jointly. Although one co-leader may take the lead momentarily, the other is ready to come in at an appropriate point and continue in the same general direction. Although in this model they lead together, at times one co-leader will take charge momentarily, such as when conducting an exercise.

EXAMPLE . . . .

Leader 1: Maybe to get started with the group this evening we'll ask for people to report on how the week went. (*Pause*)

Leader 2: John, you were going to visit your dad. How did that work out?

John: It was great. When he brought up my going to medical school, I just told him I was still thinking about it instead of arguing with him. We got along a lot better.

Leader 2: I'm really glad you found avoiding an argument helpful. What happened with other people?

Amy: I went ahead and told my mom I was going to work at the beach this summer. She took it pretty well, but I know she'll bring it up again.

Leader 1: I'm glad you went ahead and took that risk. Maybe we'll talk more about how you'll handle your mom if she brings it up again.

Leader 2: Amy and John had a chance to handle some important issues for them this week. Did others of you do something similar?

In this example, the co-leaders are actively working together, drawing out and encouraging members. Both leaders have a common goal in mind, getting members to share events that happened during the week in the expectation that a worthwhile topic or some individual work may emerge. If this does not happen, the leaders will move on to an activity they have planned for the session.

. . . .

When using the shared leading model, co-leaders should be careful not to echo each other's words too frequently or to build a dialogue with one another to the exclusion of the members.

The Apprentice Model

In this model one leader is much more experienced than the other; the group is led mostly by the more experienced leader. The co-leader is there to learn by watching and by trying his hand at leading at various times. The benefit of this model lies in the fact that the less experienced leader knows someone is there to help out if necessary.

In summary, whether or not you choose to co-lead will depend on a number of factors. Among the most important are your style of leadership, the needs of your group members, and the availability of a compatible co-leader who is willing to make the commitment to plan and cooperate in this joint venture. Regardless of the co-leading model selected, it is important for co-leaders to pay close attention to each other to maintain a consistent tone in the group and work toward common goals. This requires careful listening to each other along with an awareness of each other's nonverbal cues. In addition to paying attention to each other, co-leaders should watch the members for clues to the impact of their co-leading styles. If members seem confused or if momentum fails to build, the co-leaders should consider their co-leading as a possible cause.

ETHICAL CONSIDERATIONS

Over the last ten years, much has been written about ethics in counseling and ethical behavior in group work (Corey & Corey, 1992; Gladding, 1991). Most ethical problems and situations deal with therapy groups and growth groups, although ethical standards apply to leaders of all kinds of groups. Leaders' ethical behavior centers on their competency and behavior with the members.

Ethical Standards

All professional associations, such as the American Counseling Association, the National Association for Social Workers, or the American Psychological Association, have ethical standards regarding working with clients in groups. Aside from these organizations, there are special organizations that consist of professionals who do group work—the American Group Psychotherapy Association and the Association for Specialists in Group Work (ASGW). These associations have their own codes of ethics. It is very important that you become familiar with the standards of any organization with which you affiliate. We have found that many people who lead groups either are unfamiliar with the ethical standards pertaining to groups or are not affiliated with one of these organizations and therefore do not realize that any ethical standards exist. The ethical standards for ASGW can be found in the appendix.

Lanning (1992) discusses ethical codes as guidelines for responsible decision making. He talks about counselors using a "systematic process of ethical reasoning" (p. 21). We agree with Lanning that many ethical situations are not so cut-and-dried as some make them out to be. In our discussion below of ethical issues, we try to present a realistic view of ethical behavior and situations that occur for group leaders.

Leader Preparation and Qualifications

Just as it is unethical to practice dentistry or surgery without training, it is unethical to practice any kind of counseling without proper preparation. Helpers must realize that it is unethical to lead groups, especially therapy groups, without proper preparation. ASGW spells out in great detail excellent standards for the training of group leaders. If every group counselor had this kind of preparation, there would be no question as to whether the person had been properly trained. Unfortunately, most group leaders are not prepared at this level, and yet, many feel qualified to lead groups because they have a degree in one of the helping professions.

We want to emphasize that a degree alone does not make one qualified to lead groups. We have talked with many therapists with master's or doctorate degrees who are leading groups but have no understanding of what it takes to lead an effective group. It is the ethical responsibility of any group leader to understand group dynamics, group process, group skills, and group development. Also the leader needs to have thorough knowledge of the subjects being discussed in the group. So often we have heard leaders at our workshops say they did not realize there was so much to leading groups. They thought you just "went in and did a group—just let the members take charge and go with the flow." This is unethical leadership!

Leaders in private practice should understand that they must have the necessary skills for conducting any group they establish. Although the same standard applies in agencies, this is not as clear as it may first seem. Confusion results because administrators in agencies, hospitals, schools, and prisons force their employees (the helpers) to violate the ethical standard of being properly prepared by mandating that the helpers conduct group counseling even though they lack the qualifications and knowledge to do so. Often, the helpers have never been trained in group work or have had only minimal training. Every day, counselors, nurses, social workers, and drug and alcohol therapists are required to conduct groups even though they are not qualified. This is unethical according to the standards of all the professions mentioned above.

If you are asked to lead groups and do not feel qualified, you should make sure you get training before you start. If you are currently leading groups without proper training, it is important that you seek training immediately. Also, if you are not properly trained, you need to be aware that you and your agency are at risk of being charged with an ethics violation. More and more clients are becoming aware that therapists have ethical standards that they should abide by; thus, an increasing number of clients are challenging the ethical behavior of professional helpers.

Knowledge

It is unethical to lead a group without having a good grasp of the material being discussed. Too often, we hear of leaders who have little or no knowledge of the subject of the group they are leading, such as groups on eating disorders, panic attacks, anger, or grief. In each of these groups, there is potential for members getting into some deeply emotional material; it is the leader's ethical responsibility to know how to deal with such material. The leader cannot count on the members to know how to help other members with such complex issues as these.

Personal Growth

Leaders should not use a group for their own personal growth. We see the need and value for therapists to experience personal growth through groups, but this should not be done in the group that the person is leading. We have heard of numerous instances of leaders drawing the focus to themselves and using the group for their own therapy. This is unethical.

Dual Relationships

For group work, we define a dual relationship as one that exists in addition to the therapeutic relationship established between the leader and the members. Dual relationships are not harmful in and of themselves; many dual relationships can be very beneficial to clients and group members. We feel that often dual relationships cannot be avoided because helpers often have more than one relationship with their clients. For instance, some group leaders are also the group members' residential house counselor or the person who takes them to the movies, on hikes, or bike trips. There are times, especially in small towns, when group leaders will find themselves at the same party as members of their group. We do not feel that the leader is being unethical if he socializes with a member of his group as long as the leader is aware that potential problems could arise. It is the leader's responsibility to make sure that the therapeutic relationship is not being jeopardized.

Our position is that any exploitative dual relationship is unethical and should be avoided and any other dual relationship should be entered into with caution. By *exploitative,* we mean any relationship in which the group leader exploits a group member in any way. The dual relationship that creates the most concern is that of a sexual or romantic nature. Other dual relationships that can be exploitative involve social or business relationships between the leader and group members. Any time a leader enters into a dual relationship, the leader must proceed with great caution to ensure that it is not harmful to the member or the group.

A different kind of dual relationship exists when the group leader sees a member for individual counseling. Some argue that group leaders should not conduct individual counseling with members of their therapy groups. We disagree with this position and, in fact, we think it is unethical not to provide therapy if it would be in the best interest of the member. The purpose of group therapy is to help clients get better, and if individual therapy aids in the client's improvement, then it should be seen as a valuable tool in the therapeutic process. Also, many times groups are formed as a result of clients being in individual counseling with the leader and the leader deciding that a group would be beneficial.

Confidentiality

There are two issues regarding confidentiality that we believe any group leader should understand: the leader's ethical responsibility for keeping material confidential and the leader's lack of total control regarding members' keeping matters confidential.

It is unethical for the leader to divulge information to anyone about any member of the group. Leaders must be very careful not to give a member's friends, family members, or business associates any information, including whether or not the person is a member of the group. There are exceptions to this rule, when breaching confidentiality is required by law, such as when a member threatening harm to himself or others. Also, in certain institutional settings, the leader may be required to write notes in a file that is open to other staff members. The best way to deal with such a situation is to inform the members what is required of you by the law and the administration so that the members understand from the beginning what your requirements are regarding confidentiality. Corey (1990) states, "If you are candid about your actions, you have a better chance of gaining the cooperation of group members than if you hide your disclosures and thereby put yourself in the position of violating their confidences (pp. 31–32).

Regarding members' keeping what is said confidential, it must be understood that leaders cannot guarantee complete confidentiality because they have no control over what members say once they leave the session. The best way to prevent any breach of confidentiality is to stress its importance and discuss the subject whenever it seems necessary (Corey, 1990).

Informing Members about the Group

Prospective members have the right to know the purpose of the group and how it will be conducted. They should also be informed of any possible risks they might encounter, such as a heightened awareness of unpleasant material from their past or the need to make decisions that could lead to stressful consequences, such as getting a divorce. For voluntary groups, informing the potential members will give them a chance to decide if they want to join a group in which such activities and explorations will occur.

For nonvolunteers, where members do not have a choice about being in the group, it is very important that the leader explain what is going to happen and what is minimally expected. This prevents any disgruntled member from saying he was never told how the group was going to be conducted and what was expected of him.

It is best, whenever possible, for the leader to use a screening interview to determine if a person should be a member of the group and to have an open exchange about the risks involved.

The Ethical Use of Exercises

Leaders should keep several ethical considerations in mind when using structured activities or exercises during a group session. Most ethical problems involving exercises result from a lack of skill or sensitivity on the part of the leader. Leaders may use exercises that generate reactions they are unable to handle due to their lack of skill. Any leader who goes beyond his skill level in this respect is operating unethically. The following are examples of operating without adequate skills:

- Conducting an exercise on death, such as writing your own epitaph, and then not being able to deal with the pain, fears, and other emotions that arise
- Conducting an exercise on guilt and shame and then not being able to deal with the material that surfaces, such as incest, child abuse, or affairs
- Conducting a feedback exercise and allowing one member to be viciously attacked by the rest of the group

Additional leader behavior that is considered unethical includes the following:

1. Not informing members of what they are about to experience if they participate in any group exercise. Any potential risk must be pointed out.

2. Forcing a member to participate in any exercise. If, for whatever reason, a member states he does not want to take part in a given activity, the leader must allow the member this right. It is not unethical to encourage participation, but it is unethical to force it.

3. Demanding continued participation. Members must be allowed to stop participation at any time.

4. Tricking a member into revealing something personal that the member might not want to reveal. For example, an exercise called "Secrets" involves members anonymously writing on an index card a secret that might be hard for them to tell others. These cards are then shuffled, and the leader or each member picks a card and presents the issue as if it were his or her own. The purpose is to allow each member to hear his or her secret discussed more objectively and to defuse negative self-evaluation surrounding it. It would be unethical for the leader to coerce members into identifying their secrets, allow them to guess at one another's secrets, or allow several members to identify their secrets so that other members' secrets can be more easily identified.

5. Using exercises that tend to involve members in "heavy," emotional material without leaving adequate time for processing. In other words, it is unethical to "unzip" members and leave them hanging. A leader must be aware of the potential emotional reactions of any exercise and be sure there is enough time for working through what has been stirred up.

The Leader's Role in Making Referrals

Depending on the setting in which the leader is employed, she may see members for follow-up counseling or refer members to other therapists. With therapy groups, in which personal sharing and problem solving is the purpose, it is the ethical responsibility of the group leader to make sure members are made aware of proper follow-up treatment possibilities. Too often, this ethical standard is violated in that no follow-up treatment is outlined.

LEGAL ISSUES

Group leaders can become involved in lawsuits if they do not exercise due care and act in good faith. Therefore, as a leader, you will want to be sure to practice within your limits of expertise and not to be negligent in performing your duties as a group leader. A leader may be considered negligent who uses techniques and practices that are very different from those commonly accepted by others in the profession. It is your obligation to make sure that members are not harmed by you, the other members, or the group experience. Paradise and Kirby (1990) list the obligation to protect the client and other members as one of the main legal issues in group work. We have heard too many stories of members being harmed by the leader's inappropriate use of exercises or the use of very powerful exercises when members were not ready for such experiences. We also have heard of groups in which members were allowed to viciously attack other members. These practices are not considered ethical and the counselor could be brought up on charges of malpractice if a member felt harmed by such experiences.

The most important point to remember regarding legal issues is to know the laws in your area regarding counseling, clients' rights, and the rights of parents and minors. Also it is important that you do not practice outside your level of training and that you demonstrate at all times care and compassion for your group members. If you desire more information regarding the legal issues of group work, we found two books to be very informative: *The Counselor and the Law* (Hopkins & Anderson, 1990) and *Ethical and Legal Issues in Counseling and Psychotherapy* (Van Hoose & Kottler, 1985).

EVALUATING GROUPS

Most group leaders do not evaluate their groups, often because it takes extra time and forces them to look at the outcome of their professional work. Professionals can more easily believe that their work with clients has been helpful when they lack data to the contrary. While group leaders should not become preoccupied with evaluating their groups, periodic evaluation can give them useful feedback about their approach to groups as well as information on the kinds of experiences that are most helpful in meeting the goals of their members.

Three kinds of evaluations are possible: (1) evaluation by the group leader, (2) evaluation by the members, and (3) evaluation of the changes that actually occur in members' lives as they meet their goals. There are advantages and limitations to each, and each type of evaluation serves a particular function.

The Leader's Evaluation

The leader will want to evaluate the group from his own vantage point; the beginning leader might do a self-evaluation after each session. This self-evaluation should be simple and straightforward. Immediately following the session the leader should write down the major goals accomplished, both overall and with individual members, along with strategies used. The leader might also want to recall the content covered, which members worked on what issues, any dynamics that seemed especially important, and to make comments about the leader's role in the group. (For example, "My instructions for doing the 'Family Sculpture' exercise were confusing" or "I could have cut off Dan earlier and kept the group from getting so restless" or "Sarah attacked Bill and I didn't do anything about it.") Given this information the leader can compare what was planned with what was actually done in the group. The leader can ask such questions as these:

- How closely did I follow my plan?
- When I deviated from my plan, was it because I thought of a more appropriate strategy at the moment or because I felt lost or overwhelmed by the group?
- How closely was I able to meet the needs of the individual members?
- Did things happen in the group that I did not plan for or anticipate? Could I have second-guessed these with more forethought?
- What have I learned from the session that I can implement next time?
- On a 1-to-10 scale, how would I rate my overall satisfaction with the session? Is this rating higher, lower, or the same as my rating for the last session?

The leader should keep these self-evaluations and periodically review them to observe the progress that he is making. If there are areas in which the leader feels he is not improving, he may wish to give them special attention or ask a fellow group leader or supervisor for help.

The Members' Evaluations

The leader will find it helpful to have members evaluate the group. An informal evaluation can be done as part of the closing of any session. The leader might say: "What happened in the group during this session that was particularly valuable for you?" A more formal evaluation can be done a third of the way or halfway through the group. This might involve a checksheet with questions about the process that takes place in the group as well as its content and ways in which the group has been helpful. An evaluation that is done midway through the group allows the leader to make changes that seem desirable based on the members' feedback. A final written evaluation is also helpful for the leader in planning future groups.

A useful evaluation form for the end of groups could contain the following questions, plus some additional ones that are specific to the given group.

- What was the most important thing you gained from being in this group?

- What activities, discussions, topics stood out for you?
- What did you like most about the group?
- What did you like least about the group?
- What would have made the group better for you?
- What could the leader have done differently that would have made the group better for you?

Leaders should exercise caution when reading member evaluations. Members may have a need to please and therefore give only positive feedback to the leader. Or they may feel threatened by a leader who they feel is not open to criticism and therefore may be dishonest in their evaluation. For example, if the leader continually asks members if they like the group or if it is being helpful to them, members may conclude that the leader is fishing for positive feedback and may be reluctant to offer constructive criticism. Some members develop what can be termed a "groupie" mentality; they identify so strongly with the power of the leader that no matter what happens in the group, they believe it is for the good of the group. Since it is natural to look for positive feedback, such feedback may lull leaders into thinking that their groups are terrific when in fact there are problems that should be corrected.

The leader also should be aware that some members might lack commitment to the group or might not like him. These members are probably more likely to give inaccurate negative feedback, especially earlier in the group. The leader should be careful not to set himself up for this type of feedback by seeking an evaluation prematurely. Because of all these cautions, it is best that member feedback not be the sole source of group evaluation.

Evaluation of the Changes in Members' Lives

Probably the most important type of evaluation, yet the most difficult to obtain, is the evaluation of how the group experience has had an impact on the members' behavior. Do students get better grades in school or have fewer reported incidents of misbehavior? Do spouses communicate more effectively? Do teen mothers, having given birth to their babies, provide better care than they would have if they had not been in the group? Do unemployed workers from the group get jobs sooner than those not in the group? These are difficult questions for which to obtain answers. Members' self-reports are one method of determining if they are actually changing. Throughout the life of the group, the leader will want to ask members to comment on changes that they are making. Of course, such responses are not always accurate but the leader can often get some idea of the impact the group is having on the members. Another method of evaluating behavioral change is to have other people in the members' lives give a more objective evaluation. These outside evaluators may be teachers, employers, spouses, friends, pro-

probation counselors, primary care medical treatment staff, or individual therapists. The leader may receive informal comments or anecdotes such as "Yes, Billy is definitely paying more attention in class" or more formal feedback through the use of a written behavioral checklist. Presuming that Billy's behavior in class had a negative impact on his academic work, checking Billy's grades at the end of the next full marking period would also be a way to evaluate the influence of the group.

External evaluations are more easily obtained in such settings as schools, hospitals, or businesses where all the members and people providing evaluation data are part of one system. Evaluation becomes more difficult when the leader must go into the community or to other agencies or organizations to get information. For example, to evaluate the impact of a group on recovering drug addicts who return to the community, the leader may want to get information from spouses and friends, employers, probation counselors, and others who can report on a member's behavioral changes in everyday living. This requires permission from the member and explanations to the person from whom an evaluation is being sought. Although this takes extra time, such periodic evaluations can provide valuable information for leaders in determining the effectiveness of groups they have led.

Outcome-Based Evaluation

There is an increasing demand for outcome-based evaluation, meaning that agencies and institutions want to see data showing that the group work has been effective in bringing about changes. Thus, the leader has to try to produce lasting changes, since measurable positive changes in the members are becoming the gauge of a successful group. This is one more reason that the intrapersonal model is being seen as the wave of the future in group work, since the intrapersonal group leader focuses more on the individual member's needs rather than on the group as a whole. Some groups will easily lend themselves to outcome-based evaluation while in others it may be difficult to quantify changes in the members.

To produce data measuring the outcome, the leader must follow a procedure that includes these steps:

1. Determine the outcome goals of the specific group (for example, students stay in school, students reduce the number of days of skipping school, grades increase, members stop smoking, members have fewer panic attacks, members get jobs). For some groups, the leader may need to determine goals for each member.

2. Collect pre-group data (for example, the number of panic attacks, number of days skipped, number of fights at work, number of work days missed).

3. Focus the group sessions on the desired outcome goals. Allow members to work on their goals.

4. Develop an appropriate form for members to complete regarding their progress toward the established goals. It is very important that the form contain questions that allow you to measure the outcome of the group.

5. Determine whether people other than the members can be involved in evaluating outcome and, if so, obtain permission from the members and contact those people.

6. Collect data periodically, using the form.

7. At the end of the group collect data, using the form.

8. Plan for follow-up data collection by either mailing forms to the members (and others if appropriate) at certain intervals or giving members extra forms and asking them to send the completed forms to you at designated intervals. Collecting data at three months after the group ends, then six months, then one year, would be an excellent way to evaluate the group based on lasting changes in the members.

It is hardly possible to sufficiently stress the utility of evaluating your groups. Much can be learned from evaluations, using any of the methods of evaluation mentioned above. The ultimate evaluation may lie in experimental research, with experimental groups and control groups. Research of this nature is difficult to design, of course, in that accurate assessment of outcomes is not easy.

RESEARCH

Gladding (1991) sums up the research section in his recent book by saying, "Overall, research on the effectiveness of groups has a long way to go before it reaches the level of research on the effectiveness of individual counseling" (p. 337). Numerous articles have been written on why group research is difficult and why there is so little quality research in the group field (Bednar et al., 1987; Morran & Stockton, 1985; Robison & Ward, 1990). Cited as reasons are lack of time, lack of money, and lack of interest. Another major reason for the lack of research is the difficulty of designing a research project in which the variables can be controlled enough to study different aspects of group counseling.

Although there have been many articles published encouraging group research, no one has come to the front with ongoing quality research on either the training of group leaders or the effectiveness of group work. As Corey and Corey (1992) state, "Current research efforts are addressing questions that have been answered before" (p. 253). With greater emphasis being put on group therapy, we remain hopeful that more research will be conducted both at the university level and in the private sector.

TRAINING OF GROUP COUNSELORS

We have been group educators for a number of years and currently conduct workshops throughout the United States and Canada on group counseling. The major lack in training that we have identified is that trainees do not get to practice using specific skills such as cutting off, drawing out, holding and shifting the focus, deepening the focus, and introducing and conducting an exercise. Many report that their group course consisted of being a member of a group, with part of the class time being spent on processing the group. Being a member of a group does not prepare someone to lead groups! Some reported courses with a practice component consisting of leading a group with their peers. It is definitely beneficial to practice but, unfortunately, this kind of practice usually does not accurately simulate what they will be doing in work settings when they graduate.

Our belief is that group skills can be taught like individual counseling skills; that is, the skill is described, demonstrated, and then practiced. We believe that effective training should include delineating specific skills, practicing those skills, and practicing leading groups similar to those the student will be leading after she graduates.

Another area of training that seems lacking concerns the ability to plan effective groups. As we said in Chapter Three, good planning is essential for good leading, and yet, at our workshops, many counselors comment that they did not learn how to plan their groups. This planning can and should be taught to anyone leading a group.

Our last comment about training deals with requiring a group experience during a graduate program. If group experience is required, it should be productive; the leader should model some of the skills necessary for leading groups in various settings. Too often, we hear workshop participants describe a boring or bad group experience at the graduate level. They complain of "just sitting there with the leader doing nothing." Workshop participants have said that a combination of lack of adequate training and their graduate group experience turned them off to groups.

THE FUTURE

Most experts seem to agree that group work will continue to be a major force in the field of therapy. Gladding (1991) is very excited about the potential for groups in the nineties: "There is little doubt that in the future group work will be robust and permeate almost all segments of society" (p. 339). Corey and Corey (1992) have listed as one of the major trends of the last decade the increase in short-term structured groups for special populations. We are finding more and more professionals seeking training in leading specific kinds of groups in which the leader takes much responsibility for what happens in the group. Many school districts are requesting training in group leadership because the counselors see the need for many different kinds of groups in the schools. More specific skills training in group leadership is what we see as the next trend.

We believe that the future of group work lies in the integration of counseling theories with an intrapersonal model of leading. We also believe leaders need to learn more ways to involve the members in the therapeutic process while using counseling theories and the intra- personal model. Therapists will need and demand better training as they become more aware of the legal and ethical issues surrounding group work.

FINAL THOUGHTS ABOUT LEADING GROUPS

Now that you are at the end of this book, our hope is that you feel much more prepared to lead groups and are excited about trying to master the skills presented. At the beginning we commented that we thought this book would give you an understanding of group dynamics and the skills necessary to allow you to lead almost any kind of group. We hope we have accomplished this and that the book has been helpful and thorough enough to provide you with the basic tools for leading a group. We en- joy leading groups and have enjoyed the challenge of writing about what we do. We would like to hear your comments. Please contact us if you have any questions, comments, or reactions to share.

Ethical Guidelines for Group Counselors

ASGW 1989 Revision
Association for Specialists in Group Work

PREAMBLE

One characteristic of any professional group is the possession of a body of knowledge, skills, and voluntarily, self-professed standards for ethical practice. A Code of Ethics consists of those standards that have been formally and publicly acknowledged by the members of a profession to serve as the guidelines for professional conduct, discharge of duties, and the resolution of moral dilemmas. By this document, the Association for Specialists in Group Work (ASGW) has identified the standards of conduct appropriate for ethical behavior among its members.

The Association for Specialists in Group Work recognizes the basic commitment of its members to the Ethical Standards of its parent organization, the American Association for Counseling and Development (AACD) and nothing in this document shall be construed to supplant that code. These standards are intended to complement the AACD standards in the area of group work by clarifying the nature of ethical responsibility of the counselor in the group setting and by stimulating a greater concern for competent group leadership.

The group counselor is expected to be a professional agent and to take the processes of ethical responsibility seriously. ASGW views "ethical process" as being integral to group work and views group counselors as "ethical agents." Group counselors, by their very nature in being responsible and responsive to their group members, necessarily embrace a certain potential for ethical vulnerability. It is incumbent upon group counselors to give considerable attention to the intent and context of their actions because the attempts of counselors to influence human behavior through group work always have ethical implications.

The following ethical guidelines have been developed to encourage ethical behavior of group counselors. These guidelines are written for students and practitioners, and are meant to stimulate reflection, self-examination, and discussion of issues and practices. They address the group counselor's responsibility for providing information about group work to clients and the group counselor's responsibility for providing group counseling services to clients. A final section discusses the group counselor's responsibility for safeguarding ethical practice and procedures for reporting unethical behavior. Group counselors are expected to make known these standards to group members.

From *AGSW Ethical Guidelines for Group Counselors*, Volume 15, Number 2, May 1990, 119–126. © American Association for Counseling and Development. Reprinted with permission. These guidelines were approved by the Association for Specialists in Group Work (ASGW) Executive Board, June 1, 1989.

ETHICAL GUIDELINES

1. *Orientation and Providing Information:* Group counselors adequately prepare prospective or new group members by providing as much information about the existing or proposed group as necessary.
   - Minimally, information related to each of the following areas should be provided.
     a. Entrance procedures, time parameters of the group experience, group participation expectations, methods of payment (where appropriate), and termination procedures are explained by the group counselor as appropriate to the level of maturity of group members and the nature and purpose(s) of the group.
     b. Group counselors have available for distribution, a professional disclosure statement that includes information on the group counselor's qualifications and group services that can be provided, particularly as related to the nature and purpose(s) of the specific group.
     c. Group counselors communicate the role expectations, rights, and responsibilities of group members and group counselor(s).
     d. The group goals are stated as concisely as possible by the group counselor including "whose" goal it is (the group counselor's, the institution's, the parent's, the law's, society's, etc.) and the role of group members in influencing or determining the group's goal(s).
     e. Group counselors explore with group members the risks of potential life changes that may occur because of the group experience and help members explore their readiness to face these possibilities.
     f. Group members are informed by the group counselor of unusual or experimental procedures that might be expected in their group experience.
     g. Group counselors explain, as realistically as possible, what services can and cannot be provided within the particular group structure offered.
     h. Group counselors emphasize the need to promote full psychological functioning and presence among group members. They inquire from prospective group members whether they are using any kind of drug or medication that may affect functioning in the group. They do not permit any use of alcohol and/or illegal drugs during group sessions and they discourage the use of alcohol and/or drugs (legal or illegal) prior to group meetings which may affect the physical or emotional presence of the member or other group members.
     i. Group counselors inquire from prospective group members whether they have ever been a client in counseling or psychotherapy. If a prospective group member is already in a counseling relationship with another professional person, the group counselor advises the prospective group member to notify the other professional of their participation in the group.
     j. Group counselors clearly inform group members about the policies pertaining to the group counselor's willingness to consult with them between group sessions.
     k. In establishing fees for group counseling services, group counselors consider the financial status and the locality of prospective group members. Group members are not charged fees for group sessions where the group counselor is not present and the policy of charging for sessions missed by a group member is

clearly communicated. Fees for participating as a group member are contracted between group counselor and group member for a specified period of time. Group counselors do not increase fees for group counseling services until the existing contracted fee structure has expired. In the event that the established fee structure is inappropriate for a prospective member, group counselors assist in finding comparable services of acceptable cost.

2. *Screening of Members:* The group counselor screens prospective group members (when appropriate to their theoretical orientation). Insofar as possible, the counselor selects group members whose needs and goals are compatible with the goals of the group, who will not impede the group process, and whose well being will not be jeopardized by the group experience. An orientation to the group (i.e., ASGW Ethical Guideline #1) is included during the screening process.
   - Screening may be accomplished in one or more ways, such as the following:
     a. Individual interview,
     b. Group interview of prospective group members,
     c. Interview as part of a team staffing, and,
     d. Completion of a written questionnaire by prospective group members.

3. *Confidentiality:* Group counselors protect members by defining clearly what confidentiality means, why it is important, and the difficulties involved in enforcement.
   a. Group counselors take steps to protect members by defining confidentiality and the limits of confidentiality (i.e., when a group member's condition indicates that there is clear and imminent danger to the member, others, or physical property, the group coun-

selor takes reasonable personal action and/or informs responsible authorities).
   b. Group counselors stress the importance of confidentiality and set a norm of confidentiality regarding all group participants' disclosures. The importance of maintaining confidentiality is emphasized before the group begins and at various times in the group. The fact that confidentiality cannot be guaranteed is clearly stated.
   c. Members are made aware of the difficulties involved in enforcing and ensuring confidentiality in a group setting. The counselor provides examples of how confidentiality can non-maliciously be broken to increase members' awareness, and help to lessen the likelihood that this breach of confidence will occur. Group counselors inform group members about the potential consequences of intentionally breaching confidentiality.
   d. Group counselors can only ensure confidentiality on their part and not on the part of the members.
   e. Group counselors video or audio tape a group session only with the prior consent, and the members' knowledge of how the tape will be used.
   f. When working with minors, the group counselor specifies the limits of confidentiality.
   g. Participants in a mandatory group are made aware of any reporting procedures required of the group counselor.
   h. Group counselors store or dispose of group member records (written, audio, video, etc.) in ways that maintain confidentiality.
   i. Instructors of group counseling courses maintain the anonymity of group members

whenever discussing group counseling cases.

4. *Voluntary/Involuntary Participation:* Group counselors inform members whether participation is voluntary or involuntary.

   a. Group counselors take steps to ensure informed consent procedures in both voluntary and involuntary groups.

   b. When working with minors in a group, counselors are expected to follow the procedures specified by the institution in which they are practicing.

   c. Within voluntary groups, every attempt is made to enlist the cooperation of the members and their continuance in the group on a voluntary basis.

   d. Group counselors do not certify that group treatment has been received by members who merely attend sessions, but did not meet the defined group expectations. Group members are informed about the consequences for failing to participate in a group.

5. *Leaving a Group:* Provisions are made to assist a group member to terminate in an effective way.

   a. Procedures to be followed for a group member who chooses to exit a group prematurely are discussed by the counselor with all group members either before the group begins, during a pre-screening interview, or during the initial group session.

   b. In the case of legally mandated group counseling, group counselors inform members of the possible consequences for premature self-termination.

   c. Ideally, both the group counselor and the member can work cooperatively to determine the degree to which a group experience is productive or counterproductive for that individual.

   d. Members ultimately have a right to discontinue membership in the group, at a designated time,

if the predetermined trial period proves to be unsatisfactory.

   e. Members have the right to exit a group, but it is important that they be made aware of the importance of informing the counselor and the group members prior to deciding to leave. The counselor discusses the possible risks of leaving the group prematurely with a member who is considering this option.

   f. Before leaving a group, the group counselor encourages members (if appropriate) to discuss their reasons for wanting to discontinue membership in the group. Counselors intervene if other members use undue pressure to force a member to remain in the group.

6. *Coercion and Pressure:* Group counselors protect member rights against physical threats, intimidation, coercion, and undue peer pressure insofar as is reasonably possible.

   a. It is essential to differentiate between "therapeutic pressure" that is part of any group and "undue pressure," which is not therapeutic.

   b. The purpose of a group is to help participants find their own answer, not to pressure them into doing what the group thinks is appropriate.

   c. Counselors exert care not to coerce participants to change in directions which they clearly state they do not choose.

   d. Counselors have a responsibility to intervene when others use undue pressure or attempt to persuade members against their will.

   e. Counselors intervene when any member attempts to act out aggression in a physical way that might harm another member or themselves.

   f. Counselors intervene when a member is verbally abusive or inappropriately confrontive to another member.

7. *Imposing Counselor Values:* Group counselors develop an awareness of their own values and needs and the potential impact they have on the interventions likely to be made.
   a. Although group counselors take care to avoid imposing their values on members, it is appropriate that they expose their own beliefs, decisions, needs, and values, when concealing them would create problems for the members.
   b. There are values implicit in any group, and these are made clear to potential members before they join the group. (Examples of certain values include: expressing feelings, being direct and honest, sharing personal material with others, learning how to trust, improving interpersonal communication, and deciding for oneself.)
   c. Personal and professional needs of group counselors are not met at the members' expense.
   d. Group counselors avoid using the group for their own therapy.
   e. Group counselors are aware of their own values and assumptions and how these apply in a multicultural context.
   f. Group counselors take steps to increase their awareness of ways that their personal reactions to members might inhibit the group process and they monitor their countertransference. Through an awareness of the impact of stereotyping and discrimination (i.e., biases based on age, disability, ethnicity, gender, race, religion, or sexual preference), group counselors guard the individual rights and personal dignity of all group members.

8. *Equitable Treatment:* Group counselors make every reasonable effort to treat each member individually and equally.
   a. Group counselors recognize and respect differences (e.g., cultural, racial, religious, lifestyle, age, disability, gender) among group members.
   b. Group counselors maintain an awareness of their behavior toward individual group members and are alert to the potential detrimental effects of favoritism or partiality toward any particular group member to the exclusion or detriment of any other member(s). It is likely that group counselors will favor some members over others, yet all group members deserve to be treated equally.
   c. Group counselors ensure equitable use of group time for each member by inviting silent members to become involved, acknowledging nonverbal attempts to communicate, and discouraging rambling and monopolizing of time by members.
   d. If a large group is planned, counselors consider enlisting another qualified professional to serve as a co-leader for the group sessions.

9. *Dual Relationships:* Group counselors avoid dual relationships with group members that might impair their objectivity and professional judgment, as well as those which are likely to compromise a group member's ability to participate fully in the group.
   a. Group counselors do not misuse their professional role and power as group leader to advance personal or social contacts with members throughout the duration of the group.
   b. Group counselors do not use their professional relationship with group members to further their own interest either during the group or after the termination of the group.
   c. Sexual intimacies between group counselors and members are unethical.
   d. Group counselors do not barter (exchange) professional services with group members for services.

e. Group counselors do not admit their own family members, relatives, employees, or personal friends as members to their groups.

f. Group counselors discuss with group members the potential detrimental effects of group members engaging in intimate inter-member relationships outside of the group.

g. Students who participate in a group as a partial course requirement for a group course are not evaluated for an academic grade based upon their degree of participation as a member in a group. Instructors of group counseling courses take steps to minimize the possible negative impact on students when they participate in a group course by separating course grades from participation in the group and by allowing students to decide what issues to explore and when to stop.

h. It is inappropriate to solicit members from a class (or institutional affiliation) for one's private counseling or therapeutic groups.

10. *Use of Techniques:* Group counselors do not attempt any technique unless trained in its use or under supervision by a counselor familiar with the intervention.

a. Group counselors are able to articulate a theoretical orientation that guides their practice, and they are able to provide a rationale for their interventions.

b. Depending upon the type of an intervention, group counselors have training commensurate with the potential impact of a technique.

c. Group counselors are aware of the necessity to modify their techniques to fit the unique needs of various cultural and ethnic groups.

d. Group counselors assist mem-

bers in translating in-group learnings to daily life.

11. *Goal Development:* Group counselors make every effort to assist members in developing their personal goals.

a. Group counselors use their skills to assist members in making their goals specific so that others present in the group will understand the nature of the goals.

b. Throughout the course of a group, group counselors assist members in assessing the degree to which personal goals are being met, and assist in revising any goals when it is appropriate.

c. Group counselors help members clarify the degree to which the goals can be met within the context of a particular group.

12. *Consultation:* Group counselors develop and explain policies about between-session consultation to group members.

a. Group counselors take care to make certain that members do not use between-session consultations to avoid dealing with issues pertaining to the group that would be dealt with best in the group.

b. Group counselors urge members to bring the issues discussed during between-session consultations into the group if they pertain to the group.

c. Group counselors seek out consultation and/or supervision regarding ethical concerns or when encountering difficulties which interfere with their effective functioning as group leaders.

d. Group counselors seek appropriate professional assistance for their own personal problems or conflicts that are likely to impair their professional judgment and work performance.

e. Group counselors discuss their group cases only for professional consultation and educational purposes.

f. Group counselors inform members about policies regarding whether consultation will be held confidential.

13. *Termination from the Group:* Depending upon the purpose of participation in the group, counselors promote termination of members from the group in the most efficient period of time.

a. Group counselors maintain a constant awareness of the progress made by each group member and periodically invite the group members to explore and reevaluate their experiences in the group. It is the responsibility of group counselors to help promote the independence of members from the group in a timely manner.

14. *Evaluation and Follow-up:* Group counselors make every attempt to engage in ongoing assessment and to design follow-up procedures for their groups.

a. Group counselors recognize the importance of ongoing assessment of a group, and they assist members in evaluating their own progress.

b. Group counselors conduct evaluation of the total group experience at the final meeting (or before termination), as well as ongoing evaluation.

c. Group counselors monitor their own behavior and become aware of what they are modeling in the group.

d. Follow-up procedures might take the form of personal contact, telephone contact, or written contact.

e. Follow-up meetings might be with individuals, or groups, or both to determine the degree to which: (i) members have reached their goals, (ii) the group had a positive or negative effect on the participants, (iii) members could profit from some type of referral, and (iv) as

information for possible modification of future groups. If there is no follow-up meeting, provisions are made available for individual follow-up meetings to any member who needs or requests such a contact.

15. *Referrals:* If the needs of a particular member cannot be met within the type of group being offered, the group counselor suggests other appropriate professional referrals.

a. Group counselors are knowledgeable of local community resources for assisting group members regarding professional referrals.

b. Group counselors help members seek further professional assistance, if needed.

16. *Professional Development:* Group counselors recognize that professional growth is a continuous, ongoing, developmental process throughout their career.

a. Group counselors maintain and upgrade their knowledge and skill competencies through educational activities, clinical experiences, and participation in professional development activities.

b. Group counselors keep abreast of research findings and new developments as applied to groups.

SAFEGUARDING ETHICAL PRACTICE AND PROCEDURES FOR REPORTING UNETHICAL BEHAVIOR

The preceding remarks have been advanced as guidelines which are generally representative of ethical and professional group practice. They have not been proposed as rigidly defined prescriptions. However, practitioners who are thought to be grossly unresponsive to the ethical concerns addressed in this document may be subject to a review of their practices by the AACD Ethics Committee and ASGW peers.

• For consultation and/or questions regarding these ASGW Ethical Guidelines or group ethical dilemmas, you may contact the Chairperson of the ASGW Ethics Committee. The name, address, and telephone number of the current ASGW Ethics Committee Chairperson may be acquired by telephoning the AACD office in Alexandria Virginia at (703) 823-9800.

- If a group counselor's behavior is suspected as being unethical, the following procedures are to be followed:

  a. Collect more information and investigate further to confirm the unethical practice as determined by the ASGW Ethical Guidelines.
  b. Confront the individual with the apparent violation of ethical guidelines for the purposes of protecting the safety of any clients and to help the group counselor correct any inappropriate behaviors. If satisfactory resolution is not reached through this contact then:
  c. A complaint should be made in writing, including the specific facts and dates of the alleged violation and all relevant supporting data. The complaint should be included in an envelope marked "CONFIDENTIAL" to ensure confidentiality for both the accuser(s) and the alleged violator(s) and forwarded to all of the following sources:

1. The name and address of the Chairperson of the state Counselor Licensure Board for the respective state, if in existence.
2. The Ethics Committee
   c/o The President
   American Association for Counseling and Development
   5999 Stevenson Avenue
   Alexandria, Virginia 22304
3. The name and address of all private credentialing agencies that the alleged violator maintains credentials or holds professional membership. Some of these include the following:

National Board for Certified
   Counselors, Inc.
5999 Stevenson Avenue
Alexandria, Virginia 22304

National Council for Credentialing of Career Counselors
c/o NBCC
5999 Stevenson Avenue
Alexandria, Virginia 22304

National Academy for Certified
   Clinical Mental Health
   Counselors
5999 Stevenson Avenue
Alexandria, Virginia 22304

Commission on Rehabilitation
   Counselor Certification
162 North State Street, Suite 317
Chicago, Illinois 60601

American Association for
   Marriage and Family Therapy
1717 K Street, N.W., Suite 407
Washington, D.C. 20006

American Psychological
   Association
1200 Seventeenth Street, N.W.
Washington, D.C. 20036

American Group Psychotherapy
   Association, Inc.
25 East 21st Street, 6th Floor
New York, New York 10010

REFERENCES . . . .

Adler, A. (1927). *Understanding human behavior.* New York: Greenberg.

Bandura, A. (1977). *Social learning theory.* Englewood Cliffs, NJ: Prentice-Hall.

Banik, S. N., & Mendelson, M. A. (1978). Group psychotherapy with a paraplegic group. *International Journal of Group Psychotherapy, 28*(4), 123–128.

Bednar, R. L., Corey, G., Evans, N. J., Gazda, G. M., Pistole, M. C., Stockton, R., & Robison, F. F. (1987). Overcoming obstacles to the future development of research on group work. *Journal for Specialists in Group Work, 12*(3), 98–111.

Berne, E. (1964). *Games people play.* New York: Grove Press.

Blaker, K. E., & Samo, J. (1973). Communications games: A group counseling technique. *The School Counselor, 21,* 46–51.

Canfield, J., & Wells, H. C. (1976). *100 ways to enhance self-concept in the classroom: A handbook for teachers and parents.* Englewood Cliffs, NJ: Prentice-Hall.

Capuzzi, D., & Gross, D. R. (1992). *Introduction to group counseling.* Denver, CO: Love.

Carroll, M. R. (1986). *Group work: Leading in the here and now* [Film]. Alexandria, VA: American Counseling Association.

Casriel, P. (1963). *So fair a house.* Englewood Cliffs, NJ: Prentice-Hall.

Cavanaugh, M. E. (1990). *The counseling experience.* Pacific Grove, CA: Brooks/Cole.

Chase, L. (1975). *The other side of the report card.* Santa Monica, CA: Goodyear.

Corey, G., Corey, M. S., Callanan, P. S., & Russell, J. M. (1988). *Group techniques.* Pacific Grove, CA: Brooks/Cole.

Corey, G. (1990). *The theory and practice of group counseling* (3rd ed.). Pacific Grove, CA: Brooks/Cole.

Corey, G., & Corey, M. S. (1992). *Groups: Process and practice* (3rd ed.). Pacific Grove, CA: Brooks/Cole.

Dinkmeyer, D., & Muro, J. (1979). *Group counseling: Theory and practice.* (2nd ed.). Itasca, IL: F. E. Peacock.

Dyer, W., & Vriend, J. (1980). *Group counseling for personal mastery.* New York: Sovereign Books.

Egan, G. (1986). *The skilled helper* (3rd ed.). Pacific Grove, CA: Brooks/Cole.

Fisher, B. (1992). *Rebuilding* (2nd ed.). San Luis Obispo, CA: Impact.

Gazda, G. (Ed.). (1981). *Innovations to group psychotherapy* (2nd ed.). Springfield, IL: Charles C Thomas.

George, R. L., & Dustin, D. (1988). *Group counseling.* Englewood Cliffs, NJ: Prentice-Hall.

Gladding, S. T. (1991). *Group work: A counseling specialty.* New York: Merrill.

Glasser, W. (1965). *Reality therapy: A new approach to psychiatry.* New York: Harper & Row.

Hansen, J., Warner, R., & Smith, E. J. (1980). *Group counseling: Theory and practice.* Chicago: Rand McNally.

Harvill, R., Masson, R., & Jacobs, E. (1983). Systematic group leadership training: A skills development approach. *The Journal for Specialists in Group Work, 8*(4), 16–20.

Hopkins, B. R., & Anderson, B. W. (1990). *The counselor and the law* (3rd ed.). Alexandria, VA: American Counseling Association.

Jacobs, E. (1992). *Creative counseling techniques: An illustrated guide.* Odessa, FL: Psychological Assessment Resources.

Johnson, D. W., & Johnson, F. P. (1991). *Joining together* (4th ed.). Englewood Cliffs, NJ: Prentice-Hall.

Kees, N., & Jacobs, E. (1990). Conducting more effective groups: How to select and process group exercises. *Journal for Specialists in Group Work, 15*(1), 21–30.

Kemp, G. C. (1964). Bases of group leadership. *Personnel and Guidance Journal, 43,* 760–766.

Kormanski, C. (1991). Using group development theory in business. *Journal for Specialists in Group Work, 16*(4), 215–222.

Kottler, J. A. (1983). *Pragmatic group leadership.* Pacific Grove, CA: Brooks/Cole.

Lakin, M. (1969). Some ethical issues in sensitivity training. *American Psychologist, 24,* 923–928.

Lanning, W. (1992). Ethical codes and responsible decision making. *Guidepost, 35*(7), 21.

Lewin, K. (1944). The dynamics of group action. *Educational Leadership 1,* 195–200.

Lewis, H. R., & Streltfeld, H. S. (1972). *Growth games.* New York: Bantam Books.

Liberman, M. A., Yalom, I. D., & Miles, M. (1973). *Encounter groups: First facts.* New York: Basic Books.

Maples, M. F. (1988). Group development: Extending Tuckman's theory. *Journal for Specialists in Group Work, 13,* 17–23.

Maslow, A. (1962). *Toward a psychology of being.* New York: Van Nostrand Reinhold.

Masson, R., & Jacobs, E. (1980). Group leadership: Practical pointers for beginners. *Personnel and Guidance Journal, 58*(3), 52–55.

Mitchell, J. E., Hatsukami, D., Goff, G., Pyle, R. L., Eckert, E. D., & Davis, L. E. (1984). An intensive outpatient group treatment program for patients with bulimia. In D. Garner & P. Garfinkle (Eds.), *A handbook of psychotherapy of anorexia nervosa and bulimia.* New York: Guilford Press.

Moreno, J. (1946). *Psychodrama* (Vol. 1). New York: Beacon Press.

Morganett, R. S. (1990). *Skills for living: Group counseling activities for young adolescents.* Champaign, IL: Research Press.

Morran, D. K., & Stockton, R. (1985). Perspectives on group research programs. *Journal for Specialists in Group Work, 10*(4), 186–191.

Newlon, B. J., & Arciniego, M. (1992). Group counseling: Cross-cultural considerations. In D. Capuzzi & D. R. Gross (Eds.), *Introduction to group counseling* (pp. 285–307). Denver, CO: Love.

Ohlsen, M. M., Horne, A. M., & Lawe, C. F. (1988). *Group counseling* (3rd ed.). New York: Holt, Rinehart & Winston.

Paradise, L. V., & Kirby, P. C. (1990). Some perspectives on the legal liability of group counseling in private practice. *Journal for Specialists in Group Work, 15*(2), 114–118.

Passons, W. R. (1975). *Gestalt approaches in counseling.* New York: Holt, Rinehart & Winston.

Perls, F. (1969). *Gestalt therapy verbatim.* Lafayette, CA: Real People Press.

Pfeiffer, J. W., & Jones, J. E. (1972–1980). *A handbook of structured exercises for human relations training* (Vols. 1–8). San Diego, CA: San Diego University Associates.

Posthuma, B. W. (1989). *Small groups in therapy settings: Process and leadership.* Boston: College-Hill.

Project Adventure 1992 Workshop Schedule (1992). Hamilton, MA: Project Adventure.

Pyle, R. I., Halvorson, P. A., & Goff, G. M. (1986). The successful maintenance of treatment gains for bulimic clients. *Journal for Counseling and Development, 64*(7), 445–448.

Robison, F. F., & Ward, D. (1990). Research activities and attitudes among ASGW members. *Journal for Specialists in Group Work, 19*(4), 215–224.

Rogers, C. (1958). The characteristics of a helping relationship, *P & G Journal, 37*(6), 6–16.

Rogers, C. (1961). *On becoming a person.* Boston: Houghton Mifflin.

Rogers, C. (1970). *Carl Rogers on encounter groups.* New York: Harper & Row.

Shapiro, J. L. (1978). *Methods of group psychotherapy and encounter: A tradition of innovation.* Itasca, IL: F. E. Peacock.

Shulman, I. (1984). *The skills of helping: Individuals and groups* (2nd ed.). Itasca, IL: F. E. Peacock.

Shutz, W. (1967). *Expanding human awareness.* New York: Grove Press.

Simon, S., Howe, L., & Kirschenbaum, H. (1978). *Values clarification.* New York: Hart.

Starak, Y. (1988). Confessions of a group leader. *Small Group Behavior, 19,* 103–108.

Stevens, J. (1972). *Awareness.* Lafayette, CA: Real People Press.

Taubman, S. (1986). Beyond the bravado: Sex roles and the exploitive male. *Social Work, 31*(1), 12–18.

Trotzer, J. (1989). *The counselor and the group* (2nd ed.). Muncie, IN: Accelerated Development.

Ullman, I. P., & Krasner, L. (1975). *A psychological approach to abnormal behavior.* Englewood Cliffs, NJ: Prentice-Hall.

Van Hoose, W., & Kottler, J. (1985). *Ethical and legal issues in counseling and psychotherapy* (2nd ed.). San Francisco: Jossey-Bass.

Vorrath, H. (1974). *Positive peer culture.* Chicago: Aldine-Atherton.

Yalom, I. (1985). *The theory and practice of group psychotherapy* (3rd ed.). New York: Basic Books.

Hansen, J., 33
Harvill, R., 118, 154
Hopkins, B. R., 410
Horne, A. M., 34, 112
Howe, L., 214, 215

Information giving, 113
Interpersonal leadership style, 25
Intrapersonal leadership style, 25

Jacobs, E., 118, 143, 154, 231, 261
Johnson, D. W., 32, 242
Johnson, F. P., 32, 242
Jones, J. E., 214, 215

Kees, N., 261
Kirby, P., 410
Kirschenbaum, H., 214, 215
Kormanski, C., 23
Kottler, J. A., 4–5, 410

Lakin, M., 25
Lanning, W., 405
Lawe, C. F., 34, 112
Leader
  characteristics of, 28–30
  direction, 24
  energy of, 128
  role of, 85
Leadership
  continuum, 25
  function, 27
  style, 23–27
Legal considerations, 409–411
Length of sessions, 37
Lewin, K., 32
Lewis, H. R., 214
Listening, 108–109
Love, P., 386

Maples, M. F., 44
Maps, 51
Maslow, A., 4
Masson, R., 118, 154
Members
  attitude of, 43
  composition, 55
  involuntary, 40–41
  level of commitment, 42
  level of goodwill, 41
  level of trust, 42
  voluntary, 40–41
Mendelson, M. A., 393

Middle sessions (middle stage), 46, 269–290
  assessing, 269–273
  common mistakes in, 284–286
  leadership skills for, 273–278
  planning, 269–270
  tactics for specific groups, 287–290
  topic outlines, 278–284
Minilecturing, 113
Modeling, 117
Moral-dilemma exercises, 241
Morganett, R. S., 214
Morran, D. K., 414
Movement exercises, 223–224
  cautions, 229–230
  introducing, 250
  kinds of, 224–229
  reasons for using, 229
Muro, J., 5

Narcotics Anonymous (NA), 386
Newlon, B. J., 7, 29

Ohlsen, M. M., 34, 112
Open groups, 39–40

Paradise, L. V., 410
Parenting groups, 4
Passons, W. R., 317
Perls, F., 21, 26, 235, 317
Pfeiffer, J. W., 214, 215
Planning, 55–75
  the beginning phase, 62–65
  the ending phase, 67
  the individual session, 60–61
  the middle/working phase, 65–67
  mistakes in, 71–75
  pregroup, 55
  sample plans, 67–71
Posthuma, B. W., 24
Problem situations
  asking member to leave, 377–378
  chronic talker, 361–364
  crying, 373–375
  "get the leader," 369–371
  hostile members, 375–377
  negative members, 366–367
  prejudiced, narrow-minded members, 379–380
  rescuing, 364–366

Please remember that this is a library book,
and that it belongs only temporarily to each
person who uses it. Be considerate. Do
not write in this, or any, library book.

158.35 J17g 1994

Jacobs, Edward E., 1944-

Group counseling :
 strategies and skills /
        c1994